GENNADEION MONOGRAPHS IV

Acrocorinth, from the Air, Northwest Sector; Pendeskouphi in the background. *Frontispiece.*

CASTLES
OF THE MOREA

BY

KEVIN ANDREWS

THE AMERICAN SCHOOL OF CLASSICAL STUDIES AT ATHENS

PRINCETON, NEW JERSEY

1953

PRINTED IN GERMANY *AT* J.J.AUGUSTIN, GLÜCKSTADT

PREFACE

In 1938 the Director of the Gennadius Library in Athens discovered in Venice a folio of plans of medieval fortresses in the Peloponnese, drawn during the Venetian occupation of 1685–1715. I first saw these plans in 1948, during a year as a fellow of the American School of Classical Studies at Athens. Undertaking their publication, I remained in Greece four years longer.

This book is an attempt to gather together the historical sources relative to the castles figuring in the collection, and to present the results of my archaeological investigation, illustrated by early travellers' descriptions, by photographs of my own, and by the plans of the XVII century Venetian engineers. I have arranged the fortresses in the order as they fell to the armies of the Holy League in the campaigns of 1685–1692, whose course may be traced through the opening sections of the following chapters. In each chapter the fortress' history is recapitulated from its earliest known beginnings to its last military engagement, followed by an analysis of its architecture.

The history of the long Greek Middle Ages is viewed generally in the introduction, treated locally in the chapters, and listed by dates in the chronological table. Throughout the book, and specifically in the conclusion, I have sought to establish — with humility — evidence for the identification of the different periods and builders of the castles of the Morea from the Roman conquest to the Greek War of Independence.

This work has been made possible by the support of Harvard University, the American School of Classical Studies, and the Fulbright Foundation. The opportunity to write it I owe to Dr. Shirley H. Weber, Director of the Gennadeion, whose discovery of the plans and whose keen interest first stimulated an exploration of my own, and whose encouragement and kindness added constantly to its pleasure. To Dr. Lucy T. Shoe I am most fortunately indebted for vigorous and heartening assistance in the editing of my manuscript, and for the sympathetic intelligence for which a writer longs. I wish to express also my thanks to Dr. John L. Caskey, Director of the American School of Classical Studies, to Miss Eurydice Demetrakopoulou, Mrs. Alexandra Dervys, Dr. Peter Topping, and Mr. Takis Demodos of Methone.

To Professor Antoine Bon of Montpellier my obligations are too many to number. To his twenty-five year study of the archaeology of medieval Greece I owe all I know of method and examination. Without his previous publications I would not have known how to begin; without our acquaintance and correspondence I could hardly have continued. To his generosity, which placed at my disposal the unpublished manuscript of his history and monuments of Frankish Achaea, I owe the correction of many mistakes, the relief from uncertainty, and the greater deliverance from unwise certainty. The free choice from his collection of photographs has enabled me to include twenty-three illustrations (Figs. 21, 25, 27, 31, 32, 33, 89, 94, 96, 98, 99, 116, 117, 120, 131, 132, 133, 135, 144, 145, 147, 182, 183), together with the plan of Argos (Fig. 119), drawn by himself and M. Henri Ducoux.

The photographic reproductions of the Grimani plans I owe to the skill of Miss M. Alison Frantz. Nine of the photographs of Acrocorinth (Figs. 151–156, 160–162) were taken by Hermann Wagner. Except for the above mentioned, and the air views of Acrocorinth, New Navarino, Methone, Nauplia, and Canea (Frontispiece, Figs. 48, 61, 97, 226), the photographs in this book are my own. The sketches and diagrams have been re-drawn from my own originals by Mr. Thomas Fisher, Mrs. Grace Norcross Fisher, and Miss Patricia Baker.

Finally, to Greece as a country the debt of the spirit is, fittingly, not to be measured. I am obliged for many occasions of assistance to the agencies of the Greek Government, whose good faith was particularly welcome in an era when ξένος ἀρχαιολόγος has become almost synonynous in the language with προπαγανδιστής. During a civil war, at a time when communications and accommodation barely existed, one could do no more than throw oneself on the forebearance of the people of the country, who know only one word for stranger and guest, and whose hospitality, generosity, and trust provided a more valuable education than may be found in histories or monuments.

Athens, March, 1948
New York, January, 1953

KEVIN ANDREWS

CONTENTS

ABBREVIATIONS

Annuario = *Annuario della Regia Scuola Archeologica di Atene.*

Ἀρχ.Βυζ. Μνη. = Ἀρχεῖον τῶν Βυζαντινῶν Μνημείων τῆς Ἑλλάδος

B.C.H. = *Bulletin de Correspondance Hellénique.*

B.S.A. = *Annual of the British School of Archaeology.*

Bory de Saint-Vincent, *Relation* = J. Bory de Saint-Vincent, *Relation du voyage de la Commission Scientifique de Morée* (Paris, 1836–38), 2 vols.

Byz-Neu. Jahr. = *Byzantinisch-Neugriechische Jahrbücher.*

C. di M. = *Cronaca di Morea*, in Hopf, *Chroniques gréco-romanes* (Berlin, 1873).

Cappelletti = G. Cappelletti, *Storia della Repubblica di Venezia* (Venice, 1850–5), 13 vols.

Χ. τ. Μ. = Τὸ Χρονικὸν τοῦ Μορέως (*The Chronicle of the Morea*) ed. J. Schmitt (London, 1904).

Corinth = *Corinth.* Results of Excavations conducted by the American School of Classical Studies at Athens (Cambridge, Mass, 1925–1947. Princeton, N.J., 1948–   ).

Coronelli, *Description* = V. Coronelli, *Description géographique et historique de la Morée* (Paris, 1686).

Coronelli, *Memorie* = V. Coronelli, *Memorie Istoriografiche del Regno di Morea*, 2nd ed. (Venice, 1688).

Corp. Scrip. Hist. Byz. = *Corpus Scriptorum Historiae Byzantinae* (Bonn).

Daru = P. Daru, *Histoire de la République de Venise* (Paris, 1821), 8 vols.

Δελτίον = Δελτίον τῆς Ἱστορικῆς καὶ Ἐθνολογικῆς Ἑταιρείας τῆς Ἑλλάδος

Foscarini = M. Foscarini, *Historia della Republica Veneta* (Venice, 1722).

Garzoni = P. Garzoni, *Istoria della Repubblica di Venezia in Tempo della Sacra Lega* (Venice, 1705), 2 vols.

Gerola, *Napoli di Romania* = G. Gerola, "Le Fortificazioni di Napoli di Romania," *Annuario*, XIII–XIV, 1930–31, pp. 347–410.

J.H.S = *Journal of Hellenic Studies.*

L. de C. = *Livre de la conqueste de la princée de l'Amorée. Chronique de Morée (1204–1305)* ed. Longnon (Paris, 1911).

L. de F. = *Libro de los Fechos et Conquistas del Principado de la Morea* (Société de l'Orient latin) ed. A. Morel-Fatio (Geneva, 1885).

Leake, *Morea* = W. Leake, *Travels in the Morea* (London, 1830), 3 vols.

Locatelli = A. Locatelli, *Racconto historico della Veneta Guerra in Levante* (Cologne, 1691), 2 vols.

Miller, *Essays* = W. Miller, *Essays on the Latin Orient* (Cambridge, 1921).

Miller, *Latins* = W. Miller, *The Latins in the Levant, a History of Frankish Greece, 1204–1566* (London, 1908).

La Morea Combattuta (Bologna, 1686) = *La Morea Combattuta dall' Armi Venete* (Bologna, 1686).

La Morea Combattuta (Venice, 1686) = *La Morea Combattuta dall' Armi Venete* (Venice, 1686).

Paruta = P. Paruta, *Historia Vinetiana* (Venice, 1703).

Phrantzes, ed. Bonn = G. Phrantzes, *Annales*, in *Corpus Scriptorum Historiae Byzantinae* (Bonn).

Pouqueville, *Voyage* = F. Pouqueville, *Voyage de la Grèce* (Paris, 1826), 6 vols.

Rev. arch. = *Revue archéologique.*

Romanin = S. Romanin, *Storia Documentata di Venezia* (Venice, 1853–1861), 10 vols.

Tafel und Thomas, *Urkunden* = G. Tafel und G. Thomas, *Urkunden zur älteren Handels- und Staatsgeschichte der Republik Venedig mit besonderer Beziehung auf Byzanz in die Levante*, in *Fontes Rerum Austriacarum, II. Diplomataria et Acta*, XII–XIV (Vienna, 1856–7).

Zakythinos, *Despotat*, I = D. Zakythinos, *Le Despotat grec de Morée*, I (Paris, 1932).

ILLUSTRATIONS

FIGURES IN THE TEXT

PLATES

CASTLES OF THE MOREA

Fig. 1. Map of Medieval Greece.

INTRODUCTION

The title of this book is brief and correspondingly indefinite. More exactly, it is a description of sixteen of the larger medieval fortresses in the Peloponnese, occupied by the Venetians during the period 1685–1715, and drawn by their engineers round the year 1700. More generally, it is about Greece during the Middle Ages, in the sense that in Greece the Middle Ages have continued, without major interruptions, into the present day. Deprived of the Renaissance, admitted to Europe only in the XIX century, still waiting for her industrial revolution, Greece presents a peculiar and unfamiliar history as background for a book on castles.

This medieval aspect of Greece needs to be taken into account, no less, as the background to the present epoch, if either are to be comprehensible. In the V century B.C. Greece resisted and threw back the invasions of Asia. Three hundred years later she fell captive to Rome, which transmitted Hellenistic civilization to the western half of Europe. The legacy of Greece has come to us third-hand, filtered and re-filtered through Rome and the Renaissance. What we have is a painting of a painting. The original living image has been transformed. The great myths of a primitive tribe that covered the mysteries of man and nature wend their way through weary Roman epics, emerge again in courtly lyrics, declaim themselves upon the stage of Madame de Maintenon's school for young girls, and finish up as the musty devices of a literature of revivals. The aesthetic predilections of a different time and place have embalmed Antiquity and varnished it over with concepts of restraint, rationality, and remoteness, like an object under a glass bell. Modern scholarship has smashed the glass, and exposed what lay beneath it to the rough winds of reinterpretation, so that we begin to make out the image of a hot, turbulent, uncomfortable country, and a race whose peculiar genius was to curb the meridional violence of its nature with the forms of art. Still, however, in the popular mind, and for most of the western world, ancient Greece remains a sort of cool, ideal condition, decorated with snow-white pediments in a Mediterranean as tranquil as Baedeker or *The Tanglewood Tales*, peopled with eminent Victorians called Themistocles and Plato. For the most part we are still children of the Enlightenment, and cling to this ideal Antiquity as the direct and fitting parent of our civilization, while we keep our gaze averted from the age between, the centuries which swallowed up the last of the Legions and the *Pax Romana*.

In Greece to-day the traveller may note, among the ruins of the Ancient World, the erection of the barracks and pillboxes guarding communications through the mountains of Arkadia, and the regiments raising the defense lines across the coastal plain between Mount Olympos and the sea; and be reminded of that other age given over to danger, less chronicled

1

but closer to us than Troy or Actium, whose memorials cover the mountain passes and valleys, clifftops and harbors, from Crete to Macedonia. Where, he may ask, is the classical Greece he has been brought up with, in the long afterglow of the Renaissance? Instead of shining templestones chiselled with the resources of perfection, these fortresses of medieval Greece crouch to the contours of the land with crumbling, roofless walls of rubble, built with the mark of haste, as if there were not time between one invasion and the next to build them. The columns have fallen, and the upright bodies of the gods and charioteers have given way to the murky features of the saints, in whose melancholy slit-eyes or open glare of pity we read the warning of an age that has seen the columns fall and gone into the defensive, waiting for invasions and the Judgment.

They strike a familiar note to-day, after the bombs have fallen, among our underground lines and our research laboratories, whose hint of destruction sets us far off from the sunnier centuries of Metternich or Pericles, Louis XIV or Gladstone or Augustus Caesar. Our affinity is rather with that intervening period of disorder, where we can see the familiar crises preenacted among the crumbling social fabrics, the frightened governments, and the towering efforts of the unheroic.

Yet though our civilization claims to have been born in Ancient Greece, with its one or two centuries so bright that a squabble of two villages has set the pattern of world wars, still it is the whole of Greece, from the beginning to the present, whose history serves as the compass of human events. Let it guide us past Alexandria and Rome into its darkest period, where we shall find more signposts and read more oracles. Here in a small space are empires fighting, measuring their fortunes in the grip or loss of colonies; wars waged in the name of Christianity and civilization; native peoples fighting the encroachment of outsiders, fight-

ing against each other with the outsiders' help; and the technique of civil war so fully developed that the crisis of one country reflects the conflict of nations. It is the Middle Ages which determined Greece's relation to the world of to-day.

With the end of the Roman Empire, however, the East Mediterranean world vanishes from our Western textbooks. Side glances at medieval Greece are mostly accompanied by attempts to squeeze it, together with classical Antiquity, into the framework of a single European history, despite the divergence of their strains. Europe has been endlessly revolutionized. Its geography and institutions have been cut up into sections, and with each change the past has been set off always at further and further removes. Its present is the end of a road with many turnings. The vanishing of the empire that had unified the world, the rise of independent cities while Rome crumbled, the rise of nation-states, the blotting out of tradition and learning, the rediscovery of learning in a new tradition, the Reformation and the breakdown of a single church, the discovery of the New World and the expansion of Europe, colonization, imperialism, industrial and political revolutions, the replacing of religion by science and the class war: all this on one hand. And in contrast, the Eastern Mediterranean where the Emperors of the Romans ruled down to the century that saw the discovery of America.

Here was a huge state, always on the defensive, gradually shrinking over a thousand years, while bit by bit was broken off its edges in the long fight against the Arabs from the South, the Turks from the East, the Slavs from the North, and the Franks from the West of Europe. Within these limits it preserved its political integrity and its traditions unbroken. The palace revolts of Constantinople were not enough to destroy the Empire. Orthodox Christianity was again and again asserted over the heresies which shook it, while Christian and Moslem walked together in the holy places. The Empire did not extend across oceans. Missionaries were not sent to continents on the other side of the globe to spearpoint the subjugation of primitive or drowsing peoples. Those who came to Greece as conquerors, Romans and Avars, were hellenized. Venetian magistrates in the coastal places of the Aegean grew rebellious against *la Dominante*. Frankish barons in the castles of the Peloponnese and Thessaly died without issue. The Greeks themselves, gradually enslaved and at last robbed of all political independence, retained during the long Turkish night the religion and language which had provided the unity of Byzantium. Even with the Turkish conquest, the Empire itself remained in place, and only partially changed hands. The Sultans set their state upon foundations laid by Constantine. After the master of the house, the Emperor and Steward of Christ, was gone, the servants still remained in service. The war, commerce, and administration of the Ottomans depended largely on the hands and brains of Greeks, the subject people who knew the business of ruling better than their rulers. Geographically, after the Turks fell back from central Europe, the East returned to the limits which Alexander had set, between the Balkans and Afghanistan.

The Turkish conquest drew down a curtain upon the Eastern Mediterranean, which cut it off from the western world, and had the effect of holding time in suspension. Europe forged ahead in discovery and material advancement, but Greece, by the XIX century, had fallen again into the backward and primitive condition of life that marked her when abandoned to provincial desolation as an outpost of the new East Rome.

An organic unity and a concentration of space pervade the history of this corner of the world, and set it apart from Europe during those centuries when its tribes became nations and covered the hemispheres. A unity perhaps the result of that historical force which restricted the beginnings of civilization to the East, and later split the Roman Empire in two, and sundered the Christian Church; or perhaps the legacy of Byzantium, superimposed on that of Alexander, which left behind it, underneath a confusion of tongues, the pattern of a commonwealth of nations. The pagan civilization that had spread from Greece and Ionia out over the Mediterranean was transformed into the Christian civilization of Byzantium, which drew back from Europe and returned into its eastern half. Today's remnant of it has returned to the territorial limits of the South Balkan peninsula. Here, finally, concentrated in the language, the religion, and the vicissitudes of a continuing race, we may read that single history whose past and present reflect each other like broken mirrors.

During the III century after Christ the land of intellectual light entered its Dark Ages. Our study begins at the point where Greece vanishes from history, and re-emerges to view as the "Scythian wilderness" of the early Byzantine period. For centuries nothing is visible but the floods of invasions. Herulians, Vizigoths, and Huns pour into the country from the North, obliterating the boundaries of Empire. The old Roman law forbidding local fortification within the Imperial dominion becomes a danger before the rising tide. During the IV century the towns of Greece gird themselves with walls once more. In the VI century Justinian draws up the lines of resistance at Thermopylae and the Isthmus, and then for two hundred years Avars and Slavs sweep down into Greece, while the Hellenic population vainly tears down the temples of Antiquity to build fortresses against them. In places the Greeks are engulfed by the invasions, in others Byzantine rule is driven out entirely. In this anarchy of decentralization the invasions give impetus to the rise of local war-lords and powerful ruling clans, whose private fights perpetuate the pattern of Greek

1*

history from ancient times, and determine the progressively disastrous course of Greek events up to the Turkish conquest and beyond.

Shortly after the year 800 the tide of the Slavic invasions was halted. The barbarians settled in the land and adopted Christianity, while Greece came back under the sway of Byzantium. The great Byzantine churches of the following centuries and the record of the landowners' riches indicate that Greece at last regained prosperity. Its only history, however, was the record of strife under the alternate oppression of Byzantine officials and the local archons, who preferred to wage wars against each other rather than turn their eyes to the danger fast approaching from outside.

With all of its principal enemies Byzantium had in turn achieved some sort of *modus vivendi*. Barbarian tribes had been assimilated into the Empire. Slavs had been converted to Orthodox Christianity. Islam had come to terms, allowing religious freedom to the Christians in Arab-occupied lands. But now a new power had arisen with whom there was to be no peace, the Christians of western Europe. Since the V century these had looked to Palestine, in the territory of the Eastern Empire, as the source of relics and the end of pilgrimages. In later centuries Europe remembered how Charlemagne had endowed a pilgrims' hostel in Jerusalem. After the capture of Jerusalem by the Arabs in 638 pilgrimages continued: the tourist trade was welcome. In the X century the Byzantine navy cleared the seas of Arab corsairs, securing the way for the pilgrims who, in the next century, came flocking into the East from every corner of Europe. Pilgrimages as such were harmless, but the results were not. In the V century, after the Eastern Councils had established Christian dogma, a jealous bishop of Rome ordered the Emperor to submit to his own *ex cathedra* decisions. The rivalry of the churches of East and West grew with time and insult, until in 1054 the schism was declared final. The unity

of Christendom could be re-established now only by conquest or infiltration. The pilgrims were the vanguard. Next, the bellicose instincts of the military society of western Europe were channelled by the Church into the concept of a holy war, directed first against the Infidel in Spain, and then towards the Arabs in the East.

The Byzantine Empire had long been suffering the depredations of its enemies, the Normans on its west and the Turks on its eastern flank. Over a period of centuries the Empire had been undermined by its own internal policies, first of taxation and religious persecution, which drove its subjects to live under the kindlier and more orderly rule of the Moslems, and next by the replacing of the old agrarian system of independent landholders by a hereditary aristocracy. The new wardens of the Anatolian marches soon developed into local tyrants and rivals of the Emperor. Their vast estates were given over to sheep grazing, and the land gradually fell open to invasions. The defeat of the Byzantines at Manzikert in 1071 lost them Armenia, proclaimed the advance of the Turks, and gave western Europe the belief that the Eastern Empire was no longer capable of defending Christendom. At the close of the XI century the needs of Byzantium and the expansionist urge of western Europe came into harmony. The Emperor Alexios I appealed to the Pope to recruit troops for the defense of the Greek Empire. Pope Urban II raised the army which in 1099 overthrew the Arab Caliphate, and set up the Latin Kingdom of Jerusalem. The land-hungry, uncivilized knights and peasants of the West who had come to reclaim the Sepulchre, stayed to enjoy the charms of the Eastern Mediterranean. In vain Alexios and his successors tried to preserve their empire by keeping a balance of power between the Franks and the Infidel. Now it was too late: Europe had found its natural outlet, and learned the fatal secret of Byzantium. The sprawling, undefended wealth of the Empire inspired two more crusades during the next hundred years. The infiltration of the East at last came to a head at the turn of the XIII century, when Innocent III launched the Fourth Crusade. But religious authority, even in the age of St. Thomas Aquinas, was less a force than money. The plutocracy of Venice was swift to submit a plan for the partitioning of the Byzantine Empire. Long expert through her devious business interests in the ways of the Levant, Venice commanded the flotilla which was to bear the crusaders to the Holy Land. The Doge Enrico Dandolo changed the course of the ships, and deposited the crusaders not on the shores of Palestine, but at the Golden Horn, offering them there a prize more tempting than Jerusalem. The riches of Constantinople called to a rougher appetite: the Sepulchre was forgotten. The City was sacked, the Empire of East Rome systematically dismembered. The reigning dynasty fled into Anatolia, while the Frankish knights, descendants of the barbarian tribes that had overrun the old Roman Empire eight centuries before, now found themselves heirs to the sumptuous civilization of Justinian and Constantine.

The Western Church had now achieved temporal dominion over Eastern Europe and the shores of Asia Minor, with a Flemish count named Baldwin installed as head of a feudal Latin Empire in Constantinople. Salonica, Crete, and Cyprus became subsidary Kingdoms, the Peloponnese a Principality, Athens and the Aegean Islands Duchies, Boudonitza a Marquisate, Salona a County, distributed among the crusading barons of Burgundy, Champagne, Lombardy, and Flanders. The merchants of Venice, who had originally allotted one third of the Byzantine Empire to themselves, came off with a sizable portion including the Ionian Islands, the coasts of Albania and Epiros, the Messenian ports of Methone and Corone, the entire Cyclades, the islands of Kythera, Salamis, Aegina, Crete, and finally Euboea. This chain of islands and harbors extending down the Adriatic, through the Aegean to Constantinople, the Black Sea, and the trade-routes of Mongolia and Cathay confirmed Venice as the commercial capital of Europe.

In 1205 the Peloponnese was conquered by a band of Frankish knights who set up the semi-independent, feudal *Princée de l'Amorée* under a Prince and twelve vassal barons. The castles captured from the Greeks — Acrocorinth, Argos, Nauplia, Kalamata, Arkadia, and Patras — were improved with the arts of fortification imported from the West. New castles arose at Mistra, Maina, Passava, Karytaina, and Chlemoutsi. From these places the Franks kept the Greeks in subjection, and hemmed in the wild Slavic tribes that still inhabited Taygetos owing allegiance to none. The Principality reached its zenith in half a century. By 1259 William Villehardouin, the reigning Prince, was a captive of the Greeks. In 1261 the Greeks recovered Constantinople, drove out the Latins, and reinstated the Byzantine Empire. The Prince of Frankish Achaea was ransomed, "and as an earnest of his freedom ... gave three places, the strongest in the Peloponnese, to the Emperor of the Romans, Monemvasia and Leuktra in Mani and Lakonian Sparta. And once again the Greeks (Ῥωμαῖοι) set their hands upon the Peloponnese, and from those three places the entire island came back into their sway even as it had been before, except for a few forts and cities of which the aristocracy of Venice was possessor."[1]

The Morea was now divided among three powers. In 1311 most of the French nobility of Greece was wiped out in battle by a band of Catalan mercenaries, who established themselves in the old Burgundian Duchy of Athens. The Frankish Principality of Achaea passed into the hands of absentee rulers. New adventurers from Europe, Navarrese soldiers of fortune, the Knights of Rhodes, bankers and princes from Flanders, Florence, Naples, and

[1] Phrantzes, ed. Bonn, p. 17.

Genoa, arrived in Greece to share the spoils of the disputed successions which, during the XIV century, stimulated the expansion of the Byzantine province in the southeastern Peloponnese. Its territories gradually widened, as the foreigners fought among themselves. The Venetians, from their listening posts in Methone, Corone, Navarino, Argos, and Nauplia, studied first the disintegration of the Frankish state, and then in the early XV century turned their hostility against the Despotate of Mistra, whose rapid growth had upset the political balance. Under the threat of the Turkish invasions, Venice at the last moment tried to make peace between the Greeks and Latins in the Morea.

Her efforts were disregarded. In 1430 Constantine Palaiologos, Despot of Mistra, captured the fortresses of Patras and Chlemoutsi, and so put an end to the last remnant of Frankish Achaea. Except for the five Venetian colonies, the whole Morea was re-united under Greek rule. The Byzantine Empire now consisted of a city and a province. The fall of each demonstrated that clash of heroism and jealousy, dominant in the individual Greek nature, and motive force of Greece's history. In 1453 Constantinople was captured. The last Constantine died fighting on the walls even while the Turks were entering the city. Seven years later his two brothers, Thomas and Demetrios, ruling the Morea between them, preferred a fratricidal civil war to a common defense of their people. Each sold out, one to the Pope, the other to the Sultan. The Despotate of Mistra ended in betrayal, and by 1460 Greece disappeared as a political entity.

The Venetians busily looked to the safety of their trading posts by signing treaties with the Turks. "Essendo noi mercanti non possiamo viver senza loro" was a motto characteristic of that expediency which won Venice four centuries of greatness and at last caused her downfall. The Turks of the XV and XVI centuries could not be lived with. After 1460 the Vene-

tian colonies awaited their fate one by one. The year 1463 saw the outbreak of the first of the Turco-Venetian Wars, the long struggle of implacable expansion against the death-grip of a commercial empire. Venice's interests in the Levant dated from the XI century: Venice had engineered the Fourth Crusade, fed herself upon the rivalry of Byzantium and the Latin states of the East, and then sought to keep at peace with the power which had destroyed them all. But the Turkish capacity for destruction was not to stop with the end of the East Roman Empire. First fell Venetian Argos, then Euboea by the end of the war in 1479. In 1500 Venice lost Methone, Corone, and Old Navarino, in 1540 Nauplia and Monemvasia, in 1566 Chios, in 1571 Cyprus, and at last in 1645 the loss of Canea marked the beginning of the War of Candia. By 1669 Crete passed from Venetian to Ottoman domination.

Venice had already entered her decline. During the XIV century her North Italian dominion had begun to slip away from her, while she concentrated her energies upon the sea-borne empire in the Levant. But the conquest of Egypt by the Turks cut off her Red Sea trade, and finally the discovery of a sea-route to the Indies in 1499 shifted the stream of commerce from the Mediterranean to the Atlantic. The foundations of Venice's greatness were swiftly shored away. The Turks, meanwhile, spread over the Aegean, then north through the Balkans and Hungary into the heart of Europe.

Europe in the later XVII century was divided between two rival camps, round whom the lesser nations, independent and dependant, ranged themselves in fixed or shifting order. Louis XIV was struggling for the mastery of the continent, first bringing France itself under his heel; reducing the Stuart Kings of England to a subsidized neutrality; seizing the Spanish Netherlands, the Saar, Strassburg, Luxemburg, and Lorraine; and then securing to his house the succession to the Spanish throne.

Over a period of fifty years there formed and re-formed against him a series of alliances between Holland, Spain, Austria, the Electors of Brandenburg, Saxony, Bavaria, and the Palatinate, the Prince of Savoy, and William of Orange, King of England. The chief constant in this flux of leagues was Leopold I of Austria, whose Holy Roman Empire had become the bulwark of western Europe against the Turks. Ceaselessly the agents of France worked among the German princelings to wean them away from their submission to the Emperor. Sums were lavished on the election to the throne of Poland, while Louis XIV joined the Turks in fomenting the rebellious nationalism of Hungary and Transylvania. The Hapsburg was kept safely busy on his eastern flank when the Turks opened war in 1663. Twenty years later the political vacuum of Europe's disunity precipitated the last of the Turkish invasions. For fifty-seven days the walls of Vienna withstood the Turkish siege. Finally the tide was turned, and the great age of Ottoman expansion came to an end. Six months after the relief of Vienna, Austria, Poland, and the Republic of Venice formed the Holy League to drive the Turks out of southeastern Europe.

In the spring of 1684 an army of Venetian, Dalmatian, Florentine, Maltese, and Papal troops under the leadership of the Venetian general, Francesco Morosini, moved against the Turks in Greece. The Poles drove into Roumania, while the Austrians followed up with advances into Hungary, Serbia, Bulgaria, and Transylvania. The Venetians took the islands of Leukas, Baltos, and Xeromeros, Missolonghi, and Preveza in the first campaign, and during the ensuing winter entered into alliances with the Duke of Brunswick and the peoples of Cheimarra in Epiros and Mani in the southern Peloponnese. The year 1685[2] saw the capture of four castles in Messenia and

Mani, Corone, Zarnata, Kalamata, and Kelepha. In 1686 the Venetians took the remaining places in western Messenia, Old and New Navarino, Arkadia, and Methone, and then attacked the Turks from the side of the Argolid, capturing Argos and Nauplia. The campaign of 1687 saw the Venetians masters of Achaea and the central Peloponnese. First fell Patras, with the Castle of Morea and the Castle of Roumeli at the mouth of the Corinthian Gulf, Naupaktos (Lepanto), Acrocorinth, Chlemoutsi, and finally Mistra. Having conquered the Peloponnese in three campaigns, Morosini moved the allied armada north to Athens, which also capitulated after the bombardment of the Acropolis and the destruction of the Parthenon. In 1688 the resistance of the great fortress of Chalkis (Negroponte) threw the Venetians back into the Peloponnese. Monemvasia surrendered, and in 1699 the Peace of Carlowitz gave the Venetians a new Levantine dominion, consisting of the seven Ionian Islands, the three forts of Souda, Spinalonga, and Grabousa in Crete, the islands of Tenos and Aegina, and the "Kingdom" of the Morea. By the same treaty Poland, which had stimulated the portentous hostility of Russia against Turkey, recovered Podolia in the Ukraine, while Austrian ascendancy was reinstated in the eastern provinces of Transylvania and Hungary. The Turkish power in Europe was broken.

Now Venice had reversed the order of her losses. With the aid of powerful allies she had struck, while the striking was good, at an Ottoman Empire which had begun suddenly to show its weakness. The conquest of the Peloponnese avenged the loss of those islands and maritime places, guardians of the traderoutes to Asia on which her might and prosperity had been built. But that age lay removed by three or four centuries: it was a memory of the past, and what had happened in the intervening time gave little hope for its survival in the future. Venice had conquered

---

[2] The course of the Venetian campaigns in the Morea may be followed in greater detail in the opening sections of the consecutive chapters below.

the Morea in the belief that territorial expansion would recover her trade, her monopoly, and her ancient position among the nations of Europe. But unless the Ottoman Empire were crushed entirely, Venice could hardly hope again to do business on the Bosporos. The Ottomans were weak, but not yet shaken, and for purposes of foreign trade Istanbul was not Constantinople. Venice could exploit the Morea from all the harbors on its coast, but the enemy was still at hand. Beyond the Isthmus of Corinth lay the dominions of the Ottoman Empire, and a Turkish fleet still prowled in the Aegean. Since 1499 the East Mediterranean was a backwater. Commerce was flowing now through different oceans and round other continents. Venice had entered the War of the Holy League with the intent of recovering her vanished empire, but the conquest of the Peloponnese could not repay the sacrifice endured by her previous generation in the Cretan War.

Nevertheless, the Venetians organized the Morea with much of their old administrative skill, in accordance with the policies and institutions developed by the Most Serene Republic over a period of centuries. The record of their rule is told in the despatches of the Venetian governors, magistrates and census-takers, painting a minutely detailed picture of the country, with its sources of wealth, its needs, its fall and growth of population, and the condition of its defenses: the harbors silted up, the ports unguarded, and the fortresses fallen into neglect and ruin. From 1690 to 1715 the reports call with increasing urgency for repair and refortification of the castles on which depends the safety of the population, and of Venice's last great gamble. Plans are drawn up for their renovation, well illustrated by the collection of Francesco Grimani, reproduced in this book. The elaborate legends of the drawings tell the story of the Venetians' ambition. The directions grow monotonous: "Posto da farsi ... Recinto da farsi ... Ter-

rapieno da farsi ... Quartiere da farsi ... Altro posto da farsi ... La mura deve esser serata ... deve esser ristaurata ... ha bisogno del suo Parapeto ... Turrion S. Marco vole un cannon ... Posto vole due Colunbrine ... Turrion S. Gaetano vel una petriera ... Sitto dove si deve diruppare per impedire la Sorpresa ..." A comparison of all these projected schemes with the fortresses in their actual state are a testimony to what Venice failed to accomplish.

What Venice did accomplish in the way of fortification in the Morea at this late date seems to indicate she believed she was there to stay. But her allies of the Holy League left her for the more profitable pursuit of gnawing off sections of the Ottoman territories nearer home. In 1715 she found herself defending the Morea alone with 8,000 troops concentrated in five coastal fortresses. In a three months' campaign an enormous Turkish army drove the Venetians out of Greece forever. A conquest Venice had undertaken in a dream of past greatness ended in reducing her to the shadowy pomps and festivals of her final century, while Greece settled down under the somnolent corruption of the last hundred years of Turkish rule. This was the end of the two aged empires of East and West, which had imposed the tyrannies of their rise and fall upon a people who were at last re-emerging as a nation.

*   *   *

NOTE ON THE GRIMANI PLANS

The "Collection of the Drawings of the Plans of all the Fortresses in the Kingdom of the Morea and Part of the Harbors of the Same" contains forty-one plans, drawings, and maps of two fortresses in Crete and Euboea, three in Albania and Montenegro, and seventeen in the Peloponnese, with ten large bays around its coast.

Twenty- eight of these plans were drawn, as is known either by direct reference to his name or by the presence of his coat of arms, expressly for Francesco Grimani, a Venetian soldier and magistrate active in the Venetian conquest and occupation of the Peloponnese, 1685–1715. Wounded at the siege of Monemvasia during the summer of 1689,[3] he also fought with the rank of Lieutenant General at the capture of Valona and Canina in Albania, September 17–18, 1690.[4] From 1699–1701 he held the office of *Provveditore Generale dell' Armi in Morea,* a position of military command, at the end of which he wrote to the Venetian Senate the report dated October 8, 1701, which describes, better than any other document of the time, the condition of the Peloponnese and the details of the Venetian administration. In 1706 Grimani was called back to duty in the Peloponnese, this time as governor. At the end of his tenure his report of January 8, 1708, written to the military commander, da Mosto, completes the long record[5] of his concern and accomplishments in the castles of the Morea. Ten of these, he says, are garrisoned, four are ruled by local proveditors, six others dismantled or destroyed. Generally, he continues, the walls are in ruin; the fortresses ill supplied with troops, food, and munitions; their treasures low. He mentions the explosion of powder-stores and the consequent damage to the walls of Monemvasia, Argos, Corone, the two Navarinos, and Acrocorinth. He has repaired the cisterns, barracks, hospitals, and storehouses in Nauplia, Patras, the Castle of Morea, Argos, and Acrocorinth. At Methone he has built four new barracks, two storehouses, and a hospital, and offers an elaborate proposal for the refortification of the citadel's landward front. Notable is his ommission of any of the works built by him to strengthen the land defenses of Nauplia: the great bastion of 1706, and the two caponiers sealing off the neck of

the peninsula, built after he had withdrawn his earlier insistent demands for the fortification of the Palamedi. He suggests improvements in Old Navarino, and a plan to demolish Chlemoutsi (Castel Tornese) and build a new harbor fortress on the sea near by at Glarentza (Chiarenza). He gives particular care to the Peloponnesian harbors: Nauplia, where he recommends dredging; Drepanon with its unique facilities for dry-dock repairs, already in process of improvement, which nevertheless, with Poros, needs some fortified work to protect the entrance; Porto Longo on Sapienza; and the Bays of Tolos, Methone, and Navarino. He speaks also of a mole which the Venetians began building at Monemvasia during the siege of 1690. Finally he mentions "drawings attached to the report in Book 5, and certain despatches, notably despatch 79," and refers to a plan of Acrocorinth by La Salle.

The reference may be set beside the collection of plans reproduced in this volume. With their numerous proposals for refortification, yet without showing any of the major works actually carried out, these drawings appear to have been made, for the most part, shortly after the Venetian conquest of the Morea or, presumably, during Grimani's first period of office (1699–1701).

Those plans which bear neither Grimani's crest nor title may still have been part of his original collection. Plate X of Old Navarino is dated 1706, the first year of his governorship. The plan of Drepanon (Plate XXV) bears no reference to his name, but it was Grimani who in 1701 first suggested its fortification. La Salle's drawing of Acrocorinth (Plate XXXII) may well be the one spoken of by him in his report to da Mosto. His connection with the abortive siege of Canea (Plate XXXVIII) is unknown, but the two panoramic views of Monemvasia (Plate XXXVII) and the map of Valona and Canina (Plate XXXIX) may have been included in the series as showing scenes of his military activity. The two views of the

---

[3] Garzoni, I, p. 331.
[4] See Plate XXXIX, (I, K, V, and P).
[5] Published by Sp. Lampros in Δελτίον, V, pp. 448–561.

Navarinos (Plate XIII), the small drawing of Methone dated 1731 (Plate XVII), and that of Dulcigno, 1751 (Plate XL) are later insertions.

Seventeen out of the forty-one drawings are unsigned. The remaining twenty-four are signed by eight different hands. Six are by a French engineer, in Venetian service, who signs himself Levasseur, Le Vaseur, Vaseur, Vasieur, and Vassor.[6] His drawings of Kelepha (Plate VI) New Navarino (Plate XII), the Castle of Morea (Plate XXX), Mistra (Plate XXXIV), and Monemvasia (Plate XXXVI), are characterized by clear, large, detailed plans of the fortresses and, in two cases, carefully colored elevations. His map of the Bay of Navarino (Plate VIII) is, unlike the others, out of proportion. Five plans are by a German called Beler (variation, beller), whose meticulous draughtsmanship is sometimes obscured by liberties of proportion, and lost under the weight of Teutonically baroque ornamentation (see Plates II, III, IX, XI). Another draughtsman is Bortolo Carmoy, whose name appears on Plate XXI of Nauplia ("Copied from the original of Giovanni Bassignani..."), on Plate XXIII of Nauplia (signed B. C.), and on Plate XXXIX of Valona. The plan of the siege of Canea (Plate XXXVIII) is unsigned, but appears, stylistically, to be his also. An extreme accuracy justifies his mention in the reports of Grimani and Loredan[7] as "sopra Intendente Ingegner." The signature of Van Deyk (or Vandeyk) appears on the plans of Argos (Plate XXVIII), Patras (Plate XXIX), the Castle of Morea (Plate XXX, together with that of Levasseur), and Chlemoutsi (Plate XXXIII, together with the initials of another draughtsman, A. D.). Of these great skill is shown in the drawings of Patras and the Castle of Morea, while those of Argos and Chlemoutsi

are out of proportion. Vandeyk is mentioned in the report of Francesco Grimani[8] among the engineers as "il capo di tutti," helping also in the census of the Morea. The plans of Corone (Plate I), Acrocorinth (Plate XXXI), and Chlemoutsi (Plate XXXIII) bear the signature A. D. The last mentioned is out of proportion, but the first two are perfectly exact. The two charts of the South Argolid coast, Plates XXIV and XXVII of Karathona, Tolos, Kouverta, and Kastri, are signed by Niccolò Franco. Plates XXXII of Acrocorinth and XXXVII A of Monemvasia are the work of two Frenchmen, La Salle and Erault Sieur Desparées respectively.

Twenty of the drawings give large scale plans of the fortresses themselves. Fifteen show castles on a small scale, with large sections of the surrounding country. Eleven others are topographical coastal charts, with or without indication of castles. Six show the sieges and battles in action at Kalamata, Negroponte, Monemvasia, Valona, and Canea. Remains of an early form of tracing are evident in six of the plans, where the various lines of the fortifications are impressed with a stylus or outlined in pin-pricks.

It is interesting to note that, with one exception, this collection shows only the plans of places on or near the coast. Mistra is the only inland fortress represented. The great Frankish castle of Karytaina on the upper Alpheios is not included in the series, nor Byzantine Zaraphona in the foothills of Parnon. A clue to this omission may be found in a sentence of Corner's report of 1690: "Karytaina is a district rich in minerals, from which the Turks make their gunpowder, with a castle in good condition — as far as I was able to penetrate." The wild and mountainous interior of the Peloponnese had to take care of itself. For the Venetians the sea was all.

---

[6] A plan for the fortification of Corinth by François Levasseur is reproduced in *Corinth*, III, ii, fig. 97.

[7] Δελτίον V, pp. 501, 735.

[8] *Ibid.*, V, p. 501.

CHAPTER I

CORONE

(Plates I, II)

In the early summer of 1685 a Venetian fleet of twenty-six vessels moved down the Adriatic to the island of Sapienza, off the southwestern tip of the Messenian peninsula. There the chiefs of the allied armies of the Holy League held a council of war, where to launch the first attack against the Peloponnese. Venetian agents from the Ionian Islands were sent to negotiate with the inhabitants of Mani, the harsh, waterless ridge extending from Taygetos to Tainaron, which had long defied the efforts of the Turks to enter. The word came back that the Maniates were ready to revolt in their own good time, but for the present begged the Europeans not to land upon their coasts, since the Turks had recently made hostages of their wives and children. The Venetian commander, Francesco Morosini, decided then to set his forces against Corone, where on the other side of the Messenian Gulf he could still keep in touch with the Maniates who, fierce but self-willed allies, needed both encouragement and surveillance.

So the fleet sailed round Cape Gallo, and on June 25 disembarked 10,000 troops on the south shore of the small promontory on which stands the citadel of Corone, projecting out into the Gulf (Fig. 2). The small town below the fortress walls was occupied without resistance, and within two days the lines of circumvallation were dug, a mile long, sealing the peninsula off between both its shores.[1] Toward the mainland all the olive trees, the chief wealth of the region,[2] were cut down to remove any natural cover for the Turkish reinforcements who would arrive to raise the siege. Batteries were set up in the captured suburb and on the high ground west of the castle. Six ships fired on the stout double bastion, which rises above the sea in the fortress' northeast corner (Figs. 3 and 4), while the strongpoint of the fortifications, a great redout at the western end, became the target of a bombardment which continued until the final assault. On July 7 the Turkish relieving force arrived from Kalamata, and took up positions one mile from the Venetian earthworks (Fig. 2). Between the two camps was a small hill, which the Venetians fortified with a bonnet and covered way, upon which seemed to hang the fall or resistance of the fortress itself, for the fighting which raged around it, and the frequency with which it changed hands.[3] On the other side the Venetians ceaselessly tried to

[1] Locatelli, I, pp. 123–152.

[2] The olive orchards of Corone were noticed as early as 1191 by a pilgrim, Benedict of Peterborough, *Gesta regis Henrici Secundi*, ed. Stubbs (London, 1867), II, p. 200: "Et super gulfum illum est civitas episcopalis quae dicitur Curun, et ibi crescit copia olivarum, adeo quod dicitur quod in toto mundo non est locus ubi sit tanta copia olei olivarum."

[3] Garzoni, I, pp. 100, 107–118.

FIG. 2. CORONE, BESIEGED BY THE VENETIANS JUNE-AUGUST, 1685. TURKISH RELIEVING FORCE ENCAMPED, RIGHT.
From a drawing by Coronelli.

open a breach at the strong west bastion, while making a feint with a flank assault in the castle's south curtain. Under the direction of the engineer Verneda,[4] the Maltese troops prepared a charge of a hundred barrels of powder, which succeeded only in dislodging a small quantity of earth, while the stones of the wall filled up the breach. The explosion was enough, however, to provoke a Turkish attack from the side of the mainland, in which the Venetians were driven from the bonnet and the outermost arc of their defenses.[5] It became doubtful now whether, with the enemy in the rear, the Venetians would ever succeed at the main breach. So on August 7, before sunrise, Moro-

sini launched an attack which drove the Turks from the field. The allied army, now concentrating on the siege, dug two parallel galleries extending beneath the west bastion, where they placed a charge of 250 powder barrels salvaged from the Turkish camp. At dawn of August 11 the mines were exploded, and the breach opened. The Venetians and their auxiliaries attacked immediately. After three hours of fighting, they were repulsed, but fought their way back in the middle of the day, at the same time that a picked body of troops put to shore on the small tongue of land beyond the fortress, and prepared to storm the eastern defenses. The sign was given for a general assault from all sides, but the white flag was raised and the attack halted. During the parley that ensued one of the Turkish

[4] Better known for his plans of XVII century Athens. See W. Miller, "The Venetian Revival in Greece," in *Essays*.

[5] Coronelli, *Memorie*, pp. 66,

Fig. 3. Corone, North Curtain, Outer Enclosure, showing Outer Gate and Round Sea Bastion, looking East to Mount Taygetos.

cannons exploded accidentally, and the army of the Holy League entered the castle and massacred its 1,500 defenders and inhabitants. A Te Deum was sung after the carnage, and the Venetians turned to the repair and refortification of the citadel, which now after nearly two centuries had returned into the hands of its original builders.[6]

*　　*　　*

In the middle of the XII century the Arab geographer Edrisi described Corone as a "small town with a fort over the sea" in the outlying Byzantine province of the Morea.[7] In the year 1205, after the Fourth Crusade had dismembered the Byzantine Empire, the Frankish barons who were subjugating the Morea sent a detachment of a hundred knights, led by Guillaume de Champlitte and Geoffroy de

Villehardouin, to occupy the valuable Messenian ports of Methone, Corone, and Kalamata. Each place surrendered on terms,[8] and Corone, described in the chronicle of the conquest as weak in walls and towers but strong in its position,[9] was bestowed as a fief on Villehardouin.[10]

Venice, however, in the following year sent out a fleet of galleys to occupy her new Ionian and Aegean stations, which also took the opportunity of sailing into Methone and Corone and expelling the Frankish garrisons.[11] Villehardouin was compensated for his loss by his suzerain, the Prince of Achaea, with the two fiefs of Arkadia and Kalamata.[12] A few years later, when he himself had succeeded to the Principality, the need of naval aid forced him to make his peace with Venice. In a treaty of

[6] *La Morea Combattuta* (Venice, 1686), pp. 89–95; *Relation de la prise de Coron* (Amsterdam, 1686); Rossi, *Successi dell' Armi Venete in Levante nella Campagna di 1685* (Venice, 1686), pp. 35–139; *Il Regno della Morea sotto i Veneti* (Venice, 1688), pp. 17–31; *The History of the Venetian Conquests* (London, 1689), pp. 34–59; Foscarini, pp. 166–174; Cappelletti, XI, pp. 42–44; Romanin, VII, pp. 48f.

[7] *Géographie d'Edrisi*, tr. Jaubert, in *Receuil de voyages et de mémoires* (Paris, 1840), VI, p. 124.

[8] X. τ. M., lines 1651–1714; *L. de C.*, §§ 108–113; *L. de F.*, § 113; *C. di M.*, pp. 425f.

[9] X. τ. M., lines 1695–7:
Καὶ ἀπάυτου ἐκίνησαν κ' ὑπάουν στὸ κάστρο τῆς Κορώνης, κ' ηὗραν τὸ κάστρον ἀχαμνὸν ἀπὸ τειχέα καὶ πύργους· εἰς βράχον σπηλαίου ἐκείτετον, ἀφιρωμένο ἦτον.

[10] G. de Villehardouin, *La Conquête de Constantinople*, ed. Faral (Paris, 1939), §§ 328–330.

[11] Miller, *Latins*, p. 39.

[12] X. τ. M, lines 1864f.; *C. di M.*, p. 426.

1209 he confirmed her in possession of Methone, Corone, and all of the Messenian peninsula south of Navarino Bay.[13] The same deed was ratified later in the century by William Villehardouin, who like his father Geoffroy before him, was ready to trade land for ships. Four Venetian galleys helped him in 1249 at the siege of Monemvasia, the last corner of Greece to admit the fall of Byzantium.[14] Venice, swift to seize when the prize was there for the asking, had skillfully covered her action at Methone and Corone with judicious loans of her unique commodity, naval power, and won for her posterity the two most valuable ports in Greece.

FIG. 4. CORONE, NORTHEAST SECTOR, WITH OUTER GATE AND DOUBLE SEA BASTION.

The half-way point along the great chain of communication stretching from the Adriatic to Crete and Egypt, Syria, the Holy Land, Constantinople, and the trade routes of Asia,[15] the two towns became known as the chief eyes of Venice. Under her rule Methone and Corone had a common history, or rather absence of history, since it was Venice's concern to keep history as far as possible removed from her possessions. Business, safety, and self-interest

were the keynote of her dominion, while Methone and Corone escaped the major turmoils of three centuries. After the recapture of Constantinople by the Greeks, Venice hastened to conclude a treaty in 1265 with the Emperor Michael VIII Palaiologos, who promised to respect her colonies in the southwestern Peloponnese.[16] The pledge was subsequently renewed and largely adhered to, throughout most of the ensuing struggles of Greeks, French, Angevins, and Florentines for supremacy in the Morea.[17] A state of disorder among numerous small powers served Venice's purpose best, who through her officials at Methone and Corone worked out a technique of playing off one against the other. However, as the Frankish dominions weakened or reverted into Greek hands, and the greater part of the Morea came under the sway of one master, the ancient jealousy of Venice and Byzantium broke out. Even while the shadow of Turkish conquest spread towards the shores of Greece, the Greek Despot of Mistra, anxious to drive the last of the Latins from the soil of the Peloponnese, took to inciting raids along the borders of Messenia. In 1387 and 1388 the Turks finally invaded the Morea, and in 1428 attacked and pillaged Methone and Corone by sea.[18] Still a common peril was not enough to unite the Christians of East and West. On the eve of the Turkish conquest, while the Despot Theodore I struggled to unify the Peloponnese, Venice only saw in his efforts a danger to her own interests, and refused to contribute to his plan for a concerted defense. Precautionary measures on her part consisted in strengthening her Messenian fortresses, and trying to win, at the eleventh hour, the loyalty of the Greek inhabitants by lowering their taxes and allowing the Orthodox bishop to live within the walls of Corone. They continued nonetheless to

[13] Tafel und Thomas, *Urkunden*, II, pp. 97–100.

[14] X. τ. M., lines 2778–2790; *C. di M.*, p. 435; *L. de C.*, §§ 190, 197; *L. de F.*, §§ 210f.

[15] See *Canon Pietro Casola's Pilgrimage (1494)*, (Manchester, 1907), p. 50: "... Corone,... a very large town and a powerful fortress... The people are very wealthy, for these places are the ports of discharge for Greece and the Black Sea for all classes of merchandise."

[16] Tafel und Thomas, *Urkunden*, III, p. 68.

[17] A. Mompherratos, Μεθώνη καὶ Κορώνη ἐπὶ Ἑνετοκρατίας (Athens, 1914), p. 6.

[18] Phrantzes, ed. Bonn, p. 83; Zakythinos, *Despotat* I, p. 212.

emigrate, leaving the land empty behind them. The doom of the Venetian colonies only lingered when the conqueror of Constantinople invaded the Peloponnese in 1458, and put an end to the Greek Despotate of Mistra. When the Byzantine Empire no longer existed, Venice, as indeed all Europe, found herself at last face to face with the enemy of Christendom, with the outer defenses gone.

Venice had recourse once more to commercial treaties, which saved her for a few years longer. But the Turks of the XV century were more intent on territorial and religious expansion than on doing business with any European power which still retained possessions in Greece. The conflict broke out in 1463, which after seventeen years lost Venice her two colonies of Argos and Euboea. In 1500 the inevitable blow was struck against Messenia. The Sultan Bayezid II fell upon Methone, and captured it after a siege of three months. At Corone the Venetians were ready to withstand a siege, but the inhabitants, terrified by the bloody example of Methone, and persuaded by Turkish promises of life if they surrendered, mutinied against their governors, and gave up the citadel, only to be banished by the Turks to Cephalonia. The long Venetian rule came to an end, and all the Peloponnese, except for Nauplia and Monemvasia, which held out forty years longer, passed under Turkish sway.[19]

Corone again suffered a brief change of masters in 1532 when the Holy Roman Emperor sent his admiral, the Genoese Andrea Doria, with eighty-three vessels to harass the coasts of Greece as a countermeasure to the Turkish expedition against Vienna nine years before. The Imperial and Ottoman fleets lingered many months, equally balanced, off the Akarnanian shore, each dubious of victory, until the Turks withdrew to Euboea, and Doria seized the initiative. He attacked Corone, and after three assaults from the side of the small peninsula below the fortress on the east

(see Plate I, *Penisola con diuersi Pozzi senz' Aqua*, and Fig. 12, right), captured the place and installed a garrison of 8,000 Imperial troops. A year later the Turks returned under the veteran admiral Khaireddin Barbarossa, and laid siege, while in the outside world the Emperor Charles V cast about him for an ally. In turn, Venice and the Knights of Malta refused his offer of Corone, no longer able to support a new commitment in Turkish Greece. Meanwhile the defenders of the place came to the end of their resources. When a squadron of Sicilian ships made their appearance in the port, ostensibly to bring relief, the soldiers together with 5,000 of the population, now mainly Albanian, embarked and were transported to Sicily and Naples. For the second time Corone was empty of life, when the Turks re-entered.[20]

* * *

Corone's history is reflected in the architecture of the fortress. The first Byzantine castle occupied what is now the inner enclosure: perhaps originally a simple fort on the small eminence at the top of the peninsula ridge, the position which remained its strongpoint through the succeeding centuries. To the east of this stretches a high plateau girdled with sandstone cliffs above the sea, which dwindles abruptly to a small tongue of land at the tip of the peninsula. The fortress which the Byzantine Greeks surrendered in 1205 consisted of a triangular court enclosing a section of this area with a redout on top of the ridge. After 1209 the Venetians overlaid these constructions with new towers, walls, and bastions, while the east curtain of the Byzantine fortress became the dividing wall for another great loop of curtain and artillery bastions enclosing the whole plateau into an outer court four times the area of the inner. Finally the Turks added to the east wall of this outer enclosure

---

[19] Miller, *Latins*, p. 497; Mompherratos, *op. cit.*, p. 68.

[20] Paruta, I, p. 328; Coronelli, *Memorie*, p. 64; Miller, *Latins*, pp. 505f.

a heavy guard of artillery fortifications during the XVI century. From its western apex to its eastern flank Corone shows an organic growth from the nucleus of an early medieval hilltop castle through the proliferating cells of inner and outer courts, to the terraced ramparts and embrasured bastions of developed artillery warfare.

The oldest section of the castle still standing is the wall which divides the two enclosures. Built of a heterogeneous combination of rubble and re-used fragments of earlier construction, column drums and carved elements of marble, it dates to a period when materials were quarried out of the ruins of both classical and Byzantine buildings, as in the time of the Slavic invasions between the VI and the IX century.

From the harbor town a road leads up to the entrance gate, along a ramp retained by a battering and buttressed wall, through the foundations of a propylaea which once flanked the curtain (Plates I, II; Fig. 5). This consisted of a low screen guarded by tall, decorative piers, and an elaborate structure bearing a carved plaque of the lion of St. Mark, a slotted and embrasured parapet, and a small hexagonal turret or sentry-box at the corner.

The section of the outer curtain immediately west of the gate is built of thirty courses of massive ashlar blocks measuring upwards of 8 feet long. These are a relic of the classical Messenian Asine, but the wall itself as in certain similar sections at Methone (see below p. 66), is more probably a re-use of Greco-Roman materials. So powerful a wall does not accord with the description of the Byzantine castle of Corone in the *Chronicle of the Morea*, and the presence of more blocks of the same size in the gateway would seem to indicate

FIG. 5. CORONE, THE PROPYLAEA, AS IT STOOD IN 1829. *From a drawing by Boccuet in Expédition scientifique de Morée, Architecture, I.*

that the builders who availed themselves of the ancient stones were the Venetians of the XIII century.

The gate (Plates I, A; II, F) is set in a large, square pylon, projecting forward from the curtain, standing 50 feet high, similar in form and dimensions to the early Frankish and Venetian gateways at Methone and Chlemoutsi (see below, pp. 66, 149–150). A pointed archway, reminiscent of the Gothic century of the Fourth Crusade, leads into a high, narrow, vaulted passage, pierced also, at the top, with a semicircular window (Fig. 6). The interior

FIG. 6. CORONE, THE MAIN GATE, INTERIOR.

face of the structure is built of the masonry which predominates throughout the Venetian fortresses in Greece: small ashlar blocks of an average length of 1 foot, square or oblong, carefully fitted in strong mortar. Eastward from the entrance the curtain carries an artil-

2

lery parapet 10 feet thick, curved on the exterior, and pierced with five gun embrasures and a number of long, slanting, tunnel-shaped loopholes for musketry. A stout cordon, or torus molding, a structural hallmark of artillery fortification, runs the length of the wall, marking the level of the embrasure floors.

The northeast corner of the fortress is occupied by two huge, round, adjacent bastions set on different levels of the sand bluff. The base of the lower is made of large, squared blocks, similar in form and size to those in the west flank of the first gate and the stretch of curtain next to it on the west. At the base of this bastion no mortar is visible between the joints, but in the upper section, and in the higher bastion next to it, the masonry conforms to the characteristic Venetian pattern of ashlar blocks, 1 foot square, showing like the design of a honeycomb through the thick, white mortar. A number of round, stone bosses ornament the surface of the walls. A vaulted passage leads from the interior of the fortress enclosure down to the platform of the lower bastion (Figs. 3, 4, left), which measures 35 feet between the parapets. These contain five embrasures with sloping floors, 12 feet deep and 12 feet wide at the openings. Several long, square musket holes, bored through the parapet, cover the closer points of danger, the shore and the base of the adjacent walls. A torus molding encircles the bastion at the embrasure level, and another follows round the exterior crest of the parapet, which connects with the parapets of the curtain and bastion above it by means of two large, sloping buttresses flanking the passageway. The embrasures of the upper bastion cover the Messenian Gulf in the direction of Mount Taygetos. Its wall next to the lower tower is vertical, but on the eastern side gradually spreads out into an enormous talus, which batters at an angle of 60 degrees on to the rocks at the water's edge 80 feet below (Fig. 7, right). Rounding the angle of the circuit, this scarp sheaths the bluff and forms a great, armored front to the sea along the fortress' northeast corner. This sector is the best example in Greece of the plasticity of Venetian military architecture which molds itself to the forms of nature, cliffside and shoreline. The sea has encroached up to its base

FIG. 7. CORONE, EAST SCARP, OUTER CURTAIN, LOOKING TOWARD THE NORTH SEA BASTION.

since the drawing of the Grimani plans, and the activity of clay diggers has caused the collapse of a long section of its scarp (Fig. 7), exposing the sand hill beneath it to the more patient destruction of wind and rain.

Below the fortress on this side lie the level wheatfields of the eastern point. Directly under the curtain is a platform (Plate II, *Piaza Bassa*), 50 feet across and 200 feet long. Along its outer edge runs a faussebraye, a low, thick parapet wall parallel to the curtain, pierced alternately with embrasures and deep, tapering musket-holes. Forty feet below it is a ditch, in which four pointed buttresses reinforce the scarp (Fig. 8). The counterscarp is topped with a wall, which stands a man's height above the level of the fields. The long

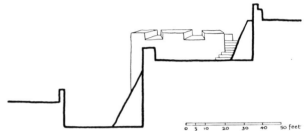

FIG. 8. CORONE, EAST ARTILLERY DEFENSES, ELEVATION.

platform is blocked at both ends by huge, round bastions. The northern of these was used as a storehouse for explosives by the Germans in 1944, who blew it up in their retreat. Its fragments show it to have been a hollow tholos, domed in brick. The southern bastion (Figs. 8–12) is a vast drum built over

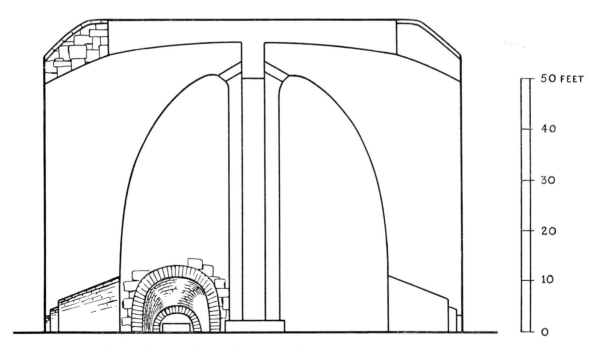

FIG. 9. CORONE, SOUTH BASTION OF EAST ARTILLERY DEFENSES, SECTION.

FIG. 10. CORONE, SOUTHEAST ARTILLERY BASTION, NORTH SIDE.

an ovoid tholos supported by an octagonal central pillar 50 feet high. Inside, at floor level, four tapering casemates, 15 feet deep, cover the water on the south and the peninsula on the east. In the bastion's west wall a wide ascent by long, sloping steps curves round to the platform above. The whole structure measures 90 feet wide and stands to a height of 70 feet on the southern side. The exterior walls are made of small, rectangular blocks of varying size. Larger blocks of sandstone and poros are used in the embrasure walls of the parapet (Fig. 10, left), around the inner mouth of the casemates in the domed chamber, and in the supporting column. Large, flat, square tiles form a covering to the upper slope of the parapet (Fig. 10). Tile is used extensively in the vaulting of the casemates, which show in wide fans on the interior walls of the tholos (Fig. 9). Fifteen feet from the ground the walls begin to incline together, built of long, flat tiles laid one upon the other in rings and rings up to the summit of the dome. The upper gun platform slopes outward from the center, where a hole admits light to the chamber below (Figs. 9, 12). A quantity of deep musket holes, square or vaulted, point in every direc-

2*

FIG. 11. CORONE, SOUTHEAST ARTILLERY BASTION, FROM THE SOUTH.

tion through the parapet, which contains five sloping embrasures, covering an arc of 200 degrees of the compass from Mount Ithome on the north to the island of Venetiko to the southeast. This complex of fortifications on the castle's east flank resembles in size the monumental works of the Venetians, but the style of construction and the materials, particularly

FIG. 12. CORONE, SOUTHEAST BASTION, PLATFORM AND PARAPET, LOOKING EAST ACROSS THE LOWER POINT.

the tile, are more closely related to the Turkish fortifications of the XVI century. After the battle of Lepanto in 1571 and the raids of Don John along the Messenian coast, the Turks were busy adding to the defenses of Methone and building a new castle at Navarino. Corone, the strongest citadel of all, would hardly have been neglected.

The curtain proceeds round the south side of the enceinte along the edge of high sandstone cliffs. All that stands above the present interior ground level is a thin rubble wall (Fig. 13). Curving round towards the northwest, it develops into an artillery parapet, which leads in turn to a small polygonal bastion built out on a point of rock, made of regular ashlar blocks and girdled with a torus at the level of its embrasures (Fig. 14). At this point the curtain jogs back, with two westward facing embrasures, 12 feet deep, piercing its parapet. This, like the parapet of the great southeast corner bastion, is topped with a covering of broken tile and brick set in a thick mortar.

FIG. 13. CORONE, SOUTH CURTAIN, OUTER CIRCUIT.

FIG. 14. CORONE, POLYGONAL BASTION, SOUTH OUTER CIRCUIT.

A long stretch of parapet leads to a second indentation of the trace (Plate I, E), where a parapet of small, carefully cut blocks and sharply defined superior slopes contrasts with the heavy, round, tile-plastered slopes of the parapets predominating in the fortress. A torus molding marks the level of three gun

FIG. 15. CORONE, VENETIAN PLAQUE IN SOUTH CURTAIN.

embrasures on the south side, set obliquely to cover the south shore of the peninsula, and two more facing west in the re-entrant wall. Beneath the torus is a plaque (Fig. 15), which identifies this section as Venetian repair of the unsuccessful Maltese breach of 1685[21] with the inscription:

1690
IS IV
IACOBVS CORNELIVS IACOB GIOR
PROV GENERAL MORAE PRAETOR

A short distance beyond the indentation begins the south curtain of the inner enclosure. A great talus, built of large, rough hewn stones, battering at a 50-degree angle, extends as far as the bastion at the fortress' west end. An inner wall with parapet and chemin de ronde runs along its top, set back from its crest, but flanked with three square towers projecting over its slope (Fig. 16). This second wall is built of small, squared blocks, and the towers

carry artillery parapets of neat ashlar masonry which enclose three of the chapels and cells of the Old Calendar convent now occupying the inner enceinte. Between the first and second towers is a cistern which communicates with an aqueduct built into the scarp (Plate I, *Condoto della Fontana*; Fig. 16, upper left). On the Grimani plans the source itself is shown to lie in the open country to the west, where sections of tile piping have been found along the course indicated. Until recently a fountain existed at the point marked G on Plan II. The fortress' external water supply probably came from both sources, while the cisterns within the castle walls were enough to hold a year's supply.[22]

At the western end, at the crucial point of the fortifications, stands a bastion built originally by the Venetians in 1463, destroyed and rebuilt by their descendants after the siege of

FIG. 16. CORONE, CURTAIN, TALUS, AND FLANKING TOWERS OF INNER ENCLOSURE, SOUTH SIDE.

[21] See report of Giacomo Corner, Δελτίον, II, p. 307.

[22] Δελτίον, V, p. 443.

1685 (Fig. 17). A contemporary account of the siege[23] describes a plaque, found between two wings of the ruined bastion, which bore the inscription:

HOC OPUS FECERUNT
MAGNIFICI
ET CLARISSIMI DD
BERNADUS DONATUS CASTELLANUS
ET
LUDOVICUS CONTARENO CAPITANEUS
ET PROVISORES CORONI
MCCCCLXIII

From what remains of the earlier construction, and from the indications given on the two Grimani plans, drawn before the new bastion was completed, it appears that the eminence of the peninsula ridge was terraced into some sort of platform for artillery. The highest section of the work remains an oblong platform raised above the interior of the inner enclosure by a buttressed retaining wall, and protected on the west side by an artillery parapet, with three shallow embrasures, and a small lower platform (Plate I, G. *Piazza bassa*) imme-

diately below it. To-day the parapet of the upper platform is an isolated fragment; the *Piazza bassa*, as drawn on Plate I, disappeared in the rebuilding of 1685–1693.[24] A large quadrilateral bastion with battering ashlar walls 100 feet high, was placed to enclose the base of the topmost platform. The parapet of this work resembles both in style and material the contemporary repair of the Maltese breach. Its western side is built doubly thick, while on the south side it is ruined for all but one fragment, which contains a line of steps, probably a communication between a lower level and an upper gun emplacement, of the form used extensively by the Venetians of 1700 in their works at Nauplia (Figs. 18, 115). Not shown

FIG. 18. CORONE, SOUTHWEST CORNER OF WEST BASTION, RECONSTRUCTED AFTER 1685.

on the plans is the 50-foot long passageway, which descends under a projection of the southwest corner of the quadrilateral (Fig. 19, right), and would have originally communicated with a third level of defense never completed. This was to have been a triangular ravelin projecting into the ditch, which was dug across the ridge in an attempt to cut the fortress off on its peninsula. Only one side of

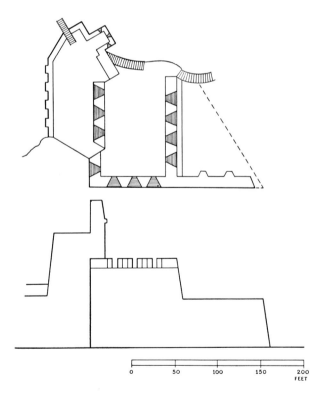

FIG. 17. CORONE, WEST BASTION, PLAN AND ELEVATION.

[23] *La Morea Combattuta* (Bologna, 1686), p. 94.

[24] Δελτίον, V, p. 435: writing in 1693, Antonio Molin, governor of the Peloponnese, calls Corone "primo acquisto e vivo preludio de successivi progressi nel Regno," and speaks of the restoration of the west bastion, nearly completed by the end of his tenure. He says, however, that the work "fu decrettato diverso dalla pristina figura."

FIG. 19. CORONE, WEST BASTION, SOUTHWEST CORNER, EXTERIOR.

this work was built: a piece of wall extending the line of the quadrangle's north flank, which, strengthened with buttresses on its inner side, ends short of its projected termination as indicated on Plate I by two dotted lines. Plate

FIG. 20. CORONE, NORTH TALUS AND CORNER OF WEST BASTION.

II shows it in its present state. Beneath the wall runs a vaulted subterranean gallery similar to those in the other late Venetian constructions at Methone and Nauplia (see below, pp. 70, 97).

Next to the high, fragmentary gun platform at the height of the fortress, there stands within the inner enclosure an octagonal Turkish tower, whose use as a cavalier (Plate I, H) was superseded by the new Venetian works. The north rampart of the inner enceinte is another great talus (Fig. 20), which contains high up on its face, under the foundations of one of the towers it supported, an empty niche framed in a heavy stone molding. A gigantic carving of the lion of St. Mark lies fallen at the foot of the wall, hidden by the houses clustering beneath it, the forgotten memorial of an empire of harbors.

CHAPTER II

ZARNATA

(PLATES III, IV)

With the capture of Corone the army of the Holy League had established a foothold on the mainland of Greece. The first major objective was the southern section of Lakonia, or Mani, geographically and politically the acropolis of the Peloponnese. Its inhabitants were the only Greeks yet ready to take up arms against the Turks, or who had any reason to be well disposed towards the Venetians. It was now necessary for Morosini to capture the castles, with which the Turks hemmed them into their peninsula, and to secure the Maniate alliance, before proceeding to attack the enemy on a larger field.

However, the warlike energies of the population, as 3,000 of them set siege to the castles of Zarnata and Kelepha, was scattered by the jealousy of their particular chieftains, none of whom would submit to a single leadership. The result was less than what the Italians had expected, who, like most foreigners who take Greek interests to heart, were mainly concerned with subordinating the revolt to their own ends. Late in August, 1685 Morosini sent six galleys to the port of Armiro on the northwest coast of Mani to encourage the attackers, and to stop any aid coming to the Turks by water.

Meanwhile the Capitan Pasha, admiral of the Turkish fleet, arrived in Kalamata with an army gathered from every part of the Morea, purposing to rouse the Greeks against the Italians, and divert the Maniates with offers of release from tribute. These were not heeded by the chiefs, who still continued to wrangle among themselves. Finally, on September 6, 1685, Morosini arrived to conduct the siege in person. Terms were sent to the defenders, who answered that not they but the Capitan Pasha must decide. Morosini let their messages pass, but intercepted the reply which came back from Kalamata. This bade them resist until the Turkish army, 10,000 strong, should come to their relief. A false message was sent instead, that no assistance could come as long as the Venetian ships held Armiro. Then Morosini sent two of his Greek agents to arrange terms. The aga in command of the fortress, fearing the vengeance of the Maniates, was allowed to surrender to Morosini alone, and on September 11 a garrison of 600 Turks was carried off in Venetian ships to the shores of Kalamata. The evacuation furnished an example of order and clemency to the neighboring castles which still held out, and the Venetians gained a good report among the local population for a victory carried off while the Turkish commander sat with his army only a few leagues away.[1]

* * *

[1] Locatelli, I, p. 153; Rossi, *Successi dell' Armi Venete*, pp. 145 ff.; *La Morea Combattuta* (Bologna, 1686), p. 96;

The history of Zarnata can barely be traced further back than the darkness of the Turkish domination. Phrantzes, writing in the XV century the history[2] of the Turkish conquest, says that the "castle of Zarnata" was bestowed by the Despot Theodore II Palaiologos on his successor, Constantine, in 1427. After the latter's death in the fall of Constantinople, Zarnata was besieged and captured in 1461 by Thomas from his brother, Demetrios Palaiologos, in the last of the civil wars before the conquest.

Not till two centuries later do we find any light cast upon the origin of the present fortress. A contemporary account of the Venetian campaign of 1685[3] states that Zarnata was one of the castles built by the Turks to keep the population in subjection. The Proveditor Giacomo Corner, in his report dated 1690,[4] likewise says it was built by the Turks "per solo freno alla licenza dei Mainotti." Wheler and Spon, who travelled through the Peloponnese in 1676, make the following respective comments:

They (the Maniates) have always bravely defended themselves against the Turks, and maintained their Liberty, till lately by this strategem the Turks were too hard for them. They got their consent to build two forts upon their Coasts, which they did so advantageously, as soon made them masters of their City, and them. And now none of them are exempted from paying Tribute, but a few in the Mountains.[5]

Ils nous dirent que depuis quelques temps le Turc les avoit obligez par adresse à consentir qu'il batit deux Forteresses sur leurs côtes, et qu'il n'y avoit que ceux des montagnes qui pussent éviter de luy payer tribut.[6]

In 1670 three forts were built in the Mani by the Grand Vizier Achmet Kiuprili, to quell the ferocious independence of its inhabitants.[7] The sources combine to place the building of Zarnata at some point shortly before the Venetian invasion of 1685.

* * *

FIG. 21. ZARNATA, FROM THE SOUTHEAST.

Coronelli, *Memorie*, p. 80; *Il Regno della Morea sotto i Veneti*, pp. 33 ff.; Foscarini, pp. 174 ff.; Garzoni, I, pp. 119 ff.; K. N. Sathas, Τουρκοκρατουμένη Ἑλλάς (Athens, 1869), pp. 336 ff.

[2] *Annales*, ed. Bonn, pp. 131, 390 f.

[3] Rossi, *Successi dell' Armi Venete*, p. 148.

[4] Δελτίον, II, p. 306.

[5] G. Wheler, *Journey into Greece*, 1st ed. (London, 1682), p. 47.

[6] J. Spon, *Voyage d'Italie, de Dalmatie, de Grèce, et du Levant*, 1st ed. (Lyon, 1678), I, p. 161.

[7] J. von Hammer-Purgstall, *Histoire de l'empire ottoman*, tr. J. J. Hellert (Paris, 1838), XII, p. 220; Miller, *Essays*, p. 385.

The fortress is described in Garzoni's history of 1705:[8]

Zarnata non v'è più di cinque miglia fra terra; giace sopra una collina di greppo in figura rotonda; girano le sue mura solo trecento sessanta passi geometrici in circa senza fossa, ma difese da alcuni torrioni che spuntano all' intorno. Ha il difetto d'esser circondata da eminenze, e tra queste una ne sorge, che la infila in parte anche col moschetto.

It is a type of small frontier fort, built to subjugate an ill-armed native population rather than to withstand the sieges of artillery. Situated on a conical hill (Fig. 21), it has neither ditch nor platforms for heavy guns. Its position is strong only on the northeast,

FIG. 22. ZARNATA, COURSED POLYGONAL MASONRY AND TURKISH SUPERSTRUCTURE, SOUTH CURTAIN.

where it dominates the plain of Kambos; on the other sides it lies open to fire from high ground.

Zarnata is built upon an ancient site, which has been identified with Pausanias' Alagonia, one of the Free Lakonian cities, which lay

[8] I, p. 119.

"inland from Gerenia about thirty furlongs."[9] The remains of a classical wall of polygonal and ashlar masonry, standing in some places to a height of 12 feet, serves as foundation for the medieval curtain, and can be traced, with a few gaps, round most of the circuit (Fig. 22). Two round towers were added to this plan at the north and east angles (Fig. 23), one containing a cistern. The masonry of the curtain is uniform throughout, consisting of small, rough limestone blocks, fitted against each other with precision, their flat sides set outwards so as to produce an unbroken surface. In certain sections tile is used in abundance between the blocks (Fig. 22). The curtain is in a ruinous condition, though in some stretches it stands to a height of 30 feet on the outside.

FIG. 23. ZARNATA, ROUND TOWER, EAST CURTAIN.

Within the enclosure, the interior ground level has almost everywhere filled up to the chemin de ronde. The parapets have all gone. Breaches exist where the medieval wall has disappeared down to the Hellenic foundations. Not even these remain in the southern corner, where the

[9] Pausanias, III, xxvi, 8; W. Leake, *Peloponnesiaca* (London, 1846), p. 180; J. G. Frazer, *Pausanias' Description of Greece* (London, 1898), III, p. 403.

entrance is shown on Plans III and IV. The wall here was torn down entirely to make room for a more effective defense of barbed wire during the civil war of 1943–1949, when the fortress served as stronghold of the neighboring villages of Malta and Varoussi.

The top of the hill is crowned with a fortified house. A two-storey dwelling was destroyed by earthquake in 1947, but a crenellated parapet of slotted merlons still stands on top of one of the walls. Below the house a semicircular line of parapet, clumsily built of rubble and tile, and pierced with shallow embrasures, covers the high ground to the south and east, where the actual curtain is set too low to be of use against the opposite hillsides. Next to the ruined building stands a strong, square tower, consisting of three storeys, 50 feet high, with small, arched windows and a parapet of slotted merlons and turrets on corbels at the four corners, all surrounded by a torus molding (Fig. 24). Rectangular blocks are used in the angles, jambs, and arches, while four stone cannon project from beneath the corbels. The building is an elaborate form of the characteristic Maniate πύργος, of which a similar example is to be seen in the fortified house of Tzanetbey at Gytheion. The style of construction belongs to the XVIII century, or to the period preceding the Greek Revolution, when Zarnata achieved ecclesiastical and military importance as the metropole and one of the four captaincies of Mani.[10]

The plans show two cisterns, one of which, in the southeast corner of the enclosure, has been converted into a subterranean chapel.

Other additions, signs of the castle's more recent habitation, are a church, built in 1847, and a windmill, now ruined.

Nothing remains to show, either from the architecture or from historical texts, whether the Venetians added anything to its defenses.

FIG. 24. ZARNATA, THE CENTRAL TOWER, SOUTH FACE.

In 1685 they found it strongly fortified. In 1690 Giacomo Corner dismissed it as "irregular and of little consequence."[11] In 1701, however, Francesco Grimani was already counting it among the eight most important fortresses in the Morea.[12] The Venetians planned to hold it against the Turkish attack, but in 1715 they abandoned Zarnata before they had a chance to defend it.[13]

[10] P. Zerlendis, Τάξις Ἱεραρχικὴ τῶν ἐν Πελοποννήσῳ Ἁγίων τοῦ Θεοῦ Ἐκκλησιῶν (Hermoupolis, 1922), p. 12.

[11] Δελτίον, II, p. 306.
[12] Ibid., V, p. 481.
[13] G. Finlay, *Greece under Othoman and Venetian Domination, 1453–1821* (London, 1856), p. 274; Miller, *Essays*, p. 424.

CHAPTER III

KALAMATA

(PLATE V)

By the beginning of September, 1685, a large section of Mani was in Venetian hands, and a popular rebellion had shut up the Turks in their fortresses. However, the presence of the Turkish army at the head of the Messenian Gulf remained the chief obstacle to further conquest. Morosini sent a detachment of troops to the region of Kalamata, where the Capitan Pasha was encamped with 9,000 infantry and spahis in the plain between the castle and the olive groves at the mouth of the Nedon River. The regiments of the Holy League spread out along a stream bed one mile to the east. The order of battle was drawn up (see Plate V), with the Dalmatians forming the vanguard, and the Venetians the main body of the line, with the Hanoverians and Saxons on the right and left wings. Two batteries were set up at the head of the stream, while the galleys ranged themselves along the shore from the Christian camp to the olive woods, firing constantly into the Turkish lines and making a feint of disembarking in the western quarter. On September 14, before dawn, the army moved forward. A force of Turkish infantry was sent into the hills to await the arrival of the Hanoverian right wing. The spahis attacked on the left, and were repulsed by the Saxons. The Venetian line continued to advance, while the Maniate auxiliaries captured the heights on the right flank. The armies met, and both Turkish horse and foot were routed. The allied commanders occupied the hill overlooking the fortress, to see if the retreat might be leading the Venetians into a trap, but the Turks were fleeing in earnest, and the Maniates followed hard on their tracks into the town, which lay behind the castle rock. Soon after, smoke and flames were seen rising from the fortress. The Turks were firing their stores.

The explosion of the munitions caused the ruin of some of the more important sections of the castle. Designed for a simpler form of warfare, barely renovated for the uses of artillery, and dominated by a hill on the east, the Venetian leaders pronounced it to be now more a liability than a refuge. In their haste to press the offensive to other regions, the Venetians removed the guns, burned down the houses within the enclosure, and blew up the gates and bastions. Morosini, who had arrived two days after the battle, returned to Mani to finish his conquest of the peninsula. The fortress was left, for the time being, in ruins.[1]

* * *

[1] Locatelli, I, pp. 165 ff.; Coronelli, *Memorie*, p. 79; Rossi, *Successi dell' Armi Venete*, pp. 175 ff.; Garzoni, I, pp. 120 f.; Foscarini, p. 176; *Il Regno della Morea sotto i Veneti*, p. 40: "questa fortezza tanta considerata da Turchi per il freno che imponeva à Mainotti, non si acquistasse intatta, diedero pria fuoco alle monitioni, che ... diroccarono i più egregi edificij, portando anche qualche nocumento alle sue difese."

Kalamata had already undergone more changes of hands than any other castle in Greece. Byzantine sources preserve their usual silence about its origins, but Edrisi in the mid-XII century mentions a large, populous town called Maita, twenty miles distant from Corone.[2] The existence of an early Byzantine fortress is attested by the *Chronicle of the Morea*, which tells how the *kastro*, transformed into a monastery, put up a brief resistance to the Frankish knights in 1205.[3] After the conquest of the Peloponnese, Champlitte bestowed on his vassal, Villehardouin, *le noble chastel de Calemate* as one of the twelve baronies of the new Frankish Principality.[4] It remained the family fief for a hundred years, saw the birth and death of William Villehardouin, and passed to his daughter, Isabella, and her husband, Florent of Hainault, who succeeded William as Prince of Achaea in 1278.[5] His rule was prosperous outwardly, but within a century of the conquest the position of the Franks in the Morea had become precarious. Undermined by the organic weaknesses of the feudal state, their early strength was also spent in the effort to possess a country and a people who have absorbed or exhausted the domination of other foreigners before and since. In 1293 this was already felt among the Slavic tribes of the near-by district of Gianitsa on the slopes of Taygetos. One of the tribesmen, imprisoned in the donjon of Kalamata, measured its height with a cord let down from his window. After he had been set free, he returned one night at the head of a band of 50 men, and scaled the walls with a ladder of equal height, "a ce que l'une partie dou donjon estoit toute dehors dou chastel," overpowering the garrison within. At dawn 600 Slavs descended from Taygetos, and drove the Franks out of the castle. Florent besieged it from without, and sent an embassy to the Greek Despot of Mistra, demanding assistance to put down the uprising. But the small Byzantine province in the southeastern corner of the Peloponnese had begun its period of expansion: the Despot answered that since the Slavs had never owned his authority, their actions were beyond his jurisdiction. Florent then sent to the Emperor in Constantinople, who now, with the change of fortunes in the Morea, was able to receive, then stall, and at last refuse the Frankish petition. However, without his knowledge, the Protostrator of the Despotate, who was half French by blood and Frank by sympathy, undertook to capture Kalamata and return it to its owner.[6]

In 1300 the castle passed to Guy II, Duke of Athens, upon his marriage to Isabella Villehardouin's daughter, Mathilda.[7] A few years later it was bought by the Florentine banker, Niccolò Acciajuoli. In 1364 Kalamata is listed among the fifteen castles of the Peloponnesian domain of Marie de Bourbon, widow of Robert of Anjou, who, like the other absentee Princes of Achaea, preserved only a tenuous and shifting authority in the Morea during the XIV century.[8] In the second quarter of the next century, the Despotate of Mistra extended its sway over all the Peloponnese, and around 1425 Kalamata came back once more into the possession of the Greeks. It was held first by the Despot Constantine Palaiologos, and passed, on his accession to the Imperial throne, to his younger brothers, Thomas and Demetrios, who fought over it in the final anarchy of the Byzantine Morea.[9]

After the Turkish conquest, it was held for a time by the Venetians, together with twenty-five other fortresses, during the first Turco-Venetian war of 1463–1479.[10] The place next

---

[2] *Géographie d'Edrisi*, p. 124.
[3] *C. di M.*, p. 426; Χ. τ. Μ., lines 1684 f., 1711–1714:
Τὸ κάστρον ηὗραν ἀχαμνόν, ὡς μοναστῆριν τὸ εἶχαν.
Τὸ σώσει τὸ ἐπολέμησαν, ἀπὸ σπαθίου τὸ ἐπῆραν·
μὲ συμφωνίες τὸ ἔδωκαν κι' ἐκεῖνοι ὡσὰν κ' οἱ ἄλλοι.
[4] *L. de C.*, § 124.
[5] Χ. τ. Μ., lines 7761 f.; *C. di M.*, pp. 433, 459.

[6] *L. de C.*, §§ 693 ff.
[7] *Ibid.*, § 839.
[8] Hopf, *Chroniques gréco-romanes*, p. 227; Miller, *Latins*, pp. 271, 287.
[9] Zakythinos, *Despotat*, I, pp. 206, 245, 265.
[10] *Estratto degli Annali Veneti di Stefano Magno*, in Hopf, *Chroniques gréco-romanes*, p. 206.

FIG. 25. KALAMATA, NORTHEAST ANGLE OF OUTER ENCLOSURE,
AND THE DONJON ABOVE THE NEDON RIVER BED.

appears, nearly two centuries later, in 1659, when Francesco Morosini attempted to divert the Turks from the siege of Candia by a raid on Kalamata with the help of a local uprising of Maniates and Albanians. The Turks abandoned the town, leaving the fortress to be sacked and the inhabitants to be carried off to the galleys. The Venetians withdrew, satisfied with slaves and plunder. The time was not yet ripe for any larger undertaking.[11]

*   *   *

Kalamata is a typical early medieval castle, with donjon, inner redout, and outer enclosure. Its original character was preserved throughout the centuries of more developed warfare, because its natural deficiencies, restricted space and eminent but not pre-eminent position, made it of little use as an artillery fortress. It crowns the hill (Figs. 25, 27) on the northern outskirts of the modern town, where the Nedon, descending from the gorges of Taygetos, curves southward into the Messenian

Gulf. It is divided into two oblong terraces, walled into an inner and an outer circuit. The former is defended by a keep at the highest point over the river.

The curtain of the lower enceinte presents evidence that the Venetians were active architecturally, even after they had dismantled the place and destroyed its key points.[12] The gate is a large, square, vaulted structure in the form of a redan, with an arched opening in its southwest face (Fig. 26). Above the door is a plaque, carved with the winged lion of St. Mark. The salient angle and the jambs and arch of the door are made of large, squared, toolmarked poros blocks. The main wall faces are of rubble, heavily plastered. Immediately behind the outer arch is a short, vaulted passage, which leads into the broad vault of the inner chamber. The platform on top is surrounded by the remains of a straight, slotted parapet.

Within the circuit, the inner angle of the redan contains the traces of an earlier gate,

[11] Coronelli, *Memorie*, p. 78; Sir T. Wyse, *An Excursion into the Peloponnesus* (London, 1865), I, p. 222; Finlay, *Greece under Othoman and Venetian Domination*, p. 213; Miller, *Essays*, p. 384.

[12] Δελτίον, V, p. 434: in 1693 the Proveditor Antonio Molin wrote "La fortezza di Calamata ... restò demolita ..., non già nella pianta, che pur intatta permane, ma ne soli parapeti, ingressi e difese."

which originally entered directly through a line of curtain now replaced by the present redan. Three large blocks, one upon the other, jut out from the wall at ground level, containing a squared recess for a gate-post. Ten feet above ground a hinge-block projects from the wall, above which three wedge-shaped blocks of poros mark the springing of an arch. The entrance indicated by these fragments does not appear on the Grimani plan, which shows the gate in its present alignment, in the redan's re-entrant flank. The gate of the original outer

Northeastward from the gate, the curtain is projected forward by the redan, and is built of similar masonry: uncut stones, roughly coursed with the help of broken tile, covered with a plaster which shows the mark of profuse application with the trowel, standing to a height of 30 feet on the exterior. A jog in the wall 100 feet from the gate, not indicated on

FIG. 27. KALAMATA, THE CASTLE FROM THE SOUTHEAST.

FIG. 26. KALAMATA, OUTER GATE.

circuit would have been one of those sections destroyed in 1685, while the present structure may be claimed to antedate the year 1701, if, as is reasonable to suppose, the plans were drawn before the end of Francesco Grimani's first tenure of office in the Morea.

the plan, is built of large, squared poros blocks in the angle. The chemin de ronde stands 2–8 feet above the interior ground level, varying with the extent to which the enclosure has filled up with the ruin of habitations and storehouses. Slight remains of a crenellated parapet show the merlons to have measured 6 feet wide, each pierced with a two-way loophole — an innovation of the XVII century. A change in masonry occurs at a point where the plastered face ends in a sharp, vertical break, disclosing an exposed stretch of bare rubble behind it (Fig. 28). Plate V shows next to it a small, square flanking tower, built with long, flat, roughly squared stones in the corners.

The northeastern extremity of the fortress is defended by a rude bastion in two levels, whose salient angle (Figs. 25, left; 29) points into the Nedon gorge, and falls beneath the fire of any artillery an enemy might set upon the high hill to the east. The angle's base is made of re-used classical blocks. Above it is a

FIG. 28. KALAMATA, MASONRY OF OUTER CURTAIN.

section of round poros and conglomerate boulders, and the parapet on top continues the masonry of smaller, plastered rubble predominating along the south flank of the outer enceinte. On either side of the angle is an

FIG. 29. KALAMATA, INTERIOR OF NORTHEAST ANGLE, OUTER CURTAIN.

artillery embrasure, built of carefully squared and fitted blocks. The fragment of a thin, circular turret or sentry-box, similar to those in the late Venetian fortifications of Nauplia, occupies the top of the parapet at the salient angle. This corner of the fortress would have been among the defenses blown up in 1685, and shortly after rebuilt by the Venetians around the turn of the XVIII century.

A narrow curtain wall turns back from the angle, and rises westward up the steep ground on the north side over the river, to join the rock on which sits the donjon of the inner redout (Fig. 25). Two features distinguishable near the ground level of this stretch of wall indicate the earliest and latest types of Byzantine masonry. Forty feet west of the salient angle are the remains of an earlier corner, with which the wall from the original outer gate presumably once connected. Its materials are visible through a fall in the masonry: great, squared poros blocks and three column drums re-used in an outer enclosure of the early post-classical refortification. Nearer the rock the curtain is made of minor rubble, peppered with pieces of bright red, broken tile, characteristic of a time when building materials had shrunk to the smallest possible dimensions. This stretch may belong to the thirty-five or forty years preceding the Turkish conquest, when the Palaiologoi held Kalamata.

The southern half of the outer curtain is, again, a continuation of the masonry and construction of the redan and its adjacent wall. A thick, buff-colored plaster, streaked with trowel marks, covers most of the rubble surface. One jog in the wall, like that in the northern half, contains rectangular blocks in the angle, measuring 1 by 1½ feet wide. The parapet has gone completely, and the interior filled up to the level of the chemin de ronde. At the southwest extremity of the enclosure the curtain forms an angle, its walls vertical as in the rest of the circuit, but strengthened with two set-backs on one side. From here it turns northeastward to the higher level of rock which provides the base of the inner enceinte.

The gateway to the inner redout is set in a heavy bastion flanking the southeast side of the enclosure (Fig. 30). A ramp leads up beneath the wall to a wide, low, brick-arched entrance piercing the bastion's east flank (Fig. 31). Above the arch is a small, rectangular, empty niche, and the salient angle of the bastion beside it strengthened with a massive buttress. The bastion contains a chamber within, vaulted in courses of flat, rough stones, separated by string-courses of brick at 1-foot intervals. The vault is divided into two sections by a reinforcing arch. One enters through the outer doorway in the bastion's east flank, turns right under the vault, and then, through a second opening in the wall which occupies the line of the actual curtain, turns left up a ramp into the interior of the enclosure. The west side of the bastion consists of a thick, square, terrepleined tower, which projects forward from the vaulted chamber on the south. The faces and flanks of the structure are built

FIG. 31. KALAMATA, OUTER ARCH OF SECOND GATE.

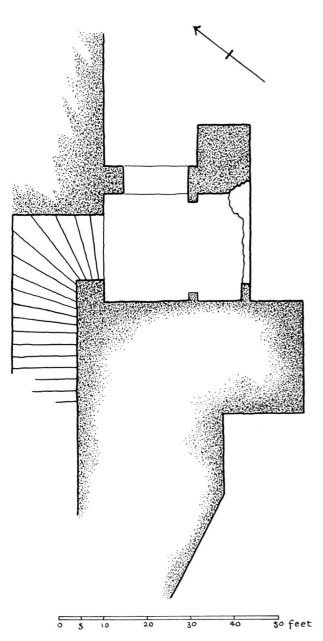

FIG. 30. KALAMATA, PLAN OF SECOND GATE.

3

of rectangular poros blocks, measuring 1 by 2 feet, with wide, flat bricks between the courses and the vertical joints, in the pattern of cloisonné masonry most characteristic of Byzantine wall construction.

On either side of the gate the inner curtain is built of big poros ashlar (Fig. 31, right). Blocks of monumental size are used in certain faces and angles. The spaces between those of disparate size are filled with small ladders of broken brick or tile. At the southwest end of the inner enclosure the rock is underpinned by a big, curved talus of small stones extending down to a lower terrace, which also buttresses the adjacent stretch of the outer curtain. A similar form of buttress serves to strengthen a square flanking tower facing the second gate on the northeast side. The northwestern flank of the upper enceinte is guarded only by a thin screen wall along the cliff over the Nedon river.

FIG. 32. KALAMATA, THE DONJON, NORTHEAST CORNER.

At the north end of the upper enclosure stands the donjon, or strongpoint of the castle. This is a conglomeration of constructions juxtaposed and superimposed upon each other, built for different uses at different times. Basically a rectangular structure, measuring approximately 40 by 60 feet wide, it projects on the eastern side into a stout, but roughly proportioned talus of small, coursed blocks (Fig. 32, left). A rectangular addition on the north side (Fig. 32, right), 34 feet long by 16 wide, built of large ashlar blocks, upwards of 4 feet long and separated by horizontal courses and upright slabs of brick, contains a vaulted cistern, 25 feet deep. The blocks themselves may date, by their size, to the late classical period, while a column drum and the shaft of a Byzantine colonnette are embedded in the donjon's south flank. Within the main body of

the donjon, largely ruined by the demolition of 1685, is an irregular chamber, oriented on a different axis from that of the outer walls, in which may be seen, entirely surrounded by their masonry, two small saucer domes, part of a trapezoidal apse in the northeast corner, and the traces of vaults and arches, made of poros voussoirs and brick, in the middle of the north, south, and west walls. A reconstruction

FIG. 33. KALAMATA, SOUTHEAST ANGLE OF THE DONJON.

of these remains[13] proves the existence of a church, of a style antedating the XIII century, encased within the donjon walls (see Fig. 33): built on the plan of a Greek cross, roofed with barrel vaults for nave and transepts, and a dome over their intersection; and preceded by a narthex on the western side, with lesser domes at the four corners over the north and south compartments of narthex and bema. This buried relic accords with the description of Kalamata castle in the *Chronicle of the Morea*: a weakly defended place made over

[13] See A. Bon, "Eglises byzantines de Kalamata," *Actes du VIᵉ Congrès international d'Etudes byzantines* (Paris, 1951), II, pp. 35–50.

into a monastery before the advent of the Franks in 1205. The present donjon would belong to the XIII century, when the French barons of the Morea rebuilt the neglected Byzantine fort,[14] and later increased the height of its walls after Florent of Hainault recaptured it from the Slavs.[15]

We conclude that a castle in two enclosures existed on the rocky hill at Kalamata in the period preceding the Frankish conquest, which fell into disuse as a purely military post before the time of the Fourth Crusade; that the Franks themselves renovated the defenses with the addition of a keep built over an earlier Byzantine church, and heightened the castle walls after 1293; and that the Venetians, who condemned the place as indefensible and demolished its gates, bastions, and parapets in 1685, later changed their opinion and rebuilt the outer circuit, together with a new entrance gate, around the turn of the XVIII century.

[14] See A. Bon, "La prise de Kalamata par les Francs en 1205," *Rev. arch.* XXIX–XXX, 1949, (*Mélanges Charles Picard*, I), pp. 98–104.

[15] *L. de C.*, § 693: "... et a cellui temps li mur n'estoient pas si haut comme il sont orendroit, car il furent haucie depuis."

CHAPTER IV

KELEPHA

(Plate VI)

The southern ridge of Taygetos descends in a rocky spine, which separates the Lakonian from the Messenian Gulf. Near the head of these bodies of water it is cut through by a pass from east to west, dividing the regions of Outer and Inner Mani, which was defended in medieval times by the castles of Passava, near the east coast, and Kelepha, situated on a high plateau overlooking the bay of Vitylo on the west.

In August, 1685, when the news of the fall of Corone reached the peninsula of Mani, the inhabitants set siege to Kelepha, which outlasted by a few days the Turkish capitulations at Zarnata and Kalamata. The arrival of Francesco Morosini at Vitylo on September 23 hastened the surrender of Kelepha, which was carried out under the same terms as at Zarnata. The keys of the fortress were handed over to Morosini on board his galley, and a garrison of 500 Turkish soldiers were transported to the island of Elaphonisi, near Cape Malea. The campaign of 1685 came to a close with the fall of Passava, whose defenses were blown up in the interest of a near-by mountain pass which could be held more easily, while Zarnata and Kelepha were considered sufficient to remind the Maniates of their alliance.[1]

The campaign of the following year was opened by the Turks, who descended into Mani in the early spring, won several victories over the inhabitants, and laid siege to Kelepha, entrenching themselves within pistol shot of the walls. These they bombarded, and almost succeeded in opening a breach, when Morosini arrived on March 31, 1686, with a light army from Corfu. Joined by a local force of 2,000 Maniates, they advanced upon the Turks, and routed them without a struggle.[2]

* * *

For the Venetians, Kelepha possessed only limited importance. It was described by the Proveditors as "irregular and of little consequence," and "built rather to impress upon the sullen nature of the Maniates the obedience due to the high Dominion, than to provide a post capable of strong resistance."[3] In 1708 the Governor Angelo Emo described Kelepha and Zarnata as "little forts, weak and outmoded in construction, built by the Turks more to control that contumacious population than to serve as bulwark to assaults from overseas."[4] The policy of the Venetians in this area, however, was not of a repressive sort. They owed

---

[1] Garzoni, I, p. 121; Foscarini, p. 177; Sathas, Τουρκοκρατουμένη Ἑλλάς, p. 339.

[2] Locatelli, I, p. 194; Foscarini, p. 196.

[3] Δελτίον, II, p. 306.

[4] Ibid., V, pp. 433, 684.

to the Maniates much of their early success in conquering the Morea,[5] while these in their turn probably felt as much friendliness for the merchants of the Adriatic as they did for any of Greece's other masters. Corner in his report of 1690 advocates a greater delicacy in dealing with them than the Turks were accustomed to use, who, though they left the people mostly to their own devices, sometimes made sudden and terrible descents. Francesco Grimani found too, during his term of office, that persuasion was a better means of administering justice than actual punishment, since in the chaotic society of Mani the plaintiff was generally as culpable as the defendant. As a result, the region which had been at first the most independent from the Venetians became, says he, the calmest in the Peloponnese. His successor, Marco Loredan, was forced to give way over the matter of taxation, from which the Maniates claimed exemption as one of the original favors granted them by Morosini. Loredan reports: "There was no force available to put down the defiance of these people, protected by the terrain of their country, harsh and mountainous, with impenetrable recesses, by reason of which they have never suffered total subjugation in any change of dominion. I, on the other hand, had to use a cautious, accommodating manner." Gentleness on his part succeeded, and the tax was paid.[6] The fiscal district, of which Kelepha was the capital, brought in a revenue in 1692 of 7,518 reals, one sixth of the average income of the other districts of the Morea.[7] It would appear for its poverty alone, if not for the autonomous spirit of its inhabitants, that the Mani was not a region in which the Venetians wished to interfere, any more than the Turks. At this date they neither could afford nor needed to concern themselves with matters inland. With resources severely limited, their chief interest was for their ancient sea trade, for which the whole Morea merely furnished a periphery of useful ports. Mani was important mainly for the harbor of Vitylo, which they tried to hold with the help of a Maniate garrison in Kelepha, when the Turkish armies swept back into the Peloponnese in 1715. But by then the Maniates had lost enthusiasm for their old ally, and a change of masters made little difference to them. The place surrendered on the first summons.[8]

* * *

Fig. 34. Kelepha, West Curtain, looking toward Vitylo Bay.

Kelepha is a large, almost rectangular enclosure, occupying an area of some 15,000 square yards, above the gorge of Milolangadho, which descends from the foothills of Taygetos to the waters of Vitylo. The ambitiousness of its size and strategic location is offset by its rigidity of plan. The curtains are straight, instead of being broken up into defensible salient and re-entrant angles, and extend to attenuated lengths beyond the effective range of its four corner bastions. The plan bears a striking similarity to that of Canea (see Plate XXXVIII), the great citadel which the Venetians built in Crete in the early XVI century. If Kelepha

---

[5] The Maniates were called by Gradenigo, Δελτίον, II, p. 239: "... anzi li primi autori del acquisto del Regno."

[6] L. von Ranke, *Die Venezianer in Morea*, Greek translation in Ἐρανιστής, II, 1843, pp. 851 f.

[7] Report of the Venetian census-taker, Domenico Gritti, translated in Φιλίστωρ, II, 1861, p. 222.

[8] Finlay, *Greece under Othoman and Venetian Domination*, p. 274; Ranke, Ἐρανιστής, II, 1843, p. 864.

corresponds to one of the two fortresses mentioned by Wheler and Spon,[9] erected by Achmet Kiuprili after his victories in Crete, it may well be that Canea furnished the model, even though its defenses had already proved obsolete by the time of its fall in 1645.[10] In which case the Turks, bad but persistent imitators, repeated its defects in Kelepha, while ignoring its virtues as an artillery fortress.

Like Zarnata, Kelepha is a frontier post, built for the limited uses of local oppression. Its curtains, unlike the great, wall-encased dykes of contemporary Italian fortification, are thin walls of masonry throughout, with chemin de ronde and small-arms parapet above. The elevation drawn at the bottom of Plate VI shows this to have been crenellated with low merlons, of which there remains only a trace in the southeast corner. The bastions at

is a semicircular bastion, also hollow, divided inside by a wall pierced with a pointed arch, into two segmental chambers, each covered with a tapering barrel vault. The northwest corner bastion contained a cistern, as the ruins of its plastered walls still show.

Large breaches to-day mark the sites of the main and postern gates. The entrance of each was situated in the side of a small, square

FIG. 35. KELEPHA, NORTH CURTAIN, LOOKING SOUTHEAST ACROSS ENCLOSURE.

FIG. 36. KELEPHA, MASONRY OF EAST CURTAIN.

the four angles, of which only the one at the southeast still stands intact, are round and hollow, and vaulted in brick as at Corone and New Navarino, with battering exterior walls and thin parapets inadequate for guns of any size. In the middle of the short south curtain

flanking bastion, vaulted within and crowned with crenellated parapets (Plate VI).

The whole circuit is undefended by any exterior works such as ditch, counterscarp, or glacis to provide concealment for the curtain and an impediment to assault. In 1701 Francesco Grimani proposed to remedy this defect. Foreseeing which fortresses would be the most crucial for resistance in the event of a Turkish

[9] *Journey into Greece*, p. 47; *Voyage d'Italie, de Dalmatie, de Grèce, et du Levant.* I, p. 161. See also above, p. 25.
[10] See below, p. 212.

counterattack, he urged the Venetian Senate to spare no effort to maintain and garrison Zarnata and Kelepha,[11] submitting also a proposal for a faussebraye to be built around three sides (Plate VI, K, K). This shared the fate of most of the Venetian schemes, and never came to fruition.

The masonry of the fortress consists largely of rubble and broken tile. The southeast corner bastion is made of small ashlar, and ornamented with a line of stone bosses under the level of the gun platform. The south side of the east curtain resembles the masonry of Zarnata, where irregular limestone blocks, cut with one flat face, are carefully fitted together without mortar to produce a uniform wall surface (Fig. 36). The tower chambers with their domes of brick, the pointed arch, and the eccentric vaults in the semicircular bastion on the south side are features of Turkish building, with analogies in other fortresses of the XVI and XVII centuries; and combine with the place's clumsy conception of defense to substantiate the conclusion that Kelepha was one of the castles built by the Turks, to enforce the payment of tribute on the border of Interior Mani.

[11] Δελτίον, V, p. 481.

CHAPTER V

OLD NAVARINO

(Plates VII–X, XIII)

The War of the Holy League entered its third year, and on June 2, 1686 the Venetian army landed at Navarino Bay. The castle guarding the northern channel was defended by a garrison of 100 Turks, who submitted to a show of force, when Königsmark, the new general of the army, set up his batteries on the high ground of Sphakteria, which commands its one approach across the channel. The Venetians found 43 cannon abandoned by the Turks, and a relic of Venice's earlier dominion, two plaques over the gate with the arms of the Morosini and Malipiero families. The standard of St. Mark was hoisted over the highest tower, to announce the victory to the Turks in Neokastro on the other side of the Bay.[1]

*   *   *

Old Navarino dates from the late XIII century. The Flemish family of St. Omer, which had taken part in the conquest of Constantinople, and become lords of Frankish Thebes, extended their power south of the Isthmus when one of their number, Nicholas II, succeeded to the rank of Marshal of Achaea, married the widow of the Prince, William Villehardouin, and became ruler of the Prin-

cipality. Around the year 1278 he built the "castle of Avarinos" for his nephew, Nicholas III, who in 1300 held the rank of bailie of Achaea, and was still alive after 1311, when most of the nobility of Frankish Greece had been slaughtered by the Catalans in the Battle of the Kephissos.[2]

Forty years later, when the Venetians and Genoese were engaged in a war over the Black Sea trade, the Bay of Navarino, which the Franks called Port de Jonc from the rushes that still grow along its sandy shores, fell into the hands of the Genoese, who used it as a base for raids on the Venetian colonies in Messenia.[3] In 1366 the castle was held by Marie de Bourbon, widow of the Prince of Achaea, Robert of Taranto, against the combined forces of the barons of Achaea, the archbishop of Patras, and her brother-in-law, whom she tried in vain to dispossess in a war over the succession to the Principality.[4] In 1381 Navarino acquired new importance as a base of operations for the Navarrese Grand Company, who came to Greece as a band of soldiers of fortune, and ended by taking over the rule of the weakening Frankish state.[5]

---

[1] Locatelli, I, pp. 210 ff.; *La Morea Combattuta* (Bologna, 1686), p. 108; Scalletari, *Condotta Navale ... del Viaggio da Carlistot a Malta del ... Gioanni Gioseppe d'Herberstein* (Graz, 1688), p. 83.

[2] Χ.τ.Μ., line 8096; *L. de C.*, §564; *C. di M.*, p. 462; Buchon, *La Grèce continentale et la Morée*, p. 461; Miller, *Latins*, pp. 144, 147, 165 f., 195, 238.

[3] *Ibid.*, p. 301; Miller, *Essays*, p. 109.

[4] Zakythinos, *Despotat*, I, pp. 109 f.

[5] *Ibid.*, pp. 146 ff.

In 1423, shortly before the downfall of Achaea, the Venetians bought Navarino from its last reigning Prince, Centurione Zaccaria, to prevent its passing to his countrymen, the Genoese. Venetian Messenia was enlarged to comprise Methone, Corone, Old Navarino, and four dependent castles, which remained the last outpost of western Christendom on the mainland of Greece after the Turkish conquest. The treaty which the Venetians made with Mohammed II in 1460 confirmed their possession for another forty years until, in 1500, the Sultan Bayezid II descended on the Venetian colonies, attacking first Nauplia, then Navarino, which both held out against him, and finally Methone, which fell after a three months' siege. Bayezid returned to Navarino, which surrendered on the first summons, in spite of abundant provisions and a garrison of 3,000. The governor of the castle was beheaded for his cowardice, but the following year it was recaptured by a Greek ensign called Demetrios, who had previously served in the garrison of Methone, with a band of 50 men. Soon, however, the Turks returned by land and sea, and the Venetian force was constrained to make its escape on some merchant vessels which chanced to be anchored outside the harbor.[6]

In 1572 the walls of Old Navarino suffered their last bombardment. Don John of Austria, who had defeated the Turks at the Battle of Lepanto the preceding year, conceived the idea of carving himself out a domain in the Peloponnese: attacked Methone, failed, and tried once more at Navarino. Turkish reinforcements came to the aid of the garrison in the castle, and from its strategic points harassed the Spanish and Italian troops, who in three days could hardly set up their batteries. The terrain afforded no shelter, and the attackers ran out of provisions. After they had gone, the Turks filled up the mouth of the Bay on the northern side, and erected a new fortress to guard the channel on the south.[7] During the next two centuries Old Navarino fell first to the Venetians in 1686, then back to the Turks in 1715, and at last to the Greeks in the War of Independence. But in all this there was no fighting, and the only damage to the defenses was caused by the more gradual warfare of time.

Fig. 37. Old Navarino, East Cliffs of Koryphasion Point; Osmanaga Lagoon below; Sphakteria, Navarino Bay, and New Navarino in the background.

By 1686 the castle had fallen into disrepair. Still, its remarkable natural position made it, in the opinion of the Proveditors Corner[8] and Molin,[9] a fitter place for defense than the much larger artillery fortress of New Navarino. Francesco Grimani lists it among the eight

---

[6] Coronelli, *Memorie*, p. 50; Cappelletti, VII, pp. 227 ff.; Miller, *Latins*, pp. 306, 385, 449, 497.

[7] Paruta, II, pp. 182 ff.; B. Randolph, *The Present State of the Morea* (Oxford, 1686), p. 5; Foscarini, p. 198.

[8] Δελτίον, II, p. 308.

[9] *Ibid.*, V, p. 438.

most strategic castles in the Peloponnese, and recommends a refortification of the second enclosure, and the erection of two bastions and a demi-bastion at advantageous points along the first.[10] But the plans in the present collection show no such proposals, and the fortress itself is bare of any distinct trace of late Venetian building. The key to the great harbor was New Navarino, which protected the one navigable entrance. The northern channel of Sikia was blocked, and Old Navarino's guns were ineffective inside the Bay, where enemy ships could withdraw out of range. Plate X of the collection, dated 1706, the first year of Grimani's office as Proveditor General of the Morea, shows, among all the artillery positions, only five guns of any appreciable size. It is probable that the Venetians gradually abandoned the idea of defending it. In 1715 both Navarinos were marked for demolition, but by then the Italians were already making their escape from Greece.[11]

*   *   *

400 feet high over the sandy reaches of Voidhokilia and the Osmanaga Lagoon (Figs. 37, 38; Plates VII–X, *Peschiera, Pesquiere, Peschira*). The ascent to the fortress begins at the southernmost tip of the point. Near the shore is a ruined stretch of wall (Plate X, 31, *Mura Anticha*), which follows the edge of the lower cliff down to the channel of Sikia. A round tower projects from the wall, containing a vaulted chamber, open on the inside, with three small embrasures facing north, east, and south; two are vaulted, and one is built with three lintel-blocks placed in descending order over the tapering side walls, a form of window-construction borrowed by the Turks from the Byzantines.

The path leads up the gradual south slope of the peninsula past the Turkish cemetery (Plate X, 30), turns west under the castle's south curtain (Figs. 39, 40), and along a walled ramp to the gate of the outer enclosure (Figs. 40, 41; Plate X, C. *Tore Sopra la Porta*). This is in the form of a square flanking tower, which projects

FIG. 38. OLD NAVARINO, VIEW TO NORTHEAST OVER THE COVE OF VOIDHOKILIA.

FIG. 39. OLD NAVARINO, SOUTH SECTOR, OUTER CURTAIN.

The castle crowns the precipitous peninsula of Koryphasion, which closes the north end of Navarino Bay, along a line of cliffs that continue the serrated scarp of the island of Sphakteria (Fig. 37, extreme right), towering

the trace of the curtain out into a curve over the seaward-facing slope. The east face of the tower is slightly recessed, half-way up its height, by means of a line of square blocks set slantingly, with a course of brick above and below it. The outer doorway (Plate X, A. *Prima Porta Magior*) is built with a portcullis

[10] *Ibid.*, V, pp. 481, 484.
[11] Miller, *Essays*, p. 424.

Fig. 40. Old Navarino, South Curtain and Gate of Outer Enceinte, looking West.

shaft and several arches one behind the other. The outermost of these is made of brick, set fanwise. Behind this is the portcullis shaft, then three arches built in varying degrees of depression. The central arch of the three is supported on scroll-shaped corbels, as may be seen also in the Turkish doorways of New Navarino. The chamber inside the tower is spanned with a wide barrel vault entirely of brick. The inner section of the structure has collapsed in recent years (Figs. 41, 44, left), but in its north side is a depressed arch of

Fig. 41. Old Navarino, Outer Gate, South Flank, showing Submerged Level of Crenellations.

alternate wedge-shaped blocks and brick, which admitted into the interior of the enclosure (Plate X, B. *Seconda Porta*). A small sentry-box in the angle between these two openings, and three recessed niches in the south and east walls of the chamber, are also arched in brick, with a line of tile forming a repeating arch over the top. By all its features the gate is Turkish, and belongs to the period after the castle's capture by Bayezid in 1500, and probably within the XVI century. The tower is crowned with a parapet of notched merlons, built over a line of earlier crenellations, whose elaborate double notches are preserved in the masonry (Fig. 41). Within the parapet the platform, 25 feet square, remains at its original level, 14 feet below the top of the upper row of merlons. A narrow chemin de ronde was built up against this heightened parapet to afford communication for defenders on the tower. The platform is reached from the chemin de ronde of the adjacent curtains on either side by means of small, depressed brick archways through the parapets of the north and south flanks. One small artillery embrasure in the east face enfilades the south curtain.

The south sector of the outer curtain supports a strong artillery position (Plate X, H, H, *Bataria Moresina*), which defends the castle's one vulnerable flank, on the side of the channel below Sphakteria. Eastward from the tower gate a passage leads to a short rampart, guarded by a parapet of broad merlons alternately pierced with loopholes, beneath which, at the level of the chemin de ronde, are two miniature casemates, arched in poros blocks. Below the chemin de ronde the curtain is pierced by a vaulted casemate, which tapers down to a small arch of poros wedges and brick, edged with a drafted line. At the interior ground level a rudely built, vaulted passage extends obliquely through the wall to an opening, whose original form is lost in a collapse of the surrounding masonry. The rampart widens into a heavy gun emplacement, extending for

100 feet, as far as the square tower which marks the mid-point of this sector. It consists of a terrepleined platform and a parapet 7 feet high and 10 feet thick, pierced with two embrasures (Plate X, I. *Canon di Bronzo da 60 Segado*; K. *Canon di Bronzo da 40 Segado*) and numerous deep, tunnel-shaped loopholes.

Between the outer gate and the square tower, the lower half of the wall is built in a talus of rough limestone blocks, small chips, and broken tile. Above the talus are traces of a line of merlons, filled in and superimposed with the masonry of the higher parapet. Within the buried crenellations, at five points, are the small, round mouths of casemates, arched with brick and poros wedges, which were put out of use by the terreplein behind the parapet. Thus the curtain in this sector shows three periods: on the lowest level a simple, crenellated parapet; then a filling-in of the spaces between the merlons with masonry, pierced by small casemates; and finally a raising of the entire rampart with a new terreplein and embrasured artillery parapet. Near the middle of the wall stands the relic of one of the flanking towers of the classical acropolis of Pylos. A few blocks of both flanks project 10 feet from the curtain in three descending courses of massive, quarry-faced, trapezoidal masonry (Fig. 42, left). Nothing remains of any medieval tower built over it.

FIG. 42. OLD NAVARINO, SOUTH CURTAIN, LOOKING EAST THROUGH OUTER GATE.

The eastern half of the outer south curtain is built with a much slighter talus than in the western, and employs a number of re-used classical blocks in its lower zone. It supports, instead of a gun platform, a thin parapet, still standing near the eastern end, of alternately slotted, notched merlons (Fig. 42). The terreplein, walled along the interior and strengthened with a line of buttresses, is only half as wide as in the preceding western sector. Near the base of the curtain the wall face contains the mouth of a casemate arched in a single curved block of limestone, with a fan of wedge-shaped blocks and a repeating arch of tiles set over it. This corresponds with the position marked on Plate X: L. *Falconeto di Bronzo da 3.*

The curtain jogs forward, with a westward-facing casemate at ground level in its re-entrant side, and ends in a round tower (Fig. 42; Plate X, M. *Posto Precipicio*), 35 feet high and 30 feet wide, built with a number of re-used classical blocks at the base, and an abundance of broken tile in its upper section. The ruin of the platform above reveals a domed chamber within, vaulted in brick like the round bastions at New Navarino, Corone, and Kelepha. Three casemates point out to the south, east, and west, their vaults, 8 feet deep, tapering down to round openings cut out of single squares of poros, recessed within frames of limestone blocks. A short extension of its wall connects the tower with the unscalable cliffs that guard the castle's whole east flank.

To the west of the outer gate is another southward-facing gun position (Plate X, D, D, *Posto Sᵃ Barbara*). The outer face of its wall is broken into three obtuse angles, describing a rough arc, built with a slight talus on to steep rocks crowning the western slope of the hill. Near the bottom of the wall two small, depressed arches mark the mouths of vaulted, tapering casemates, 7 feet deep, rendered obsolete by a terreplein built up against the curtain on the inner side. Immediately beyond

this, at the southernmost angle of the enclosure, stands a round tower (Figs. 40, left, 43; Plate X, G. *Passavolaᵉ da 9*), 22 feet high and 20 feet in diameter, topped with a crenellated parapet, one of whose remaining merlons is built with large, flat bricks laid between the squared blocks of the angles. Steps ascend to the tower platform from the chemin de ronde

Fig. 43. Old Navarino, South Corner Tower, Outer Enclosure.

of the curtain on the east and north. It contains a small chamber, vaulted in brick and completely open on the tower's inner side, and a brick-vaulted casemate within, piercing its southern flank.

The curtain now turns north in a wide arc for 450 feet to meet the inner enclosure on the uppermost part of the hill. The slightly battering wall is built of rough, tightly fitted limestone blocks, crowned with a spiny palisade of swallow-tail merlons, facing out over the Ionian Sea (Figs. 44, 45). Beneath these, again, may be traced the immured outline of earlier crenellations. The present chemin de ronde, which stands 15 feet above the interior ground level of the enceinte, provides further indication of two periods of construction by not bonding with the parapet's inner face.

A small, rectangular tower, 15 feet wide, flanks the curtain near the southern end. Its angles are built of square blocks with large, flat bricks set between the joints. A number of

FIG. 44. OLD NAVARINO, WEST CURTAIN, OUTER ENCLOSURE, LOOKING SOUTH TO OUTER GATE, LEFT. SPHAKTERIA AND NEW NAVARINO, UPPER LEFT.

other bricks set vertically give a pseudo-Byzantine impression of cloisonné masonry. Underneath the tower platform, at the interior ground level, is a brick-vaulted chamber, open on the inner side, and providing access to a brick-vaulted casemate in one of the flanks, exactly as in the round tower at the south corner. Near the north end of the outer circuit stands another round tower, measuring 20 feet wide (Figs. 45, 46; Plate X, 1. *Turion San*

FIG. 45. OLD NAVARINO, WEST CURTAIN, OUTER ENCLOSURE, WITH ROUND FLANKING TOWER, LOOKING SOUTH.

Gaetano). This western curtain contained, at its point of juncture with the inner circuit, a postern gate (Plate X, 5. *Porta Stopa*), which to-day has disappeared in a large breach immediately below the inner curtain wall. The latter, however, remains untouched by the breach, without any panel of truncated masonry to show that the outer curtain ever bonded with it.

The inner circuit is in the form of a horseshoe, with its eastern flank unwalled. Its south flank is the most demolished section of the fortress. The original construction has largely disappeared in the collapse of its towers and ramparts, and the jungle of dwarf ilex covering its ruins. At the eastern tip (Plate X, R. *Posto Bel Veder*) stood a round tower, of which the only traces are a buttress on the cliff side and a great piece of fallen masonry, which shows the curve of its wall and the vaults of two of its casemates, originally $4\frac{1}{2}$ feet deep. The east half of this south curtain was a vertical wall, topped with a thin parapet, and masked by a stout, low talus of a later period. Plates VII, IX, and X show a pair of round towers in the middle, with the gateway to the inner enclosure immediately to their west. Both structures have been almost entirely destroyed. Of the eastern tower, portions of the two flanks still stand, of which one penetrates the talus and the parapet of the adjacent curtain. Its

FIG. 46. OLD NAVARINO, WEST CURTAIN, OUTER ENCLOSURE, LOOKING NORTH.

inner wall is pierced by a depressed arch, communicating with an upper chamber. Of the other tower next to it on the west, nothing remains in place but its interior wall, which shows the mark of a vault in its masonry. Below these towers the fragments of their rounded fronts lie about among the ruins of other buildings in the lower enclosure, marked on Plate X (17, 19) as a cistern and a Latin church. Between the towers, at the present ground level, may be seen two large, slightly curved blocks, belonging to a vaulted passageway, which passed through the wall at a level originally much lower. Yet on Plates IX and X the entrance to the inner enceinte is drawn

west of the two towers, not between them. Breaches now mark the sites of the *Porta del Castel* (Plate IX, D) and the round tower that occupied an angle of the wall west of the gate (Plate X, 2. *Turion del Sendardo*). There still stands, however, amid great slopes of fallen stone, the western section of a piece of wall, which ran parallel to this flank of the upper enclosure, and originally tangent to the fronts of all three towers (Plate X, P, P. *Traversa*). It is built of limestone and tile rubble, $2\frac{1}{2}$ feet thick, and rises to a height of 20 feet on the outer side, with a parapet of square merlons on top (Fig. 47). The curtain on the side of the open sea stands 40 feet high, again distinguished by the feature of a crenellated parapet built over a level of lower battlements, still showing in the masonry.

At the western corner of the enceinte the curtain is flanked by a large, square tower

FIG. 47. OLD NAVARINO, TRAVERSE IN FRONT OF SOUTH FLANK OF INNER ENCLOSURE.

(Fig. 46, left; Plate X, Z. *Turion S. Marco vole un Canon da 12*), 35 feet high, built with big angle blocks of poros and limestone. On top, the whole southwest corner of its parapet is cut out so as to form a gun embrasure 90 degrees wide, with the peculiar construction of a floor which slopes to south and west on either side of the angle.

From this point all the way round to the cliffs on the eastern side of the castle, the wall stands upon 2–5 courses of trapezoidal blocks, which once supported the curtain of the classical fortress. Near the northwest corner of the inner enclosure is a round tower, whose rubble walls contain near the top two circular holes for casemates, enclosed in a square, recessed stone frame similar to those in the outer circuit. On the north side the lower courses of two small, round, classical towers provide, in each case, the base for a later medieval superstructure. The tower on the west contains a small, vaulted chamber, accessible through a hole in the platform above (see Plate X, 3. *Turion Serue per pregion*). Between both towers the curtain supports a parapet of notched and slotted merlons, one of which is notched twice in the outline of a W, like those in the lower parapet of the outer gate (Fig. 41). The last stretch of curtain near the east end is marked with a string course of squared poros blocks. It forms an obtuse angle, built of bevelled ashlar poros, a few feet from the point where it ends above the cliff. Along the eastern side a few stretches of low, thin parapet are embedded in the uppermost rocks.

Out of the mass of ruins which fill the enclosure, the only distinguishable remains are the circular foundations of the *Casa del Ajutante* (Plate X, 15), and a number of cisterns with plastered walls.

The fortress has undergone so many transformations at the hands of its different masters, Frank, Genoese, Navarrese, Venetian, and Turk, that it is as hard to tell the form of the original St. Omer castle as it is to distinguish between the subsequent periods of its architecture. Portions of the classical acropolis *in situ* probably formed the base of the XIII century Frankish fortifications, while the lower section of the circuit walls, characterized by the Italian form of their submerged battlements, may belong within the 77–year occupation of Old Navarino by the Venetians (1423–1500). On the other hand the heightening of these same ramparts may well have taken place during the latter part of the XVI century, after the Battle of Lepanto and Don John's raid had frightened the Turks into fortifying Navarino Bay. These higher parapets preserve the earlier notched form, even in sections which are distinctly Turkish, such as the outer gate and the southern sector of the outer curtain, with its round flanking bastions and its piecemeal adaptation to the uses of artillery. The other towers and bastions along the rest of the circuit, with their restricted width and their brick-vaulted inner chambers and casemates, appear to belong also within the unrecorded years of the XVI century.

CHAPTER VI

NEW NAVARINO

(PLATES VII, VIII, XI–XIII)

New Navarino is placed at the mouth of the Port, at the widest part of the entrance, which it was built to guard. Its figure is irregular, and its walls lacking in height, built without terreplein, but founded directly on the living rock. They are defended by two great bastions, which have a double order of Artillery, and two others, smaller, for guns of lesser size. The side facing the Port is flanked by two platforms of restricted size, roughly quadrangular, set at the opposite corners of that sector. In the south-south-east quarter there stands next to the enclosure a Citadel of hexagonal shape, which contains in its angles six bastions of identical construction. But so narrow are its works that its plan resembles more a model than a Fort: its whole exterior circuit measuring no more than 225 geometric paces.

So Foscarini[1] described the fortress as it appeared at the time of the Venetian occupation. Immediately after the fall of Old Navarino, the Venetian galleys proceeded to secure the Bay, and batteries were set up on the heights of Sphakteria at the southern end. Though the ground around the fortress was too rocky for the walls to be mined, the Turks nevertheless surrendered after Königsmark routed a relieving force a few miles away. On the night of the capitulation certain fires, which had been started by the bombardment, caused the explosion of a powder store in one of the bastions of the hexagonal fort. The evacuation of 3,000 Turks was carried out, however, without the usual reprisals, and

Francesco Morosini entered the citadel on June 18, 1686.[2]

* * *

New Navarino was built by the Turks in 1573, two years after the Battle of Lepanto, to guard the most strategic point along the western shore of the Peloponnese.[3] It is one of the best preserved fortresses in Greece, with probably the least history.

The plan is a simple enclosure broadly disposed over a slope of ground, descending from the edge of a plateau to the shore of Navarino Bay, where two large, independent works cover the entrance. The highest part of the fortress is guarded by a small, but elaborate defense, which presents an obstacle to attack from the side of the plateau. The curtains are thin walls of masonry, built of tightly fitted, smooth-faced limestone blocks, of the sort used also at Zarnata and Kelepha. A chemin de ronde, 4–8 feet wide, follows all the way round their top, protected by parapets of varying forms of crenellation. The east and north-

[1] *Op. cit.*, p. 199.

4

[2] *La Morea Combattuta* (Bologna, 1686), pp. 111–117; *History of the Venetian Conquests*, p. 66; *Il Regno della Morea sotto i Veneti*, pp. 52–57; Locatelli, I, pp. 214–225; Foscarini, p. 200.

[3] Coronelli, *Description*, p. 64; Randolph, *The Present State of the Morea*, p. 5; Miller, *Essays*, p. 377.

Fig. 48. New Navarino and Pylos (Neokastro), from the Air, 2500 feet, looking Southeast.

west curtains, built with a slight batter, carry parapets with a curved crest, pierced by small embrasures at 30-foot intervals, alternating with loopholes (Fig. 49). On the southwest side the curtain faces the more dangerous quarter of the open coast, and is built correspondingly stronger (Fig. 50). Two casemates, 10 feet deep, pierce its lower section next to the western sea bastion (Fig. 50, left). The wall stands 30 feet high, and supports its chemin de ronde on a line of recessed arches for its entire length from the plateau to the sea (Fig. 51). The parapet is higher than those of the other curtains. Near the sea the merlons are large and square, alternately pierced with loopholes. Further up the hill, the crenellations have been alternately filled in with masonry, leaving space for loopholes between the merlons themselves. Beyond the round flanking bastion, at the point where the ground begins to rise steeply, the individual merlons again detach themselves, while the crenellations slope parallel to the terrain (Fig. 51, left). Toward the top

of the hill, where the ground falls away steeply below, the crenellations disappear, leaving a straight-topped parapet, pierced with loopholes that present a square opening on the inside, and diminish with a pronounced pitch to a tall, narrow slot on the exterior. At the top, over the ditch which encircles the hexagonal citadel, the loopholes lose their pitch, and open horizontally over the glacis. This

Fig. 49. New Navarino, East Curtain, looking North across the Bay toward Sphakteria.

long parapet, which varies according to the terrain outside, shows a certain adaptability on the part of its Turkish builders, whose understanding of fortification seems to have stopped short, however, in the matter of the curtain's actual thickness and strength against

who probably borrowed the form from the dome construction of the Byzantines.[4] The largest of these bastions are situated in the east and southwest flanks.[5] Near ground level their walls are pierced by vaulted casemates, 12 feet deep and 10 feet wide at the opening,

FIG. 50. NEW NAVARINO, SOUTHWEST CURTAIN, WITH CASEMATES AND FLANKING BASTION.
AT THE TOP, THE HEXAGONAL FORT, WITH ITS SOUTHWEST GLACIS, UPPER RIGHT.

artillery. Communication between the interior of the enclosure and the chemin de ronde is provided by flights of steps at three points around the north and east.

The curtains are defended by four round flanking bastions. All five drawings in the Grimani collection agree in placing a fifth at the angle directly north of the gateway on the east side (Plates VII, VIII, XI, XII, XIII), but there is no trace of any such construction (Fig. 49, right). These towers vary from 25 to 65 feet in diameter, with embrasured parapets upwards of 7 feet thick. The chambers within are domed in brick, like those in the east defenses at Corone and in the flanking bastions of Zarnata, Kelepha, and Old Navarino. This use of brick-vaulted tholoi in works of fortification appears to belong exclusively to the Turks,

4*

with vaults and side-walls built of cut voussoirs and ashlar blocks (Fig. 50). Plain buttresses reinforce the outer walls (Figs. 50, 52, 56, right).

At the northernmost corner of the castle, by the inner shore of the channel, the trace of the eastern curtain projects out into a work, designated on Plate XII as *St. Maria*, which an inner wall seals off into a separate quadrangle. Its outer walls are pierced by a line of casemates at ground level, two in each flank and four in the north face, which measure at their opening 8 feet high and 9 wide, with side walls

[4] I know of no instance in Greece where the Venetians used domes of brick, except to cover the tiny turrets and sentry-boxes along the ramparts of the Palamedi and in their XVIII century works at Methone and in the ditch of New Navarino (Fig. 60, left).

[5] The latter was destroyed in 1943 by an explosion of Italian munitions. The breach appears in Figs. 48, 51.

and vaults of cut poros blocks. The east corner of the structure is rounded, while that on the west is chamfered and built of large, rectangular blocks, extending for a width of 5 feet into the wall faces on either side of the angle. The narrow parapet of the adjacent curtains

built over the outer entrance to the channel. It was probably the first section of the place to be built, as may be judged from the masonry of its north flank, which penetrates the adjacent certain wall. Like its companion to the east, it is in the form of a quadrangular

FIG. 51. NEW NAVARINO, SOUTHWEST CURTAIN, INTERIOR, SHOWING ARCADES, PARAPETS, AND RUINED FLANKING BASTION. WESTERN SEA FORT, LOWER RIGHT.

runs round the top of the walls, containing on the east side shallow embrasures placed at wide intervals, and on the west a series of loopholes every 4 feet. The eastern casemates are built with depressed vaults and monolithic limestone jambs on the outer face; on the west their vaults are lower, and the construction throughout is of smaller poros blocks. Inconsistencies such as these do not imply, in Turkish architecture, different periods of building. The whole fort is unified, at the level of the chemin de ronde, by a string course molding, of a weightiness indicative of an early period of artillery fortification. It is distinguished, however, by the unusual feature of a drafted edge above and below the bulge of the torus.

The primary purpose of the castle is embodied in the western sea fort (Plate XI, D. *Bateri a marini*; Plate XII, *forte Stᵃ Barba*),

enclosure, with provision for a double level of guns, shut off by a wall from the main enclosure of the fortress (Fig. 51, right). A narrow chemin de ronde and parapet follow round the top of this inner wall and the north and south

FIG. 52. NEW NAVARINO, SOUTHEAST CORNER TOWER, THROUGH A CASEMATE IN THE FLANKING BASTION IMMEDIATELY NORTH.

flanks, communicating directly with the artillery platform along the west face. This measures 100 feet long by 25 feet wide, enclosed on three sides by a parapet 10 feet thick, containing eight embrasures (Fig. 53), and carried on a row of short barrel vaults, which lead into a

FIG. 53. NEW NAVARINO, THE WESTERN SEA FORT, INTERIOR, SHOWING RAMP AND NORTHWEST ARTILLERY PLATFORM.

second row of saucer domes on pendentives (Fig. 54), vaulted in brick and poros voussoirs. The interior face of the bastion's west wall is marked by the arcade of these vaults, with their double arches of poros blocks (Figs. 53, 55), a feature that may be seen again in the

south bastion of the Castle of Roumeli. A single transverse unit is formed by each separate barrel vault and domed compartment, enclosed within piers and reinforcing arches, with an extension through the outer wall in the form of a casemate, one to each compartment, which slopes down to the rocks along the sea's edge. From the great platform above these structures, a thin ramp communicates with the slanting court of the quadrangle, develops into a paved path, and so leads out through the doorway in its inner wall.

The openings throughout the fortress are distinctive, and resemble nothing built either by Byzantine predecessors or contemporary Venetians, although the imitation is transparent. The entrance to the west sea bastion is a depressed arch (Fig. 55), made of six large, wedge-shaped poros blocks, topped with a bigger block of similar form, which in its proper place would be a keystone, and two much wider, eccentrically carved elements, which serve on either side to modulate between the curving line of the arch and the horizontal courses of the wall face. Above it four stone brackets project from the wall,

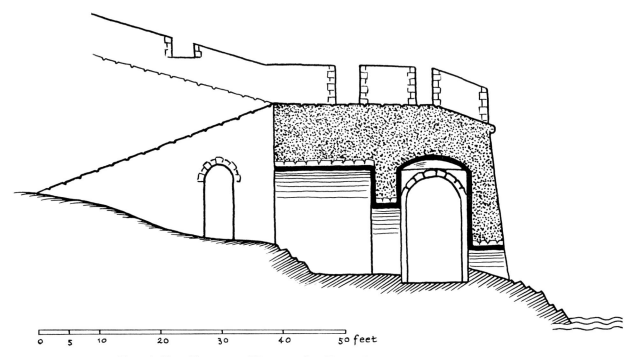

FIG. 54. NEW NAVARINO, WESTERN SEA FORT, SECTION OF NORTHWEST FACE.

interrupting the line of the string course molding with its small cornice on either side of the torus, to accommodate a balcony now fallen. The gateway in the fortress' east curtain (Fig. 49), now the chief entrance from the side of the modern town of Pylos, is built in sections, like

of the hill. It is built in the form of an avant-corps, containing a wide, pointed vault, with a smaller, pointed door in one of its walls, flanked on both sides by pyramidal buttresses, and topped with a string course to mark their talus (Fig. 56).

Fig. 55. New Navarino, Entrance to the West Sea Bastion. In the background, the Vaulted Gun Platform.

Fig. 56. New Navarino, Southeast Gate.

the outer gate at Old Navarino or the gates in the land walls of Constantinople: on the outside a depressed arch of wedge-shaped blocks; behind it, a straight lintel, supported on scroll-shaped corbels; then a short passageway, vaulted in poros voussoirs. The round flanking bastion in the curtain directly south of the eastern gate is entered from within the enclosure by an opening in five sections: a vaulted passage, 5 feet deep; a small depressed arch; a scrolled door like that in the preceding; a round arch in brick; and finally another small poros vault. The main gate of the castle is situated in a short stretch of curtain immediately east of the hexagonal fort at the top

The hexagonal citadel, which defends the enclosure from the side of the higher plateau, forms the apex of New Navarino's fortifications, both in plan and elevation (Figs. 48, 50). Its short, broad ramparts contain a series of high, narrow, transverse, barrel vaulted chambers, six to eight to a side, each with a door, transom, and small, round window under the vault, the voussoirs of whose arches carry through to the inner façade of the walls (Figs. 57, 58). A century and a half later the Venetians used the same construction in the ramparts of the Palamedi forts at Nauplia, while in the XIII century the Franks had already built at Chlemoutsi an inner hexagonal redout with hollow ramparts containing a single longitudinal vault. The redout at Navarino encloses a six-sided court, divided later into sections by transverse walls when the castle, having served its original purpose, prolonged its life as a prison, useful in times of civil war. Five of the six angles of the fort are defended by big, prominent bastions (Fig. 59), each containing a brick-domed cistern, into which

Fig. 57. New Navarino, Interior of Hexagonal Fort. In the background, Sphakteria, and Old Navarino, extreme right.

water is collected by means of a hole in the platform above. The outer walls of the citadel are built with a talus, predominantly of rubble masonry, though with some patches of brick and of poros ashlar. Large, rectangular blocks are used in the angles of the bastions. The heavy torus, set one foot below the level of the embrasures, follows round the elaborate trace, with its close succession of salient and reentrant angles. The broad gun platform, shaped like a snowflake in outline, and paved in square limestone slabs as in the western sea fort, crowns the ramparts and angle bastions, supported on the vaults and domes beneath. The parapet contains numerous well built artillery embrasures: four round the outer walls of each bastion (not ten as indicated on Plate XII), and five to six along the curtains between them. The parapet is strongest in the south and southeast quarter, standing 11 feet high and 10 feet thick, pierced with tapering, square loopholes between the embrasures. Only in one sector of the citadel is its regularity broken. Plate XI (M) shows an arsenal in the northeast corner bastion just within the curtain of the

Fig. 58. New Navarino, Hexagonal Fort, Interior, showing Repair of the Demolition of 1686, with Entrance, lower right. In the background, the South Channel to Navarino Bay and Southern Tip of Sphakteria.

outer enclosure. The absence of a bastion at this angle substantiates the historical record of the explosion in the powder store in 1686.

It remains to consider what additions were made, after this date, to a fortress mainly remarkable for its uniformity of style and

FIG. 59. NEW NAVARINO, ANGLE BASTION OF HEXAGONAL FORT, WITH DITCH AND COUNTERSCARP, LOWER RIGHT.

materials. At the turn of the XVIII century New Navarino became the capital of the province of Messenia under the Venetians,[6] who seem to have preferred it for purposes of administration against the far stronger, but outlying cities of Methone and Corone. As a fortress, however, its position was dubious. In 1690 Giacomo Corner described its exposure to higher terrain, and its lack of a ditch or palisade.[7] In 1693 Antonio Molin[8] deemed the place of little use in a bay that was itself too large to be defended, although its aqueduct[9] and cisterns together were enough to provide a year's supply of water. The plan drawn for Francesco Grimani by Levasseur (Plate XII) shows an ambitious scheme for its refortification: a ditch to surround the entire fortress, with counterscarp, covered way, and glacis; three ravelins on the two long flanks; and an extended hornwork to protect the vulnerable south side of the hexagonal citadel. In addition

a *Torre projettato* was to be built on the rocky islet at the mouth of the channel, where now stands the tomb of the French philhellenes killed in the Battle of Navarino: a semicircular bastion with a small ditch, facing the fortress, containing nine embrasures and a gun platform supported on vaults, and a cistern in the center.[10] The plan was realized only in small part. A shallow ditch, 40 feet wide, was dug around the southern sector of the hexagonal citadel, to enclose its three outer bastions. The counterscarp is vertical, and measures 8–20 feet high, forming salient and re-entrant angles in conformation with the indentations of the trace. At two points, opposite the south and southeast curtains of the fort, the covered way is projected forward by miniature pentagonal ravelins (Fig. 60), of a form similar to those proposed on Plate XII in another sector. Part of the ditch is walled off into a small compartment by the two interior flanks adjacent to the

FIG. 60. NEW NAVARINO, RAVELIN IN THE DITCH BELOW SOUTH CURTAIN OF HEXAGONAL FORT.

counterscarp, each pierced by three loopholes, and the inner face of the work, which admits entry from the ditch through a low door. The inner corner is flanked by a domed sentry-box. The glacis descends to the natural ground level opposite the westernmost of the angle bastions

---

[6] Miller, *Essays*, p. 419.

[7] Δελτίον, II, p. 308.

[8] *Ibid.*, V, pp. 437, 443.

[9] Traces of which may be seen in the plateau to the southeast. See also Plate XI, I, *Condutta daqua*.

[10] Δελτίον, V, p. 493, report of Francesco Grimani: "Anche a sicurezza di questo mio devotissimo parere sarebbe eriger un forte sopra il scoglietto all' incontro della Piazza che quasi inaccessibile e angusto potria con poco presidio lungamente sostenersi."

(Fig. 50, upper right). This system of outworks belongs to the turn of the XVIII century, and may be considered as a modification of Levasseur's original plan.

The demolition of the northeast angle bastion was repaired by a plain obtuse corner, without additional defense to match the other five. The broad gun platform over the ramparts stops abruptly just short of the middle of the north curtain of the hexagon (Fig. 58), which rounds the corner with a thin masonry wall, topped by a chemin de ronde and a straight parapet without loopholes, backed by a line of steps (Fig. 58, right) in the manner of construction used by the Venetians in their later works at Corone and Nauplia (Figs. 18, 115). The adjacent curtain on the east also lacks the artillery platform which occupies the other four and a half sides; its place taken by a ramp, which descends into the court. The entrance to this court from the area of the larger enclosure is situated in the hexagon's north wall: a plain, vaulted passageway, faced on the outside by an avantcorps in the form of a ponderous Roman arch, which can hardly have been built by the Turks either before or after the Venetian occupation. The angle ruined in 1686 lay within the main circuit of the fortress walls, and as such was not of crucial danger. Yet if the Venetians troubled themselves to carve a ditch out of the rocks of the plateau, it is unlikely that they would have left any section of the defenses in a state of collapse. The Grimani drawings show the hexagonal fort intact, indication that the repair was carried out after Grimani's tenure and, presumably, before 1715. By this date, however, the Venetians had decided to destroy the fortress as a place incapable of defense.[11]

Plates XI and XII show a rectangular edifice, flanking the interior of the short stretch of the outer curtain wall, which contains the castle's southeast gate. The passage into the enclosure leads through this building, which consists of two compartments, formed by massive, round, longitudinal and transverse arches, with two domes carried on the pendentives that spring between their angles. The building as it stands to-day has been extended to form an integral part of the hexagonal work, and supports a gun platform above, guarded by a plain, straight parapet on the side of the enclosure, and a thicker, embrasured parapet covering the approaches from the high ground on the south. It is possible the Venetians, after the drawing of the Grimani plans, incorporated the western end of this structure into the upper citadel, and yet its parapets show no trace of age or weathering. In the decentralization of Turkish rule during the XVIII century, the fortified places of Greece fell into universal disrepair. It remained, at Neokastro, for the liberating French troops under Marshal Maison to raze the town within the walls, and rebuild it round a small harbor just inside the mouth of Navarino Bay (Fig. 48, left). The fortress was left empty of habitation, as at Methone and the Castle of Morea, but its hexagonal citadel was to serve a longer term, and probably underwent some reconstruction in the years after 1828.

[11] Miller, *Essays*, p. 424.

CHAPTER VII

METHONE

(Plates XIV–XVII)

On June 22, 1686, the army of the Holy League disembarked at Methone. The Turks withdrew into the fortress, and the Venetians occupied the small *borgo* outside the ditch, sealing off the peninsula with circumvallations and a row of earthworks to the rear to guard against the arrival of the Seraskier, who was now gathering his forces at Nisi. Morosini summoned the Turks to surrender the fortress, reminding them of Navarino and Corone, respective examples of Venetian clemency and vengeance. The disdar in command of the place answered, in Mohammedan fashion, that since all men were born to die, he would defend it till death. So the Venetians resorted to bombardment, which caused such havoc within the place that the women and children had to be shut up in the small island fort at the southern end of the peninsula, where their cries could not be heard by the defenders on the walls. After four days Morosini sent another summons and the Turks asked for a night's truce. They occupied this time in transporting munitions up to the ramparts from a quarter previously under fire, while the Venetians dug their trenches forward to the edge of the counterscarp. The next morning the disdar sent back a second answer of defiance. Morosini, reluctant to damage the fortifications, demanded a surrender for the third time. The Turks were dismayed by the continued abeyance of the Seraskier, and by the sight of the Venetians already moving their materials into the ditch in preparation for mining the walls. The white flag was hoisted, and on July 10 four thousand Turks came out of the fortress, leaving 100 cannon behind them, together with all their slaves, black and white, to the questionable liberty of Venetian rule.[1]

* * *

Methone first appears as a Byzantine city in A.D. 533 when Justinian concluded the Persian peace and sent Belisarius to attack the Vandals in North Africa. On his way to Sicily, Belisarius and his armada "approached Methone and found both Valerianus and Martinus arrived there shortly before. And since the wind had fallen, Belisarius moored his ships there, and disembarked the whole army. Putting to shore, he mustered his officers and drew up the troops in order."[2] Six centuries later, Methone is mentioned again, in the *Geography* of Edrisi,[3] as "a town defended by a fort, which commands the sea."

In the early XII century Methone sheltered a squadron of corsairs which preyed on Venetian merchant vessels as they plied their way

[1] Locatelli, I, pp. 226 ff.; Coronelli, *Description*, pp. 85 f.; *The History of the Venetian Conquests*, pp. 78 ff.

[2] Prokopios, *History of the Wars*, ed. Loeb, III, xiii, 9, 10.

[3] *Géographie d'Edrisi*, p. 124.

between the Adriatic and the Aegean. Piracy was encouraged by the Emperor John II Comnenus who, trying to halt the commercial and military infiltration of his Empire by the Crusaders and western traders, rescinded the privileges granted to the Venetians in 1082 by his father, Alexios I.[4] They in turn answered by sending a fleet into the Aegean, which ravaged the islands and carried off the women and children into slavery, and in 1125 the Doge Domenico Michieli, *Terror Graecorum*, descended on Methone and razed it to the ground. Three quarters of a century later we find the Venetians enjoying free trade in the "district of Methone," and finally laying claim to the place in the Partition Treaty on the eve of the Fourth Crusade.[5]

In 1204 Geoffroy de Villehardouin the younger, bound for Constantinople but driven by contrary winds into the harbor of Methone, took refuge for the winter with the archon of the place, and joined him in a private war against his neighboring landlords. From his Messenian reconnaissance the Burgundian knight learned that the Morea was, like the rest of the Byzantine Empire, rich and divided against itself.[6] The following year, when he returned with his companion, Champlitte, and a band of knights to carry out its conquest, Methone, it is said, still lay ruined and abandoned from the time of Michieli's raid.[7] Messenia was occupied as a part of the newly founded Principality of Achaea, but in 1206 a Venetian fleet took possession of Methone and drove out the Frankish garrison under the eyes of Villehardouin, the Prince. In 1209 he consented to Venice's legal possession, and for the next three centuries Methone owned uninterrupted Venetian sway.[8] Colonists were

sent out, and the place was fortified and developed into the chief port between Venice and the shores of Asia. Situated, as it was said, "half way to every land and sea," it offered a stopping place for the pilgrims whom the Venetian navy had the monopoly of transporting to the Holy Land.[9] For nearly 200 years the twin colonies of Methone and Corone enjoyed freedom from both the Franks of the Principality and the Greeks of the Despotate of Mistra. Then, toward the end of the XIV century, the Despot Theodore I Palaiologos began the policy of expansion which, under his successors, was to end in the complete absorption of the Frankish State. The Venetians vainly tried in 1394 to unite both Greeks and Franks against the Turks, whose raids drew ever closer, but the Greeks were following their own plans for unification of the Morea.[10]

The first half of the XV century was a perilous period for Venice's Messenian and Argive colonies, continually raided by the Despot's troops and threatened from a decreasing distance by the Turks. In 1415 the Emperor Manuel II, who had previously plotted to capture Venice's Greek colonies, asked her to contribute to the unified defense of the Morea. She refused, and furthermore ordered the governors of Methone, Corone, Argos, and Nauplia not to allow the Emperor or his officials into their territory. In 1417 the *Castellani* of Methone and Corone provoked a rupture between the Prince of Achaea and the Despot of Mistra. War followed, and for the next forty years the Despot's troops overran that part of the Morea where Frankish rule had ceased to exist, and periodically ravaged the Messenian boundaries. The Venetians retaliated with measures against the Greek inhabitants of the colonies. In 1444 the number of Greeks in the

---

[4] Daru, I, pp. 167f.; Tafel und Thomas, *Urkunden*, I, p. 53.

[5] *Ibid.*, I, pp. 264, 469.

[6] Villehardouin, *La conquête de Constantinople*, I, §§ 226–232.

[7] X. τ. M., lines 1690–4; *L. de C.*, § 110; *C. di M.*, p. 425.

[8] Daru, I, pp. 167f.; Miller, *Latins*, pp. 39, 59f.; S. Luce, "Modon-a Venetian Station in Medieval Greece," in *Studies in Honor of Edward Kennard Rand* (New York, 1938), p. 196.

[9] *Le saint voyage de Jherusalem du Seigneur d'Anglure, 1395*, ed. Bonnardot and Longnon (Paris, 1878), p. 99: "De droicte ordonnance les Veniciens envoyent chascun an V galées en la Terre Saincte, et arrivent toutes a Barust qui est le port de Damas en Surie."

[10] Zakythinos, *Despotat*, I, pp. 138, 143.

garrison of Methone was reduced. Greeks were forbidden to congregate or form associations. Their property was confiscated, and in Methone they were forbidden to hold land in fief. Emigration resulted, and the land was left wide open, so that the Venetians could find none to work it. When it was too late, they abolished some of the taxes, in hopes of inducing their subjects to return.[11]

When the Despot Thomas Palaiologos escaped to Venice in 1460, and the last outpost of East Rome had fallen, the Sultan Mohammed II paid a visit to the Venetians in Messenia. He was sumptuously entertained, but his troops pillaged the land and killed a number of the inhabitants. The Republic at last realized the full danger, and began to refortify Methone. In 1494 a traveller noted:

> There are 2000 inhabitants, and the sea encloses it on both sides. It is well walled and sufficiently strong, but flat ... The soil is very productive ... Lodging is good... The sea washes the walls, and it has a port capable of receiving the largest ships. It has strong walls with drawbridges at every gate, which are four ... It is well furnished with towers, and on the towers and the walls there are pieces of artillery of every size. Toward the mainland it is very strong, and it is being continually strengthened. The *Signoria* is adding there a large moat and a double line of thick walls, and it will be a stupendous thing when it is finished.[12]

The Greeks, however, were still moving out, through fear of invasion, to other Venetian possessions.

In 1499 war at last broke out. A Turkish vessel was sunk in the Aegean for not saluting the Venetian flag, and the Sultan Bayezid II retaliated with an armada of 250 ships against the Venetian ports in Greece. Naupaktos fell, and in 1500 Bayezid moved against Methone.[13]

In preparation for the attack, all the houses outside the fortress were burned down, and a dam was built across the harbor to allow only one ship to enter at a time. The women were deported to Crete. The garrison numbered 7,000. For a month Bayezid besieged the place by land with an army of 100,000 and 500 siege guns, while the Turkish ships blockaded it by sea. The Venetian fleet arrived under Melchior Trevisan, and with 27 sail drove off 100 enemy vessels. These returned, however, at a moment when the largest Venetian galleys were immobilized by a calm. The Venetians withdrew with losses, leaving the fortress unguarded. Then Trevisan returned with his whole fleet in battle order to force an entry into Methone Bay. On August 9, 1500, four of his vessels loaded with food, munitions and reinforcements, made their way through a double line of Turkish ships to the mouth of the harbor. In a fatal moment the defenders abandoned the ramparts to remove the chain and let the ships into port. The Janissaries entered the citadel at the ruined tower of the governor's palace, and swarmed over the town, preventing the inhabitants who tried to set fire to their houses and munitions. The garrison made its last stand on the island fort at the end of the peninsula. Those who escaped could see the flames of the burning citadel from Zakynthos. The Turks slaughtered the entire adult population, and took the governor and all the children under twelve into slavery. They repaired the walls, and repopulated Methone with families from villages all over the Peloponnese.[14]

In 1531 an attack was made on Methone by the Knights of St. John, driven from their stronghold on Rhodes. First an advance guard of Greeks was smuggled into the town on two schooners, with the connivance of the Greek port authorities, who had once been servants of the Order. Then the tower on the mole was captured, and all of the town occupied as far as the governor's palace at the north end. But the rest of the forces were late in coming out from their hiding place behind the island of

---

[11] *Ibid.*, pp. 167, 169, 171, 181 f., 192, 218, 237, 242, 244.
[12] *Canon Pietro Casola's Pilgrimage, 1494*, (Manchester, 1907), pp. 50, 191 ff.
[13] Mompherratos, *op. cit.*, pp. 57 ff.

[14] Cappelletti, VII, pp. 226 ff.; Daru, III, p. 285; Miller, *Latins*, pp. 496 ff.; Mompherratos, *op. cit.*, pp. 66 f.; Luce, *op. cit.*, p. 203.

Sapienza, and the rumor of a Turkish relieving force caused the Knights to withdraw, after sacking the town and carrying off 1,600 prisoners.[15]

In 1572 Methone was the object of a raid by Don John of Austria, following on the victory of Lepanto, but his enterprise failed both at Methone and Navarino, and the coasts of Greece remained free from European invasions until the time of Francesco Morosini.

In 1715 the Venetians tried to defend the Morea with a feeble concentration of troops at Methone and four other points of resistance. Again the great Venetian fortress suffered a Turkish siege, while for five days the army of the grand vizier kept up a vigorous attack, until the white flag was raised, and the Venetians asked for terms. But the Turks continued bombarding the place, and the garrison, who had heard of the massacres at Nauplia and the Castle of Morea, laid down their arms and ran out of the fortress by the sea gate toward the Turkish galleys.[16]

The fortifications, which had suffered severe damage from the siege of 1686, were repaired and enlarged by the Venetians with new works along the land front. During the XVIII century they were left to crumble. Colonel Leake, who visited Methone in 1805, described their

wretched state of repair, though in construction they are far more respectable than those of Neokastro (New Navarino); the land front has a much higher profile, and there is a ditch intended to be wet and to communicate from sea to sea, but now dry and full of rubbish. Towards the sea both towers and walls are falling to ruin. Mothoni is one of those convenient and important situations which have always been occupied: and hence it is that we find no remains of Hellenic antiquity, the materials having long been converted to the repair of modern dwellings and fortifications.[17]

In 1825, Ibrahim Pasha landed at Methone, on the campaign that was to end in the waters of Navarino. After 1828, the liberating French troops under Marshal Maison rebuilt the town outside the walls, dismantling for this purpose the city which had existed within them.[18]

*   *   *

Foscarini[19] describes the city of Methone, built

on a promontory extending into the sea, which bathes it on three sides. The north side, facing the land, is occupied by a citadel which defends its front. This is provided with a large ditch which passes from sea to sea, and is for the most part dug out of the rock, with a high counterscarp faced in stone. The citadel is dominated by an eminence, which sweeps it horizontally and overlooks the city enclosure, the gateway, and the bridge. At the other end, where the circuit projects into the sea, at a distance of 30 paces from the walls, there stands a small work of octagonal form, commonly known as the lantern, which defends the canal. Under cover of the work, beneath the east wall of the city is a small port, once capable of holding seven or eight galleys, but now through long neglect barely sufficient for a few small craft. The circuit wall of the city is of moderate height, without terreplein, flanked by a number of narrow, square towers not built for artillery, which serve it more for decoration than for defense.

The peninsula juts out 1000 feet into the sea off the southwestern corner of the Messenian cape (Fig. 61), forming, together with a deep curve of shore on one side and the island of Sapienza opposite, the great stretch of sheltered water which Venice first coveted for her merchant fleet. The fortress is separated from the mainland by a ditch, which describes a wide arc across the neck of the peninsula. Its counterscarp supports a covered way and glacis, which slopes out over a space 60 feet wide. On the western side may be seen traces of an outwork, which corresponds partially to recommendations by Francesco Grimani[20] and

---

[15] Miller, *Latins*, p. 504; Luce, *op. cit.*, p. 204.

[16] B. Brue, *Journal de la campagne que le Grand Vézir a faite en 1715 pour la conquête de la Morée* (Paris, 1870), pp. 42–49; Cappelletti, XI, p. 48; Daru, V, p. 191; Luce, *op. cit.*, p. 205.

[17] Leake, *Morea*, I, pp. 431 f.

[18] Buchon, *La Grèce continentale et la Morée*, p. 455.

[19] *Op. cit.*, p. 202.

[20] Δελτίον, V, p. 483: "A Ponente poi coglierei il favore del sito, facendovi una Tanaglia semplice con il suo Camin coperto e con spalto..."

FIG. 61. METHONE, FROM THE AIR.

Agostino Sagredo.[21] The counterscarp itself
dates from several different periods. For the
line of the ditch was changed by the Venetians
in the last years of their second occupation, to
include the prominent bastion built on the
eastern shore by the General Antonio Loredan.[22] These innovations[23] do not appear on

Plate XVI, which appears to have been drawn
before 1701, while Grimani still held the office
of *Provveditore Generale dell' Armi*. However,
a small plan of 1731 (Plate XVII) shows the
north defenses almost exactly as they remain
to-day. Since the building of the modern mole
in 1870, the whole inner corner of the harbor
has silted up with deposit from the neighboring
stream and the action of sea currents, so that
for half their length the eastern walls of the
fortress, once washed by the waves, now stand
isolated on an enormous beach (Fig. 62).

On the east side the counterscarp rises out of
the sand, parallel for 300 feet with the face of

[21] *Ibid.*, V, p. 748: "... Con le Fortificationi soprariferite,
il compimento delle quali non richiede fatica di lungo tempo,
quella Piazza, ch'è della ben nota importanza per la sua situa-
tione, può esser in stato di buona difesa, ma per esser meglio
assicurata, viene da Professori creduta conferente anche la
proposta opera a Corno su la croppa del Monte, col suo fosso,
e camin coperto; sopra di che alla generosità Publica sarano
riservate le risolutioni, ne tempi, che riuscissero più oppor-
tuni."

[22] *Ibid.*, V, p. 748: "... La fossa ... avanti la faccia del
mezzo baluardo predetto (the Loredan bastion), quasi tutta
restò formata di nuovo, e così la contrascarpa opposta alla
faccia sudetta fu eretta da fondamenti con sua galeria
paralella al di dietro del muro, e con tre rami di altra Galeria
inoltrata ottanta piedi sotto lo spalto. Alla strata coperta
mancavano due piedi d'elevatione al suo parapetto, ma in
quella opposta alla faccia del mezzo Baloardo era compito il

suo giusto inalzamento, e piantate anco le palizzate. Lo
spalto era poi avvanzato a buon termine in qualche sito."

[23] Brue, *Journal de la campagne*, p. 42: "Les Vénetiens ont
parfaitement fait reparer les fossés et joint aux anciennes
fortifications une espèce de bastion sur la gauche et quelques
autres ouvrages sur la droite."

the Loredan bastion: a low, battering wall of rough, coursed stones with great, square blocks in the outer angle. Opposite the middle of the Loredan's face, it bears a plaque carved with the lion of St. Mark. Along the whole stretch of this wall as far as the bridge, underneath the curved bay, and then proceeds in a straight line to the western shore.

It terminates on this side in a work not shown on the Grimani plans, but built in the last years before 1715. This is a long, quadrangular, terrepleined redout (Figs. 72, B; 87), in which

FIG. 62. METHONE, THE EAST CURTAIN, FROM THE LOREDAN BASTION TO THE BOURTZI FORT.

covered way, there runs a vaulted passage, 6 feet high by 4 wide, communicating with the ditch by means of five small entrances, arched in heavy, curved poros blocks marked with a drafted edge. Several other galleries run off at right angles from the main passage, leading in under the glacis for the purpose of counter-mining. On the northwest side of the stone bridge is a double ramp built into the corner of the counterscarp where it forms an obtuse salient angle. This ramp, which appears only on the drawing of 1731, descends both faces of the counterscarp on either side of the angle. It is made of long, sloping steps, with cut lime-stone blocks along the outside edges. On the west the counterscarp is a vertical rubble wall, which stands to its greatest height opposite the heavy bastion at the fortress' northernmost extremity, around which it forms a large,

the counterscarp forms the rear wall, built to cover the sector where the terrain, sloping down to the shore, would otherwise reduce the effective capacity of the ditch and leave the northwest front of the citadel open to attack. The work is built with battering walls of large, uncut, but well fitted limestone blocks. Its sea flank, 35 feet high, is built in its lower half of monumental ashlar courses, laid on a pro-jecting base set among the ragged rocks at the edge of the water. Its north face contains a plaque of the Venetian lion and a heavy torus molding along the top. Above, on the south, east, and west sides, are the foundations of a stone parapet 8 feet thick. Along the north side, facing up the shore toward the heights of Ayios Nikolaos, are the traces of an earth-filled parapet, pierced with embrasures 15 feet deep.

The ditch measures 130 feet across at its widest, in the middle section between the Bembo and Loredan bastions. Round the

fortified projection. Originally the sea must have washed well into the ditch on the east, but another 20 feet of rock-cutting would be

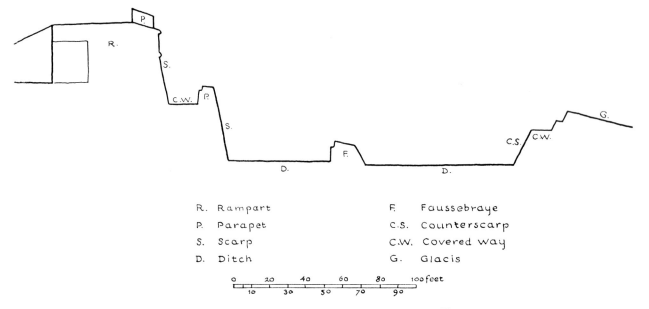

R.   Rampart   F.   Faussebraye
P.   Parapet   C.S.   Counterscarp
S.   Scarp   C.W.   Covered way
D.   Ditch   G.   Glacis

FIG. 63. METHONE, THE NORTH DEFENSES: WESTERN HALF, ELEVATION.

salient curve of the former, it dwindles to a width of 50 feet. Here it is excavated 25 feet out of the rocky ridge of the peninsula, severing the backbone of the mainland from its

needed to bring the water all the way through. As Leake observed, this was probably what the Venetians intended, both when they began the work in the last years of the XV century,

FIG. 64. METHONE, THE NORTH DEFENSES: DITCH, FAUSSEBRAYE, BRIDGE, SCARP, AND ENTRANCE GATE.

and at the beginning of the XVIII, when they returned to it again.[24] The capture of Methone in 1715 halted the work, but we are told that the French occupying force of Marshal Maison continued to excavate and widen the ditch, among other labors of construction at Methone in the early XIX century.[25]

A faussebraye (Figs. 63, 64, 70) runs down the middle of the ditch between the flanks of the two terminal bastions. Its exterior slope is made of big, flat paving-stones, rough in outline, but accurately fitted together. Beneath the west flank of the Loredan bastion, a passage through it admitted to the original entrance of the fortress, as shown on Plate XVI.

The main portion of the ditch belongs to the end of the XV century, together with the Bembo bastion, the faussebraye, and the central section of the counterscarp and glacis. The Loredan bastion, the lower platform flanking the east side of the Bembo bastion, the realignment of the eastern counterscarp, and the artillery work at its western end all carry the winged lion of Venice, and are enumerated in Agostino Sagredo's report of 1714 as recent additions to the fortress.[26]

The north rampart of the place (Fig. 63, left), extends between the two big artillery bastions at either end, comprising the "double line of thick walls," whose erection was noted in 1494 by the pilgrim, Casola. The outer line, or scarp proper, rises 35 feet above the ditch. It is broken into two sections by an obtuse angle at the center, and supports a covered way, communicating with both bastions. The western half is built with a battering face of rough limestone, strongly mortared, with a

low, thick parapet above. The southeast half has only the slightest talus, covered in a thick, red mortar, and is built with a large proportion of soft, greenish sandstone, with two courses of ashlar blocks marking the level of the covered way. Here the parapet is straight-topped and vertical, thinner and twice as high as that on the other side.

The original entrance to the fortress is shown on Plate XVI to have been situated in the middle of this southeast side, approached across the ditch through an opening in the faussebraye. All that remains to-day is a mass of masonry built on a small limestone spur, projecting from beneath the scarp. One may discern from it two flanks of the gate, with outer sides set obliquely to the wall, and something resembling a step between them. It was put out of use when the present parapet was built over its foundations and a new gate erected. The question arises, when was the second bridge built? The Grimani plan shows only the first. The present entrance, then, must be attributed either to the Venetians after Grimani, or to the Turks during the XVIII century, or else to the French, at the end of the War of Independence, who built the present bridge of fourteen arches which leads to it across the ditch. During the XVIII century the Turks were for the most part inactive architecturally, and the French of 1828 only built the present structure along the line of an earlier wooden bridge, carried on stone pillars, mentioned in the descriptions of Grimani and Foscarini quoted above and noticed by French travellers in the early XIX century.[27] It would be reasonable to assign to the Venetians of 1700 the present monumental gateway (Fig. 64) at the head of the bridge: a small pylon pierced by an arch between fluted Corinthian pilasters, crudely carved with a baroque array of flags and pikes in either corner.

The powerful rampart of the north front

---

[24] Δελτίον, V, pp. 747f.: "La fossa avanti la Piattaforma S. Maria era profondata in sei piedi nel grebano."

[25] Bory de Saint-Vincent, *Relation*, I, pp. 126, 128.

[26] Δελτίον, V, p. 747: "L'antico antemurale, che dividendo la larghezza del Fosso stesso s'estende dal Fianco del mezzo Baloardo sudetto sino alla Piattaforma S. Maria è abbassato al segno, che fu creduto necessario, ne altro manca, che di formarvi inanzi un breve spalto, e stabilirvi, dietro il parapetto, la sua palizzata... La vecchia falsabraga, che dalla Porta della Piazza communica al fianco basso sudetto, è aggiustata ne suoi piani, restando da farsi solamente li parapetti."

[27] Pouqueville, *Voyage*, VI, p. 68; *Expédition scientifique de Morée, Architecture*, I, (Paris, 1831), plate XII.

5

rises above the trace of the outer scarp, flanked with square towers in the southeast section and a round, battering bastion at the central angle (Figs. 64, 66). This projects on its eastern

FIG. 65. METHONE, THE NORTH DEFENSES: COVERED WAY AND UPPER SCARP, LOOKING WEST TO THE BEMBO BASTION.

side into a square buttress, which accounts for its mistaken delineation on Plate XVI as a square tower. It is crowned with a torus molding and a plain parapet without embrasures or loopholes. The western half of the rampart batters in the lower portion, divided at the north end into talus and vertical scarp by a short torus, or string course molding (Fig. 65). The wall in this flank is built of the most characteristic form of Venetian masonry: squared blocks in courses, showing through the mortared joints. The regular torus runs along the top of the wall. The parapet is set back from it 3 feet, and contains, between the round central tower and the Bembo bastion, six deep embrasures built with sloping floors and side walls of ashlar. In the southeast sector, on the other hand, the wall is vertical, and consists mostly of finely cut, rectangular blocks, measuring up to 5 feet long, many of them marked

with dowel holes. These are classical materials, but the layers of tile and chips between the courses indicate their re-use in the present structure of the wall. Similar blocks are used in the lower portion of a large, square flanking tower, which projects into the covered way (Fig. 66).

Near the southeast end this road passes under a round archway, set in a tall, narrow, vaulted passage, flanked on each side by a casemate, 15 feet deep, tapering to a round hole from an arched opening in the inner face, edged with a drafted line (Fig. 67). This

FIG. 66. METHONE, THE NORTH DEFENSES: COVERED WAY AND UPPER RAMPART, LOOKING SOUTHEAST TOWARD THE INNER GATE.

entrance forms a bottleneck for the final 70 feet of the covered way, which here turns slightly more to the south, and leads to the third gate (Plate XVI, A. *Porta di terra ferma*). This is a great, square pylon, of a form reminiscent of the gate at Corone, which contains a round arch, 20 feet high, backed by a pointed arch 10 feet higher (Fig. 68). Cut poros blocks are used in the vaults of both arches, in the jambs of the outer, and in the angles of the pylon. The wall faces, however, together with the stretch of curtain between these two inner gates, are made of a soft, green, local stand-stone, cut in small, squared, oblong blocks, which wind and rain have eroded into smooth hollows between the hard, mortared joints.

Loredan bastion. The Grimani plans, which do not indicate the latter, show the triangular bulwark to be the chief artillery defense in this corner of the citadel. Beyond its rounded end, Plate XVI shows a small, rectangular bastion, with artillery parapet pierced by embrasures on the northeast and northwest sides, situated in the middle of the ditch, with the faussebraye terminating against the northwest wall and the

FIG. 68. METHONE, INTERIOR OF THE THIRD LAND GATE: THE GRANITE COLUMN OF 1493/4 AND THE LOREDAN PLAQUE OF 1714.

FIG. 67. METHONE, THE NORTH DEFENSES: INTERIOR OF SECOND GATE.

The section between these two gates is enclosed on the east side by a terrepleined bulwark supporting a triangular platform, 120 feet long, with a parapet containing four embrasures over the eastern shore, and two more which enfilade the interior portion of the ditch, whose southeast end it serves to block. It contains on this same side two tall, narrow vaults, the outer of which admits to three 15-foot casemates, distinguished again by the feature of a drafted line round the inner arches, tapering down to small, arched openings covering the ditch near ground level. The bulwark itself has a curved apex, pointing over the

FIG. 69. METHONE, EAST FLANK OF LOREDAN BASTION, INCORPORATING A CORNER OF THE ORIGINAL SQUARE TOWER.

5*

FIG. 70. METHONE, THE DITCH, LOOKING EAST TO THE LOREDAN BASTION.

sea coming up beneath its outer flank. Its only relic today is the short east flank above the sands of the beach, set between the earlier and later masonry of the wall face on either side. Its own wall of bulging limestone and hollowed sandstone rubble abuts on the fragment of a small, square corner tower shown on Plate XVI, whose base and angle of big, cut poros blocks remain embedded in the surrounding masonry (Fig. 69).

This northeast corner of the fortress does not appear to-day as shown on the Grimani plan of 1699–1701. The small rectangular work below the triangular bulwark was judged inadequate on this "side most easily attacked" of the crucial land defenses, and replaced by a huge, trapezoidal bastion (Figs. 70; 72, C), projecting so far out into the moat that the counterscarp had to be re-aligned for its accommodation (Figs. 70; 72, A). Set in the middle of a much widened ditch, the bastion masks the whole southeast end of the scarp itself (Fig. 71). There is a small entrance on this inner side, opposite the scarp, connecting with a ramp which leads up to the wide, terrepleined parade. On the side of the sea the parapet stands 18

feet high and 5 feet thick, with three wide, vaulted embrasures. Another ramp ascends from the parade to a raised gun platform, which occupies the north face and part of the northwest flank. On these sides the parapet is a terrepleined defense 20 feet thick, of which a line of earth mounds is all that remains to-day. In the bastion's west corner, however, it diminishes to a thickness of 6 feet, built of stone throughout. The terrepleined gun platform terminates near this corner at a point

FIG. 71. METHONE, THE NORTH DEFENSES: SOUTHEAST END OF THE DITCH AND PLATFORM OF THE LOREDAN BASTION.

adjacent to the curved salient angle of the original bastion, the foundations of whose northeast parapet can still be traced across the parade, a broad band of masonry just showing above the platform level, and whose northwest parapet (Fig. 71, foreground) stands almost intact, 8 feet thick, pierced by one embrasure and several long, straight, loopholes. A small quadrangle is enclosed in the west corner of the parade by this parapet and the adjacent walled-up end of the gun platform. The walls of this bastion stand 35 feet

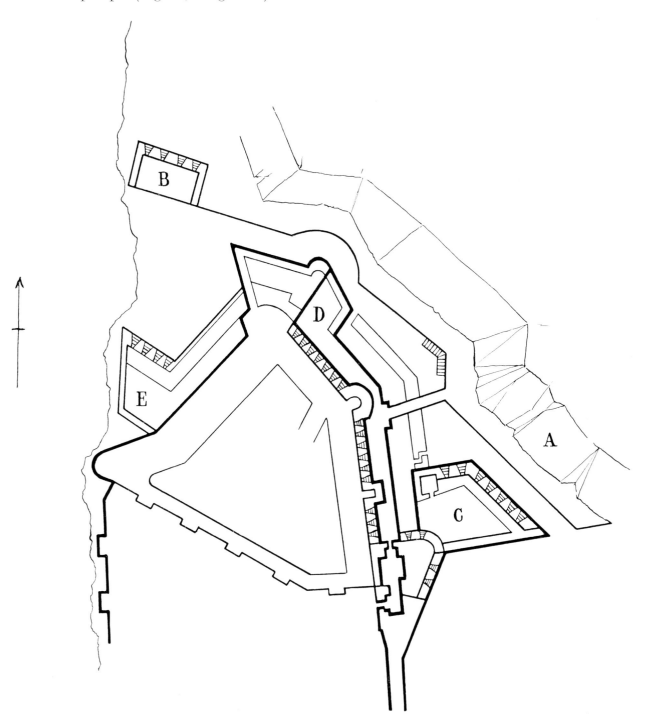

Fig. 72. Methone, Plan of the Land Defenses, showing Late Venetian Constructions, not indicated on Grimani Drawing: A. Reconstructed Counterscarp, B. Terminal Outwork at West End of Counterscarp, C. Loredan Bastion, D Flanking Platform below Bembo Bastion, E. Work in the Western Ditch.

above the floor of the ditch.[28] They are built with a slight talus, of small limestone blocks roughly squared, set in neat, regular courses (Fig. 69, right). Large, squared blocks of the dimensions of classical ashlar are used in the angles and in several courses along the base of the southeast flank. A heavy torus surrounds the top of the walls, and above this the parapet shows a ruined facing of small blocks and brick similar to the early XVIII century Venetian parapets at Nauplia. In the northwest corner is a ruined, hexagonal turret built out on a corbel-supported projection of the torus. The turret's pointed cap, domed and plastered inside, lies fallen in the moat below. The bastion's north face contains a large and wind-worn lion of St. Mark, with a plaque beneath it, bearing the inscription

ANTONII LAVRETANI
PROV GLIS ARM IN PELOPONESO
REGIMINE ET CVRA
ANNO MDCCXIV

The northwest flank of the bastion is built in two sections, separated by a clearly defined rift, which extends all the way up the talus; is marked by the abrupt termination of the cordon, and continues up the crest of the parapet. This line also marks the division between the thick, terrepleined gun platform and the thinner masonry parapet near the western corner. The right hand half is built of small, neatly squared ashlar blocks, characteristic of late Venetian architecture. The rest is of the prevailing rough, coursed limestone, up to the rift itself which is edged on the left with large, squared blocks. Though this edge is built as an angle, the two sections are probably contemporary. For a system of vaulted galleries of the same size and pattern as those in the counter-

scarp and those of the Grimani bastion of 1706 at Nauplia, following round all four sides of the trapezoid at the level of the moat, extends under both sections of the northwest flank, providing an organic unity not evident on the surface.

The moat in its northwestern side is dominated by a strong work whose original section is a large, three-sided bastion projecting fan-wise from the northernmost angle of the fortress (Fig. 74). Its northeast corner projects into a rounded tower. The bastion's whole outer face is divided by a string course molding into vertical and battering planes. The talus of the lower section is built on the edge of the rock-cut ditch, out of square blocks with drafted edges. The north face of the bastion consists of a terrepleined gun platform 50 feet long. The parapet, which commands the ridge of the mainland, has the inexpert quality of Turkish authorship. The crest is clumsily curved, and in this important position contains six gun embrasures only. The spaces between are filled with numerous musket holes of different shapes and sizes, pointing steeply down into the ditch. Some of these openings are square, others constricted, others pointing

PRETORE   NE · C A V· ON
IO · BEMBO VRBS HOC ASILLO OR
NATA Ē AÑO O · MC CC LX· XX· OC

FIG. 73. METHONE, PLAQUE IN THE BEMBO BASTION.

two ways. Several of the openings on the inner face are arched in brick. Underneath the platform runs a long vaulted passage, off which there branch three enormous casemates, piercing the bastion's north face. Twenty feet deep and bottle-shaped, they are vaulted in voussoirs of sandstone, and taper to small, circular

[28] Sagredo, Δελτίον, V, p. 747: "A Modon nell' estremità destra al Mare s'è eretto un mezzo Baloardo intitolato S. Antonio dalla parte del Porto, e lo devo creder gia perfettionato, mentre quando mi staccai dal Regno erano formate sino le Garitte su gl' angoli, e si travagliava ne parapetti. È contaminato lungo le sue faccie e fianchi, con un altra Galeria di communicatione, che lo traversa nel mezzo, et ha una Porta di sortita sul roverzio dell' orecchione per communicar nel Fosso."

mouths, 16 inches in diameter, made of narrow, wedge-shaped blocks of poros. The passage itself is entered from a big vault beneath the platform of the round tower at the angle, which opens in turn on to a long, narrow, sunken court, extending the length of the bastion behind its terrepleined front. The flank which encloses it on the west is a thin wall, against which a flight of steps leads up to the terreplein, while the flank on the east contains two great, bottle-shaped casemates, which

cavalier, the highest point in the fortress. The east wall of the bastion contains, just above the cordon which marks its mid-point, a plaque with the three shields of the Foscarini, Bembo, and Foscolo families, and a partly obliterated inscription which ascribes the bastion to a Venetian official called Bembo and a date after the year 1480[29] (Fig. 73).

The re-entrant angle between this flank and the fortress' northwest scarp is occupied by a demibastion (Figs. 72, D; 74), whose trapez-

FIG. 74. METHONE, THE NORTH DEFENSES: DITCH, FAUSSEBRAYE, BEMBO BASTION, AND LOWER FLANKING PLATFORM.

once enfiladed the ditch. Out of this court, on the south side, rises a high cavalier (Fig. 74, upper left), built on a projecting, battering base, whose front is broken up by three widely obtuse, slightly rounded angles, built of finely squared stones. A small string course molding crowns its wall. Three concrete observation posts, relics of the Italian occupation of 1942, are crowded into the small space on top of the

oidal parade communicates directly with the covered way of the scarp and, by means of vaulted passages, with the lower court of the Bembo bastion above and the ditch below it. Its battering walls are ringed with a torus molding. Its parapet is 15 feet thick, and con-

[29] Hopf, *Chroniques gréco-romanes*, p. 381, lists among the *castellani* and *rettori* of Methone and Corone: 1494. Francesco Bembo, q. Giovanni.

tains two embrasures to enfilade the ditch. A plaque of the lion of St. Mark stamps its eastern flank. The structure does not appear on the plans of this collection, but was recommended to be built by Francesco Grimani in his report of 1701, as a work to cover the gate and the bridge,[30] and by Agostino Sagredo as nearing its completion thirteen years later.[31] The parapet, on the side facing out over the glacis, is built with added height, as a continous wall unbroken by embrasures, with a line of steps backing its inner face (Fig. 70, foreground).

The long circuit of the outer curtain contains many periods and styles of building, some belonging, no doubt, to the original XIII century Venetian fortification of Methone, though largely overlaid with additions from the later Venetian and Turkish centuries. Beginning on the east side, a 150-foot stretch of stoutly battering talus runs southward from the *Porta di terra ferma*. It is topped with a torus and a parapet made largely of brick, with a superior slope of thickly plastered rubble. It contains only three embrasures, but a multitude of deep, slanting musket holes of the form seen already in the parapets at Corone and Navarino: loopholes of a length out of all proportion to the width of their openings, allowing for the least possible visibility and angle of fire. The gun platform behind the parapet measures 20 feet wide and is supported on its inner edge by a series of arches, vaulted some in sandstone, others in brick, of Turkish construction. Reaching up to the base of this arcade is a great bank of earth, which may be presumed to have been raised on the recommendation of Francesco Grimani's engineers. The legend on Plate XVI refers to the section as *Terrapieno da farsi*.

This battering stretch of curtain ends at a big, square tower, 40 feet high, with a frontage of 35 feet, built almost entirely of great poros ashlar blocks measuring $2\frac{1}{2}$ feet high by 1–4

feet long, similar to those used in the inner wall of the north curtain (Fig. 75). These blocks appear so well in place, without insertions of smaller material between the joints or any additions other than a few patches of repair where cannon balls must have struck,

FIG. 75. METHONE, SQUARE FLANKING TOWER IN EAST CURTAIN.

that we may suppose the tower to date to Greco-Roman[32] or early Byzantine times.

Beyond the tower runs a long stretch of straight, slightly battering curtain wall. Its north half is made chiefly of small, flat, green sandstone blocks. The southern half is built in part of miscellaneous rubble, in part of close-fitted, rough limestone. The base is strengthened by a long, low buttress not bonding with the wall, but added later. Where the buttress

[30] Δελτίον, V, p. 483.
[31] *Ibid.*, V, pp. 747 ff.

[32] See A. Bon, *Le Péloponnèse byzantin jusqu'en 1204* (Paris, 1951), p. 4, on Methone in Roman times.

has worn away, the wall base itself is seen to be of the same sandstone masonry as the other side. This is an indication that the use of sandstone at Methone implies an early date of building, an hypothesis which fits certain other sections of the fortress where sandstone prevails among the walls. The whole stretch is surmounted by a thin parapet, of which a few tall merlons still stand.

FIG. 76. METHONE, EAST CURTAIN: POSTERN GATE AND TOWER, INTERIOR.

In the middle of this stretch of curtain, and integral with it, stands a square tower, 55 feet high (Plate XVI, C. *Posto alla Porta Stoppa*; Figs. 62, 76). This projects inside the enclosure, instead of out from the curtain wall. Its front is extended on either side by two wings to form a wide façade, decorated along the top with a line of six brackets, a rude Venetian lion flanked by two shields of the Foscarini,

and a plaque below it containing, in a scalloped frame, a horned helmet carved above a slanted shield of the Michieli family, with the initials P and M carved in Gothic script in either corner. Round the outer entrance of the tower the talus has fallen away, revealing an earlier, vertical wall which contains the original round poros arch through which one passes into the fortress. This inner, earlier façade is of poros ashlar and contains above the arch a winged and haloed lion set full-face, with two shields on either side weathered beyond recognition. Behind the arch are a narrow, open shaft for portcullis, and another round arch of flat sandstone blocks in the tower's inner face. A later wall, extending up to the level of the chemin de ronde of the adjacent curtain, encases the tower's three inner sides. The extension of the chemin de ronde thus formed is supported on the inner face of the tower by a large, pointed arch built over the entrance, which dates the addition to the Turkish period (Fig. 76). Next to the tower, on the south side, is a chemin de ronde, distinguishable also as Turkish by the presence of a recessed pointed arch in one of its sides.

At the end of the long, straight stretch the curtain projects forward into a redan, which supports a rectangular platform with wall and parapet on its two inner sides, well enclosed in the terreplein, banked up to the adjacent chemin de ronde, which the Grimani plan recommends raising. Points D and E on Plate XVI indicate the terreplein to be built at the curtain of the postern gate and "at the position called Piazeta."

A short distance beyond this redan is a gate (F. *Porta del Mandrachio*) which Plate XVI shows flanked by a group of buildings, which were partly destroyed by an explosion in 1944. A square tower once stood beside the gate on the north side, at the head of a landing which leads down to the water on the south (Fig. 77). The gate itself is backed by an avantcorps of Turkish construction, containing a tall, pointed arch filled with a low, round, vaulted passage whose outer angles are made of squared poros blocks. On the outside, next to the gate, is another piece of masonry with a groove for portcullis (Fig. 77, left), which also fails to bond with the curtain. The traces of another

to the open sea, carrying with them the muddy deposit from the stream which empties into the harbor. At the point where the new mole crosses the mouth of the *Mandrachio*, traces of the original wall may be seen just at the surface of the water. It was built with a battering

FIG. 77. METHONE, HARBOR GATE AND EAST CURTAIN, LOOKING NORTH.

structure, projecting from the curtain at the south end of the landing, is shown on Plate XVI as a square tower. Only the foundation of this remains, and the springing of an arch in the wall immediately above it. The ramp itself is retained by a vertical wall of big poros ashlar, encased in a later, battering wall of sandstone blocks. Plate XVI, G shows, inside the circuit at this point, a *corpo di guardia da farsi*, of which there are no traces.

Just beyond the landing, the modern mole, built in 1870, extends 300 feet out from the castle wall, garnished with eight Venetian cannon stuck upright among its boulders. It cuts directly across the mouth of the original port, which still bears locally the name of Mandraki. The original mole hugged the shore, parallel with the southeast sector of the curtain. It was built partly open at the south end, so that the currents could flow unimpeded out

outer face of great, square blocks, probably of classical provenance, banked by rough boulders. A marble column shaft, embedded among these stones, sticks up at the point of intersection of the two harborwalls.

Plate XVI indicates on the curtain, just south of the new mole, an artillery position, which consists of a line of six embrasures set in a stout parapet, backed by a wide, walled terreplein. The rest of the curtain as far as the south end of the circuit is terrepleined, as recommended on Plate XVI (I. *Terrapieno da farsi al posto S. Filipo*).

At the point where the long east curtain begins to curve round toward the southern end, there stands a tower whose front projects from the face of the wall and rises 60 feet above the water, standing to conspicuous height above the ramparts, and containing two tall, narrow vaults, open on the inner side (Figs.

78, 79, 88). The six corners thus formed in this inner face are built of large, squared poros blocks, and the vaults of cut voussoirs spring from delicately molded cornices. The arch in

the wall dividing the two chambers and an arch in the northeast flank of the tower are both pointed, and constructed of curiously spliced blocks. In the outer corner of the partition wall is another small pointed arch over a flight of three steps. These are broken off, owing to the collapse of the wall in the south corner. The southwest flank contains part of a depressed arch issuing on to steps which lead up to the top of the tower. Too much of the upper and outer sections are ruined to give any sign of what purpose the tower served in the age of artillery warfare. Despite its dangerous prominence as a target for bomb ketches, it is certain that it belongs to the period after 1500. The pointed and depressed arches, the pseudo-Venetian neatness of the construction, and its complete impracticability as a fortified work assign it definitely to the Turks. Beyond it, as indicated on the plan, is a short stretch of artillery parapet with a curved crest covered in flat, yellow brick, like the Turkish parapets of Corone. It is backed by a broad terreplein, walled on the inside.

The sea gate at the southern tip of the peninsula (Plate XVI, M. *Porta di San Marco*)

FIG. 78. METHONE, TURKISH TOWER, SOUTHEAST CIRCUIT WALL.

FIG. 79. METHONE, TOWER AND SEA GATE AT SOUTH END OF CIRCUIT.

consists of tall twin towers, 55 feet high, with the entrance set between the two, and an upper vault joining them, providing a single platform above, 60 feet long by 20 wide (Fig. 80). The whole structure is built of large poros ashlar. The eastern tower has vertical walls

this opening is pointed, the outer topped with a flat lintel supported on molded cornice blocks, and surmounted by a flat, recessed, semicircular tympanum. Inside the chamber are several loopholes. The chemin de ronde from the adjacent curtain follows behind the

FIG. 80. METHONE, THE SOUTHERN SEA GATE, SHOWING BRIDGE AND MOLE, LEFT.

made of blocks 1 foot high by 1–4½ feet long. Its base is of big, weathered sandstone. The western tower is built differently, with a base battering on the two outer sides, marked along the top by a torus molding. In the middle of the outer face is a round ornamental boss enclosed within a square, molded frame. The east tower contains in its upper level a vaulted chamber, entered from the chemin de ronde under a small double arch in two sections, pointed outside, depressed within. The chamber's outer walls contain wide, tall, arched windows, ill-conceived for defense, a defect which the Italians of 1942 remedied by blocking them up with masonry and leaving only a small opening in each. There is another vaulted chamber in the west tower, also entered through a double doorway from an extension of the chemin de ronde. The inner section of

two towers, on the west side supported on a machicoulis of plain poros corbels (Fig. 81). Between the towers is an avantcorps, which contains a large pointed arch springing from the same kind of molded cornice blocks as are used in the doorway of the western chamber and under the arches of the double vaulted tower to the east. Inside this opening is the smaller, depressed arch of the passageway itself. On the outside, the face of the passage is recessed between the two towers and rises to slightly over half their height. The passage is divided within by an open shaft for portcullis, in whose inner wall are embedded three carved blocks above the arch of the vault, a winged lion of Venice flanked by two rampant heraldic beasts. In the east flank of the inner entranceway another relic of Venice is immured, a block carved with the shield of the Foscolo family, placed on its side at ground level. The position of the latter obviates the claim which might be made on behalf of the former blocks, that the presence of a winged lion assigns the building to the Venetians. Such disrespectful use of a Venetian armorial crest combines

Turkish Towers of Yedi Kule at Constantinople and Rumili Hissar on the Bosporos. Each level is surmounted by a crenellated parapet and the whole is crowned with a round dome (Fig. 82). The wall of the outer enclosure contains, in all but the two landward faces, wide

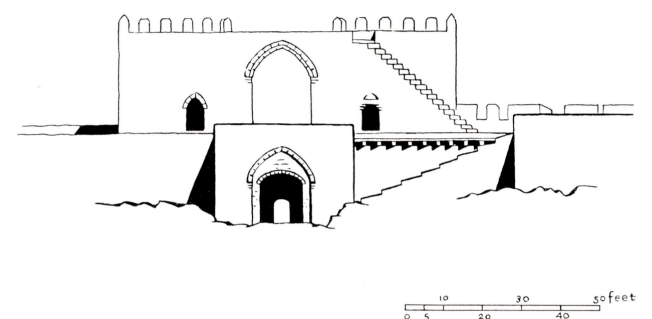

FIG. 81. METHONE, THE SOUTHERN SEA GATE, INTERIOR.

with the other features of the gateway, the depressed and pointed arches, the molded cornice blocks, and the parapet of tall merlons with pointed copes crowning the upper platform, to ascribe it to the Turks.

Outside the gate are the ruins of a small landing with a crenellated parapet. This connected with the bridge, now half collapsed, which crossed the channel at the bottom of the port to the little limestone reef where the Venetian defenders of 1500 made their last stand. Two arches of the bridge still stand (Fig. 80), leading directly to the mole, which passes out beyond the island, intact for a few paces, and then submerges, just visible below the surface of the water.

The little island fortress, locally known as Bourtzi, belongs to the period after 1500. It consists of an octagonal enclosure forming a low platform round a high, octagonal, lantern-shaped tower in two levels, reminiscent of the

arches of brick set low over the rocks, as if intended originally for casemates, but now filled up with masonry. One enters from the mole through an avantcorps built of alternate courses of ashlar blocks and double courses of brick, under a pointed arch built of four superimposed fans of dense brickwork. Within,

FIG. 82. METHONE, THE BOURTZI, OR ISLAND FORT. SAPIENZA IN THE BACKGROUND.

ramps lead up on both sides to the paved platform round the base of the tower. The five outer sides of the parapet each contain three embrasures 4 feet deep. Two of the angles are occupied by round turrets. Toward the land the parapet is pierced with loopholes. A low, depressed arch in the tower leads into a passage, which curves up round two of its sides to an upper level, in whose wall four tapering casemates, 15 feet deep, point out over the lower enclosure. Inside the tower, at the bottom, is a square cistern. The upper walls are recessed at the level originally occupied by wooden flooring. The tower's outer walls and the angles of the lower enclosure are made of ashlar blocks. Stone bosses are embedded in four of the tower's sides. The whole building is unmistakably Turkish, both in style and in its lack of any functional purpose. Its only strength lies in the thick walls of the lower section of the tower. The rest is mere symmetry and decoration. It probably predates the near-by fortress of New Navarino, where the Turks of 1573 showed a similar enthusiasm for symmetry, but somewhat more understanding of artillery fortification.

Inside the sea gate, on the west side, the chemin de ronde is reached by a ramp (Fig. 81, right), underneath which a small, brick-vaulted passage leads out to the rocks of the shore next to the battering flank of the western tower. Beside it is a position of five embrasures, as shown on the plan, backed by a wide, walled platform, the terreplein recommended by Grimani's engineers at the upper of the two points marked N on Plate XVI.

The defenses along the west side of the fortress are laid out on a more simple scheme than on the east or south. The long stretch of curtain is flanked by five plain, square towers. Despite certain variations in the masonry, it seems to belong largely to the earliest period of the Venetian fortifications. There is little provision for artillery. The rocks and shoals below and a prevailing northwest wind would have prevented the approach of enemy ships up to the walls, so that little was needed beyond the thin parapet whose traces appear all along the curtain. This is one reason, too, why the walls, having suffered less damage and consequently less repair, are probably also older than those in other quarters of the fortress. The flanking towers are roughly of one size, but differ in minor points. The tower nearest the south end of the circuit, unlike the others, is built on a battering base. Next to it, Plate XVI shows a line of five embrasures, which to-day do not exist. The position, however, was deemed fit, more recently, for artillery, as is attested by the rusted remains of an old Russian field gun bearing the mark of a Petersburg foundry, captured by the Germans and passed on to the Italians in the Second World War. For 200 feet north from this tower the curtain is faced in large poros ashlar. This stretch is terminated by a breach from an explosion of 1944, where pieces of the wall cover the rocks below, and a great semicircle of earth blown out behind it reveals a cross section of the buried walls of the old city of Methone. These extend down to the base of the curtain, 30 feet below the wide expanse of earth, level with the chemin de ronde, which has piled up through the slow ruin of buildings. Another tower, with a platform raised above the chemin de ronde, projects from the curtain with chamfered corners of small, square poros blocks, and sandstone blocks in the face and flanks. An unusual feature is the string course molding carved in a rope pattern (Fig. 83). There is a third tower, ruined for all but one flank, which stands high above the chemin de ronde (Figs. 84, 88, right) next to the traces of a large, rectangular building marked on Plate XVI as P. *Quartiere novo gia fatto.* The next tower to the north (Fig. 84) has an artillery parapet, curved on the outside, neatly built with cut blocks in the corners and several loopholes bored through it. The fifth tower is perhaps the earliest. It is a slender, fragile edifice belonging to an age when height was the primary element of defense (Fig. 84, left). Only 10 feet wide, it rises 70 feet above the sea. The walls are built of rubble, tile, and stones of all sizes, a miscellany not found in the more

wall which divides the main enclosure from the triangular inner circuit (Plate XVI, i. *Castel da Terra*) joins the west curtain at a point where it projects out in a prominent round bastion with upper vertical and lower batter-

FIG. 83. METHONE, POLYGONAL FLANKING TOWER, WEST CURTAIN.

FIG. 84. METHONE, FLANKING TOWERS ALONG THE WEST CURTAIN.

developed architecture of the Venetians. The curtain for 100 feet beyond it contains, near the bottom, a quantity of drums and bases of fluted columns, blocks with sections of pilasters, and pieces of architrave, remnants of the ancient Methone. Along most of the curtain the wall facing has fallen away, but what remains indicates a construction of very small pieces of stone held in a strong mortar. Some sections of the wall are of big, rough, closely fitted limestone blocks. Others are built on foundations of classical ashlar.

A hundred feet north of the high tower, the

ing walls (Fig. 85). The base is of limestone ashlar, built out on the edge of the rocks, while the upper section of its wall is made of the same materials as the tall tower next to it on the south.

The northwest flank of the *Castel da Terra* is an artillery rampart with a Turkish parapet, curved in outline, plastered on top with tile chips, and pierced with embrasures and obliquely pointing, square musket holes. Behind it a terreplein, 20–40 feet wide, extends up to the northernmost angle of the enclosure. Two raised works, or cavaliers, stand upon this

FIG. 85. METHONE, WEST FLANK AND ANGLE BASTION OF
INNER ENCLOSURE.

terreplein, built with curved fronts, each containing two vaulted chambers with tapering ends, supporting a semi-ovoid platform girdled with a parapet (Fig. 86). These are similar in plan and construction to a round flanking bastion in the Turkish fortress of Kelepha (see above, p. 38), while the depressed, pointed arches in their walls are further evidence of Turkish authorship. The outer face of this flank of the citadel stands 35–60 feet high, and is built with a pronounced talus (Fig. 85). Next to the round angle bastion at the lower corner, the base of the wall is built of large ashlar. Most of the wall, however, is made of flat-faced limestone blocks, rough but coursed, with chips of stone and tile held in strong mortar. A plaque with a winged lion and three shields of the Bembo, Foscarini, and Foscolo families, the same triad which appears on the

Bembo bastion in the north defenses, serves to date this wall to the period of the late XV century.

On the Grimani plans this northwest flank is drawn unguarded. They do not show the 150-foot long rampart built below it where the ditch opens out to the sea, extending parallel with the talus, and projecting forward into an artillery position, supported on five deep vaults, facing north over the mainland, and walled into an enclosure along the rocky shore (Figs. 72, E; 87): another structure recommended by Grimani[33] and reported by Sagredo to be nearing completion in 1714[34]. Its battering walls are made of rough, coursed limestone, and show the familiar features of late Venetian architecture, the ashlar foundation courses, the vaulted subterranean passage following

FIG. 86. METHONE, TURKISH CAVALIERS AND PARAPETS
ALONG WEST RAMPART OF INNER ENCLOSURE.

the length of the walls, the St. Mark lion, and the torus molding. Built after the Grimani

[33] Δελτίον, V, p. 483: "A Ponente ... una caponiera nel mezzo della fossa, la sua strada coperta, la sua piazza d'armi, bagnata da due mari, oltre a Cavalieri et altri miglioramenti interni."

[34] Ibid., V, pp. 747 ff.: "L'altra falsabraga opera nuova avanti il lato della Piazza verso Ponente, et il fianco della medesima, che fa fronte verso la contrascarpa, erano quasi alla loro intiera elevatione, e non restavano da terminarsi, che le Casematte, ed il lato, che deve chiudere, su l'orlo del Mare l'opera stessa, a continuare ad unirsi all' estremittà della contrascarpa della Piazza."

plans were drawn, it would presumably ante-date the bastion on the opposite counterscarp, which masks it for the purpose of artillery.

The two enclosures of the fortress are divided by a stout, low wall, only 20 feet high, flanked with five towers. The two on the west

and Marshal Maison in the War of Independence.[35]

Outside the wall stands a pillar of red granite, 12 feet high by 3 in diameter, with a rudely carved poros capital of Byzantine pattern encircled with an inscription, now

FIG. 87. METHONE, THE LATE VENETIAN WORK IN THE WESTERN SECTION OF THE DITCH, LOOKING NORTH. IN THE BACKGROUND, THE WEST COUNTERSCARP AND OUTWORK.

side, one square and one octagonal, are little more than projections of the wall face. The other three are taller, containing upper chambers and platforms girdled with tiny parapets. These chambers are entered from the wide chemin de ronde through doorways arched in brick. In the central tower is situated the *Porta di Castel da Terra* (Plate XVI): a wide, pointed archway of brick, placed in a wall face of the elaborate cloisonné masonry borrowed by the Turks from the Byzantines. The whole wall belongs probably to the period shortly after 1500, when the Turks were busy rebuilding and repopulating the battered city. To the east of the gate, the inner enclosure contains the cistern and the foundations of the house used as headquarters by Ibrahim Pasha

almost obliterated, which Leake[36] in 1805 read as follows:

COL   CCCCLXXXXIII
HLICER HIC [LEO SVPER
RORI FRANCISCI BR
IIUSPICIT ALTA MARIS

Thirty-six years later, Buchon[37] read the letters as a reinscription in honor of Francesco Morosini:

RECTORI FRCISCI MOROS(INI)
RESPICIAT ALTA MARIS
    CEPETES... EPO...
COL ... MCCCCLXXXIII
.... VICER LEO SVPER

Examination of the stone proves Leake's reading to be the more correct. The date 1493 can

[35] A drawing of this by Boccuet appears in the *Expédition scientifique de Morée, Architecture,* I, plate XII.
[36] *Morea,* I, p. 431.
[37] *La Grèce continentale et la Morée,* p. 457.

be clearly read, together with the words below it, HIC LEO SVPER, and on the other side of the capital the fragment .. SPICIT ALTA MARIS. The name of the official to whom the column was raised has weathered away beyond all recognition.[38] If however, Leake could have mistaken BR for BE, and the date CCCCLXXXXIII for CCCCLXXXXIIII, it could be construed that the inscription commemorrates the name of the Rettore Francesco Bembo, who held office at Methone in 1494,[39] and appears to have been active in architectural construction. The supposition seems more probable in view of the presence of a flat, rectangular stone, placed on top of the capital, which is carved with the three Bembo, Foscarini, and Foscolo shields.

Close by the base of the column lies a slab of marble, 10 feet long by 2 feet, 8 inches wide, with an inscription[40] referring to the refortifications of the year 1714:

of earth indicating the sites of houses, although from the air (Fig. 61) is revealed the plan of the streets and intersections, which the eye cannot detect at ground level. All that remains to-day are a Turkish bath, a small minaret at the corner of what was once the Latin cathedral (Plate XVI, Y), numerous cisterns, and a small, square building with pyramidal roof at the northwest of the outer enclosure (Plate XVI, T. *Deposito per polvere*). This is drawn on the plan in yellow, the color of the works which the Venetians were proposing to erect around the year 1700, and in style and dimensions resembles two contemporary storehouses built by the Venetians at Nauplia. There stands also a church, which dates from the French occupation of 1828. There are no traces of the buildings proposed and colored in yellow on Plate XVI, nor of those which Francesco Grimani claimed to have built in his report written from Methone at the end of his second

D   O   M
METHONEM   COMMVNIRI
VALLIS MOENVS ET PROPVGNACVLIS TERRA MARIQVE
MANDAVIT SENATVS
ANTONIO LAVRETANO PRO^ri G̅N̅ALI ARMO^vm IN PELOPONNESO
QVI TANTI OPERIS CVRAM SVSTINENS
AD VRBIS ET REGNI TVTAMEN
FORTITIORA MVNIMENTA EREXIT ET CLAVSIT
ANNO SALVTIS MDCCXIV.

Of the town which once existed within the circuit, barely a wall remains among the piles

tenure in January, 1708.[41] Nor does anything remain of the two long buildings near the

---

[38] Buchon's reading of MOROS seems inaccurate, since Leake distinguished only the letters BR. In any case, as Luce points out, the latinized form of the name, Mavrocenus, would have been used.

[39] Hopf, *Chroniques gréco-romanes*, p. 381.

[40] Another inscription of the second Venetian occupation of Methone may be seen on a plaque, broken down the middle, immured above a door of one of the houses in the new town:

AD   MDCLXXXVIIII   DIE   XV
AVGVSTI   M   V
HOC   SACELLVM   DICATV   VIRGINI MARIAE DE
SALVTI   PROTOR   NOS   RUCTVM FVIT
AD A   NDAM MILITA   IVM   DEVOCTIONE EX
IVSSV ILL^mi   ET   EX^mi PROR^i   DONATI PROVISORS
EXTR^ii HVIVS   CIVIT   ETHONIS PRAESTANTISS^mi
ET VIGILANTIS^mi   ETAT   MEMORIAM.

[41] Δελτίον, V, pp. 540–548. The buildings mentioned are four barracks, a storehouse for grain and biscuit, a powder store, and a hospital. The engineer and author of four of the plans in the Grimani collection, Van Deyk, was in charge of the works.

granite pillar, the *Quartiere che si Fabrica su la piazza grande d'Armi*, and the *Altro Quartiere simile capace di due compagnie*. In their place one sees only the four low walls of the cemetery of the British prisoners of war, killed in the wreck of the Italian ship *Sebastiano Veniero*, which was torpedoed off the Messenian coast in 1941, and now lies at the west end of the moat, a rusty skeleton sticking out of the sea, monument to Italy's latest attempt in the Eastern Mediterranean.

FIG. 88. METHONE, INTERIOR OF OUTER CIRCUIT, LOOKING SOUTH TOWARD SAPIENZA.

CHAPTER VIII

ARKADIA

(PLATE XVIII)

While Morosini's army was besieging Methone during the summer of 1686, three galeots were sent out from Navarino to the shores of Arkadia, fifteen miles up the coast, whose castle on a hill just inland had been abandoned by the Turks with a small booty of 14 cannon, and its towers exploded.[1]

*   *   *

The medieval history of this place dates to the early Byzantine period, when the classical Kyparissia was colonized by refugees from the hinterland of the Arkadian province in the time of the Slavic invasions.[2] In the XII century Edrisi described it as "a large and populous town, where ships put to shore and set sail from".[3] In 1205 the Franks besieged it during the campaign led by William de Champlitte and his hundred knights against the coastal places of Messenia. The strong donjon of the castle resisted, in the words of the French *Chronicle*, "pour ce qu'il estoit assis sur une pierre bise, et avoit une bonne tour dessus, de l'ovre des jaians."[4] After seven days the Frankish siege-engines brought the Greeks to submission. In the formation of the new Principality, Arkadia became one of the twelve baronies of the Morea, and was bestowed as a fief on Geoffroy de Villehardouin. In 1261 it passed to Vilain d'Aunoy, one of the French nobles who took refuge in the Principality of Achaea after the fall of the Latin Empire of Constantinople.[5] In 1391 Arkadia came into the hands of the Genoese family of Zaccaria, who in the XIV and early XV centuries were the most powerful barons in the Frankish Morea. Centurione Zaccaria, lord of Arkadia and nephew of the previous Constable of Achaea, became in 1404 the last ruler of the Crusader state. What remained of it, a small tract of land in the northwestern Peloponnese, passed to the Greek Despot of Mistra, Thomas Palaiologos, as the dowry of Centurione's daughter, whom he married in 1430. The castle of Arkadia and the title of Prince alone remained to Zaccaria, who died two years later. Thomas lived at Arkadia until the approach of the Turks in 1460, when he made his escape to Venice, leaving the Morea in the hands of Mohammed II.[6]

By the end of the XVII century the castle had outlasted its use, for a steep mountainside immediately above it made it an easy prey to

---

[1] Locatelli, I, p. 232; Garzoni, I, p. 174; Giacomo Corner, Δελτίον, II, p. 208.

[2] See A. Bon, *Le Péloponnèse byzantin jusqu'en 1204*, p. 61.

[3] *Géographie d'Edrisi*, p. 124.

[4] *L. de C.*, § 115.

[5] X. τ. M., lines 1370 ff., 1865, 8462; *L. de C.*, §§ 108, 110, 114–117; *C. di M.*, pp. 425–427; *L. de F.*, §§ 112–114.

[6] Miller, *Latins*, pp. 370, 391 ff., 449.

artillery. An account of 1688 speaks of "cotesta mal difesa Citta, ... hora desertata & disabitata,"[7] while Coronelli makes no mention of it in his description of the Peloponnesian forts. The Proveditor Corner claims that a single squadron of soldiers is sufficient to hold it.[8] In 1693 the Proveditor Molin writes that it is inadequately situated for its scant artillery to cover the shoreline, which lies open to enemy landings.[9] The castle's diminished importance in this period is indicated by the Grimani drawing (Plate XVIII), which affords it a space of barely two inches square and represents it inaccurately in plan. The map is drawn rather to show the neighboring coastline and the anchorage. Nevertheless, it indicates also a military headquarters and an Italian church in the lower town, which proves at least that a garrison was maintained here in the time of Francesco Grimani.

*   *   *

The lower enclosure is entered from the southeast by a long ramp (Fig. 89), retained on

the south side by a Turkish wall of rough limestone and tile, coated with thick gravel mortar, supporting a straight-topped parapet with loopholes. The higher ground on the other side is walled with a scarp of roughly squared

Fig. 90. Arkadia, South Angle Tower, Outer Enclosure.

blocks in courses, interspersed with tile and scaffold holes, which projects into an outwork guarded by a loopholed parapet. This does not figure on Plate XVIII, and would have been built either by the Venetians after Grimani, or by the Turks after 1715. The fortress' outer gate has collapsed, together with its tower, which shows in the panorama at the top of Plate XVIII. In its place are the remains of a small mosque, a simple, quadrangular building with a dome on spandrels.

The south corner of the enclosure, just below the entrance, is occupied by a large tower, whose bottom nine courses are built of re-used classical poros blocks, all 2 feet high and upwards of 5 feet long (Figs. 90, 91). Most of these are bevelled along the lower edge. Three have one or two edges drafted. Five are engraved with mason's marks: four with individual letters, Σ, Δ, I, Π; and a fifth with ΔH.

Fig. 89. Arkadia, the Fortress from the East.

[7] Scalletari, *Condotta Navale*, p. 118.
[8] Δελτίον, II, p. 208.
[9] *Ibid.*, V, p. 439.

FIG. 91. ARKADIA, RE-USED CLASSICAL BLOCKS IN SOUTH
ANGLE TOWER.

Another contains a square dowel-hole. Between the joints are tile and limestone fragments. These courses belong to an early post-classical refortification of the acropolis of Kyparissia. The upper section of the tower (Fig. 91) is built of small, flat, roughly coursed limestone and poros blocks, in a style which prevails throughout most of the fortress walls. The tower's southwest flank is masked by a long buttress, of a later period, made of lesser limestone rubble with flat, rectangular blocks in the corners (Fig. 90). The curtain of this outer enclosure is built of trimmed, oblong blocks in fairly regular courses (Fig. 92). The upper zones are of limestone and brick rubble, belonging probably to a reconstruction in Turkish times. What remains of the parapet above is crenellated, with square loopholes in the merlons. Near the western corner is a small flanking tower, which projects forward from, but not above the level of the curtain (Fig. 92, right). At the west angle of the circuit a spur of rock supports a round eyrie of miniature dimensions, from which the curtain rounds back up the hill to join the west face of a great

FIG. 92. ARKADIA, SOUTHWEST CURTAIN OF OUTER ENCLOSURE, SQUARE FLANKING TOWER.

tower, built with six courses of large blocks, 2 feet square, set with some brick and limestone fragments between the joints (Fig. 93). The upper face is of smaller, squared poros and uncut limestone blocks, with a greater admixture of broken tile. Remains of an arched

FIG. 96. ARKAI

between thi corner,[10] no tion inside

FIG. 93. ARKADIA, WEST TOWER, LOWER ENCEINTE.

window pierce the upper wall in a collapse of the masonry. The retaining wall, which the plan shows round the base of the tower on the south, contains the characteristically Turkish profusion of scaffold holes on the exterior, and carries a parapet with an embrasure 100 degrees wide, the work of an apprentice in the technique of artillery fortification.

The details of the upper enclosure, or *Castelo*, are wrongly drawn on the Grimani plan. Instead, the curtain continues the line of the west face of the tower, and further to the north is built with re-used ancient blocks of mon-

umental size. Flanking the curtain on this side is another square tower, drawn on the plan, which faces out over the sea. It contains a large cistern, half-subterranean, 25 feet deep and 18 square, divided into two vaults by a single square pier, forming an arcade. Beyond it, almost nothing is left of the castle's northeast sector. Some isolated fragments of masonry stand above the steepest part of the hill, with battering outer faces of plastered rubble, with a number of large poros blocks in the angles. Nothing is to be distinguished of the two small, square towers, which the plan shows on the northeast side. The wall is more substantial in its eastern half. There is a curved corner of battering masonry; then a stretch where the rough limestone is carefully set to form a smooth wall surface; and then a 40-foot stretch of ashlar blocks of poros, 4 by 2 feet in size, interspersed with smaller pieces of poros, limestone, and tile — probably the repair of an earlier Byzantine wall, which had itself been built out of ancient materials. The northeast was the side of the fortress least exposed to attack; a makeshift parapet wall was enough to defend the cliff top, and was the structure soonest to crumble and most often rebuilt. It is difficult to distinguish the various periods suggested by its diversity. Further down the hill below it, three courses of great ashlar blocks descend the slope in the one visible fragment of Kyparissia *in situ*.

The east angle of the castle is strategically the most important, since it is on this side that the saddle joins the hill to the mountainside above it. It is guarded by a stout bastion, which jogs forward from the north curtain (Fig. 94) and curves out into a round tower, of a form not seen in Greece before 1205, battering on to the steep rocks (Fig. 95). This also is built of small, rectangular, oblong blocks, trimmed in courses. The parapet above is an addition of the artillery period, made of smooth poros ashlar and pierced by two embrasures of Turkish pattern, covering the road marked on

CHAPTER IX

NAUPLIA

(Plates XIX–XXIII).

After the fall of Methone, Morosini transported his forces by sea to the southwestern coast of the Argolid. On July 30, 1686 they disembarked at the harbor of Tolos (Plate XXIV), marched overland to Nauplia, occupied the Palamedi mountain, and trained their guns on to the lower town. The Turkish garrison of 1,500 was outnumbered four to one, and dispatched a call for help. The Seraskier had spent the two months since his defeat at Navarino ravaging the countryside rather than fortifying the castles in his territory, but now drew near, and sent a force of 300 Janissaries into Nauplia by water. On August 6 Königsmark drove him from the field in a pitched battle in the plain of Argos. Morosini, who had received intelligence of the damage being done to the wooden houses inside the fortress by the Venetian mortars and bomb ketches, sent an ultimatum to the defenders. This was rejected, and the Venetians continued to dig their way toward the counterscarp on the east side of the city. After three weeks the Seraskier returned with reinforcements from Euboea. The Turks inside Nauplia made a sortie, but the relievers missed the chance to coordinate the attack with an assault on the Venetian rear, and the defenders withdrew again with losses into the fortress. A slave, escaped from the Turkish camp, reported to Morosini that the Seraskier was planning a surprise attack for daybreak of August 29. The Christian troops were put on guard, and when the fight came routed the Turks completely. Those in the citadel attempted to break out, but were driven back. Then they surrendered, and opened the gates to the Venetians, who found the place stored with 26 cannon, and 17 more on the Bourtzi, or small island fort in the bay.[1]

*　　*　　*

The commercial relations of Venice with Nauplia date from the year 1199, when the Emperor Alexios III granted them free trade in this and four other cities of the Peloponnese.[2] Already in 1153 Anaboli was numbered by Edrisi among its thirteen principal towns.[3] In 1180 its powerful archon, Theodore Sgouros, was given an Imperial fleet to clear the Greek coasts of piracy. His son, Leon, added to the family dominion by capturing the mountain castles of Argos and Corinth in 1203.[4] The Franks arrived the following year, led by Boniface of Montferrat, the King of Salonica, who

---

[1] Locatelli, I, pp. 243–273; Garzoni, I, pp. 165–173; Scalletari, *Condotta Navale*, pp. 148–190; Coronelli, *Memorie*, p. 104.

[2] Tafel und Thomas, *Urkunden*, I, p. 265.

[3] *Géographie d'Edrisi*, pp. 122–125.

[4] M. G. Lamprynides, Ἡ Ναυπλία (Athens, 1950), p. 28.

laid siege to Nauplia with the help of four Venetian galleys. It was during the winter of 1204–5 that Geoffroy de Villehardouin reached Nauplia from Methone, and proposed to an old companion in arms, William de Champ-

Grand Company had made an end of their Duchy, a bailie still held them in the name of the exiled Walter of Brienne, son of the last Burgundian Duke. After his death and the marriage of his sister, the fortresses passed

Fig. 97. Nauplia, from the Air (3000 feet).

litte, whom he found in the besiegers' camp, that a band of the crusaders undertake the conquest of the Morea. Long after the rest of the country had been subjugated, Nauplia at last fell in 1210. The Franks occupied one of its two fortified enclosures, and the other remained in the hands of the Greeks.[5] The castle of Argos fell two years later, and was given with Nauplia to Othon de la Roche, Lord of Athens, in recompense for his aid at the siege of these places.[6] He and his successors held them for a century, and then, after the Catalan

to the family of Enghien, and continued in that line till near the end of the XIV century.

In 1377 the last of the family, Marie d'Enghien, was orphaned at the age of thirteen. Her relatives, apprehensive at the expansion of her Greek and Florentine neighbors south and north of the Isthmus, placed Argos and Nauplia under the protection of Venice, who was careful to arrange a marriage between Marie and a Venetian citizen called Pietro Cornaro. When this man died in 1388, the young widow was prevailed upon to sell her two castles to the Venetian Republic. But before the new governor could arrive to take over his duties, both places were seized by coup de main of the Greek Despot of Mistra, Theodore I Palaiologos, in conjunction with his father-in-law,

[5] X. τ. M., lines 2871–3:
Τὸ ᾿Ανάπλι γὰρ εὑρίσκετον κάστρον εἰς δυὸ τραχώνια·
ἐν τοῦτο ἐσυμβιβάστησαν νὰ δώσουσιν τὸ πρῶτον
καὶ τὸ ἄλλο τὸ ἀχαμνότερον νὰ τὸ κρατοῦν οἱ ῾Ρωμαῖοι.
See also C. di M., p. 436; Miller, Latins, pp. 37, 62.

[6] X. τ. M., 2875 ff.; L. de C., §§ 190, 195–202; L. de F., § 212.

Nerio Acciajuoli, Duke of Athens. Nauplia was taken by the Venetians in 1389, but Argos was only given up to Venice after six years of open war with the Byzantine Despotate.[7]

The Venetians established themselves in Nauplia and developed it, together with Methone and Corone, into one of the strongest coastal positions in Greece. It repelled the attack of Bayezid II in 1500, who from there moved down on his fateful expedition against Methone. During the early XVI century, however, Nauplia's state grew dangerous. The fortifications became inadequate against the increasing power of artillery, and the garrison of the place diminished; few Venetians could be enlisted for the growing perils of service in the Peloponnesian colonies. The Greeks and Albanians, whom they employed in their corps of *stradioti*, or light horsemen, clashed with the inhabitants and among themselves, while the Turks from near-by Argos, lost by Venice in 1463, entered and departed from the city without hindrance.[8]

In 1537 the Turks began the campaign to drive the Venetians from their last footholds in the Morea. The island of Aegina fell first, and then the Turkish army arrived before the walls of Nauplia. The town was bombarded from the heights of the Palamedi, but the Venetians had command of the sea, and were able to send in supplies and reinforcements. The *stradioti* made bold sorties as far as Argos, and counterattacked so consistently that after fourteen months the Turks withdrew. However, a fleet of combined European powers was defeated off Preveza by the Turkish admiral, Khaireddin Barbarossa, and Venice, left to carry on the fight alone, was forced to make peace in 1540. Seven thousand had died in the defense of Nauplia. The city was surrendered

to the Turks, together with Monemvasia, some of whose inhabitants were removed and given lands in the Venetian colonies of Crete, Cyprus, the Ionian Islands, and Dalmatia.[9]

During the XVI and XVII centuries the Turks used Nauplia as their capital of the Morea. Its fortifications were neglected, and in 1619, when the Duc de Nevers, a descendant of the Palaiologoi, tried to instigate a rebellion in Greece, there were only 800 Turks in the garrisons of Nauplia, Methone, Corone, and Navarino.[10] It remained for the Venetians of 1686, who kept Nauplia the capital, to repair the damages of time and war, and extend the fortifications far beyond the limits of the medieval castle.

* * *

FIG. 98. NAUPLIA, THE THREE CASTLES OF ACRONAUPLIA, LOOKING WEST.

The city is built along a peninsula, which extends westward into the Argolid Gulf below the precipitous height called Palamedi (Fig. 97).

Upon it lies Napoli di Romania bathed on three sides by the waves, and on the fourth joined by a ridge to the Mainland; not cut off from the said Palamida, which communicates with the Place

[7] G. Thomas, *Diplomatarium Veneto-Levantinum* (Venice, 1880), I, pp. 211 ff.; Χρονικὸν Σύντομον, ed. Bonn, p. 516; Hopf, *Chroniques gréco-romanes*, pp. 236–8; Miller, *Latins*, pp. 339 ff.; *Essays*, pp. 111, 121, 124 f., 136; Zakythinos, *Despotat*, I, pp. 132 ff.

[8] Miller, *Latins*, pp. 495, 501 ff.; *Essays*, pp. 241 ff.

[9] Miller, *Latins*, pp. 507 ff.

[10] Miller, *Essays*, p. 382.

by a narrow way left open... The City faces North, contained on the side of the port within a masonry wall, flanked with towers round and square in the ancient manner. Toward the land it is defended outside by a wide ditch, faussebraye, traverses, and counterscarp. By a steep ascent, covered with a long traverse, one climbs from the Town to the first of three castles above it, called Toro from a great bastion facing East; then one passes to the second, called Castle of the Franks; and finally through a passage to the Castle of the Greeks — all three enclosed by circuit walls, and each defended from the other by a higher level of terrain. Of the batteries which fortify the City, two on the West-Northwest are close together and furnished with a greater number of various kinds of artillery, which in this quarter guard the entrance to the port. Directly opposite these, about two hundred paces off, the Island Castle stands on a little reef, surrounded by a deep bottom.

So Garzoni described the fortress as it appeared in the first years of the XVIII century,[11] and as the Grimani plans substantially show it.

In classical times Nauplia served as the naval station of Argos,[12] but was a deserted ruin by the II century after Christ.[13] Presumably it shared the fate of the other Hellenic fortresses which were demolished after the Roman conquest. Yet at the western end of the peninsula there remained a strong foundation of polygonal masonry to provide a base for the earliest post-classical fortification. From the *Chronicle of the Morea* we learn that the Byzantine castle, which held out five years against the Frankish siege, consisted of two enclosures, of which "the first" was taken over by the Franks, and "the other weaker one" given back to the Greeks. The nomenclature of these two sections of Acronauplia persisted, as we see from Garzoni's description and the Grimani plans, for five hundred years. The curtain walls of the Castel de Greci are built directly on classical foundations, and appear to belong to several different periods, though a generally prevailing form of masonry, rubble with single, double, or triple courses of broken

<hr>

[11] I, pp. 165 f.
[12] Strabo, *Geography*, VIII, 6, 2.
[13] Pausanias, II, xxxviii, 2.

tile or brick at regular and irregular intervals extending along the wall faces, continues through both the enclosures, and seems to date them at least to the time preceding the Frankish conquest.[14] The walls of the Byzantine fort belong to an age when no record was made of their building, though it is probable that in the hands of the Sgouros archons in the late XII or early XIII century Nauplia's defenses were strengthened against the menace of the roving crusaders.

Fig. 99. Nauplia, East Wall of Castel de Franchi, with Round Tower masked by Venetian Talus.

The Frankish occupation of Nauplia (1210–1377) seems not to have altered the original plan of the fortress. It remained a place of minor importance in comparison with Argos, and as an appendage of the Athenian Duchy,

<hr>

[14] G. Gerola, "Le Fortificazioni di Napoli di Romania," *Annuario*, XIII–XIV, 1930–1931, p. 354, says the two enclosures are of separate periods entirely. In support of this he cites, first, the north curtain of the Castel de Franchi which is reinforced with a Venetian talus, as if the wall here were weaker than that of the Castel de Greci. The talus, however, does not imply weakness in the original wall so much as greater vulnerability of position. The curtain is not only lower, but also placed above a more gradual slope. The *Chronicle* also says it was the weaker enclosure which the Greeks occupied after 1210. Secondly, he mentions the heavy wall which divides the two. This is an artillery emplacement (Fig. 100) with scarped face of Venetian construction. West of it, however, stands the fragment of another wall, built of squared stones and brick, which forms on Plate XXIII a separate *Recinto*.

afterwards held by a succession of bailies, only a secondary effort would have been made toward its fortification. One stretch of wall still stands, which belongs probably to the XIII or XIV century. The east curtain of the Castel de Franchi, which was later reinforced and masked by a Venetian talus, was flanked originally by two round towers and a triangular redan, now partly visible through a collapse of the surrounding masonry (Fig. 99).

The Venetians held Nauplia for a century and a half, and again for twenty-eight years at the turn of the XVIII century. The chief fortifications of the city belong to these two periods. In 1388 and for nearly a hundred years after, the Venetian officials in Nauplia reported to the Senate on the ruinous condition of the walls, urgently requesting money and materials. But it was not till the Turkish danger had been fully realized, with the loss of Argos and Negroponte, that Venice was finally driven to heed their calls. In 1470 Vettore Pasqualigo was sent out as *Podestà*, together with the engineer Antonio Gambello, to repair the medieval walls and make the place over into an artillery fortress.[15] The last thirty years

FIG. 100. NAUPLIA, VENETIAN TALUS DIVIDING UPPER AND MIDDLE ENCLOSURES, LOOKING SOUTH.

FIG. 101. NAUPLIA, VENETIAN GATE FROM CASTEL DE GRECI TO CASTEL DE FRANCHI, AT SOUTH END OF TALUS WALL.

[15] Gerola, *Napoli di Romania*, p. 355.

of the XV century is the earliest period to which any of the existing Venetian defenses can definitely be assigned. Their massive construction, inaugurating a new era in the art of war, is a prelude to the great artillery fortifications which Venice was to build soon after at Methone and Corone, and during the next century in Crete.

The heavy wall between the castles of the Greeks and the Franks belongs probably to this period. It serves to terrace the higher ground to the west, and supported six gun positions, as shown on Plates XXI–XXIII. The parapet has crumbled into a heap of earth, but the outer face of the wall is in good preservation, with the blocks showing through the thick mortar (Fig. 100). To-day the way from the upper to the lower enclosure is through a gap at the north end above the town. The original passage, as the plans show, is at the south end, through an archway surmounted by a sculptured lion with a shield (Fig. 101) on which could still be distinguished in 1936 the three bands of the Pasqualigo crest. The passage leads down into a small triangular court, bounded on the east by a three-sided, terrepleined bastion with battering walls. On the north the court is enclosed by a wall, containing an arch of finely cut and fitted limestone blocks, a distinctive feature of this period around 1500. Above the door are two notched merlons, one pierced with a loophole and the other with a small arched embrasure at the level of the chemin de ronde (Figs. 100, 102).

Pasqualigo made important additions to the walls of the Castel de Franchi. The length of

FIG. 102. NAUPLIA, NORTH FACE OF THE GATE FROM THE UPPER TO THE MIDDLE ENCLOSURE, LOOKING SOUTHEAST ALONG PALAMEDI CLIFFS TO KARATHONA BAY.

FIG. 103. NAUPLIA, NORTH CURTAIN OF CASTEL DE FRANCHI, SHOWING SUPERIMPOSED VENETIAN TALUS AND ROUND BASTION. IN THE BACKGROUND, ASCENT TO THE PALAMEDI.

its north curtain is reinforced with a talus, bearing a winged lion and the remains of a plaque, now broken away. An integral part of the talus is a round tower which projects the

marked on Plate XXI as the main gate to the fortress. The tower and the wall above it are crowned with notched battlements, which continue along the top of a talus wall that rings

FIG. 104. NAUPLIA, GATE OF THE CASTEL DEL TORO.

widely battering reinforcement of the walls out over a point of the hill (Fig. 103), and carries a parapet of notched and slotted merlons, in one of which is an empty scrolled plaque. Another talus was built round the east wall of the enclosure, sheathing the earlier curtain of which we have mentioned the Frankish tower.

The main fortifications of the late XV century consist of a third enceinte built to enclose the remainder of the hill east of the Castel de Franchi. The entrance in its northwest corner (Fig. 104) was built by Pasqualigo, as is attested by the carved stone shield, marked with three bands, set with a winged lion above the archway. This is flanked by a squat, round tower with a battering base, ringed with a torus molding at the level of the arch. It is

the north side of the third enclosure, or Castel del Toro (Fig. 105).

The strongpoint of Acronauplia is the great

FIG. 105. NAUPLIA, INTERIOR OF THE CASTEL DEL TORO, SHOWING GATEWAY AND NOTCHED BATTLEMENTS. THE BOURTZI, OR ISLAND FORT, RIGHT.

tower which gave its name to the third enclosure (Figs. 106, 107, 111). It is a stout,
double circular bastion with widely battering
walls built of large, square ashlar blocks, supporting two gun platforms on different levels.
The higher of these has a diameter of 35 feet
between the parapets, which contain six gun
embrasures, indicative by their size of the
early artillery period: vaulted and tapering to
small arched openings on the exterior. On the
south side the rampart is scarped, but on the
east loses its crest and assumes a curved outline.
A passage descends through a tall, pointed
archway under the higher platform, and

exists from the year 1500. Furthermore, if the
two shields signify two magistrates, the bastion
must date between the years 1493 and 1519,
when Nauplia was ruled by a double government of *rettore* and *provveditore*.[17] A later addition is the second passage which descends
through a depressed archway, built of small
poros blocks stippled with marks of the dressing tool, between walls of rubble and broken
tile, to a small, square door in the bastion's
northeast flank (Fig. 106), which is lined with
large, greenish yellow brick. These are all common features of materials and construction
among the works undertaken by the Venetians

FIG. 106. NAUPLIA, EAST SECTOR OF THE FORTRESS, WITH XV CENTURY ROUND BASTION AND GRIMANI BASTION OF 1706.

emerges through a small door on the south
side of the tower, facing the open bay. Above
this opening are a carved lion and two empty
shields. Gerola[16] notes, in attempting to date
the structure, that the name of Castel Toro

at Nauplia during their second occupation at
the turn of the XVIII century. The outer door
is set in a patch of rubble, which is inserted
into the bastion's uniform ashlar surface, and
issues on to a flight of steps which descend to

[16] *Ibid.*, p. 366.

[17] Miller, *Latins*, p. 495.

7

the enclosure of the huge, quadrangular fort built round its base in 1706 by Francesco Grimani (Figs. 106, 107, 111). By all indications this second passage was pushed through the round bastion's wall after this date, to provide communication from the old third enclosure

FIG. 107. NAUPLIA, THE GRIMANI BASTION.

with the elaborate system of defenses built along the land front two centuries later.

Beneath the castle, which occupies the whole rocky ridge along the south side of the peninsula, lies the lower town along the north. Gerola suggests that a suburb may have existed under the fortress walls in Byzantine times,[18] pointing for evidence to the stretch of curtain which follows down the hill in the northwest sector, in steps and angles, from the Castel de Greci to the shore. This is a thin wall, built with a diversity of rubble, which offers little clue to periods or builders. Certain sections are full of tile chips. Others are made of big, sharp stones, held in strong mortar, with carefully fitted blocks in the angles. The parapet is too fragmentary to give any idea of its original form. One short section is built over depressed relieving arches which span two clefts in the rock, its face consisting of oblong, rectangular blocks, with a quantity of brick set vertically, horizontally, and also in ladders between them. The masonry consists of the thick, yellow brick, which seems to have come

into use at Nauplia in the Venetian constructions of *ca.* 1700. It is unlikely that any sort of settlement existed outside the fortress before the end of the XV century. The sea came up to the rocks of Acronauplia, and toward the northeast the land was swampy up to the foot of the Palamedi. Dorotheos of Monemvasia writes that when the Venetians first occupied Nauplia, there were only two original castles of the Franks and the Greeks; that before the loss of Negroponte in 1470 "there existed below these not a single house, neither walls nor gate; 1502 was the year they began to build the lower walls of Anapli."[19] The Venetians filled in the marshy land, and by driving piles into the muddy bottom of the sea, extended the foundations for a city out into the water. The wall and flanking towers which they built around it assumed a new importance as the city's outer defense, while the fortifications on Acronauplia itself lost part of their original use. A strong curtain was built to face the side of the mainland, extending from the double round bastion at the east end of the Castel del Toro to the sea, protected by a full system of artillery outworks. The Grimani plans, drawn before Grimani himself had rebuilt this eastern sector, show the curtain to have been broken into two sections, to form an obtuse angle. At this point stood the city gate (Plate XXI, *Porta di Terra Ferma*), through which one passed across the ditch into the Argive plain. At the head of the ditch was a detached work girt with a small moat of its own, with two levels of guns to enfilade the ditch and cover the approaches from the northeast.

The lower circuit has disappeared in all but the western quarter. The thin rubble curtain that descends from the Castel de Greci joins a small tower at the edge of the water, supporting a parapet with three small embrasures, and built with battering walls and a torus molding which continue all the way round

---

[18] Gerola, *Napoli di Romania*, p. 367.

[19] Hopf, *Chroniques gréco-romanes*, pp. 238f.; Gerola, *Napoli di Romania*, p. 368, note 3.

what remains of the adjacent sea wall. This follows the indentation of a small cove, pierced in the re-entrant angle by a vaulted passage leading up to a wide, terrepleined platform above the walls. The inner and outer arches of this aperture are, here again, made of four or five large, curved limestone blocks, of the form which may be dated to the late XV or early XVI century. The westward-facing stretch of this wall, known as the Πενταδέλφια, or Five Brothers Bastion from the embrasures in its original parapet (Plates XXI, XXII, XXIII), is built with a battering ashlar face, turns a rounded corner at the cove's opposite end, and begins what was once the long, northward-facing arc of the sea front. To-day, however, this only stands for a stretch of 320 feet as far as the truncated flank of a square structure marked on Plate XXIII as *N. La nuova Cisterna.* An obtuse angle in the wall between this and the Five Brothers battery was flanked by a small, round tower, demolished to give way to the modern steps descending from the platform above. Two fragments remain of its curved walls, projecting from the curtain on either side, which each contain near ground level the flank of a vaulted casemate. Now a broad esplanade occupies the line once formed by these northern sea walls, built out on the silted ground which was continually filling the harbor during the XVII and XVIII centuries[20].

The only other part of the town walls still standing is a short section of the original east curtain, which was incorporated as a back wall into the big, quadrangular bastion of 1706. Its parapet, hidden behind this later work, became obsolete in the early XVIII century, and was replaced with a walled passage. The heavy torus, made of short, narrow blocks, along the top of the earlier curtain, resembles that of the adjacent round *torrione* of the period *ca.* 1500, and may be seen with the curtain's talus in cross section, outside the northwest corner of the Grimani bastion,

where it was sheared off in the demolition of the 1930s.

Another construction of the Pasqualigo period is the small fort on the islet of St. Theodore, or Castel da Mar (Fig. 108), which was built in 1471 to secure the entrance to the

FIG. 108. NAUPLIA, THE BOURTZI, OR ISLAND FORT.

harbor.[21] It consists of a tall, octagonal tower with battering walls, topped with a cordon in quarter-circle with drafted underside, and an embrasured parapet, and flanked by low, semi-circular gun emplacements on the east and west. The water gate and two smaller towers carry notched merlons which resemble, as does the masonry of the walls, the other works of Pasqualigo on Acronauplia. The artillery parapet is designed for small pieces, and contains a variety of embrasures, the oldest of which are vaulted and tapering, like those of the double round bastion. Other sections of the parapet are made of square blocks, with brick set horizontally and vertically between them, like those built by the Turks after 1715 on the postern gate of the Palamedi. In 1525, only half a century after the island fort was built, one of the Venetian bailies of Nauplia found it already antiquated, and recommended lowering the central tower, in accordance with the new principles of artillery warfare.[22] Nev-

---

[20] Δελτίον, V, p. 491; Pouqueville, *Voyage*, VI, p. 252.

7*

[21] Gerola, *Napoli di Romania*, pp. 388 ff.

[22] *Ibid.*, p. 391: "Il castello del scoglio è fatta a l'antiga e il torrion dentro è troppo alto e staria forse ben esser bassato et far le cente al modo se usa cum le bombardiere alla francese."

ertheless, it was still considered an important defense during the second Venetian occupation.[23] The Grimani plans show that the Turks, during the XVI or XVII century, had surrounded the island with a *porporella*, or barrier of stones under water, to prevent the approach of larger ships. Another barrier was built between this and the north end of the Five Brothers bastion, with a gap in the middle to allow the passage of ships. Plates XIX and XXII show that its inner half was rebuilt into a mole.

The Turks added little else to the fortifications of Nauplia. In the southwest corner of the Castel de Franchi, the small terrepleined bastion guarding the gate from the upper enclosure is surrounded by the wide arc of a thin, uncrenellated parapet, pierced with fourteen loopholes, similar to the semicircular "battery" in the fortress of Zarnata (Plates III, IV). A low parapet with musket holes at ground level, on top of the east wall of the Castel de Franchi may also be attributed to the Turks, whose careless rule otherwise left Nauplia to crumble.

After the capture of the place in 1686, Morosini wintered his army in Nauplia, where, according to Foscarini,[24] "all the galley slaves were put to work, restoring the fortress and improving its defenses ... to guard it against assault from Mount Palamedi ... Among other labors ... a way was cut in the living rock at the sea end along an advantageous covered stretch, to which the auxiliaries from the seaborne army could have easy access." The path is shown on Plates XIX, XX, XXI, and XXII leading up from the tip of the peninsula to an entrance in the curtain wall. A few rock-cut steps can be made out to-day high up in the gulley, at the head of which stands a postern gate, accommodated by the partial destruction of the classical polygonal wall, which stands particularly high at this point. The door is arched in small, wedge-shaped blocks of poros, in the same construction used by the Venetians in their works on the Palamedi — unlike their doorways of the XV and XVI centuries. The postern appears to date, together with the stairs, to that same winter of 1686–7.

It was on Nauplia that the Venetians of 1700 concentrated their architectural activity. The first of their additions to the circuit wall was a small demi-bastion, built during the governorship of Daniele Dolfin (1701–1704)[25] in a corner of the north flank of the Castel de Greci with battering walls and finely cut and fitted blocks in the angles, a torus molding, and a projecting corbel in the east corner (Fig. 112).

The Venetians concentrated, however, in the fortification of the landward front.[26] Proposals were drawn up by the French engineers La Salle and Levasseur to straighten the town's east curtain, and to replace the round tower on the sea with a new and larger bastion, which was completed by the year 1714.[27] The largest unit of these eastern fortifications, and the only one standing to-day, is the great quadrangular bastion built round the base of the *torrione* (Figs. 106, 107, 111), which took the place of the *Pezzo stacato*, or detached work, drawn on each of the Grimani plans of Nauplia. Another plan by Levasseur, drawn in 1705, published in Gerola's study,[28] refers to this work as "Ravelin which must be destroyed, being a defense of little worth, made with earth and stones, and partly ruined." The new bastion is banked inside into three terraces, of

---

[23] Garzoni, I, p. 166.
[24] *Op. cit.*, p. 242.

[25] Report of Daniele Dolfin, Δελτίον, V, p. 620.
[26] Gerola, *Napoli di Romania*, pp. 376 ff.
[27] Report of Daniele Dolfin, Δελτίον, V, p. 620: "Per migliorare le fortificationi dalla parte di terra, ch'è la piu debole, fu giudicata proficua l'erettione d'un mezzo baloardo, che dalla Porta di terra ferma termina in mare. Avvalorato dalla publica sovrana approvatione il projetto, ebbi honore di gettare li primi fondamenti, e sollecitati a tutto potere li lavori con l'opera delle ciurme, provai il contento di vederlo in breve tempo, e con tenuissimo aggravio della publica cassa interamente compito, e armata di valida batteria, che domina e rade l'unica venuta, per la quale si possa da quella parte approssimar a gl' approcci."
[28] *Napoli di Romania*, p. 378, fig. 20.

which the lower and middle levels carry parapets of embrasures 18 feet deep, which enfilade the ditch. The upper parapets on the east and south are thinner, and to-day mostly destroyed. As in the Palamedi forts,[29] built soon after, these parapets are largely of brick, and a small

east and southeast corners extending 20 feet into the flat, mortared surface of the east face. The upper courses of these angles are all of smooth ashlar. The irregular form and arrangement of these materials leads to the supposition that the Venetians were trying out a new

FIG. 109. NAUPLIA, LATE VENETIAN ANGLE CONSTRUCTION IN THE PALAMEDI FORTS.

FIG. 110. NAUPLIA, CLIFFS OF THE PALAMEDI FROM THE CASTEL DEL TORO, SHOWING CAPONIER, DITCH, AND ZIG-ZAG ASCENT TO THE UPPER FORTIFICATIONS.

brick turret supported on a corbel occupies the northeast angle. Around three sides of the quadrangle run subterranean vaulted galleries similar to the contemporary Venetian works at Methone and Corone. The bastion's outer walls are distinguished by the use of great rusticated ashlar blocks, measuring $1\frac{1}{2}$ by 4 feet, built on the north flank in ten courses rising half way up the wall, and in the north-

decorative style, perhaps inspired by the remains of the ancient Greek walls they found close by. A few years later they were to use similar blocks in a more finished pattern with a drafted line up the angles of the Palamedi fortresses (Fig. 109), as their builders described, *lavorati alla rustica*.[30] The walls of the Grimani bastion are stamped in each face with the seal of St. Mark, and on the north side a small plaque bears the initials F. G., and the

[29] For an account of their building, see Gerola, *Napoli di Romania*, pp. 394 ff.

[30] Agostino Sagredo, Δελτίον, V, p. 744.

date 1706. This was the first year of Grimani's tenure as *Provveditore Generale*, or Governor of the Morea. The plans in the present collection do not show any of these renovations in the eastern sector, and so must antedate the governorship of Daniele Dolfin: evidence that the plans were drawn largely during the two years Grimani was general of the land forces, or *Provveditore Generale dell' Armi in Morea*, an office which ended in October, 1701.

Beyond the Grimani bastion to the east are two ditches cutting across the slope under the Palamedi cliffs. That on the north is 30 feet across, and appears on Plate XXIII as N. *Caponiera Perfetionata*. It is cut into the rock on one side and built up with a wall on the other. At the bottom, affixed to the wall, is a sculptured shield bearing the Grimani arms, surmounted by a coronet such as we see in

Fig. 111. Nauplia, Castel del Toro, Grimani Bastion, Caponier and Ditch, seen from the Palamedi Cliffs.

most of the drawings of this collection. A small channel running down the middle of the ditch answers to the *Aquedotto* drawn on the same plan. A modern hydraulic installation stands to-day at its head. On the south is a larger caponier (Figs. 110, 111), not indicated on the plans: a long, arched passageway, gable-roofed on the exterior, built in successive, steeply ascending sections from a point opposite the southeast corner of the Grimani bastion to the top of the slope where, immediately under the Palamedi rock, is a small terrace with a parapet, built by Agostino Sagredo in 1714.[31] Both walls of the caponier measure 5 feet thick, pierced with single and two-way loopholes at 4-foot intervals. Walls and roof are built of rough stones in thick, strong mortar, with squared limestone blocks in the angles, and brick to form the openings. The whole length of the work is guarded on the south side by a precipitous, rock-cut ditch. The plans show nothing of these constructions, but Gerola mentions that Grimani, who considered the Palamedi too expensive to fortify, confined himself to building two caponiers in the rock beneath it.[32] The rectangular prison building in the confines of the Castel de Greci (Plate XXIII, G. *Quartieri Nuovi*)may be another of Grimani's works, who mentions in his report of 1701 the erection of barracks in the forts of Argos and Nauplia.[33] The last of the Venetian constructions on the lower rocks of Nauplia was the monumental entrance in

[31] Δελτίον, V, p. 743: "Al piede della discesa del Monte, in testa della Caponiera, s'è ridotto quasi in perfetto termine in Posto, sotto il dirupo, che fiancheggia il lato della Caponiera stessa, per la parte verso Caratona."

[32] An inscription in honor of Grimani was seen by Pouqueville inside the house of one Cassan Bey in Nauplia, *Voyage*, IV, p. 231 n.

FRANCISCO GRIMANO
SUPREMO CLASSIS MODERATORI
QVI VRBEM
EXTRA MVNIMENTA FIRMAVIT
INTVS HAC CONSILII AEDE EXORNAVIT
ANNONA PROVIDIT
LEGIBVS ORDINAVIT
NAUPLIA VOVET
ANNO DOMINI MDCCVII

[33] Δελτίον, V, p. 482.

the north wall of the Castel de Greci (Fig. 112). A zig-zag of stairs in two sections leads up to it from the town, the upper supported on four

apex is a small lion plaque carved with the coronet of the *Provveditor Generale da Mar*, or High Admiral, and the inscription:

FIG. 112. NAUPLIA, NORTH FLANK OF THE CASTEL DE GRECI: THE DOLFIN BASTION (*ca.* 1703) AND THE SAGREDO GATE (1713)

relieving arches spanning gaps over the living rock. Two of these arches are of flat, rough stones; the two others are of neat poros wedges. The steps and the coping stones of the retaining wall are toolmarked on their vertical sides. The head of the ascent abuts against the flank of the slender, battering Dolfin tower. Preceding the gateway are tall, ornamental pillars made of big blocks of alternate width, crowned each by a pyramidal stone. The gate itself consists of an avantcorps pierced by a round arch and surmounted by a pronounced cornice and a pediment above it. Beneath the

MILITVM COMMODO
AVGVSTINVS SAGREDO PROV. G̅LI̅S MARIS
COMPENDIO VIARIVM
FIERI CVRAVIT
ANNO MDCCXIII

It was in this same year that the Venetians were already carrying out their plans on the Palamedi, transforming the mountain top into a city of fortresses. The idea for such a work had been proposed and rejected in turn by Morosini, Corner, and Grimani; although the design submitted by the latter was to form the basis for the fortifications carried out by

FIG. 113. NAUPLIA, FORTIFICATIONS ON THE PALAMEDI.

FIG. 114. NAUPLIA, INTERIOR OF THE MASCHIO FORT ON THE PALAMEDI.

Agostino Sagredo soon after. Plate XXIII shows a rudimentary plan of "communicating towers which entirely fortify the mountain." Sagredo's labor was accomplished in three years, from 1711 to 1714, at a cost of 53,081 reals, the last tangible achievement in the long history of the Venetian empire.

One year after the mountain was fortified, the Turks fell upon the Morea with an army of 100,000. The Venetian garrison in Nauplia numbered 1,269. The Turks took up positions under steady fire from the guns on the Palamedi. Tradition had it later that the plans of the new fortifications were sold to the enemy by the French colonel, La Salle, who himself had executed their construction. After only eight days, during which the Turks lost 8,000 of their number, the Venetians abandoned the Palamedi and descended to the lower town. The Janissaries followed them down into the ditch, and forded it at a point where the water was shallow. Then they scaled the scarp, planted a petard under the gate, and opened a breach. Too late the Governor Alessandro Bon raised the white flag, when he saw the Palamedi fall. The guns on the Grimani and Dolfin bastions offered no resistance to the Janissaries, as they swarmed in through the breach

in the east curtain. In the heat of the assault they failed to notice the signal for surrender, and while the Bourtzi was also opening its gates, began to massacre the population. The twenty-five thousand, it was claimed, who remained alive were sold as slaves in the

FIG. 115. NAUPLIA, ARTILLERY EMPLACEMENT ON THE PALAMEDI.

Turkish camp. The Palamedi, Acronauplia, the lower town, and the island fortress all were taken in the space of two hours.[34] So Nauplia fell, and with it the whole Peloponnese was lost to Venice.

[34] Brue, *Journal de la campagne*, pp. 23–34; Cappelletti, XI, pp. 157f.; Romanin, VIII, pp. 40–42; Miller, *Essays*, p. 424.

CHAPTER X

ARGOS

(Plate XXVIII)

While the Venetians were besieging Nauplia, the Seraskier arrived in Argos with a relieving army. Morosini went out to meet him on August 6, 1686, moving his light troops across the bay, while Königsmark marched the rest of the army by land, to surround the enemy on both sides. The Turks fought and fled, despoiling the fortress of all but two of its cannon.[1]

* * *

Fig. 116. Argos, the Castle from the East.

As in all the Greek castles which antedate the Fourth Crusade, there is no record of its building. Argos held the rank of metropole from the year 1088,[2] and is mentioned by Edrisi in the XII century as one of the thirteen principal towns in the Peloponnese.[3] It was also one of the five towns where the Venetians were granted freedom of trade in 1199.[4] Six years later, while the Franks were overrunning the Peloponnese, Champlitte was told that Argos, together with Nauplia and Acrocorinth, were fortresses too strong to capture.[5] Does this strength refer only to its natural position or to some recent refortification by Leon Sgouros, archon of Nauplia, who had seized it two years before? Argos held out after all the other castles of the Morea but one had fallen to Champlitte's army, and only surrendered in 1212 to Geoffroy I Villehardouin.[6]

For two and a half centuries the history of Argos follows the fortunes of Nauplia. Both places were fiefs of the Burgundian Dukes of Athens, and remained in the hands of bailies of their exiled successors after the Catalan invasion of the Duchy in 1311. Seventy-seven years

[1] Locatelli, I, pp. 249f.; Garzoni, I, pp. 167ff.
[2] Χρονικὸν Σύντομον, ed. Bonn, p. 515.
[3] Géographie d'Edrisi, p. 124.
[4] Tafel and Thomas, Urkunden, I, p. 265.
[5] Χ. τ. Μ., line 1587.
[6] C. di M., p. 436; Miller, Essays, p. 88.

later they were purchased by Venice from the last of the Frankish line in 1388. A Venetian governor was sent out, only to find the two castles occupied by the joint force of Nerio Acciajuoli, Lord of Athens, anxious to restore his city's earlier dominion, and his son-in-law, Theodore I, Despot of Mistra, who had seized the chance to incommode his neighbors in Messenia. The Venetians drove out the Greco-Florentines from Nauplia, but failed to recover Argos. Venice in the meantime retaliated with a series of commercial interdicts against the Duchy and the Despotate, but avoided a war her treasury could not afford. Instead, acting through her agents in Methone and Corone, she induced the constable of the Franco-Navarrese Principality to invite the Duke of Athens to a conference and take him prisoner. The condition of his release was the immediate surrender of Argos. The Greek Despot, unconcerned, refused to give it up, and continued hostilities on his own, pillaging the Messenian borders and protracting fruitless negotiations over a period of five years. It was not till 1394 that a truce was signed, by which Venice recovered Argos, and Theodore was promised a safe refuge in Venetian territory in the event of a Turkish invasion.[7]

In 1395 the Turks moved into northern Greece. In 1397 a Turkish army invaded the Peloponnese and fell upon Argos. The walls withstood the first attack, but panic seized the defenders, and the Turks entered. The inhabitants were massacred, the walls demolished, and, according to different reports, fourteen or thirty thousand peasants were carried off into slavery.[8] Venice, however, continued to hold the place.

Ten years after the fall of Constantinople Venice herself was attacked by the Turks in Greece. In 1463 an escaped Christian slave of the Pasha of Athens took refuge with one of the Venetian officials in Corone, who refused to surrender him. The Pasha of the Morea answered by seizing Argos. The Venetians recaptured the castle under the leadership of the condottiere Bertoldo d'Este, but lost it again four months later.[9]

After 223 years Argos returned to the Venetians under Morosini, but by then it was no longer worth what it had been to the Franks and the Byzantine Greeks. The Proveditor Gradenigo mentions it in his report of 1692 as "di minor consideratione,"[10] and in 1708 Angelo Emo speaks of "li due piccioli Castelli di Thermis e Argos."[11] The collection of Grimani drawings devotes to it only one inaccurate plan (Plate XXVIII). Argos had held a subsidiary rank, first as a fief of Athens, then as a dependency of Nauplia under the Venetians, who in the two periods 1388–1463 and 1687–1715 concentrated their efforts on the sea-port town at the expense of the hilltop castle. In 1715 they abandoned Argos to the Turks without a struggle.

*　　*　　*

The fortress crowns the Larissa hill, which rises 870 feet above sea level, with a steep drop over the plain to the east, and is joined by a saddle to neighboring mountains on the west (Fig. 116). It is built on the plan of two concentric enclosures developed in turn by the ancient Greeks, the Byzantines, and the castle builders of western Europe, upon the foundations of the prehistoric citadel of "horse-bearing Argos"

ἵνα τείχεα
λάϊνα Κυκλώπι' οὐράνια νέμονται.[12]

---

[7] *Ibid.*, pp. 76, 111, 124f., 136; Zakythinos, *Despotat*, I, pp. 132ff., 155, 199.

[8] Phrantzes, ed. Bonn, p. 83; Miller, *Latins*, p. 358; Zakythinos, *Despotat*, I, p. 157.

[9] Laonikos Chalkokondyles, ed. Bonn, pp. 545, 556, 561; Coronelli, *Memorie*, p. 114; Daru, II, pp. 563f.; Miller, *Latins*, p. 465; *Essays*, p. 372.

[10] Δελτίον, V, p. 231.

[11] *Ibid.*, V, p. 684. Thermisi is a small rock fort near the tip of the Argolid peninsula, on the south side opposite the island of Hydra. It was built by Walter of Brienne in the first half of the XIV century. See Μεγάλη Ἑλληνικὴ Ἐγκυκλοπαιδεῖα, article: Θερμίσι.

[12] Euripides, *Troades*, lines 1087–8.

The curtains are flanked with bastions and towers, triangular, octagonal, square, and round, which cover the span from early Byzantine to Turkish times. The masonry of the

FIG. 117. ARGOS, THE SOUTHWEST FLANK.

medieval superstructure shows an unusual uniformity, which baffles the attempt to decide whether the castle is more predominantly Byzantine or Frankish. The walls are built mostly of small, roughly trimmed blocks of poros and limestone, square and oblong, coursed with the help of broken tile along the interstices (Figs. 120, 122, 125, 126). The gate of the outer enclosure (Plate XXVIII, A) is set in the middle of the long southwest flank[13] (Fig. 117); a depressed passageway leads into a small court between the short south flank of the inner enceinte, which contains its entrance, and a thin wall on the east, through which a door admits to the broad, sloping, horseshoe-shaped expanse of the outer enclosure (Fig. 120; Plate XXVIII, B, C). These main outer and inner gates are each flanked on

[13] References of orientation are made to the plan given in Fig. 119, and not to the misleading Plate XXVIII.

FIG. 118. ARGOS, CONSTRUCTIONS FLANKING THE FORTRESS GATE: ROUND FRANKISH TOWERS AND PYRAMIDAL BASE OF THE TURKISH BASTION.

the eastern side by a tall, round tower, containing a chamber in its upper section (Figs. 117, 118, 120). The lower of these two rises high above the level of the adjacent curtains. Further down the southwest flank, the outer face of the wall projects forward into a pointed redan (Figs. 117, 121). The chemin de ronde of the curtain descends here by a flight of six steps to a small, triangular platform, from which another stair on the opposite side leads down into the interior of the enclosure. The faces of the redan carry a parapet in two levels; the upper continues the parapet of the curtain above it, backed by a small chemin de ronde of its own, supported on the vaults of two gun embrasures pointing through the wall on either side beneath it.

The southeast corner of the enceinte is defended by a high, square tower, the stepped projection of whose base contains three blocks of cyclopean masonry. The angles are built of huge blocks of poros, whose dimensions indicate previous use in classical times. One angle near the top of the tower is occupied by a fluted column shaft set upright. Several column drums are built into the wall face, which is also peppered with small fragments of tile. More ancient elements, rough cyclopean boulders, column drums, and big ashlar blocks of poros, make up the stretch of the east flank of the outer enceinte for the next 18 feet, as it turns an acute angle and leads northward from the corner. This long flank of the castle is guarded by a succession of towers of different

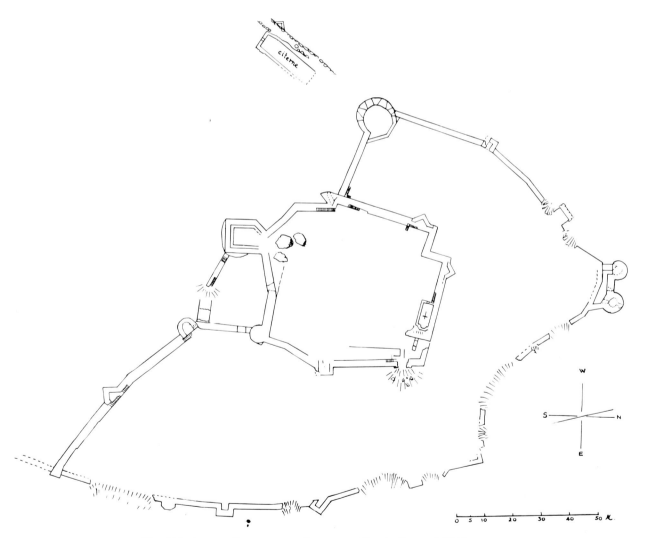

FIG. 119. ARGOS, PLAN OF THE FORTRESS. *By A. Bon and H. Ducoux.*

size and shape. Proceeding from the southeastern corner, the first is an octagonal tower
built on a jutting base, and made of a miscellaneous mixture of carefully trimmed poros

FIG. 120. ARGOS, SOUTHEAST CORNER OF INNER ENCLOSURE.

blocks, big and small, column drums, and
Byzantine marble fragments (Fig. 123), of a
form generally similar to some of the polygonal
towers in the walls of Constantinople. Next
comes a square tower, set also on projecting
courses at the base, built of rougher materials
than the preceding, with a number of marble
colonnettes. Third, a pointed redan is built of
tightly fitted, uncut stones, with ladders of

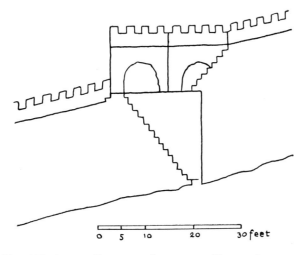

FIG. 121. ARGOS, REDAN IN SOUTHWEST FLANK, INTERIOR
VIEW.

brick in the interstices and squared blocks in
the salient angle. Further to the north, polygonal and cyclopean blocks appear along the
base, and in the upper sections of the wall
embedded in the masonry of oblong field
stones and broken tile. Above are a few traces
of a parapet with square merlons. The curtain
forms a right angle and then continues in a bay
(greatly accentuated on Plate XXVIII into a
deep re-entrant angle), to-day largely ruined
both in its wall and flanking towers, out to the
fortress' northernmost extremity.

This corner is occupied by two tall, straight,
round towers similar to those flanking the
southern gates. On either side, the polygonal
socle and the medieval superstructure of
coursed blocks separated by long, double and
triple courses of flat brick, may be seen to
penetrate the curved, projecting flanks. A
remnant of the curtain shows above the interior ground level, just behind the short stretch
of wall joining the two towers. These carry
traces of a parapet of big, square merlons, and
the connecting wall has a chemin de ronde on a
lower level, guarded by these merlons. The
towers' original roofing has gone, and instead,
in each, a clumsy, pointed dome of rough
stones is squeezed in between the circular
walls. In each tower a part of the wall beneath
the dome has been broken through, to provide
a gun embrasure, with smooth, tapering sides
and sloping roof, whose thick covering plaster
bears the marks of wooden planks. Thus this
section contains three different periods of
medieval fortification: the curtain built on the
ancient base; the two towers built up against
it, and finally the attempt to adapt these
structures to the uses of artillery by destroying
their original tops and inserting in their place
domes and vaulted embrasures.

The northwest flank of the outer enclosure
stands directly upon the lower courses of the
ancient circuit wall, which in one stretch of
100 feet rises 30 feet high. Along the top of the
medieval wall above it runs a parapet of square

Fig. 122. Argos, Masonry of Southwest Flank.

Fig. 123. Argos, Polygonal Flanking Tower,
East Outer Curtain.

Fig. 124. Argos, the West Artillery Bastion.

merlons with pointed copes. There are two square flanking towers, one built within the foundations of a larger Hellenic tower, and the other set upon a projecting base of its own. At the western extremity of the enceinte a big, circular artillery bastion (Figs. 124, 129, lower right) guards the fortress at its most vulnerable point, where the high saddle provides an approach from the side of the Arkadian mountains. The parapet of five embrasures varies in thickness from 5 to 8 feet; curves downwards over its crest, and outwards at the embrasure mouths; and is pierced with three deep musket holes. The lower section of the bastion batters slightly all round, with several cyclopean blocks immured in its surface of big, round stones that show through the fine, smooth mortar of the joints. Other elements in the

wall are carved Byzantine marble plaques, projecting column shafts, and one large, round boss. As in the round artillery bastions of Kelepha, there is no string course molding, which, with the irregular plane of the walls, produces that effect of shapelessness characteristic of much Turkish fortification. Below the tower to the southwest are the ruins of a cistern and the angle of a building made of large, rectangular blocks, marble fragments, and ladders of broken tile, which would seem to date to the same period as the greater part of the fortress. It is situated along a line of blocks, which for a short space indicate how the town walls of ancient Argos were joined to its acropolis. The curtain of the outer enclosure turns eastward from the bastion, and rises up the hill for 70 feet to meet the western angle of

FIG. 125. ARGOS, EAST FLANK OF INNER ENCEINTE, SOUTH HALF, SHOWING POLYGONAL AND MEDIEVAL MASONRY.

FIG. 126. ARGOS, EAST FLANK OF INNER ENCEINTE, NORTH HALF, SHOWING THE FLANKING TOWER.

the inner, its crenellations sloping parallel to the terrain (Figs. 124, 129, right). Four small casemates pierce the parapet at the level of the chemin de ronde.

The curtain of the inner enceinte stands upon a well preserved classical socle. In the southern half of its eastern flank the blocks are quarry-faced polygonal (Fig. 125); in the north, tool-faced and fitted with such precision as to give the impression of trapezoidal masonry[14] (Fig. 126). Along the northern flank of the enclosure the construction of the ancient base combines the features of both trapezoidal and Lesbian[15] (Fig. 127).

The northwest corner of the enclosure is planned with a sophistication reminiscent of angle construction among the castles of France. It is built on a tenaille trace, with two redans projecting from the north and west faces of the adjacent curtain (Fig. 129). Each of these supports, like the redan in the outer southwest curtain, a triangular platform, 6 feet above the chemin de ronde, enclosed by parapets in two levels, consisting of rude casemates pushed through the wall at a later date, and an upper chemin de ronde with narrow parapet.

Jutting out from the south end of the enclosure is the ruin of a heavy bastion con-

FIG. 127. ARGOS, NORTH FLANK OF INNER ENCLOSURE.

FIG. 128. ARGOS, EAST CURTAIN OF INNER ENCEINTE: CHEMIN DE RONDE, PARAPET, AND SQUARE FLANKING TOWER.

The medieval curtain built above this socle resembles that of the outer enclosure. The midpoint of the eastern side is broken into an obtuse angle, at which stands a high, narrow, square, flanking tower, hollow down to the ground, projecting forward from the trace and above the level of the curtain on either side. Both curtain and tower carry crenellated parapets of wide, square merlons (Figs. 126, 128).

sisting to-day of a pyramidal base, 33 feet square, surmounted by a smaller quadrangle with battering faces of its own (Figs. 117, 118), without provision for guns. It seems to have replaced an earlier, round tower, of which one curved fragment lies below it on the east, and whose stones and mortar resemble the materials of the round artillery bastion in the western corner. In 1715 the Venetians, according to a contemporary account,[16] blew up "the wall

[14] See R. L. Scranton, *Greek Walls* (Cambridge, Mass. 1934), pp. 64ff., 162.

[15] *Ibid.*, pp. 34, 160.

[16] *Chronique de l'expédition des Turcs en Morée*, attributed to Constantine Dioecetes, ed. N. Jorga (Bucarest, 1913), § 80, p. 164.

8

near the gate," because they were unable to defend the castle, which was found ruined when the Turks entered.[17]

The interior of the inner enclosure has been zealously excavated by archeologists in search of the *Arx Argivorum*. The area has been

Latin church, or the governor's residence indicated along the eastern quarter.

The medieval fortress follows, as much as can be seen from traces along the base of the walls, the general outline of the classical citadel of Argos. The place was in a sufficient

FIG. 129. ARGOS, NORTHWEST ANGLE OF INNER ENCEINTE, WITH THE TWO FLANKING REDANS. IN THE BACKGROUND, THE WEST ARTILLERY BASTION AND CURTAIN OF OUTER CIRCUIT.

swept clean of all post-classical remains except for a small chapel in the north side, built on ancient foundations (Plate XXVIII, *Cuartiiri*), while all that once formed the interior ground level of the medieval period has been dumped out through a breach in the east flank, like a slag-heap over the slope of the outer enceinte. Deep, narrow, vaulted cisterns exist, as shown on Plate XXVIII, in both inner and outer enclosures. A third cistern, divided by a row of three square piers, is situated in the southeast corner. Nothing remains of the mosque, the

state of defense at the beginning of the XIII century to withstand the seven-year siege of the Frankish crusaders. The circuit wall must therefore have been complete at least at the end of the early Byzantine period before 1205. It stands, in its almost complete present state, directly upon the living rock or the ancient socle. It is nearly impossible to tell if the Franks changed the castle's basic plan. Additions certainly they must have made during the 176 years of their occupation, and among these may be counted the four tall, round towers at the northern and southern ends,

[17] Brue, *Journal de la campagne*, p. 22.

which do not bond with their adjacent walls. This form seems to have been imported from western Europe. For except in rare instances, the fortress builders of Byzantium adhered over a period of a thousand years to the scheme of the square flanking tower, despite its more vulnerable front and the obstruction of its projecting angles to the uses of flanking fire.[18] The plan of the northwest corner of the inner enclosure, with the two redans placed carefully on either side of its re-entrant angle, may also date to the time of the Burgundian Dukes of Athens. From the artillery period are the round west bastion, the square redout in the southwest flank with its original and rebuilt superstructure, the upper portion of the twin towers on the north, the clumsy embrasures broken through the wall in several places, and the double parapets on top of the redans, similar to the those in certain constructions at Patras and Acrocorinth. These are all Turkish works, belonging to the period after 1463. The two Venetian occupations of 1394–1463 and 1686–1715 seem to have left Argos without a trace. In 1701 Francesco Grimani spoke of the need for repair, the walls lying open through explosions in the powder stores.[19] But the place was not even numbered among the Morea's chief inland forts, since it lay too far from the sea and had no harbor to defend.

[18] See T. E. Lawrence, *Crusader Castles* (Golden Cockerel Press, 1936), pp. 27f.

[19] Δελτίον, V, p. 481.

CHAPTER XI

PATRAS

(PLATE XXIX)

The campaign of 1687 began on July 21 when the Venetians and their allies disembarked at Patras. Two years before, a deputation of its inhabitants had come to Morosini, asking him to make Patras his next objective after Kalamata. The Seraskier had prepared for such a landing by digging trenches on either side of the town, but the Venetians discovered an unguarded, marshy spot, where they came ashore and took the Turks by surprise. On July 24 the two armies clashed after a series of skirmishes. Königsmark defeated the Seraskier in the field, while the garrison fled from the castle, leaving 65 cannon behind them.[1]

*　　*　　*

The geographical position of Patras made it during the Middle Ages what Corinth had been in Antiquity, the commercial capital of Greece. The Roman colony planted by Augustus in the northwest corner of Achaea was destined to have an important history even during the centuries when history elsewhere in Greece was dormant. Patras flourished as a religious center from the II century after Christ, when tradition associated it with the matyrdom of St. Andrew. But behind the religious importance of the place was its situation at the juncture of the Adriatic and the Corinthian Gulf, ideal for trade between Greece and Italy.

Patras preserved touch with the outside world and remained one of the strongholds of the Greeks in the Peloponnese while the rest of the country was being overrun by the Slavs. In 805,[2] at a time when the Empire was attacked by both the Saracens and the Bulgars, the Slavs of the Morea rose and besieged Patras, become now an outpost of Byzantium, while a Saracen fleet also blockaded it by sea. When the garrison approached the end of its resources, a horseman was sent out from the city to look if any relief was coming from the Imperial governor in Corinth. The signal to the watchers in the castle was to lower his flag if aid was in sight. The vigil was in vain, but on his return toward the city, his horse stumbled and the flag went down. The defenders broke out and defeated the Slavs in a decisive battle, which was to mark the gradual recovery of the Morea from their invasions and revolts. The deliverance of the city was considered a miracle of its patron saint. The arch-

[1] Locatelli, I, pp. 167, 330 ff.; Garzoni, I, p. 209; Prodocimo, *Successi dell' Armi della Serenissima Republica di Venetia nella Campagna di 1687* (Venice, 1687), pp. 16 ff.

[2] For the date 805, as opposed to 807 as originally suggested by Hopf in *Geschichte Griechenlands*, in Ersch und Gruber, *Allgemeine Encyklopädie der Wissenschaften und Künste*, LXXXIII, (Leipzig, 1866), p. 99, see Bon, *Le Péloponnèse byzantin*, p. 44 and note.

bishopric was raised to the rank of metropole, and upon the Slavs who settled in the region were imposed the first steps in their hellenization: conversion to Orthodoxy and payment of rent to the Church.[3]

During the following centuries Patras developed the political independence accompanying commercial and ecclesiastical autonomy, left, like Nauplia and Monemvasia, to the rule of its own local archons. One of these was the widow Danielis, foster mother of the Emperor Basil I, who bequeathed to his successor, Leo VI, a vast fortune consisting of estates, money, precious textiles, and slaves amounting to the thousands.[4] In the third quarter of the XII century a colony of fifty Jews was noted there by Benjamin of Tudela.[5] Venice also acquired an early footing in Patras with trading privileges granted by Alexios III in 1199,[6] and then claimed the city for herself in the Partition Treaty of 1204.[7] It was at Patras, however, in the early summer of 1205 that the Frankish knights initiated their campaign in the Morea. They built there a fort by the sea, captured the lower town, and forced the castle to surrender.[8] In the organization of the Frankish Principality, Patras was made seat of the Latin archbishopric and fief of Guillaume Aleman, a Provençal knight who had taken part in the conquest. Asserting his power in his new domain, he imprisoned the archbishop, and used the archiepiscopal church and palace to enlarge the old Byzantine citadel. A few years later, his son and successor pledged Patras to the archbishop for 16,000 hyperpers, and departed from Greece.[9]

In the XIV century the power of the Latin ecclesiastic grew, while the lay power of the Frankish state declined. In 1326 the archbishop served as bailie of the Principality. When, in 1333, the titular Latin Empress of Constantinople, Catherine de Valois, purchased Achaea for her son, Robert of Taranto, the archbishopric was practically an autonomous state. On the death of its incumbent, Catherine's bailie laid siege to the castle of Patras, causing a protest from the Pope, who ordered the Morea to be placed under an interdict. In 1338 Catherine herself came to the Morea to survey the situation from near by, and to see what could be done to defend the Principality against the Catalans, Greeks, and Turks who threatened it by land and sea. The need of papal support against all these foes forced her at last to acknowledge the Pope's temporal authority over Patras, and she withdrew her forces.[10]

When Robert of Taranto died in 1366 and his widow, Marie de Bourbon, was pressing her son's claim to the Principality, the archbishop again asserted his independence, together with the other barons of Achaea, by declaring in favor of Philip, Robert's brother. Marie attacked Patras, which was defended by one of the canons of the cathedral, the Venetian Carlo Zeno, who after six weeks broke out and drove her army back to Navarino. Peace was made at last between Marie and Philip, who four years later succeeded in buying her off with an indemnity.[11]

At the beginning of the XV century, when the Frankish Principality was disappearing from the map, Venice stepped in to rent Patras from the archbishop, who through fear of the Turks, was anxious to get rid of it. The purchase of Naupaktos in 1407 and the occupation of Patras for several years after 1408 gave Venice command of the Corinthian Gulf. A convenient treaty with the Turks confirmed

[3] Constantine Porphyrogenitus, *De Administrando Imperio*, chap. 49; Miller, *Essays*, p. 40.

[4] Theophanes, *Vita Basilii*, ed. Bonn, pp. 226–228, 317–321; Kedrenos, ed. Bonn, II, 190–193, 236–237; Bon, *Le Péloponnèse byzantin*, pp. 74, 121–122, 127, 128.

[5] *The Itinerary of Benjamin of Tudela*, ed. Adler (London, 1907), p. 10.

[6] Tafel und Thomas, *Urkunden*, I, p. 264.

[7] *Ibid.*, I, p. 469.

[8] Χ. τ. Μ., lines 1410–1421; *L. de C.*, §§ 90, 91; *C. di M.*, p. 422.

[9] *L. de C.*, § 128; *C. di M.*, p. 428; Miller, *Latins*, pp. 64, 147; Miller, *Essays*, p. 78.

[10] Miller, *Essays*, pp. 270 ff.; *Latins*, p. 261.

[11] *Ibid.*, pp. 287 ff.; Zakythinos, *Despotat*, I, pp. 109 f.

her possession.[12] With their usual efficiency the Venetians devoted the revenues of both cities to their refortification. When, after five years, the lease of Patras expired, they gave it back to the archbishop, who called them in a second time in 1417 to defend it against the Greeks of Mistra. The Pope, however, claimed Patras two years later, and Venice was forced to hand the town over to a power unable to hold it.[13]

The destruction of the Latin Principality was precipitated by the refusal of the Despot Theodore II to give up his realm of the Morea to his brother Constantine, who in 1427 came to Mistra to be installed. To make up for this loss, Constantine sought compensation in the last, weakly defended relic of Frankish Achaea. The Pope had already made an effort to protect Patras by sending as its archbishop Pandolfo Malatesta,[14] whose sister was married to the Despot Theodore. However, in 1428 the three Palaiologos brothers attacked the city. The following year Constantine attacked it alone. He was driven off, but the defenders agreed to surrender the place to him if the archbishop did not return from Italy by the following May. In June, 1429 Constantine came back and was received by the citizens in triumph. Only the castle held out until a year later. After this, the Venetians transferred their trade to Naupaktos, to which most of the townspeople of Patras emigrated during the uneasy years before the Turkish conquest. In 1446, when Murad II stormed the Hexamilion and entered the Peloponnese with his army, he found the town of Patras deserted. Four thousand only held out against him in the castle and the archbishop's palace. When Constantine Palaiologos became Emperor in 1449, his brother Thomas ruled his half of the Morea from Patras. But when Mohammed II came for the final Turkish assault eleven years later, the town was once more abandoned.[15]

At the beginning of the Cretan Wars in 1645, after the loss of Canea, the Venetians attacked Patras on one of their diversionary operations against the Turks in the Morea.[16] During the Turkish domination Patras continued as the chief commercial city in the Peloponnese, with a busy export trade in silk, wool, raisins, and leather.[17] Its population was put by Spon[18] at between four and five thousand, a third of whom were Jews. After 1574 Patras was the seat of one of the two sanjaks of the Morea, and under the Venetians of 1687–1715 it formed the capital of one of the four provinces of the "Kingdom."[19]

The decline of the fortifications dates from the XVII century. Wheler[20] describes the place as "not considerable, either for Beauty or Strength, having only one round tower toward the sea, a broadside toward the town, and ditch'd round about." The Venetian governors make slight mention of Patras in their reports. Nothing is said about repair of the fortifications, although a storehouse and several other buildings were erected by Corner and Grimani.[21] In 1708 Angelo Emo writes of the dangerous position of the province of Achaea, open on all sides to attack, and guarded only by Patras, a fortress incapable of repelling even a minor assault. He speaks of its moderate elevation and narrow dimensions, the

---

[12] Thomas, *Diplomatarium*, II, p. 202.

[13] Miller, *Latins*, p. 363.

[14] Memorial of Malatesta's incumbency was to be seen in the Museum at Patras until 1942, when the occupying Italian troops removed it: an inscription commemorating his restoration in 1426 of the church inside the fortress. See S. M. Thomopoulos, Χριστιανικαί ἐν Πάτραις ἐπιγραφαί, in Δελτίον, I, pp. 523 ff.:

CHMEION ΑΥΘΕΝΤΟΥ ΠΑΝΔΟΥΛΦΟΥ ΝΤΕ ΜΑΛΑΤΕC
ΤΟΙC ΜΗΤΡΟΠΟΛΙΤΟΥ ΠΑΛΑΙΟΝ ΠΑΤΡΟΝ ΤΟΥ ΑΝΑ
ΚΑΙΝΙCΑΝΤΟC ΤΟΝ ΤΗΔΕ ΘΕΙΟΝ ΝΑΟΝ ΤΩ ΧΙΛΙΟC
ΤΩ ΤΕΤΡΑΚΟCΙΟCΤΩ ΕΙΚΟCΤΩ ΕΚΤΩ ΕΤΕΙ

[15] Miller, *Latins*, pp. 388 ff., 409, 414 f., 434; Zakythinos, *Despotat*, I, pp. 207, 258.

[16] Miller, *Essays*, p. 194.

[17] Wheler, *Journey into Greece*, p. 298.

[18] *Voyage*, II, p. 16.

[19] Miller, *Essays*, p. 356.

[20] *Journey into Greece*, pp. 297 ff.

[21] Δελτίον, II, p. 303; V, p. 482.

vulnerability of the small, old fashioned flanking towers, and the general disadvantage of
the terrain, which covers the approach to the
walls.[22] The importance of the place in the
eyes of the Venetians may be gauged by the
space afforded to it in the Grimani plans. A
single drawing of Patras (Plate XXIX) made
by the engineer Van Deyk, is labelled *Topo-*

fortress. A street of houses has taken the place
of the *fossa* on the north. Along the east flank
a sunken roadway, some 20 feet below the level
of the surrounding fields occupies what was
once the ditch, whose inner scarp of masonry
still stands (Fig. 132). It was by means of a
bridge of two arches across this ditch (Fig.
133, right) that the fortress was originally

FIG. 130. PATRAS, THE CASTLE FROM THE NORTH.

FIG. 131. PATRAS, THE INNER REDOUT, FROM THE SOUTH.

graphia, not *Pianto,* and includes the city and
a large part of the surrounding country; the
castle itself is only three inches square. The
neglect of the fortress was due, not so much to
its natural weakness and the obsoleteness of
its defenses as to the proximity of a much
stronger fortress, the Castle of Morea, strategically situated at the entrance to the Gulf of
Corinth, eight miles away.

*   *   *

The castle of Patras occupies the spur of a
plateau above the coastal plain (Fig. 130) half
a mile removed from the sea. The outer circuit
is strengthened by an inner enclosure or keep
(Fig. 131) in the northeast corner, where the
high terrain favors the attacker. The circuit
walls were surrounded by a narrow terrace
acting as faussebraye, and a ditch round the
north, east, and south flanks, which served to
cut them off from the plateau. Today the *falsa
bruo* remains intact round two sides of the

FIG. 132. PATRAS, DITCH AROUND THE NORTHEAST CORNER AS
IT APPEARED BEFORE THE BUILDING OF THE PRESENT ROAD.

[22] *Ibid.,* V, p. 685.

Fig. 133. Patras, Northeast Sector: Gate, left, and Keep, right, with the Bridge
across the Ditch as it appeared in 1938.

entered. The main gate is a large tower, 30 feet square, projecting out from the middle of the east curtain (Figs. 133, left; 134). It is vaulted entirely in brick, with a brick reinforcing arch inside its inner face. Through this a pointed arch gives access to the fortress enclosure. The outer door, now ruined, was situated in the tower's north flank (Fig. 135): a low arch of wedge-shaped blocks was surmounted by a huchette, with an outer face arched in brick, masking the gap down which missiles could be dropped. The face and south flank of the tower (Fig. 133) have a battering base, and are pierced with a row of loopholes, of a pattern borrowed by the Turks from the Byzantines. These are built with tapering sides and sloping vault, whose depressed arch appears in a fan of brick on the inside of the wall. On top of the tower are traces of a loopholed parapet round all four sides. In the northwest corner is a small guard chamber, measuring 8 feet by 10, vaulted inside, with a plastered gable roof. Loopholes in its outer wall cover the adjacent curtain. The whole tower, with its brick vault, pointed arch, and pseudo-Byzantine loopholes, is Turkish.

Fig. 134. Patras, East Flank of Outer Circuit, showing
Turkish Gate, Talus, and Polygonal Corner Bastion.

On the south side of the gate is a 60-foot stretch of wall, containing one embrasure in the parapet, covered with a depressed, sloping vault of brick. The length of the wall a reinforcing talus of different masonry is applied against its face (Fig. 134).

The southeast angle of the fortress is occupied by a wide, squat, seven-sided tower (Figs. 134, 136), built with extravagant neatness and delicacy, of small ashlar courses of poros and limestone alternating with courses of brick, reminiscent of the traditional pattern of Byzantine masonry. It is girdled round half its height, with a thin torus molding. Various

FIG. 135. PATRAS, EAST GATE OF THE FORTRESS, SHOWING ARCHWAY AND HUCHETTE, NOW DESTROYED.

stone cannon decorate its sides, and on its outermost face is a small ornamental niche covered with an ogee arch. The platform of the tower is 35 feet wide. Its parapet in the north corner is built into a stout, domed turret, covered with a conical cap, surmounted by a flat-topped hexagon of brick, and surrounded by five other such ornaments set on a brick-covered ledge recessed from the turret walls: a more elaborate structure than the domed turrets built by Turks and Venetians at Nauplia and Monemvasia, Methone and New Navarino in the XVII and XVIII centuries. The parapet contains, in its six other sides, as many vaulted embrasures, covering the hills to the east and the low-lying city to the southwest. The embrasures are 6 feet high and 10 feet wide on the inside, and taper slightly to the outer walls. The vaults are made of stone and brick and the embrasures are arched in a similar way, covered by repeating arches of brick. This line of embrasures supports a chemin de ronde and a musketry parapet garnished with bizarre crenellations whose merlons, only 6 inches apart, are notched on either side, with a tall, central section topped with a conical, plastered cap and a peak of pointed stone. The whole tower is another relic of the Turkish period.[23]

Adjacent to it on the west side, the curtain is masked by a later talus, also Turkish, made of small, roughly squared blocks, intermixed with long irregular double and triple courses of brick (Fig. 136), which bonds neither with the curtain nor the bastion. It is built out over the base of an earlier, square flanking tower made of large, classical limestone blocks of irregular size (bottom of Fig. 136), fitted together with carved marble fragments and little ladders of brick between the joints. Where the talus ends, the curtain behind it is seen to be made of rough limestone and cut marble and poros blocks, with several broken pieces

[23] Traquair in his brief note on Patras ("Mediaeval Fortresses in the North-Western Peloponnesus," *B.S.A.*, XIII, 1906–1907, pp. 279–281) wrongly assigns it to the Italians.

of fluted column drums, which, like the preceding stump of tower, belongs to the fortress which grew up out of the ruins of ancient Pa-

(Fig. 137, right) projects obliquely forward from the preceding curtain and belongs to a different period. It supports a chemin de ronde

FIG. 136. PATRAS, HEPTAGONAL TURKISH BASTION, SOUTHEAST ANGLE OF OUTER ENCLOSURE.

tras, and already existed before the coming of the Franks.

A 40-foot stretch of vertical, mortared wall

and a parapet of high, wide merlons set close together, built of rubble with a large proportion of brick laid flat and in ladders, and pierced

FIG. 137. PATRAS, SOUTH CURTAIN, EASTERN SECTOR: EAST FLANK OF REDAN.

with tiny, square loopholes. Below the chemin de ronde, on the inner face, is a recessed arch made of wedge-shaped blocks, with a marble

FIG. 138. PATRAS, SOUTH CURTAIN: FLANKING TOWER BUILT OF CLASSICAL ELEMENTS.

left). Over its lintel is a pointed relieving arch of brick set fanwise, embedded in the masonry, with a repeating arch of brick placed over it. The upper portions of this latter section of wall are Turkish, as is the whole 40-foot stretch adjacent to it on the east, while the lower portion is made of classical elements, which date it among the earliest medieval fortifications.

The curtain joins with a small flanking tower, 15 feet square, belonging also to the original Byzantine circuit (Fig. 138). It is built with squared blocks of every size, slabs of stylobate marked with dowel holes, architrave blocks, column drums, broken Ionic volutes, and a life-size marble statue without arms or legs, set in a niche in the tower face.[24] The tower flanks are of smaller, more rubbly material, marked in the lower half with several double courses of brick, in the late Byzantine style,

FIG. 139. PATRAS, SOUTH CURTAIN, WESTERN HALF, SHOWING TURKISH ARTILLERY PARAPET.

fragment carved in a leaf and dart molding. This arch gives access to a small embrasure of well cut poros topped with a limestone lintel. A similar arch and opening appear in the next short stretch of wall projecting south (Fig. 137, left).

which could date it to the brief period in the last days of the Despotate, when the Palaiologoi

[24] This was noted by Leake (*Morea*, II, pp. 146f.) and by Pouqueville (*Voyage*, IV, p. 355), who wrongly places it in a bastion on the north side.

held Patras. It may also be Turkish, but the west flank does not bond with its adjacent curtain, which seems to be Turkish from the presence of a casemate similar to the two already mentioned built fairly low in its face (Fig. 138). This is topped with a Byzantine colonnette as a lintel, and a recessed tympanum and relieving arch of bricks above it. The wall here also contains many marble fragments, which probably continued to exist as building material as late as the Turkish period. The tower has a low parapet, 3½ feet high and 4 feet thick, curved on the outside, containing narrow embrasures in face and flanks, each covered with a piece of classical marble. A similar curved parapet continues above the curtain next to it on the west for the length of 35 feet, containing three embrasures (Figs. 138, left; 139, right). This stretch is backed by a terreplein (Fig. 140, left) whose retaining

wall is built of round field stones, a few large, square poros blocks, and several marble fragments with brick widely dispersed, set flat and upright. By their dimensions the embrasures would seem to belong to the early artillery

FIG. 141. PATRAS, SOUTH CURTAIN: ARTILLERY REDAN.

period, and in style both parapet and terreplein are Turkish.

The curtain continues above a foundation of large, re-used ancient blocks, with a narrow, straight parapet (Fig. 140), pierced by small loopholes, to a prominent redan where the parapet thickens to 4½ feet and contains a small gun embrasure on either side of the salient angle (Fig. 141). In the eastward-facing parapet of the redan are two loopholes of an unusual pattern, built in the form of small, tapering, vaulted tunnels, partially walled on the outside to make in each a double slot. From this point to the western corner of the castle, the curtain carries a chemin de ronde and parapet of varying width and function. Steps lead down from the terreplein of the redan to the chemin de ronde of the lower curtain. The parapet is first thin and straight, then crenellated for a 30-foot stretch, in which the merlons are slotted and the embrasures built with steeply sloping floors. Then, for another 40 feet, the parapet thickens to 4½ feet and contains five embrasures set high in the chemin de ronde and built so narrow as to

FIG. 140. PATRAS, SOUTH CURTAIN, EASTERN HALF.

serve, despite the wall's extra thickness, little purpose for artillery (Fig. 142, right). Below the chemin de ronde in this section, three large, brick-vaulted casemates point obliquely in different directions. The parapet is pierced with the long, narrow musket holes characteristic of Turkish artillery defenses. Again for 90 feet the parapet runs with a straight pointed cope, narrowing to $2\frac{1}{2}$ feet in width, with a regular succession of loopholes, as far as a square tower (Figs. 142, 143, right), occupying the salient angle formed by a deep recess of the curtain near the western end. This tower, 15 feet square, is built of rough materials and, at the bottom, angle blocks of irregular size. In the upper half the corners are made of small, neatly squared, toolmarked limestone blocks. A thin parapet above the tower is pierced with a few single and double loopholes. In the bay formed by the curtain at this point there is a small, vaulted postern gate,

parapet are made of squared, toolmarked limestone blocks.

At the western end of the circuit is a round artillery bastion (Figs. 142, 143): a great drum

FIG. 143. PATRAS, ROUND ARTILLERY BASTION AT THE WESTERN ANGLE.

FIG. 142. PATRAS, SOUTH CURTAIN, WESTERN END.

now used as the entrance to the fortress. The parapet here is an elaborate Turkish construction in two levels. The lower part contains three gun embrasures, over which runs a thin upper parapet, covering the embrasure mouths by means of round arches. The sides of the embrasure and the inner face of the lower

80 feet in width, dominating the entire city. A XVII century description of Patras mentions "a round tower, well built, high and strong, which has six very long guns to command the Road, but they lye too high to do any harm to the Ships, except a shot should chance to hit any of the masts."[25] The masonry consists chiefly of toolmarked, rectangular poros blocks of different sizes, some laid in ashlar courses, with a number of larger slabs and blocks of limestone. A torus molding round the middle of the tower marks the spreading of a slight talus in the lower half. What remains of the parapet is of small rubble masonry, resembling that of the south curtain. It contained originally a ring of vaulted casemates, surmounted by a chemin de ronde and upper small arms parapet of merlons, slotted, double-notched, and crowned, like those of the polygonal bastion at the southeastern corner. Of the casemates there remain only a few squared limestone blocks in the outer face of the

[25] Randolph, *The Present State of the Morea*, p. 3.

parapet. Several isolated merlons stand between the spaces fallen about the embrasures. The platform of the bastion is shut off from the fortress enclosure by a high, straight, curving parapet wall, pierced with small loopholes and a depressed brick archway with two marble column shafts for jambs. At either end of this arc of wall is a domed turret or sentry box (Fig. 139) marking the juncture of north and south curtains with the round bastion. The parapets appears to belong all to one period, being everywhere bonded together and of uniform masonry. The bastion itself belongs to the artillery period, and may be a

stones have more a Venetian than a Turkish outline, and contrast with the miscellaneous rubble of the surrounding wall face.

The curtain that defends the fortress along the north (Fig. 130), running from the round artillery bastion at the west to the inner redout at the eastern end, is the original wall of the early Byzantine castle, which existed at Patras before the Franks and withstood the Slavs in 805. It is built (Fig. 144) of huge, chiselled blocks, carved marble, poros and limestone slabs, and column drums, all fitted together in a patchwork of heterogeneous architectural members, that eloquently speaks

FIG. 144. PATRAS, NORTH CURTAIN, BUILT OF RE-USED CLASSICAL ELEMENTS.
TO THE RIGHT, TURKISH ARTILLERY EMPLACEMENT.

relic of the short Venetian occupations of 1408–1413 and 1417–1419, though the parapets are a later Turkish addition.

Around the base of the bastion is a terrace encircled by a retaining wall, the north side of which is the *Falsa Bruo* shown on Plate XXIX. It is built of squared poros, uncut limestone, and tightly packed brick. On the northwest side may be seen the curved, toolmarked blocks of the corbelled support for a turret projecting from the top of the wall. These cut

of the period when the acropolis of Antiquity was transformed into the castle of the Dark Ages.

The curtain's inner face is of rubble, stratified to some degree of regularity by long rows of brick. Near the western end it is barely standing above the interior ground level, but in the eastern half rises to a height of 15 feet. Superimposed on the Byzantine curtain, the wall is of rubble, made with the same gray gravel mortar as in the parapets of the round bastion and the south curtain, and is pierced with rude, tall, sloping, arched loopholes. A round tower near the middle of the flank projects from the curtain with walls of round, rough stones set among flat and upright bricks, girdled with a torus molding and topped with

end, where the curtain joins the inner redout, the wall still supports a few slotted merlons and a straight, loopholed parapet. The upper sections of this north curtain wall, including the parapets, the round tower near the mid-point, and the thickening of the wall to its

FIG. 145. PATRAS, SALIENT SECTOR OF THE KEEP.

an embrasured parapet of the artillery period. The upper portions of both tower and adjacent curtain bond together, while in the tower's inner face a wide, pointed arch springs from ground level and carries an ascent of steps to the chemin de ronde. The whole construction is Turkish.

Further east is a section, 35 feet long, where the wall is built with extra thickness on the inner side and projects out into a talus covering the lower face of the Byzantine wall (Fig. 144, right). Here a higher, thicker parapet is pierced with curving-sided gun embrasures and ob-liquely set, square musket holes. A minute passage leads up to a small, vaulted chamber with an arch in the inner wall that opens on to the enclosure. Another passage, 3 feet high and 20 feet long, serving as a kind of embrasure, slants at a wide angle from this chamber through to the outer face. Near the eastern

east, are all a series of artillery defenses, built as a refortification of the original early Byzantine curtains by the Turks during the XVI and XVII centuries.

The castle keep (Figs. 131; 133, right; 145), built at the highest point of the circuit and dominating the plateau above the city, is separated from the interior of the main enclosure by a faussebraye and shallow ditch, encased on both sides in battering rubble walls (Fig. 131), which extend round the salient inner angle of the keep from the north to the east curtain. A narrow stone bridge on arches crosses the ditch on the south side of the keep to an entrance through the fausse-braye. The keep itself is an irregular quad-rangle with sides 60–80 feet long, strengthened with flanking towers, compressed as to space, but filled with an aggregate of fortifications dating from every period of the castle's history. Along the north side the style of the preceding flank of the outer circuit is continued in a stretch of wall, built of ancient blocks and column drums that rises to a height of 25 feet, with a rubble superstructure, and penetrates the large, battering foundations of a tower projecting obliquely from the middle of the flank. This base is of miscellaneous, squared and uncut blocks, neatly coursed, with angles made of large, flat slabs. The face of the tower (Fig. 145, right) is marked with three double and triple courses of brick and at the top contains four brackets, or machicoulis, for balcony and huchette, as may be seen in the late Byzantine flanking towers of Mistra. The north side of the keep's salient angle penetrates this tower's short flank, but does not follow the same trace of the wall on the other side. The salient angle (Fig. 145) is of different construction also: an assortment of big ashlar blocks probably of classical origin, interspersed with sections of rubble. The oblique tower, built up against these two faces of the keep's north flank, may well date to the occupation of Patras by the Palaiologoi (1430–1460).

The east flank of the inner redout stands 40–60 feet above a wide, sloping ledge, terraced by the high rubble wall of the faussebraye over the road that follows to-day the site of the original ditch. The scarp beneath it supports a straight, loopholed parapet, and contains the ruined shell of a round tower (Fig. 132).

Other than the very early section in the north flank, there is little in the redout itself that can be definitely assigned to a particular date. The masonry of the different sections offers little clue to its chronology. The strong-point of the redout is a high bastion, built against the interior of its northeast salient and the oblique flanking tower (Fig. 146). It consists of a chamfered angle of three battering faces inside the redout, made of courses of round limestone with vertical and

horizontal brick showing through the strong mortar. An ascent of steps leads up to an oval-shaped platform surrounded by a parapet, 4 feet thick, containing embrasures and deep musket holes. The chamfered, battering construction resembles that of the near-by

FIG. 146. PATRAS, THE KEEP: REINFORCING BASTION WITHIN THE SALIENT ANGLE.

fortifications at Naupaktos and may have been added by the Venetians in the early XV century, or perhaps by the Turks after 1460 in imitation of the citadel across the Gulf.

The east flank of the redout supports a passage between an inner and an outer parapet, which leads down an incline through a small pointed arch to a square tower at the southeast corner of the quadrangle (Figs. 131, 133, right). This carries a parapet in two levels, of the same distinctive pattern as in the heptagonal and round bastions of the outer circuit. Under the chemin de ronde, which passes round three sides of the tower, are embrasures of a crude form, consisting of recessed arches with a square opening in the outer shell of each side, 2 feet above the level of the sunken tower platform. The superstructure of all the walls and towers is Turkish, as in the rest of the fortress.

The small flanking tower in the middle of the south side (Fig. 147) and the towers at the other corners are of different masonry from the walls which connect but do not bond with them, laid over also with the repair of later centuries. Nor does the western flank of the quadrangle bond with the chemin de ronde built up against its inner side on a line of seven tall arches (Fig. 148). The redout looks, in plan at least, with its rigid quadrangle and square towers, more Byzantine than Turkish. It is impossible also that this high point of the castle should not have been especially fortified in early Byzantine times. Since there is no sign or likelihood that its main body postdates the period of the Latin archbishops, one may suppose that the walls which stand today at least follow the line of an inner redout existing before the occupation of Guillaume Aleman.

A general survey shows the place to have been fortified in early post-classical times out of the spoils of ancient buildings. The whole north curtain, portions of the inner redout, the square stump of flanking tower and the piece of masked wall near the heptagonal

FIG. 147. PATRAS, THE KEEP: SOUTH FLANK AND INTERIOR ANGLE.

corner bastion, the face of the flanking tower with embedded statue, and several foundation courses along the south curtain all prove that the present circuit follows the same line as that built by the Byzantine Greeks to withstand the Slavic invasions.

A large part of the east and south curtains as they stand to-day belongs, probably, to the refortification of Patras under its Aleman,

FIG. 148. PATRAS, THE KEEP: INTERIOR OF THE WEST FLANK.

Acciajuoli, and other archiepiscopal overlords during the XIII and XIV centuries. The seven-year occupation by Venice at the beginning of the XV century has left the round bastion at the western angle, and perhaps the chamfered bastion within the keep. The second Greek period (1430–1460) probably saw the building of the oblique tower on the north face of the inner redout, and perhaps also the repaired flanks of the small tower with the embedded torso on the south side. The Turks added the entrance gate in the east side of the circuit, the heptagonal bastion, the talus adjacent to it on the west and portions of the curtain just beyond, a 40-foot stretch of thickened curtain near the west end, the upper half of the north curtain and the round tower at its mid-point, the 35-foot stretch reconditioned for artillery immediately to its east, and the parapets of all the curtains and towers of the circuit. The Venetians of 1700 added nothing, but only left the fortress in its state of advanced decay.

CHAPTER XII

THE CASTLE OF MOREA[1]

(PLATE XXX)

It was reported to Morosini that from the opposite shore of the Gulf of Corinth, or Gulf of Lepanto, a large number of small vessels were replenishing the Ottoman camp with provisions and supplies. In order to cut off this traffic it was necessary to pass under the batteries of the two castles planted at the narrow mouth of the Gulf, one the Castle of Romelia, the other the Castle of Morea. These are built like guardians of the entrance, but small and irregular, on the points of the two shores which curve toward each other, anciently known as the promontories of Rio and Antirio. These are removed one from the other not more than six hundred and twenty-five paces, the former in the Province of Aetolia, the latter in the confines of Locris. The Castle of Morea has rather the figure of a triangle. At its apex, facing directly north toward the Castle of Romelia, it has three bastions, and at the back a moat which divides and defends it from the land.[2]

On July 25, 1687, five days after the capture of Patras, the Venetian army occupied the Castles of Morea and Roumeli, with a store of 37 and 31 cannon apiece, which the Turks had abandoned, having blown up the sea front of Roumeli in their retreat.[3]

* * *

In the year 1499 the Sultan Bayezid II opened his campaign against the Venetians in Messenia with an action reminiscent of his predecessor, Mohammed the Conqueror, who before the siege of Constantinople had sealed both shores of the Bosporos with the forts of Rumili and Anadolu. In the space of three months Bayezid built twe fortresses, which became known as the Castles of Roumeli and Morea, at the two points where the mountainous ramparts of the Peloponnese and mainland Greece narrow together and sink into the low, opposing sandbars dividing the Gulf of Corinth from the Ionian Sea. With the development of artillery these fortresses were brought up to date successively by the Turks, the Venetians, and the French. Until 1715 they changed hands only once, and then without fighting or resistance.

The reports of the Venetian governors describe the vital importance of these positions. In 1690 Giacomo Corner writes:[4]

The Castle of Morea, descending to the sea shore in the lap of the marshy terrain, well fortified by a wall with double enclosure, and surrounded by the water which fills a broad ditch, will be always in a position to put up an excellent defense. Without doubt it would be well to consider enlarging some of the fortifications.

A year later the census-taker, Marino Michiel, speaks of the influx of Greeks from Levadia and Salona, received under Venetian protection, and assigned lands and houses at

---

[1] It was not possible to examine the architecture of this fortress which, during the time of writing, was serving a military purpose. The chapter is perforce incomplete.

[2] Garzoni, I, pp. 209f.

[3] Locatelli, I, pp. 332ff.

[4] Δελτίον, II, p. 309.

Castel di Morea.[5] Writing in 1701, Francesco Grimani[6] numbers it among the five chief maritime fortresses of the Peloponnese, and speaks of the recent construction of barracks, warehouses, and other buildings:

Angelo Emo[7] in his report of 1708 says that the Venetian Senate recognized the weakness of the fortress at Patras, when it "recently ordered the fortifications at the Castle of Morea," a site more advantageous both for

Fig. 149. Castle of Roumeli (Antirrhion), South End of the Enclosure and West Flank.

The Most Excellent Senate has received so many proposals from experts concerning the fortification of the Straits, every one of which expresses the necessity of a fort on either side, that I need add no further considerations of my own on the subject. On the Lepanto side this work will be much harder, though the need for it is equally, if not more pressing. For if that citadel (Naupaktos, taken by the Venetians also on July 25, 1687), together with the shores of Roumeli, goes back into the hands of the Turks, the Kingdom will possess no harbor for ships inside the Gulf. And in case (God wish it not) of new emergencies, a harbor will be indispensable for galleys and other ships to approach and anchor, safe from attack by land. The dredging of the old harbor (of Naupaktos), to make it serve the purpose, would involve the least expense. Building a mole elsewhere would be extremely expensive, although when the Castle of Morea is improved in the manner already indicated by me, as is being carried out with great urgency, it will need under its cannon at least a small port to provide some shelter for vessels along that exposed line of shore.

Venice's commerce and for the safety of the Greeks living hitherto undefended in the lower town at Patras. The report of Agostino Sagredo[8] lists the works completed:

Per il premunimento del Castello di Morea, che ha preso nome di nuova Fortezza, due furono li progetti, uno ristretto, l'altro esteso, ch'abbraciava di più del primo, un opera coronata; ma ricercando la stessa molta spesa, mezzi vigorosi, e più lungo tempo, fu creduto proprio rimetterla ad altra opportunità, e determinar in presente il ristretto proggeto, con due basse Tenaglie, e con l'aggiunta di due Rivelini, suo camin coperto, e spalto, con una larga contrafossa; operationi, che possono esser ultimate, prima della veniente campagna, quando non manchino li mezzi, onde il geloso posto s'attrovi in difesa. Tal'era la confidenza dell' Ecc.mo Sr Provr General del Regno Loredan, et in sue lettere me ne portò il motivo. Le muraglie del Recinto s'attrovavano quasi da pertutto ridotte al cordone, e non mancavano, che pochi passi di fondamenta al lato del mezzo Bastione verso il Mar, che copre la Porta, per giungere dal lato stesso al

[5] Sp. Lampros, Ἱστορικὰ Μελετήματα (Athens, 1884), p. 201.

[6] Δελτίον, V, p. 493.

[7] Ibid., V, p. 685.

[8] Ibid., V, pp. 748–750.

9*

vecchio Castello. Il terrapieno di esso s'era stabilito nella maggior parte. La Porta del soccorso del suo lato verso levante intieramente perfettionata, con tre gran Casematte: eretta la Piattaforma alla punta della linguetta. Le casematte, che corrono paralelle a' suoi lati, la maggior parte ridotte alla croppa del volto, e stabilito il Deposito da polvere. Era inalzato sino al cordone il terrapieno della faccia, a fianco dell' altro mezzo bastione fabricato per Ponente; nella gola del quale deve eriggersi un altro Deposito da polvere. La porta di sortita, dalla qual per via d'una gran Galeria, che traversa il ramparo si riferisce fuori dell' angolo del fianco dello stesso mezzo Bastione, era terminata, equalmente la sortita opposta all'angolo del fianco del Bastione di mezzo a cui solo mancava il terrapieno nella parte del fianco sinistro, dove non era compita la sua sortita. Le due basse tenaglie avanti le cortine

Giancix, il quale ha incontrato volentieri ogn' incomodo, et esercitate le parti del suo versato talento, et infervorato zelo, non solo nelle progettate idee, ma nella direttione, et effetto di esse, così a Romania per il Palamida, come con viaggi frequenti a Modon, al Castello di Morea, et altrove.[9]

This was written in November, 1714. The following year the Turks returned. The Castle of Morea was one of the five isolated fortresses from which the Venetians at that time were trying to defend the whole Peloponnese. But Corinth and Nauplia were quick to fall and the Castle of Morea surrendered after a five days' siege. The commandant received the honors of

FIG. 150. CASTLE OF MOREA (RHION), THE CHANNEL FRONT FROM THE NORTH.

erano a buon termine, e s'era dato principio alli parapetti. Era stabilito di tutto punto il gran Magazzeno, che corre paralello al lato della Fortezza, che fa fronte al Mare verso levante. Al Quartiere piantato presso il Magazzeno stesso, si travagliava nel colmo, et era fondamentato un altro Quartiere. Restavano da fabricarsi le casematte, lungo li due lati della Fortezza rivolti verso il Mare, e le altre casematte proposte per sostenere il ramparo, che deve farsi al lato dell'antico Castello, che forma una delle cortine del Recinto. Era in gran parte escavata la fossa, in tutta la sua lunghezza, fondamentato uno delli due revellini, e principiata la cisterna nella Piazza. Et a questo passo non devo tacer alla Serenità Vª il merito singolare, che si è conciliato il Sigᵣ Sargente General

war, but while terms were being discussed, a band of Janissaries entered the fortress and slaughtered a large number of soldiers and civilians. They were restrained from a general massacre, but the news of Turkish savagery spread through the Morea, hastening the fall of the last of the Venetian colonies.[10]

Nearly a century later in 1805, William Leake visited the place, and wrote:[11]

[9] For the role of the engineer, Giancix in the fortification of the Palamedi, see Gerola, *Napoli di Romania*, pp. 394–396.
[10] Cappelletti, XI, p. 159; Δελτίον, V, p. 804.
[11] *Morea*, II, pp. 147 ff.

I rode one afternoon to the castle of the Moréa, as the Turkish fortress on Cape *Rhium* is called. Like the castles of the Dardanelles, it contains an interior work which overlooks the outer. The inner is a circular fort with embrasures in the parapet, and appears much older than the exterior enclosure, which is quadrangular and fortified with ravelins on the two land fronts. If the inner castle originally stood on the shore, the sea has retired about 250 yards since it was built; at present there is a broad level between the shore and the outer wall, where boats might land and escalade the fortress. The reality of a gradual retreat of the sea is affirmed by the natives, and appears very probable ... At the opposite point of *Antirrhium* I am told that the retreat of the sea is not so rapid. The breadth of the strait appears to me to be little, if at all, short of a mile and a half ...

The castle of the Moréa is surrounded by marshes intermixed with a few plantations of currants, and the land-front is protected by a wet ditch communicating from sea to sea ... In short, it is a little Turkish fortified town, with a Greek suburb, situated, as usual, on the outside of the walls; I observed in the fortress several good English brass ordnance of the time of the Stuarts, — others of Venetian origin.

Pouqueville in 1816 found the fortress in bad repair, though belonging under the special jurisdiction of the Capitan Pasha, together with Antirrhion, the forty-three Aegean islands, the ports and narrows of Euboea, Naupaktos, and the peninsula of Mani. The Castle of Morea served as a barrier to foreign worships, none of which were allowed to enter the Corinthian Gulf. Pouqueville also mentions some marble fragments belonging to the temple of Poseidon, incorporated into the fortress walls.[12]

It was still an important position when Dodwell wrote of it in 1819:[13]

Part of the walls are washed by the sea. Here is a battery of large guns, a little above the level of the water, which might possibly be serviceable in case of emergency, but in the second tier I did not see a single gun mounted; everything, according to the custom of Turkish forts, is in disorder and neglect.

Within the walls there is a small mosque, and a few half ruined houses for the garrison. On the opposite side, on the Aetolian shore, the castle of Romelia is seen on a low projecting point ... Were these places properly fortified, the pass might be completely barred against an enemy.

In the War of Independence the Castle of Morea with its Turkish garrison held out to the end. After the Battle of Navarino the fortresses of New Navarino, Methone, Corone, and Patras accepted the capitulation imposed on Ibrahim Pasha by Marshal Maison. Only at Rhion the commanders of the fort refused to surrender. On October 10, 1828, the French and English expeditionary forces surrounded the place, and took up siege positions under the fire of the Turkish guns. On October 23 Maison arrived from Navarino to conduct the attack himself. Batteries were set up, and an ultimatum was sent to the defenders, who defiantly rejected it. The morning of October 30 the French and English delivered an artillery barrage which lasted four hours, and finally opened a breach. While the troops were preparing their assault, the place surrendered, and the Turkish crescent was lowered over the last fortress in the Peloponnese.[14]

The repairs undertaken by the French immediately after they occupied the place are described by one of the officers in charge:[15]

Le château de Morée, situé à la pointe la plus septentrionale du Péloponèse, sur l'un des côtés du détroit connu sous le nom de Petites Dardanelles, n'était primitivement composé que de quelques tours de diverses formes, réunies par des murs d'enceinte de deux mètres d'épaisseur, surmontés d'un faible parapet en maçonnerie.

Les Vénitiens voulant donner à ce château toute la force réclamée par l'importance de sa position, jetèrent en avant un bastion et trois demi-bastions qu'ils réunirent par des courtines; deux demi-lunes couvrirent les fronts opposés à la mer; un large fossé plein d'eau les préceda, et un chemin couvert à glacis coupés, précédé lui-même d'un fossé, entoura tous ces ouvrages.

Ce fut probablement au commencement du dix-huitième siècle que ces constructions furent entre-

[12] *Voyage*, IV, p. 399 and note.

[13] *A Classical and Topographical Tour through Greece* (London, 1819), I, p. 125.

[14] Mangeart, *Souvenirs de la Morée*, pp. 76 ff., 400; M. A. Duheaume, *Souvenirs de la Morée* (Paris, 1833), pp. 40–45; G. Finlay, *History of the Greek Revolution* (Edinburgh, 1861), II, pp. 192 f.

[15] Quoted in Mangeart, *op. cit.*, pp. 321–325.

prises, comme semble l'indiquer une inscription latine placée au-dessus de la porte de mer, ouverte dans le nouveau fort. Cette inscription est presque entièrement effacée; mais, avec quelque attention, on reconnaît qu'elle était ainsi conçue:

PORTA SALUS CASTRI AUXILIIS INTRANTIBUS
ARTE
INGRESSUM PANDIT MILITIBUS QUE LEO
ANNO DOMINI 1713.

Ces fortifications furent-elles totalement achevées par leurs auteurs et détériorées seulement par l'incurie des Turcs, ou bien étaient-elles encore imparfaites lorsque ceux-ci en devinrent les maîtres? Ce qu'il y a de certain c'est que les parapets en maçonnerie des demi-lunes et des bastions étaient, à l'époque du dernier siège, en assez bon état, mais que les chemins couverts étaient presque entièrement effacés, ce qui donnait la faculté de voir de loin les escarpes, et permit de faire deux brèches praticables avec une batterie située à cinquante mètres des saillants les plus avancés.

Après avoir relevé ces brèches, afin de mettre la place à l'abri d'un coup de main, la chose la plus importante était de chercher à dérober les escarpes aux coups de la campagne; c'est à quoi les ingénieurs français se sont appliqués en reconstruisant les chemins couverts du front sur lequel on a dernièrement dirigé les attaques.

Cet ouvrage est maintenant tout-à-fait terminé, et, dès à présent, les brèches aux faces des bastions de ce front seraient impossibles à faire, de l'emplacement si judicieusement assigné aux batteries de Charles X et de Georges IV, qui ouvrirent la place en quatre heures. Il faudrait aujourd'hui, pour faire ces brèches, traverser un avant-fossé, couronner le chemin couvert et descendre dans son terre-plein, pour établir une batterie, car le parapet de cet ouvrage, qui est une véritable contregarde, est trop étroit pour recevoir des pièces. Toutes ces opérations seraient si difficiles qu'elles retarderaient considérablement la prise de la place, si toutefois elles ne dégoûtaient pas tout-à-fait l'assiégeant d'une entreprise si longue et si périlleuse.

Quoique l'autre front de terre fût moins attaquable que le précédent, on continua le chemin couvert jusqu'à la partie la plus orientale de la place, ce qui n'empêcha pas de s'occuper d'autres réparations et améliorations plus pressantes; ainsi, on a relevé les parapets des demi-lunes et du corps de place. Celui du demi-bastion de l'ouest, qui avait presque entièrement été détruit pendant le siège, a été construit en terre; ce bastion pourra désormais être défendu avec plus de succès qu'auparavant, parce que les boulets, qui finissent par détruire des parapets en maçonnerie, et en enlèvent d'abord des éclats fort dangereux pour les défenseurs, se perdent d'une maniere inoffensive dans des masses de terre.

Cette amélioration pourra par la suite se faire dans les autres ouvrages du fort, quoique leur peu de capacité y puisse présenter quelque obstacle; mais pour le moment on a dû se contenter de réparer les parapets actuels en maçonnerie, pour mettre le plus promptement possible la place en état de défense. On a seulement eu l'attention de remplacer, autant qu'on l'a pu, la pierre par des briques dont les éclats sont bien moins dangereux pour les défenseurs que ceux de la maçonnerie ordinaire.

Outre ces travaux qui doubleront les moyens de défense du château, le génie s'est occupé de la réparation des bâtiments jugés propres au service: ainsi il a transformé en caserne pour trois cents hommes le premier étage d'un grand magasin, dont il a refait en entier la toiture; il a réparé trois magasins à poudre, en a disposé un quatrième dans l'une des nombreuses casemates du fort ...

CHAPTER XIII

CORINTH

(Plates XXXI, XXXII)

After the fall of Patras, Naupaktos, and the Castles of Morea and Roumeli, the Seraskier withdrew in haste to Corinth. When Morosini arrived a week later, on August 1, 1687, only a rearguard of the Turks was left, spreading the usual desolation of an army on the retreat. The powder-stores in the castle were exploded; the houses in the lower town destroyed. There was no siege, for Acrocorinth was empty. The Seraskier had fled to Thebes, abandoning the Peloponnese to a few pockets of resistance.[1]

*   *   *

Acrocorinth comes second to the Acropolis at Athens as the oldest continuously inhabited citadel in Greece. In pagan times there existed a fortress which encompassed the entire mountain top, sections of whose foundations are to be found throughout the circuit of the medieval defenses. The classical remains belong chiefly to the IV century before Christ. The size of the mountain and the absence of relevant sherds argue against Mycenaean origins, but certain stretches of rough polygonal masonry suggest that Acrocorinth may have been fortified in the age of the Cypselid tyrants in the VII or VI century.[2] During the period of prosperity which followed the Persian Wars, the city walls were rebuilt. In 243 Aratos of Sikyon with 400 Achaeans succeeded in capturing the mountain citadel from the Macedonians in a daring night assault up the cliffs to a point where the wall was only 15 feet high.[3] In 146 B.C. the armies of Rome entered Greece in order, like other invaders after them, to impose their own dominion over the factional strife between its cities and their various leagues. Corinth, the most strongly defended city in the Peloponnese, was sacked by order of the Roman Senate, whose general, Mummius, also demolished the fortifications of its acropolis. The widening circle of Roman expansion included now a subjugated Greece. Local fortification was forbidden, and existing strongholds dismantled within the boundaries of the Empire.

Five centuries later, when these same boundaries were breaking up, permission was once more granted to raise walls around the cities of the Roman world. Investigation in the lower town at Corinth has revealed the existence of

[1] Locatelli, I, p. 338; Garzoni, I, pp. 212f.; Prodocimo, *Successi dell' Armi*, p. 77; *Il Regno della Morea*, p. 84.

[2] See R. Carpenter, "The Classical Fortifications of Acrocorinth," *Corinth*, III, ii, pp. 1–43.

[3] Plutarch, *Aratus*, xvii, 4; xxi–xxii. See also *Corinth*, III, ii, p. 43, n. 2, where Professor Carpenter identifies the point of Aratos' entrance as the northeast headland of the mountain, where a couloir affords an ascent up the eastern cliffs of the north gulley (see *Frontispiece*, left).

a powerful wall dating from the IV century after Christ.[4] In the VI century Justinian was constrained to give up the complete defense of borders and turn to the protection of separate internal portions of his empire: particularly, in Greece, at the two main bottlenecks along the traditional routes of invasion, the pass of Thermopylae and the Isthmus of Corinth. The record exists[5] of the building of a wall sealing the six-mile passage overland between the Saronic and Corinthian Gulfs. Though no mention is made of Acrocorinth itself, it is unlikely that the architectural energy of Justinian would have neglected this chief obstacle to an attack of the peninsula.[6]

In 583–6 the Peloponnese was invaded by the Slavs. A century and a half later the country was swept by plague, and the Slavs entered in a second wave. In 743 the Byzantine general, Stavrakios, failed in an attempt against them. It was not till 805, with the defeat of the Slavs by the Greeks at Patras, that Byzantine authority was reintroduced into the Morea. Restored to the Empire, Corinth was made capital of the Theme of the Peloponnese, and became the seat of its ecclesiastical and military headquarters. It resisted the two Bulgarian invasions of 981 and 995, and during the XII century Edrisi and Benjamin of Tudela noted the city's commercial prosperity and the trade that flourished at its ports on either gulf. In 1147 the fortress fell to a band of raiding Normans under Roger II of Sicily, more through the fright of its commander than through weakness in its defenses. In return for help against these Normans, the Byzantine Emperor granted special trading rights to the Venetians in Corinth, among other cities of the Empire.

In 1203 Leon Sgouros, lord of Nauplia, possessed himself of Acrocorinth, to which he retired on falling back from Thermopylae, where he had planned to resist the conquest of Greece by the Frankish crusaders. Boniface of Montferrat descended through Thessaly to Corinth, Argos, and Nauplia. While the Peloponnese fell to a band of Frankish knights, Acrocorinth resisted a siege lasting five years. Sgouros made a sortie in which one of the besiegers, Jacques d' Avesnes, was wounded. The Franks built a small fort on the hill of Pendeskouphi three quarters of a mile to the southwest, to cover the main defenses of the castle, and another on a low hill guarding its eastern ascent. In 1210 Leon Sgouros committed suicide by riding his horse off the top of the cliffs, and Acrocorinth fell to Othon de la Roche, Duke of Athens, and Geoffroy I Villehardouin, Prince of Frankish Achaea.

During the first half of the XIII century Acrocorinth remained a fief of the Villehardouin family, and until 1250 contained the mint of the Principality. In the middle of the century its fortifications were augmented among the architectural works undertaken by William Villehardouin. The importance of the place increased as a Frankish stronghold when the Greeks once more established themselves in the southeastern corner of the Peloponnese. In 1311 it assumed a role it was to hold, off and on, until 1460, a frontier post for the Franks against the Catalans, then for the Byzantines against the Turks, and once again for the Venetians at the turn of the XVIII century. In 1324 Acrocorinth was refortified by the Angevin Prince of Achaea, John of Gravina, and in 1358 passed by deed from the Prince, Robert of Taranto, to Niccolò Acciajuoli, whose wealth and power, it was hoped, would protect the district against Albanian and Turkish raids. After 1385 Acrocorinth fell to secondary rank as a dependency of Nerio Acciajuoli, who seized the Athenian Duchy from the Catalans. The castle fell rapidly into

---

[4] *Corinth*, III, ii, p. 127.

[5] Prokopios, *De Aedificiis*, ed. Bonn, pp. 272f.

[6] For the history of Corinth during the Middle Ages and the description of its medieval fortifications, I am indebted to Professor Antoine Bon. This chapter is mainly a condensation of his exhaustive study: "The Medieval Fortifications of Acrocorinth and Vicinity," *Corinth*, III, ii, pp. 128–281.

FIG. 152. ACROCORINTH, BYZANTINE CISTERN.

ascents between the cliffs on the north and northeast, a slightly gentler, though more open gradient along the south, and a long, sloping approach from a saddle on the western side.

The north and west sections of the classical Greek fortress would have been those most thoroughly destroyed by Mummius in 146 B.C. (though the whole face of one Hellenic tower [Fig. 160, left] still stands among the west defenses), and correspondingly the first to be rebuilt when the subjects of Rome began once more to seek refuge on heights of land. The screen wall at the head of the north gulley is among the earliest of these post-classical defenses, built with care in its lower sections, of large ashlar blocks re-set from some ruined classical building. Piercing this wall is a postern gate, vaulted, and on the outer face square-topped with an enormous lintel block (Fig. 151). The foundations of the lookout

FIG. 153. ACROCORINTH, THIRD LINE OF DEFENSE, FROM THE SOUTH.

tower on the highest peak and a great, brick-vaulted cistern within the circuit (Fig. 152) belong also to the period of Justinian or his predecessors.

The Slavic invasions marked a time of destruction and disuse, after which fragments from earlier Byzantine buildings appear in the fabric of the walls. To this period belong, in the west defenses, the original two-storey con-

To the two centuries of the Frankish occupation belong a number of important constructions and the major part of the circuit wall as it now stands. The small fort of Pendeskouphi (*Frontispiece*, right) dates to the years of the Frankish siege, 1205–1210. The square keep in two storeys with its subsidiary courts on the mountain's southwest peak (Fig. 156) belongs to the time of William Villehardouin, who

FIG. 154. ACROCORINTH, PASSAGEWAY OF THIRD GATE.

FIG. 155. ACROCORINTH, FLANKING TOWER IN SOUTH CURTAIN.

struction of the second gate, with its doorways and windows topped by marble colonnettes for lintels; the original, half-masked second wall south of the gate, built of re-used classical and small, squared blocks alternating with heavy tile courses; the small outwork sealing off a ledge north of the second line; and most of the third line of defense, with its great, square, barrel-vaulted flanking towers (Fig. 153) built on the scale of the towers of Antiquity, with archer-slots, like them, for windows; and the inner third gate with its ashlar-vaulted passageway, portcullis-shaft, and column-lintels (Fig. 154). Also Byzantine, earlier than the XIII century, is the main body of the curtain wall in the southeastern sector, including a small, square flanking tower built of rectangular poros blocks and re-used classical and Byzantine elements, with a narrow archer-slot in the face (Fig. 155).

according to the Aragonese version of the *Chronicle of the Morea* built himself a residence at Acrocorinth. Its masonry of small, trimmed blocks and broken brick, its pyramidal base and vaulted doorway closely resemble Villehardouin's donjon at Mistra. The northeast outwork may belong to the same period. The first of the three gates on the western side (Figs. 158, 160) with its adjacent wall extending northwest, is Frankish of the early XIV century. The boldly protruding arc formed by the curtain in the northeast sector, and the two outworks on the east are distinguished by the absence of early Byzantine material between the classical base and the medieval superstructure, as well as by small, narrow, solid, square or polygonal towers, broad merlons with alternate loopholes, vaulted and tapering openings at the interior ground level, and a masonry of carefully set angles and coursed, rectangular blocks, in which the use of large, flat tile gives an impression of contemporary Byzantine authorship. From 1358 to 1394, however, the castle was in the hands of the strong and wealthy Acciajuoli, who may have been responsible for the works

holes, unique among the castle's ramparts, may also be an indication of the Knights' brief tenure. The artillery parapets in the northern and southern wings of the third line, with their shallow emplacements for short-range cannon, would belong likewise to the early XV century.

FIG. 156. ACROCORINTH, KEEP AND EAST WALL OF REDOUT.

in this sector. It is unlikely that the Despot Theodore, whose cession of Acrocorinth to the Knights of Rhodes was an act of desperation, would have added much to the fortifications during the first six years of his possession. The Knights, on the other hand, may well have put their new prize into a state of defense with the addition of such works as the heavy north section of the second line (Fig. 159), built as a firing platform for artillery now in common use. The particular style of its uniform, slightly battering wall face, unmarked by scaffold

What the later Byzantines may have added to Acrocorinth is hard to tell, although by the fatal year 1458 it was sufficiently strong to withstand for three months the siege of the Sultan Mohammed.

Turkish activity during the XV, XVI, and XVII centuries seems to have been largely confined to works of repair and the building of mosques inside the circuit. The rectangular tower at the north end of the outermost line (Fig. 158, left), with its parapet in two levels for artillery below and small arms above, to-

Fig. 157. Acrocorinth, from the West.

Fig. 158. Acrocorinth, First Line, Hollow Tower and Artillery Bastion at North End.

gether with its tall and double-notched merlons resembles the elaborate, fussy Turkish parapets at Patras, despite the careful, tool-marked ashlar of its wall faces, which would ordinarily appear Venetian. The southern half of the same first line ends in a bastion built of the distant pathway that winds up from Old Corinth and the hamlet of Anaplogha (*Frontispiece*, lower right), far out of range of the musketry of the period. Both the construction, orientation, and masonry, in which the helter-skelter appearance of broken brick

FIG. 159. ACROCORINTH, SECOND GATE AND NORTH HALF OF SECOND LINE.
IN THE BACKGROUND, THIRD LINE AND NORTHWEST BATTERY.

against the cliff, made of finely squared poros and limestone blocks, set in regular courses interspersed with broken tile. The irregular quadrangle of this bastion is terrepleined only on the inner side; paved to provide a gun platform, to which cannon could be dragged up a ramp to an embrasure in its west face. This has a wide angle of fire and a steep pitch to cover the approach to the first gate some 70 feet beneath it (Fig. 158). In the same face of the parapet is a loophole 5 feet deep, of the sort found most frequently in Turkish fortifications. The north parapet contains four similar loopholes, impractically placed in the direction

and tile contrasts with the tidiness of the actual blocks, seem less Venetian than Turkish. The whole outer line of defense appears on the Grimani plans, but without any designation of *progettato* or *fatto da nuovo* to indicate Venetian authorship. In fact the only recommendation for this line is contained in its description on Plate XXXII as an "enclosure to be destroyed."

By 1687 the entire fortress had fallen into disrepair, as we may learn from the quantity and urgency of the recommendations on these plans. The Venetians responded to the challenge as best they could. The two chief needs were restoration of the walls, which the Turks had not even tried to defend, and the rebuilding of artillery parapets in the one sector where artillery availed. The Venetians repeated the example of their classical Greek, Byzantine, and Frankish predecessors by con-

after the drawing of the Grimani plans) cut a moat out of the rock, which descends from the southwestern cliffs, turns a right angle, and ends against a lower line of cliffs some 300 feet to the north. The scarp is made of small ashlar

FIG. 160. ACROCORINTH, THE WEST DEFENSES.

centrating on the defenses of the crucial western side. Here they added parapets containing five embrasures on the second line north of the gate, thirteen embrasures on the wall and towers of the third line, seven more in the northwest sector of the curtain (Fig. 161), and four in an artillery platform built on to the west end of the Frankish redout (Fig. 162). This work is made of squared, tool-marked blocks, and contains a small store-room with a ceiling cast on a wooden form, with a sentry-box set in the parapet. Outside the first line of defense the Venetians also (but

blocks, with a characteristic Venetian batter and chamfered corner. Two stout piers (Fig. 160) on both sides of the ditch originally carried a wooden bridge. The second gate was strengthened with the addition of a new façade against the lower storey (Fig. 159), built of poros ashlar, pierced by an arched doorway framed in a double molding. Above it are three ornamental features: four stone cannon projecting from the wall, a niche, now empty, for the Lion of St. Mark, and a torus molding that marks a retreating batter to the original wall face. Flanking the gate on the west side is a large, square tower on a pyramidal base, occupying the site of an earlier edifice whose much wider foundations extend around it. The tower is also of poros ashlar, with an admixture of broken brick and marble, stone cannon decorating its face and flanks. Torus moldings mark the top of the base and the level of the gun platform above. Though similar both in masonry and construction to the two end bastions of the first line, this building may have been added by the Venetians in response to the request of Giacomo Corner for a "work to cover the gate."

The activity of the Venetians on Acrocorinth is unambitious in comparison to their other works at Methone, Corone, and Nauplia. Here, as in most of the castles of the Morea, the more extensive schemes for refortification belonged to the imagination, like the dream of the past in which they had undertaken their conquest.

FIG. 161. ACROCORINTH, ARTILLERY PARAPET, NORTHWEST BATTERY. PENDESKOUPHI IN THE DISTANCE.

FIG. 162. ACROCORINTH, VENETIAN ARTILLERY PLATFORM, SOUTHWEST ANGLE OF CASTLE CIRCUIT.

CHAPTER XIV

CHLEMOUTSI

(Plate XXXIII)

On August 3, 1687, the castle of Chlemoutsi, or Castel Tornese, surrendered without a fight to the Venetians, giving up a store of 34 cannon. The garrison was evacuated to Smyrna, but 150 Turks remained behind and were baptized. In the space of a fortnight Morosini had peacefully acquired all the northern Peloponnese.[1]

* * *

The castle owed its building to a feud between Geoffrey I Villehardouin and the Latin clerics of the Principality of Achaea.[2] When all the Morea had come under Frankish domination, Monemvasia alone still held out in the hands of the Greeks. In 1220 Geoffrey's barons pointed out to him that the Latin clergy of the Principality, who "sit at ease and take their rest, and have no fear of battle," were in possession of almost a third of the Prince's lands. Geoffrey called upon the bishops, priests, and knightly orders to compensate for military service by contributing out of this abundance to concerted action against the last Greek stronghold. They replied that they owed him nothing more than allegiance; their possessions they held from the Pope. Geoffrey answered by confiscating their fiefs. The Pope excommunicated him, but he immediately put his new revenues to use by building the castle of Chlemoutsi. In 1223, when the fortress was completed, Geoffrey sent an embassy of minor friars and two knights to lay the case before Honorius III in Rome. The conquest of the Morea, they claimed, the establishment there of the Latin rite, and the building of the new castle to protect the shores and chief harbor of the realm were all acts in the cause of the Roman Church against the schismatic Greeks.

---

[1] Locatelli, I, p. 341; *Il Regno della Morea*, p. 85.

[2] That it was Geoffrey I, and not his son and successor, Geoffrey II, who was the protagonist in the clerical controversy of 1220–1223, is demonstrated by Longnon in an article, "Problèmes de l'histoire de la principauté de Morée" (second part), *Journal des Savants*, July–December 1946, pp. 157–159. A summary of his argument runs as follows: Buchon in *Recherches et Matériaux* (followed by Hopf and Miller) places the date of Geoffrey I's death in 1218, shortly before the controversy, on the ground that he could not be excommunicated twice — Honorius III had already excommunicated and absolved him in 1218 — without mention being made of it in the papal correspondence; that consequently it must be another Geoffrey, his son, whose rash opposition to the Church is a sign of his youthfulness. This reasoning does not hold, however, in the case of Othon de la Roche, excommunicated by Honorius both in 1217 and later, together with Geoffrey, in 1220–1223. In this case neither is it a matter of youthfulness, nor was any reminder made of his earlier excommunication. In 1222 Honorius ordered the excommunication of "G. Prince of Achaea, G. his son, and his vassals." Again in 1223, when peace was made between them, Honorius took under his protection "G. de Villehardouin, Prince of Achaea, his wife and his sons, his land, and all his possessions." This must refer to Geoffrey I, since the *Chron-icle of the Morea* states that Geoffrey II was childless. Accordingly we must believe, contrary to what has been hitherto written on the subject, that Geoffrey I was still alive at the time of the controversy, and that it was he who built Chlemoutsi.

Honorius perforce lifted his interdict, and the Prince and clergy of Achaea agreed to help each other in the common effort.[3]

The Villehardouins held the territory of Elis for their princely domain, with their capital at Andravida, called Andreville, their port at Glarentza, and two strong fortresses near by at Katakolo, called Beauvoir, and Chlemoutsi, which was also gallicized into Clermont. These four places fall within a radius of 16 miles, situated on the westernmost promontory of the Peloponnese. It was believed that at Chlemoutsi William Villehardouin established the mint of the Principality, with license accorded by his suzerain, King Louis IX,[4] to issue the coins common in France at the time, the *tournois*, stamped with the Church of St. Martin of Tours and the inscription *G. Princeps Achaee de Clarentia*, which were the currency of the Frankish Morea from 1250 to 1333.[5] The Venetians in the XVI century gave Chlemoutsi the name of Castel Tornese, supposing it to have once contained the Frankish mint, an assumption due probably to the frequent confusion of Chlemoutsi with Glarentza. On the death of William Villehardouin in 1278, Chlemoutsi, with Kalamata, passed to his widow for life.[6]

In 1313 there arose one of the disputes over the succession to the Principality, which characterized the waning rule of the Franks in the Morea during the XIV century. The granddaughter of William Villehardouin was married to Louis, younger brother of the Duke of Burgundy, who in the absence of male heirs succeeded Philip I of Taranto as Prince of Achaea. However, before he arrived in his new domain, William's younger daughter, Marguerite, who held the barony of Akova in the Morea, menaced by personal enemies, all Burgundian partisans, asserted her own claim

to the inheritance of the Villehardouins. She married her daughter to Ferdinand of Majorca, one of the leaders of the Catalan Grand Company, who two years before had inflicted the disastrous defeat on the French nobles at the Kephissos, and who now claimed the Morea himself in his wife's name. The barons of Achaea confiscated Marguerite's possessions, for the crime of giving her daughter to the Catalans, and imprisoned her in Chlemoutsi, where she died soon after. Ferdinand in 1314 landed with Catalan troops at Glarentza, captured Chlemoutsi and Katakolo, and for a brief space forced the Burgundian party to recognize him as overlord. In 1316 Louis of Burgundy finally arrived in the Morea. Joined by all the barons of Achaea and by an army of Greeks from Mistra with whom he had made an alliance, he defeated and slew Ferdinand at Manolada in Elis. The Catalan garrison at Glarentza surrendered, and the Achaean fortresses which still remained to the dwindling Principality reverted to the hands of its Angevin rulers.[7]

In the last days of Achaea, Glarentza passed to Carlo I Tocco, Count Palatine of Cephalonia and Despot of Epiros. Constantine Palaiologos attacked it in 1427 during his final campaign against the Franks, and then obtained it peacefully by marrying Tocco's daughter, who brought it with her as her dowry. He also took possession of Chlemoutsi, which he made his headquarters, in preparation for the attack on Patras. After that city fell in 1430, a fleet of galleys sent by the Pope too late to aid in its defense, captured Glarentza for a short time. Constantine bought it back, and then had it systematically destroyed, to prevent its giving shelter to an enemy again.[8] Wheler, who visited the ruined city in 1674, noted the hard cement of the walls, which only gunpowder could have dislodged.[9] To-day its only remains are a few

[3] X. τ. M., lines 2626–2720; *C. di M.*, pp. 434f.

[4] Marino Sanudo, "Istoria del Regno di Romania," in Hopf, *Chroniques gréco-romanes*, p. 102.

[5] G. Schlumberger, *Numismatique de l'Orient latin* (Paris, 1878), p. 312, plate XII; *Corinth*, VI, pp. 152–156.

[6] Miller, *Latins*, pp. 87, 102, 147, 268.

[7] *Ibid.*, pp. 251–256, 287.

[8] *Ibid.*, p. 388.

[9] *Journey into Greece*, p. 290.

10*

masses of masonry standing among cultivated fields, and a long ditch which marked the city's limits.[10]

Chlemoutsi by 1700 had lost its old importance. It served for the Venetians as the capital of their fiscal district of Elis, though Corner's

FIG. 163. CHLEMOUTSI, THE CASTLE FROM THE NORTHEAST.

report of 1690 dismisses it as small in size and hardly inhabited.[11] In 1701 Grimani wrote:[12]

In addition to improving the chief places already standing, it might be well to consider building a new fortress at Chiarenza, where the remains of the ancient city are still to be seen. A number of reasons make me press this suggestion, provided it is not contrary to the conditions of the peace of Carlovitz. Your subjects would have safer refuge in such a place than in Castel Tornese, which in this case should be destroyed, being too far from the sea, and incapable of enduring a siege unless considerable money were invested in adding to its defenses. Nor would a new fortress place greater demands on the garrison, since the number which now occupies Castel Tornese would suffice there too. It would enjoy the facilities of relief by sea, since there still remain the traces of a sizeable harbor, which would offer shelter for large ships without danger and with less trouble than in any other part of those shores. It would be the richest and most fruitful center of commerce, being the closest to Venice, and the closest also to the Islands, which would be the

FIG. 164. CHLEMOUTSI, THE OUTER GATE, INTERIOR VIEW.

[10] Viz. Traquair, "Mediaeval Fortresses of the North-Western Peloponnesus," *B.S.A.*, XIII, 1906–1907, p. 272.

[11] Δελτίον, II, p. 308; V, p. 231.
[12] *Ibid.*, V, pp. 484f.

first to provide trade. Moreover the population, so much desired, would increase with time, both through the healthiness of the air,which is perfect, and through the profit of abundant commerce, such as flourished there once under the famous domination of the Greeks.

Castel Tornese lay three miles inland, and hardly suited Venice's maritime purposes. Already five centuries old, it was no longer defensible in the age of artillery warfare.

* * *

It remains to-day, however, a striking example of a Frankish castle of the first years of the Latin Principality. It comprises a hexagonal keep enclosing a courtyard, built on a high hill (Fig. 163), with an outer enclosure extending round its more gradual slope, commanding a view over the Ionian Sea, the promontory of Chelonatas, and to the east the plains of Elis and Achaea.

The entrance gate (Figs. 164, 165, 166) is placed in the northwest side (Plate XXXIII, A. *Porta principal della Fortezza*). Originally it consisted of a pylon set in a deep, narrow recess of the curtain wall, containing a passage-

FIG. 165. CHLEMOUTSI. THE OUTER GATE.

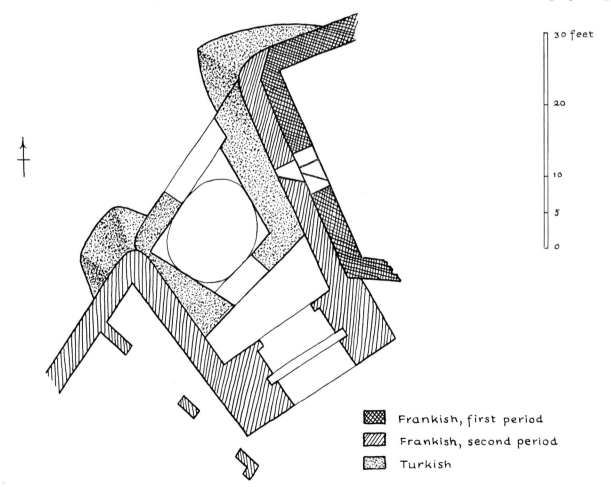

30 feet

20

10

5

0

Frankish, first period

Frankish, second period

Turkish

FIG. 166. CHLEMOUTSI, PLAN OF THE OUTER GATE.

way, 12 feet long by 9 wide, built of great, squared poros blocks, divided by a groove for portcullis, and covered with a depressed vault of smaller poros voussoirs. The space recessed between the two angles of the curtain was filled subsequently by a small, irregular quadrangle of walls with depressed archways in the outer and inner sides, covered by a low dome of small squared blocks, similar to the saucer domes in the sea bastion at New Navarino. This is a Turkish addition, which provides an unbroken front to the curtain. The

FIG. 167. CHLEMOUTSI, INTERIOR OF NORTH CURTAIN, CONTAINING FIREPLACE AND LANCET WINDOW; TURKISH CRENELLATIONS ABOVE.

juncture of its outer wall with the two points of the corners of the recess is strengthened at the bottom by stoutly battering buttresses. Between it and the vaulted passage a space is left open to the sky.

The northeast sector of the outer curtain gradually ascends the hill in three straight stretches broken by obtuse angles, up to the inner redout. The wall is made of well fitted blocks of rough-cut limestone, which here and there approximate coursing. There is little broken brick or tile. It supports a narrow chemin de ronde bordered by a small inner wall and an outer parapet now largely ruined. This is Turkish, built of square, alternately slotted merlons with steeply pointed copes and crenels with sloping sills, built with a large quantity of broken tile. The outer curtain is pierced by a number of lancet windows (Fig. 167) of a pattern reminiscent of French Romanesque, which helps to date it to the original building of the castle. The curtain appears from the beginning to have provided the back wall for buildings ranged all along it on the north, east and west sides. The windows indicate this, as well as numerous foundations and partition walls, bonding with the curtain, which project from it at right angles. Next to the outer gate, on the east side, is a well preserved specimen of a building dating from the early XIII century. It measures 30 by 100 feet, with the gable ends and the long inner wall still standing to their original height. The stretch of curtain forming the back wall contains three lancet windows with flaring sides and sloping, tapering vaults of poros voussoirs. Two of these are round-topped. One has a pointed arch. A fourth window at the east end of the building is topped with three big, rectangular slabs laid side by side. In the middle, between the two round lancets, is a fireplace: a wide recess filled with a concave backing of brick, with sides of small, cut poros blocks, inclining toward each other, like the lower half of a pointed arch, under the chemin de ronde (Fig. 167, left).

Seven such fireplaces appear along the outer curtain, and four more within the inner redout. Some are built with square recesses, others are concave, but all show the uniformity of construction characteristic of all the details of the fortress. The south or inner wall of the long building next to the gate stands in a fragmentary condition, with breaches marking the site of windows. Near the top, however, are three rectangular openings, measuring 6 by 12 inches, set each within a small embrasure built

which there remains only the lintel block, incised in a distinctive manner to fit over jambs with drafted edges (Fig. 168). These are missing, leaving a breach of masonry, which reveals a loophole built in the east wall of the recess itself. And this in its turn is blocked by the

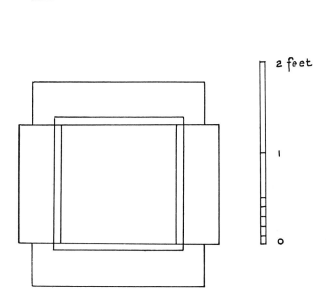

FIG. 168. CHLEMOUTSI, WEST FLANK OF HOUSE BUILT WITHIN THE OUTER GATE, SHOWING WINDOWS BLOCKED BY LATER CONSTRUCTIONS.

FIG. 169. CHLEMOUTSI, CONSTRUCTION OF WINDOWS AND NICHES IN OUTER CURTAIN.

with flat top, tapering sides, and inward sloping sill. On the outside of the wall these are encased in four cut poros blocks with bevelled edges. The short west wall of the building extends along the east side of the recess which forms the entrance gate, its south corner penetrating part of the flank of the gate pylon. This west gable end contains in its upper half a small loophole, blocked and rendered obsolete by the side wall of the recess built against it. Directly below this loophole is a window, of

later insertion of the domed quadrangle. The long building must then antedate the recessed wall of the curtain and the pylon of the gate which was built round its west gable end and blocked up both its windows. An opening was subsequently pushed through the wall of the recessed curtain to allow the lower of these to function, as a vantage point against an attacker entering the narrow throat of the gateway. But this window, too, was put out of use by the insertion of the Turkish dome. Further east, the foundation walls of other houses may be traced along the curtain, which contains more lancet windows, fireplaces, and small niches encased in cut poros with bevelled and drafted edges (Fig. 169).

On the east side the curtain rises up the hill to join the hexagon of inner walls crowning the summit. Near the top, the wall forms a jog, as shown on the plan. The angle here is built square at ground level, but in its upper portion becomes gradually rounded, forming as it were the sector of a tower, whose curve follows up into the single slotted merlon standing above it. At the top of the outer curtain, immediately beneath the entrance to the inner redout is a postern (Plate XXXIII, C). This is a low, depressed passageway, similar in shape to that in the outer gate, with vault and side walls of big poros blocks. Next to it, parallel to the front of the inner enclosure, is

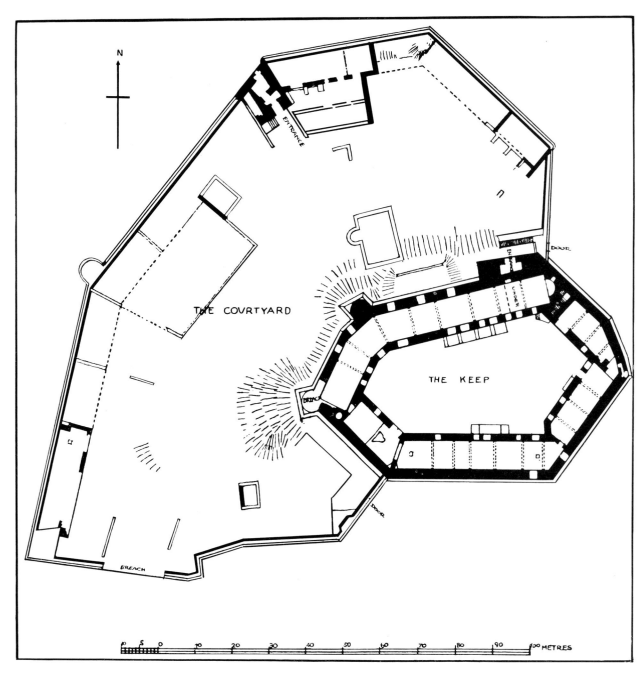

FIG. 170. CHLEMOUTSI, PLAN OF THE FORTRESS. *From B. S. A., XIII, 1906—1907, p. 274, fig. 5.*

a flight of steps with a parapet running up its north side, leading to the chemin de ronde.

The curtain in the western sector also provided the back wall for buildings contemporary with it, as shown by the presence of clean-cut, poros-arched lancet windows and brick-fitted fireplaces. Some of the windows have sloping vaults and flaring sides. In others the sides are parallel and the vaults horizontal. Two hundred feet west of the outer gate is a round tower, 20 feet in diameter, with a chamfered string course molding round its waist. The lower portion is built with a slight talus. Its walls do not bond with the curtain, and since it figures on the Grimani drawing, it may be considered a Turkish addition of the artillery period. The western corner of the enceinte is an acute angle, wrongly drawn as obtuse on the Grimani plan,[13] pointed at ground level and rounded in the upper portion. A terrepleined bastion is built into the corner. Its walls do not bond with the curtain, and it is probably another Turkish addition. On top, the corner of the parapet contains a few voussoirs originally belonging to some small domed structure, turret or sentry-box. Near this western angle, the south flank of the enclosure contains the breach made by the guns of Ibrahim Pasha in 1825.[14] From here to within 12 feet of the western angle, the wall is marked by long, parallel courses of broken tile between the stones, in a style of masonry commonly Byzantine or Turkish. The Turkish parapet above it contains wide, square, alternately slotted merlons of sloppily assembled rubble and broken tile, with steeply pitched copes. On the exterior there is no perceptible difference in masonry between the parapet and the wall itself. The whole stretch looks to be Turkish repair.

Half way along the south flank, the curtain jogs back 15 feet. The angle of the wall is

[13] For references of orientation see the plan by Traquair given in Fig. 170.

[14] P. Kalonaros, "Khlémoutsi," *L'Hellénisme contemporain*, II, 1936, p. 177.

rounded, like the outer corners of the recessed walls of the main gate. Here another Turkish structure in the form of a square tower is fitted into the re-entrant angle formed by the jog, its face flush with the outer section of the curtain wall. Its salient corner is built with

FIG. 171. CHLEMOUTSI, SOUTH CURTAIN, OUTER ENCLOSURE, LOOKING TOWARD THE WESTERN ANGLE.

squared limestone blocks at the bottom, but proceeds to a curve toward the top, perhaps in imitation of the west angle of the outer curtain and the small jog on the east side. Within the tower is a chamber 8 by 10 feet wide, covered by a saucer dome of square blocks, similar to that at the outer gate. The recessed stretch of wall east of this tower carries a double parapet of Turkish pattern (Fig. 171).

Near the junction of the south curtain with the inner redout, the wall makes a rounded obtuse angle (wrongly drawn on Plate XXXIII as occupied by a round tower). A semi-subterranean triangular chamber, covered by a splayed vault, is not marked on the plan, and is built against the inner side of the angle. Further east is a postern (also absent from the Grimani plan) whose depressed arch of poros voussoirs is similar in form and material to the other openings of the fortress, and may be considered contemporaneous with the Frankish circuit wall, which, 30 feet beyond, bonds into the high, faceted scarp of the inner enclosure (Fig. 172).

Fig. 172. Chlemoutsi, the Keep: Western Sector.

This keep is a huge, irregular hexagon, 280 feet long by 180 wide, consisting of a ring of enormous, vaulted galleries built round an inner court. The entrance (Plate XXXIII, D) is situated in an avantcorps, 50 feet high and 46 wide, projecting 15 feet from the keep's long north flank. A tall, wide, depressed arch of large poros blocks leads into a short, high, vaulted passageway inside the avantcorps. The corners of this structure are made of big, squared blocks of poros, 1–2 feet long. The walls of the inner passage carry through to the face of the avantcorps in the form of two vertical lines of cut poros blocks extending up to the springing of the vault. Here, however, the rubble masonry merges with that of the rest of the facade, in which the line of the vault does not appear. A second depressed arch, 6 feet deep, through the outer line of the north flank itself, leads up into the hexagon of vaulted halls.[15]

Though the original flooring has gone in all

but one short flank, traces in the side walls show them to have consisted of a lower storey and high upper gallery. In the north and northwest halls the crypt was made of stone vaults. On the south and southwest the floor was of wood, supported on beams, as shown by the lines of large, square holes in the walls 7 feet above the present ground level (Figs. 173, 175). This lower storey issues on to the court

Fig. 173. Chlemoutsi, the Keep: Southwest Gallery.

by means of low arches, round and depressed, made of the prevailing, well trimmed poros.

The galleries are covered by long barrel vaults of immaculate poros ashlar (Figs. 173, 174, 175). These are of western origin, although

[15] It is in a corner of the southwest gallery of the keep that Professor Sotiriou in 1918 discovered the remains of a furnace which he considered to be the actual mint of the *tournois*. See G. Sotiriou, "Le château-fort de Chloumoutzi et son atelier monétaire de tournois de Clarentia," *Journal international d'archéologie numismatique*, XIX, 1918–1919, p. 276.

in Europe the churches and monastic buildings of the XII century are built with round or pointed vaults. Here the vaults are ovoid, apparently a local interpretation. The exigencies of the hexagon impose the need of diminishing width at the ends of several galleries, where

pilasters which supported them are mostly in place (Fig. 175), made of large, squared poros blocks set one upon the other, fitted several inches into the wall, topped with plain, chamfered impost blocks of Byzantine pattern.

FIG. 174. CHLEMOUTSI, THE KEEP: VAULT OF SOUTHWEST GALLERY.

the side walls come together. Here the vaults taper to a rounded point, in much the same way as may be seen in certain Turkish bastions and cavaliers at Methone and Kelepha (see above, pp. 38, 80).

The walls of the galleries are made of rough but close-fitted limestone blocks as are the walls of the exterior. The vaults are strengthened with reinforcing arches, at intervals of 20–30 feet. These have all fallen,[16] but the

[16] When Traquair visited the fortress, the reinforcing arches were still partially in place (*B.S.A.*, XIII, 1906–1907, p. 277). He mentions their plainness, unadorned by molded or chamfered edges, which would have been the normal Gothic form.

The galleries are lighted by numerous windows of a distinctive and almost uniform construction (Fig. 176). A depressed vault is pushed through the 7-foot thickness of the wall, built of big, cut poros blocks in its soffit and angles, with side walls of rubble. Along the base is a banquette made of big, squared blocks. The whole is open on the interior. On the outside, it is divided into two small, round arches by a plain, square column under the low segment of the vault, standing on a small wall built against the end of the banquettes. The scheme of twin arches under a single vault is a common form of window in French architecture of the XII century.[17] It is not surprising to find it in Greece at the beginning of the XIII. The carefully built, depressed-vaulted passageways of the windows remain intact, together with most of the side walls and some of the banquettes. The remaining dressing stones, which form the columns and the double arches have gone in all but one, which face of the wall, which contains, instead, a low, pointed arch. Here again are the lateral banquettes along the side walls, but the outer structure of double arches has disappeared. Three openings in the western half of the same wall conform to the prevailing scheme, larger than the preceding, and set on a slightly lower level, to serve as doorways to a platform, carried on

FIG. 175. CHLEMOUTSI, THE KEEP: SOUTH GALLERY.

is situated in the outer face of the hexagon's south wall, preserved by a filling of masonry. The pattern of its double arch can still be distinguished, finely outlined in pale brown poros against the rough, white limestone of the walls. The inner wall of the north gallery contains, at its east end, four windows of a different pattern (Fig. 177). The arc of poros voussoirs which marks the outer edge of the depressed vault, is set 4 inches back from the

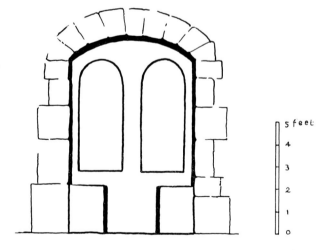

FIG. 176. CHLEMOUTSI, WINDOW IN THE KEEP.

[17] C. Enlart, *Manuel d'archéologie française depuis les temps mérovingiens jusqu'à la renaissance*: vol. II, *Architecture civile et militaire* (Paris, 1904), pp. 120 ff.

low arches, which in turn admit to the gallery's ground floor. In the east side of the keep the outer walls are pierced by three openings with side walls largely ruined, but covered in flat poros slabs, 4½ feet long, of the sort used also in the easternmost outer window of the long pilasters with pronounced, projecting capitals.

Inside the court, immediately east of the entrance, stairs ascend (Fig. 177, right) between the north and northeast halls, to the platform above the hexagon, at the head of which stands, to a height of 21 feet, one wall of a

Fig. 177. Chlemoutsi, the Keep: Inner Face of the North Gallery, with Pointed Arched Windows, right.

building next to the first gate. A further example of the stylistic uniformity of the castle is to be seen in the several small, square niches in the south and southeast halls, identical in construction to those in the east wall of the outer enceinte and the windows of the long house built against its north wall. These galleries also contain fireplaces like those in the outer curtain. Their backs form a slightly concave recess in the wall, projecting up through the vault between curved inclining sides (Fig. 175) to small, square openings in the roof. The lower sections are made of horizontal rows of broken tile, and are flanked by poros watch tower. The ascent is marked on Plate XXXIII: "stair by which one ascends to the top of the Vaults of said redout which, covered by roofs with aqueducts, carry the water to the Great Cistern." Only in one corner is there any trace of an outer parapet. Here stand two wide, capped merlons belonging, like the rest of Chlemoutsi's parapets, to the Turkish period. A straight parapet runs above the inner walls of the northeast and southwest galleries, but in all the commanding space of the continous platform round the hexagon there is no provision for guns. In the west corner of the keep is a circular shaft, in whose walls show the traces of a spiral staircase, which once communicated with the upper level. The outer wall of the keep on the north side shows, on close examination, near the top, a series of vertical joints set at regular intervals, like a line of walled-up crenellations. The breach at the west corner of the keep reveals, at the same level, the cross section of a parapet and chemin de ronde, and a sloping line of blocks descending to it from the key of the vault. From this one may conclude that the vaults of the galleries were originally covered with a sloping or gable roof, surrounded on the outside by a chemin de ronde and parapet on a lower level, and that the height of the walls was then raised, the space between them and the vault then being filled to form the present platform.

Beneath the long south hall is a cistern (Plate XXXIII, B), which measures 108 by 15 feet, and is built with a high, almost pointed vault of poros ashlar, originally held up by reinforcing arches springing from the rows of five pilasters still standing along its sides. The two square holes in the floor above its either end are marked on the plan: H. *Due Pozzi p: il qualle si estra de l'aqua di d*ᵃ *Cisterna.* The east end of the north hall contains a curved, domed niche. This corner is indicated on the plan as E. *Corpo di Guardia.* Next to this, immediately to the right of the entrance passage, the gallery once contained what the plan describes F. as *Loco qual era Chiesa Grecha qual serve p. Monitione sotto della qualle e deposito di Polvere.*

The two western corners of the hexagon are strengthened with tall, vertical round towers, 15 feet in diameter (Fig. 172, left), one almost entirely ruined, probably by the guns of Ibrahim Pasha in 1825. They are built on square bases, one of which has battering sides. It is unusual that these are placed within the outer enceinte and not in the more exposed sector of the keep outside the girdle walls.[18]

However, the Frankish builders probably trusted to the steeply falling ground on the south and east to leave those sides without extra defense.

The castle appears to date almost entirely to one period, the years 1220–1223. The round-topped lancets of the outer enclosure, the double arched windows of the inner redout, the great barrel vaults, the fireplaces, and the vertical round towers are all Western in origin. Chlemoutsi is built in the style, which the Frankish knights brought with them, of French fortress architecture of the preceding century.[19] Lacking purely Gothic features, it appears to be more a transition from the Romanesque, the earlier form surviving in colonial isolation. But the transplanted style is also modified by native conditions. Chlemoutsi shows the influence of Byzantine tradition and local Greek materials in the great poros blocks lining the passageways of the gates, the square reinforcing arches of the vaults, and the chamfered impost blocks on which they rest. The later Byzantine occupation of Chlemoutsi under the Palaiologoi (1427–1460) seems to have left no trace. Two centuries after its building, so strong a castle would still have been in good condition. The Turks, however, in the following centuries, rebuilt the parapets and made certain provisions for artillery, namely, adding the round tower in the middle of the northwest curtain, and the terrepleined bastion in the western corner. They also inserted domed chambers at the outer gate and the re-entrant angle in the south curtain, and repaired a stretch of the same curtain near its western end. The Venetians of 1700 added nothing. By their time the bulwark of Frankish Achaea had long outlasted its use.

[18] *B.S.A.*, XIII, 1906–1907, p. 275.

[19] Professor Antoine Bon calls attention to other fortresses distinguished by the use of "two parallel, concentric walls forming a series of galleries and enclosing a central court," namely, the portion of Crac des Chevaliers built before 1170, and a number of castles in Western Europe of which the prototype is Boulogne, built between 1228 and 1234. Chlemoutsi fits between these two both chronologically and geographically, and so may be a link in the development of this type of fortification. See *Rev. arch.*, XXVIII, 1947, pp. 177–9.

CHAPTER XV

MISTRA

(PLATE XXXIV)

After the fall of Corinth to the Venetians, the Turks abandoned the highland regions of Tripolis and Karytaina, and there remained only Mistra which still held out in the interior of the Peloponnese. Since the spring of 1687, six thousand Maniates had been besieging it under the command of the Venetian governor of Zarnata, Niccolò Polani. Once they had captured the outer suburbs of the town, but were driven off in large numbers by a sortie of seventy Turks. However, with the news that the Seraskier had abandoned the Peloponnese, the Turks submitted, and the offer of surrender was sent to the council of war in Corinth. But, as a contemporary account has it, the council decided against favorable terms, "in regard that they had held out to the last gaspings of the whole Kingdom and thereby had forfeited compassion."[1] The women and old men were to be set free, but all the men between the ages of seventeen and fifty were to go to the galleys, unless collectively they could redeem their freedom for a sum of 200,000 reals.

On August 25, 1687, letters from Polani telling of the submission reached Morosini who, sailing round the Peloponnese, had put into the port of Vathy on the Maniate coast. A group of Turkish emissaries arrived from Mistra, and formally surrendered on board Morosini's galley, announcing that they were unable to pay the required ransom for their liberty, but offering to leave the Peloponnese and all their goods behind them. In a signed agreement they were guaranteed their lives. The outcome, however, was changed by the news that plague had broken out in Mistra. Morosini ordered the Turks to confine themselves within the town until it passed over. Some of the emissaries were kept behind as hostages; others were sent back to Mistra to collect all the weapons and horses of the Turks and give them up to Polani. Shortly after, there arrived a band of Greeks from the region of Mistra, led as usual by their priests, who, offering to put themselves at the Venetians' disposal, were given arms and sent back to keep a watch on the Turks.[2]

During the winter of 1687–1688 the situation in Mistra became increasingly troublesome for the Venetians. The rations which they meted out to the quarantined city were insufficient, and as a result the stores of wheat were periodically rifled. Many of the inhabitants escaped to Monemvasia, where other Turks, under arms, still held out in the name of the Sultan. In January, 1688, the Venetians

---

[1] *A Journal of the Venetian Campaigne* (London, 1688), pp. 13 ff.

[2] Locatelli, I, pp. 349 ff.; Garzoni, I, pp. 213 ff.

decided to transport the Turks of Mistra to Argos and then quarantine them on ships off the coast. Those in the lower town of Mistra submitted to this decision, but the castle made a show of resistance. When after several days the Venetians entered it, they found a store of arms, which the Turks had sequestered in violation of the terms signed at Vathy. The Venetians then carried out a revenge, whose

the officers of the allied army, while 778 able-bodied men were selected for the galleys. Rather than submit to this, many of them threw themselves into the sea and drowned. The war council meanwhile decided the old men and women should be taken to Athens, which the Venetians were preparing to eva-cuate after their six months' occupation, pend-ing an eventual exchange with Christians held

FIG. 178. MISTRA, VIEW FROM THE NORTHEAST

savage perfidy was noted at the time.[3] The Turks were removed, numbering over 2000, to Argos, from which they were sent to the small island in the bay of Tolos, six miles east of Nauplia. There, after a mass baptism to initiate them into the mysteries of Christianity, 312 boys and girls were distributed as slaves among

as slaves by the Turks elsewhere. In March, accordingly, Morosini transported the captives to Piraeus, but instead of negotiating for the return of Christian slaves, he deposited the prisoners ashore as a decoy to the Turkish army which had to come to their rescue, leav-ing them there, in his own words, "to the great confusion of the enemy, and to the illustrious glory of the splendid, invincible greatness" of the Most Serene Republic. The plague, which

---

[3] Garzoni, I, p. 263: "Della descritta sentenza speculazioni sinistre ne formò il Mondo ... Molti imputarono al cambia-mento de' patti con Mistra quelli della fortuna."

had spread in the wake of war from the Morea to continental Greece, soon made short shrift of the last captives of Turkish Mistra.[4]

*　　*　　*

The city of Mistra was founded in the middle of the XIII century, when William Villehar-

Lacedaemon, which was called, after the name of the place, Myzithra.[5] The Slavs, driven into the barren interior of Taygetos, acknowledged William's rule and agreed to serve in his armies, though for many years they preserved a state of semi-independence, remaining exempt from taxes and other feudal services.[6] The building of the new fortresses established

FIG. 179. MISTRA, VIEW OVER THE DESPOT'S PALACE AND THE UPPER TOWN, FROM THE CASTLE.

douin was prince of Achaea. The capture of Monemvasia by the Franks in 1249 made him master of all the Peloponnese, excepting the Venetian stations of Methone and Corone. The only active enemy left in his realm was the Slavic tribe of Melings, who inhabited the mountain range of Taygetos. To subjugate and confine them in it, he built the castles of Old Maina and Leutron, called Beaufort, in the Mani peninsula, and a third on a hill near

a peace in the Morea, during which the Frankish Principality reached its zenith.[7]

[5] Χ. τ. Μ., lines 2985–2991:
Κι ὅσον ἐγύρεψεν καλὰ τὰ μέρη ἐκεῖνα ὅλα,
ηὗρεν βουνὶ παράξενον, ἀπόκομμα εἰς ὄρος,
ἀπάνω τῆς Λακεδαιμονίας κανένα μίλιν πλέον.
Διατὶ τοῦ ἄρεσεν πολλὰ νὰ ποιήση δυναμάριν,
ὥρισε, ἀπάνω στὸ βουνὶ καὶ ἔχτισεν ἕνα κάστρον,
καὶ Μυζηθρὰν τ᾽ὀνόμασεν, διατὶ τὸ ἐκράζαν οὕτως·
λαμπρὸν κάστρον τὸ ἔποικεν καὶ μέγα δυναμάριν.
[6] Miller, Latins, pp. 100 f.
[7] Χ. τ. Μ., lines 3038–3042:
Κι ἀφότου γὰρ ἐχτίστασαν τὰ κάστρη ὁποῦ σὲ εἶπα,
τὸ Λεῦτρον γὰρ κι ὁ Μυζηθρᾶς καὶ τῆς Παλαίας Μαίνης,
ἐδούλωσε τὰ Σλάβικα κ᾽εἶχεν τὰ ἐν Σέλημάν του,
καὶ περιεπάτει, ἐχαίρετον ἀπὸ ὅλον τὸ πριγκιπᾶτο,
ὡσὰν τὸ ἐκατακύριεψεν καὶ ἀφέντεψε τὸ ὅλον.

[4] J. M. Paton, The Venetians in Athens, 1687–1688 (Cambridge, Mass., 1940), pp. 22, 32 ff., 89 f.

11

However, there soon occurred a turn of fortune, which led ultimately to the gradual but steady elimination of Frankish rule from Greece. Ten years after the building of Mistra, William Villehardouin married Anne, daughter of the Despot of Epiros. This archon was con-

against a huge Imperial force gathered from every nation in the Near East. Villehardouin and his followers were taken prisoner and brought to the Emperor, who offered to buy the Franks off the Morea with an indemnity sufficient for the purchase of wide estates in

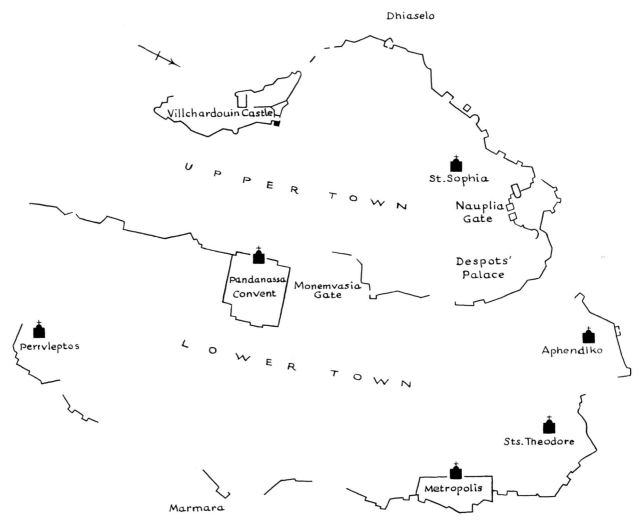

FIG. 180. MISTRA, PLAN OF THE TOWN WALLS.

tending with the Greek Emperor of Nicaea, Michael VIII Palaiologos, for the recapture of Constantinople from the Latins. To help him protect his Macedonian possessions, the Despot called in the aid of his new son-in-law, the Prince of Achaea. Michael met their combined forces on the plain of Pelagonia, but the Despot quarreled with Villehardouin at the last moment and deserted him, leaving him alone at the head of a band of Frankish knights

France. Villehardouin claimed the Principality was not his to surrender, but belonged by right to all the families which had taken part in its conquest. The Emperor declared no sum of money would ever ransom him, and Villehardouin remained in prison three years. Finally Michael Palaiologos got his bargain. On the advice of one of his companions in chains, Geoffroy de Bruyères, baron of Karytaina, William offered to give up the fortresses of Old Maina, Monemvasia, and Mistra. Bruyères was let out and sent off to Greece to arrange the transfer of the three places. At Nikli in Arkadia he held a parliament with Guy I de la Roche, Duke of Athens, and the wives of the imprisoned Prince and barons. Against the better judgment of the Duke of Athens, who offered to substitute himself for Villehardouin as the Emperor's prisoner, Bruyères persuaded the Frankish ladies that the three castles belonged to Villehardouin, to dispose of as he wished; Monemvasia he had captured himself, while Maina and Mistra were of his own building. Bruyères then handed over the three places to a representative of the Emperor, and in 1262 William Villehardouin returned to his dominion, now reduced by a fifth of its size.[8]

The formation of a Byzantine state in the Peloponnese provided the inevitable outlet for the hostility of the Greeks against the foreign occupiers of their country. When William arrived at his capital of Lacedaemonia, he found the city empty of its inhabitants; the Greeks had all moved to Mistra to live under the protection of their own nationality. The Prince's presence in Lacedaemonia gave them the excuse to withdraw even further, into the trackless wilderness of Taygetos, where they made a pact with the tribe of Melings to rebel in the name of the Emperor. They sent word to the newly installed Imperial governor in Monemvasia that Villehardouin was breaking his oath and threatening to attack them. Reinforcements of Greek troops and Turkish mercenaries began to arrive from Constantinople to attack the borders of the Principality.[9] And so began a state of war which lasted, with barely a pause, for the better part of two

centuries, during which the Byzantine power grew, while the Frank diminished.

The new Byzantine territory in the southeastern Peloponnese was governed at first by a general, appointed every year. One of these, Andronikos Asan, took advantage of the disorder in the Frankish Principality which followed the death of Louis of Burgundy in 1318, and enlarged the province by the acquisition of most of Arkadia including the castles of St. George, Akova and Karytaina.[10] From these possessions of the Franks, lands were bestowed on the various monasteries founded around the turn of the XIV century, which constitute the restored splendor of Mistra to-day. Mistra also became at this time the seat of the bishopric, which was transferred from Lacedaemonia, and from the year 1308 the Imperial governor was appointed not annually as before but for life.[11]

In spite of these gains, the country was in a dangerously unsettled state. One chronic evil, as ancient as modern, bedevilled the course of events in whatever part of Greece had liberated itself from the Franks. The fights and jealousies of the strong local families kept the Byzantine province in constant upheaval, while pirates ravaged the undefended coasts. A decisive step was taken to put down this confusion when, in 1348, the Emperor John VI Cantacuzene sent his second son, Manuel, as Despot of Mistra. Henceforward until the Turkish conquest, the Byzantine province remained directly dependent on the Imperial house, being governed either by younger sons or brothers of the Emperor. The real importance of Mistra dates from this time. The new Despot levied taxes for the creation of a navy, with which he succeeded in clearing the seas of pirates. In 1355, when a rival Despot was appointed with the support of the local archons, Manuel took the opportunity to quell their chaotic jealousy by

[8] X.τ.M., lines 4252–4534; L. de C., §§ 317–326; C. di M., pp. 442–448; Sanudo, in Hopf, Chroniques gréco-romanes, pp. 106 ff. The Aragonese version of the Chronicle of the Morea states (§§ 297, 307) that Michael VIII claimed Corinth as well as the three Lakonian castles, but that he relinquished his claim when the castelain of Corinth refused to give up the fortress to the Byzantine envoys.

[9] X.τ.M., lines 4509 ff., 5604 ff.; C. di M., pp. 448 f.; L. de C., § 330 ff.; Hopf, Chroniques gréco-romanes, p. 116.

[10] Miller, Latins, p. 259; Zakythinos, Despotat, I, p. 72.

[11] Ibid., I, p. 82; M. Hadzidakis, Μυστρᾶς (Athens, 1948), p. 15.

11*

force. He put down their opposition with the help of his bodyguard of Albanian troops, whom he afterwards settled in the depopulated and uncultivated sections of his realm.[12]

Partisan strife broke out again when John VII Palaiologos sent his son, Theodore, to replace the Despot Demetrios Cantacuzene, who had been trying to make Mistra independent of Byzantium. Demetrios was backed by his Frankish neighbors and by the ever-encroaching Turks, while Theodore had the support of the population and the equivocal aid of the Venetians. The struggle was resolved by the death of Demetrios in 1384.[13]

The reign of Theodore I marked a wide advance in the progress of the Byzantine power toward the ultimate unification of the Peloponnese. The local archons were subdued, again by means of Albanian troops, who were afterwards profitably used to clear more virgin lands for cultivation. In 1385 Theodore married the daughter of Nerio Acciajuoli, Duke of Athens, creating an alliance which, three years later, took active form against their neighbors, when Theodore siezed Argos from the Venetians. For five years he raided the borders of Venetian Messenia, until the Turkish peril forced him to come to terms. In 1394 Argos was given back to the Venetians, while the Despot was promised in return a safe refuge among the Venetian colonies in case of need. Both parties swore henceforward to respect the liberty of each other's subjects and refuse sanctuary to each other's enemies. The establishment of this friendship ensured the safety of Theodore's southwestern flank, and left him free to attack his other neighbors to the west and north. A successful war against his brother-in-law, Carlo Tocco, brought him Acrocorinth as a prize. Another war followed with the Navarrese, whose commander, Pedro Bordo de San Superan, Vicar General of

Achaea and later Prince, called in the Turks to help him. Already these had possessed themselves of Macedonia, destroyed the Serbian Empire, and descended into Thessaly as far as Neopatras. Now began a series of invasions of the Peloponnese, which were to continue at regular intervals for another half century until the final conquest. In 1395 Bayezid I sent an army across the Isthmus, and another two years later, which destroyed the Hexamilion and captured Argos. The Turks defeated Theodore himself at Leondari, and then after ravaging the Morea, withdrew again to Thessaly.[14]

In the midst of this danger Theodore looked about him for new allies, and in 1400 sold the castles of Corinth and Kalavryta to the Knights of St. John of Rhodes. Mistra also was to be handed over, but when the emissaries of the Knights came to take possession of the Byzantine capital, the indignant inhabitants attacked them and drove them off. They also refused to recognize Theodore as their Despot until he had paid back the money to the Knights and recovered the two places he had sold. The defeat of the Turks by Tamerlane in Asia Minor and the death of the Sultan Bayezid finally gave him the courage in 1404 to send the Knights away and re-occupy Corinth, annexing also the old Frankish county of Salona on the north side of the Gulf.[15]

The territorial expansion which had taken place in the Byzantine Morea under Theodore I continued during the rule of his nephew and successor, Theodore II, son of the Emperor Manuel II, who became Despot in 1407. But underneath the expansion, the Despotate was permeated by the organic dissolution of the Empire. In 1415, during Theodore's minority, Manuel II rebuilt the Hexamilion, as the last defense-line of Byzantine Greece. But Venice, trying short-sightedly to re-adjust the balance of power in the Peloponnese, refused to con-

[12] Miller, *Latins*, pp. 281 f.; *Essays*, pp. 96 f.; Zakythinos *Despotat*, I, pp. 95 ff.
[13] *Ibid.*, p. 117.

[14] *Ibid.*, pp. 131 ff., 138 ff., 143 f., 147, 152, 154, 156.
[15] Miller, *Latins*, pp. 368 f.; Zakythinos, *Despotat*, I, pp. 159 f.

tribute to the undertaking, and the archons of the Despotate turned a blind eye to the north, refusing in their turn to man the Isthmus wall. Theodore then sought help from the west, hoping to enlist the support of the Papacy by marrying in 1421 Cleopa Malatesta, sister of the Latin archbishop of Patras. Two years later the Turkish general, Turakhan, descended on the Peloponnese, and ravaged the country up to the gates of Mistra. But in the face of this advancing tide, the Christian powers of Greece remained more hostile to each other than to the Infidel. Theodore declared war first against Antonio Acciajuoli of Athens, who had indulged in devastation of his own in the wake of the Turkish armies; then against Centurione Zaccaria, the last Prince of Frankish Achaea, whom he took prisoner in 1423; and finally against Carlo Tocco, who was besieged in Glarentza and defeated by the Imperial fleet.[16]

In 1427 Theodore decided to enter a monastery, and his brother Constantine was appointed as Despot. Then Theodore changed his mind, and offered Constantine an indemnity instead among Carlo Tocco's possessions in Achaea. As a result, the Byzantine Despotate was increased by the acquisition of Chlemoutsi and Patras, and finally in 1429, when Thomas Palaiologos married the daughter of Centurione Zaccaria, who died the following year, the last remnant of the Frankish Principality became part of the unified Greek Morea.[17]

Constantine succeeded to the Despotate on Theodore's death in 1443. He rebuilt the Hexamilion, took measures to improve the agricultural economy of the Morea, and by instituting a series of public games tried to raise the nation's fighting spirit, which he himself embodied in the last acts of energy and daring to dignify the expiring Empire. He attacked Thebes and Athens, and forced Nerio II Acciajuoli to acknowledge his suzerainty, and

then carried the assault up to the Pindos mountains. But Nerio appealed to his previous suzerain, the Sultan Murad II, who in 1446 came down into Phokis, retook Lidoriki and Galaxidi, drove off the combined forces of Thomas and Constantine at the Hexamilion, and advanced as far as Patras. The Turkish army retired to the north with a train of 60,000 Greek prisoners.[18]

Venice at this time was frightened, by the Turkish victory over the Hungarians at Varna, into renewing a treaty of friendship with the Sultan. Her territories in Messenia and Argolis were threatened by the precipitate expansion of the Despotate, which was also arousing the national feeling of the Greeks inside her own colonies. The Venetians vainly enacted repressive measures against them, but they emigrated in a steady stream, leaving the Venetian lands empty, to strengthen the Despotate of Mistra against the day of resistance.[19]

In January, 1449, Constantine Palaiologos left Mistra to be crowned emperor in Constantinople. The Morea was divided between his two brothers, Thomas and Demetrios, who between them played out the unseemly and tragic last act in the history of the Byzantine Morea. The successive Turkish invasions, which had devastated the Peloponnese, had now reduced the province to the status of tributary to the Sultan. As if this had not already sealed the doom of the Despotate, Thomas in the northwest and Demetrios in the southeastern Peloponnese, with his capital at Mistra, at once entered into a conflict, which was like an invitation to the Turks of Thessaly to intervene and dictate their own terms. When Thomas seized the district of Skorta, Demetrios called in the aid of Turakhan, who forced Thomas to give up Kalamata to his brother.[20] Meanwhile in Asia Minor the Empire was fast shrinking. The victory of the Sultan Mohammed II

[16] *Ibid.*, pp. 167 ff., 188, 196 f., 198 ff.
[17] *Ibid.*, pp. 205 ff.

[18] Miller, *Essays*, pp. 100, 149; Hopf, *Chroniques gréco-romanes*, p. 267; Zakythinos, *Despotat*, I, pp. 229 ff.
[19] *Ibid.*, pp. 220 ff.
[20] *Ibid.*, pp. 242, 245.

against the Seljuks left him free to attack Constantinople. On May 29, 1453, he captured the City, on whose walls the last Emperor died fighting. During this final agony of Byzantium, while the Papacy and the states of western Europe waited for the end of its thousand-year existence, Thomas and Demetrios Palaiologos in the last corner of free Greece, waged a civil war against each other, oblivious to everything but their mutual hatred.

The year after Constantinople fell, the Morea was beset by an internal problem which brought the cataclysm closer. The Albanian population, living off lands devastated by the Turkish invasions, had grown to such an extent that the Government of Mistra increased their taxes, with the result that 30,000 of their number rose in revolt and laid siege to Patras and Mistra. A second time Turakhan was called in to prop up the tottering Despotate. He quelled the rebellion, but allowed the Albanians to keep their lands and livestock, and by confirming Demetrios and Thomas in their rule, made their existence only more dependent on the pleasure of the Sultan.[21]

At this stage of disintegration the Despotate was now powerless against the local archons, who in 1454 removed their support from the Despots and voluntarily placed themselves under the jurisdiction of the Turks.[22] But when Mohammed II demanded his tribute from the Morea, nothing was forthcoming. The Despots could not prevail on their rebellious subjects to pay it. In the spring of 1458 Mohammed came down into Thessaly and waited for the Despots' envoy. Then he advanced to the north shore of the Corinthian Gulf, where a sum of 4,500 gold pieces was finally brought him, together with a demand for renewal of the treaty of peace and vassalage. This time it was too late. Mohammed crossed into the Peloponnese, and captured Acrocorinth after a three months' siege. Next fell the castles of Patras, Kala-

vryta, and Vostitza, in which Turkish garrisons were installed. Thousands of prisoners were carried off to Constantinople, leaving the Peloponnese depopulated and defenseless. The country now lay wide open.

Early in 1459 Thomas, as spokesman of the archons' particular jealousy, revolted against his brother and the Sultan. In the middle of the year, Pope Pius II met the ambassadors of the western powers and Thomas' own envoys at Mantua to confer on what might be done to halt the Turkish advance. While empty promises issued from the papal chair, Bessarion called for a crusade to come to the aid of the Morea in revolt. Pope Pius exerted himself to save the last shred of the Greek Empire by sending, instead of a crusade, a company of 300 Italians to besiege Patras.[23]

Thomas and Demetrios added to the futility of this gesture by continuing their civil war under the very imminence of enemy occupation, in the recurrent pattern of the catastrophes of Greek history. Finally, to put an end to Thomas' revolts and to prevent the Peloponnese from falling into the hands of the West, Mohammed made his final assault. In May, 1460, he carried the attack straight to Mistra, where Demetrios made his submission. Thomas escaped from Porto Longo on the island of Sapienza opposite Methone on July 28, to live out his exile in Italy, while Demetrios was settled on the islands of Lemnos and Imbros, as the Sultan's pensioner. Except for Monemvasia, all the Morea was Turkish by the middle of 1461.[24]

The new Turkish province of the Peloponnese was divided into the two sanjaks of Mistra and Patras.[25] Early in the occupation, during the Turco-Venetian war of 1463–1479, Mistra was the target of a Venetian attack led by Sigismondo Malatesta. The commander of the Venetian troops, Bertoldo d'Este, had been

[21] Miller, pp. Latins, 429 ff.; Essays, p. 103.

[22] Zakythinos, Despotat, I, p. 250.

[23] Ibid., pp. 260 ff.

[24] Hopf, Chroniques gréco-romanes, p. 268; Miller, Latins, pp. 446 ff.; Zakythinos, Despotat, I, pp. 267 ff.

[25] Miller, Essays, p. 356.

killed in an attack on Corinth, and the *condottiere* of Rimini was chosen to succeed him. In July, 1464, he landed at Methone, but found there only 7,000 troops. He advanced to Mistra and captured the two outer circuits of the town, but the castle, defended by 120 men, held out until the arrival of Turkish reinforcements drove off his small army, which was as ill-equipped and half-hearted as all the expeditionary forces sent from western Europe into Greece during the Turkish domination.[26]

When the Venetians occupied Mistra at the end of the XVII century, the town was flourishing commercially, as the center of the Peloponnesian silk trade, with 42,000 inhabitants, 400 of whom were Jews. Although the capital of the province of Lakonia was placed at Monemvasia for its more advantageous position on the sea, Mistra was one of the seven non-provincial capitals which served as the seat of a Venetian proveditor.[27]

Coronelli[28] describes the town as it stood at this period:

It has but two great Gates, one on the North side toward *Napoli di Romania*, the other on the West toward *Exokorion*, to which answer two Highways or great Roads, one called *Aphetais* or grand *Bazar*, the other *Hellerion*.

The inhabitants are exposed to excessive heats during the summer: for besides that the City lyes full South, being seated at the foot of the Mountain, the Suns Rays by this opposition are reflected and redouble the heat ...

The City is divided into four Quarters, each of which being separated from the rest, makes of itself a disunited Body. The Castle is one of them, the City another, and two suburbs the other; whereof the one is called *Mesokorion*, that is to say the middle Suburb, and the other is called *Exokorion* or the outward Suburb, by the Turks named likewise *Maratche*.

The *Exokorion* is separated from the other three by the River *Vasali Potamos*, and has no communication with them but by a stone Bridge.

The Castle named *to Castron* is seated on an Eminence, is of a conical Figure, and has good walls;

it had some years since ten Pieces of Artillery, and a Garrison of Eighteen or Twenty Janisaries Commanded by a Disdar that seldom resides there.

This city, "esteemed the second for bigness in all the Morea,"[29] ended its long history in 1770. In that year the Peloponnese became the center of a new upheaval against Turkish rule, when Russia, pressing as usual toward the warm sea ports in a war with the Ottoman Empire, sent agents into Greece to incite the population to rebel. The Czarina Catherine II and her favorite, Gregory Orloff, contrived a scheme by which the Russian fleet should come to the aid of the Greeks in revolt, and establish Russian control over the country which has so often been regarded as the key to the Eastern Mediterranean. As in the Middle Ages Catholicism had served to justify the designs of the West against the Byzantine Empire, so now religion gave Russia the chance to stand forth as the protector of Orthodox Greece. The Russians entered into negotiations with the most revolutionary of the Greeks, the Maniates, who agreed to arouse the rest of the Morea. But the Russian fleet turned out to bring only a token force, and the Greeks lost heart on learning that, in order to be liberated from the Turks, they had first to swear themselves subjects of the Russians. However, a body of Maniates issued forth from their mountainous peninsula and captured Mistra, where they plundered Turks and Christians indiscriminately. Mistra served as the seat of a provisional revolutionary government, while the Greeks and Russians captured Kalamata and ineffectually besieged Corone and Methone. After a few months the Turks transported bands of Albanians into the Morea, which routed the Greco-Russian forces in Arkadia, Lakonia, and Messenia, recapturing Mistra and burning it to the ground.[30] The town was

---

[26] Miller, *Latins*, p. 467; A. G. Mompherratos, Σιγισμοῦν-δος Πανδόλφος Μαλατέστας (Athens, 1914), pp. 19f., 28ff.; Stephano Magno, in Hopf, *Chroniques gréco-romanes*, p. 203.

[27] Miller, *Essays*, pp. 419f.; Hadzidakis, *op. cit.*, p. 20.

[28] *An Historical and Geographical Account of the Morea*, English translation (London, 1687), pp. 94–96.

[29] Randolph, *The Present State of the Morea*, p. 8.

[30] Finlay, *The History of Greece under Venetian and Ottoman Domination*, pp. 301 ff.; P. M. Kondoyannis, Οἱ Ἕλληνες κατὰ τὸν πρῶτον ἐπὶ Αἰκατερίνης Β′ Ρωσσοτουρκικὸν πόλεμον (Athens, 1903), pp. 128–132, 362.

burned a second time by Ibrahim in 1825, and fell into the ruin which stands to-day, the charred and ghostly relic of Byzantium.

* * *

Leake[31] describes the place as he saw it in March of the year 1805:

I ride up to the Castle of Mistrá, and pass the rest of the morning at that important geographical station. The castle seems never to have been very formidably fortified, though it is strong by its position and great height; it is about five hundred feet above the level of the plain; the hill on three sides is extremely steep; on the fourth, or southern side, it is perpendicular, and separated from another similar rock by the torrent Pandeleímona, so called from a monastery τοῦ Παντελεήμονος towards its sources. This stream divides the town into two parts, tumbling over a rocky bed, like the *Hercina* at Livadhía; a little below the town it joins another rivulet which rises to the northward, near the village of Vársova: the united stream joins the *Eurotas*, to the southward of *Sparta*. There are still the remains of some fine cisterns in the castle. The view from thence is of the utmost beauty and interest; the mountains to the north, east, and south, are spread before the spectator from *Artemisium*, on the confines of *Argolis* and *Arcadia*, to the island of *Cythera* inclusive, together with a small part of the *Laconic* gulf, just within that island. All the plain of *Sparta* is in view, except the south-west corner near Bardhúnia, which is concealed by a projection of Mount *Taygetum*. Towards the mountain the scene is equally grand, though of a different nature. A lofty summit of Taygetum, immediately behind the castle, three or four miles distant, is clothed with a forest of firs, and now deeply covered with snow; the nearer slopes of the mountain are variegated with the vineyards, corn-fields, and olive plantations belonging to the villages of Barsiníko, and Vlakhokhóri, situated on opposite sides of the ravine of the Pandeleímona, which winds from the southward in the direction of the highest summit of Taygetum. This remarkable peak is not much inferior in height to ʹOlono, or any of the highest points of the Peloponnesus, and is more conspicuous than any, from its abrupt sharpness. I cannot learn at Mistrá any modern name for it, except the very common one of Ai Eliá, or Saint Elias, who, like Apollo of old, seems to delight in the protection of lofty summits.

A cultivated tract of country, similar to that about Barseníko and Vlakhokhóri, occupies the middle region of Taygetum through its whole length; it is con-

cealed from the great plain by a chain of rocky heights which immediately overhang the plain, and of which the Castle-hill of Mistrá is one. Like that hill they terminate in steep slopes or in abrupt precipices, some of which are almost twice as high as the Castle of Mistrá, though they appear insignificant when compared with the snowy peaks of Taygetum behind them. They are intersected and separated from one another by the rocky gorges of several torrents which have their origin in the great summits, and which, after crossing the upper cultivated region, issue through those gorges into the plain, and then traversing its whole breadth join the Eurotas flowing under the eastern hills. This abrupt termination of Taygetum, extending all the way from the Castle of Mistrá, inclusive, to the extremity of the plain, forms the chief peculiarity in the scenery of Sparta and its vicinity. Whether seen in profile, contrasted with the richness of the plain, or in front with the majestic summits of Taygetum rising above it, this long gigantic bank presents a variety of the sublimest and most beautiful scenery, such as we hardly find equalled in any part of picturesque Greece itself.

One of the most delightful spots in this scene is the village of Peróri, a little to the southward of Mistrá, where the mosque and houses interspersed amidst gardens are traversed by a rapid stream like the Pandeleímona, which issues from a stupendous rocky opening behind the village. It would seem, that in the time of Coronelli this village was connected with Mistrá, and formed a part of the southern quarter then called Exokhóri.

The southern part of the town is still named Misokhóri; the part occupied by the Metrópoli, under which name the cathedral and bishop's house are comprised, is Katokhóri: the houses are so much dispersed, that the town occupies a mile and a half along the foot of the hill, though there are not altogether more than 1000 houses, of which about a fourth are Turkish. Katokhóri alone, together with another quarter now deserted, called Kastro, on the north-eastern side of the castle above Katokhóri, once contained an equal number, but they were destroyed during the insurrection of 1770, or after that event, and their ruins only are now left, occupying a space equal to that of the present inhabited town. When the Albanian army was destroyed or driven out of the Peninsula, there still remained the old Albanian colony of Bardhúnia, the Maniátes, and the hungry Pashás of the Moréa, to plunder Mistrá in succession; and it was not until the Turkish fleet had reduced Mani to terms, that the Porte had the power of affording the place any protection. The remains of the house of Krevatá, once the richest family in the Moréa, but which is now extinct, in consequence of having been tempted by the Russians to engage in the insurrection, are seen in Katokhóri, between the Metrópoli

---

[31] *Morea*, I, pp. 127–131.

and the river Pandeleímona. The Krevatá, who joined the insurrection, fled into Mani on its failure, and died there.

The drawing by Levasseur in the Grimani collection (Plate XXXIV) shows the complete town of Mistra (Fig. 178), with the two torrents enclosing the castle hill. The upper town (Fig. 179) is marked *Forteza*. The Despots' Palace bears the interesting appellation of *Pallaza d'Carlo magna*. Its courtyard is called *Bazara*. The Metropolis is marked as *Archivescovo*, the monastery of Sts. Theodore as *Convente d'callori* (καλόγεροι), and the Pandanassa Nunnery as *Vescovata*. The town itself, already falling into ruin at the turn of the XVIII century, is indicated as *Cassa Parta distruta et Parta in Piede*. The hamlet of five or six houses, called Dhiaselo, in the saddle between the castle rock and the hill to the west is marked *Borgo diascolo*, while *Borgo de ebraicha* refers to the ruined Jewish suburb in the gulley which descends from Dhiaselo to the Lacedaemonian plain. The present centre of Mistra on the southeast side of the river, once known as Exokhori or outer village, is marked on the plan *Borgo da bassi*, a translation of Kato Khora, the name actually applied to the settlement of houses around the Metropolis and the church of Sts. Theodore at the north end.

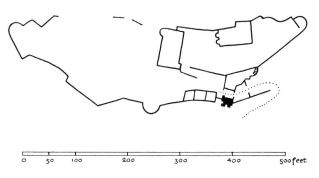

FIG. 181. MISTRA, THE CASTLE: PLAN.

The castle is drawn in outline, measuring only two or three inches square on the plan, though showing correctly the chief elements of the fortifications. The hill rises precipitously

to a narrow, rocky ridge, some 450 feet long, whose two levels are walled into a lower and an upper enclosure (Fig. 181). The entrance to the first of these is approached on the north side through a screen wall of the Turkish period, pierced with oblique and slanting loopholes, at the head of a cobbled ramp.

FIG. 182. MISTRA, THE CASTLE: OUTER GATE.

The gate itself (Fig. 182) is set in a redan of the outer curtain, consisting of a short passage vaulted in alternate rows of cut voussoirs and long, flat bricks, and a chamber, 12 feet square, covered with a pointed vault. The masonry of the redan's northwest face consists chiefly of uncut limestone with some squared poros blocks, separated by broken tile fragments set flat and upright, here and there forming ladders and double courses. Bigger blocks and thicker bricks are used in the corner to the left of the entrance. In the wall face may be seen also the end of an embedded octagonal colonnette with tile set round it in two concentric semicircles. Above the entrance is a shallow, recessed arch. The gate is connected with the inner enclosure immediately above it by a short wall, which climbs the rocks and joins the upper curtain by means of a small, rounded, tower-like structure built on a curved projecting base. This stretch of wall does not bond with the gate, though its masonry is similar, containing courses of broken tile and small tile ladders. Its parapet contains six loopholes placed low at the level of the interior platform, inside tall, domed, plastered niches, which constitute an odd combination of loophole and casemate, and belong probably to the realm of Turkish experimentation. Flanking the gate on the northeast side, set slightly back from its façade, is a tall, narrow tower with battering walls, built on two high stepped projections (Fig. 183). Its northeast and southeast sides are built with deeply

northwest side are three casemates at platform level, 4 feet wide and as many high on the inside, and 4 feet deep, tapering down to small openings, later partially blocked to allow slots for small arms. The casemates are vaulted in toolmarked voussoirs of poros and limestone.

FIG. 184. MISTRA, THE CASTLE: CONSTRUCTION OF RECESSED ARCH IN THE FLANKING TOWER OF THE OUTER GATE.

FIG. 183. MISTRA, THE CASTLE: FLANKING TOWER OF OUTER GATE.

recessed arches rising 30 feet high, spanned in the "Byzantine" construction of alternating wedge-shaped blocks and bricks. Above this runs a cavetto molding, marking the level of the platform (Fig. 184). On top, the parapet is built of rectangular blocks, separated by bricks in the horizontal and vertical joints. On the

Gate and flanking tower would both appear to belong to one period, since their walls bond together and there is no difference in masonry. The cloisonné masonry of the tower parapet, the recessed arches of the flanks, the slightly incurved splay molding round its three sides, and the projecting base all suggest the Byzantine, though perhaps equally well the Turkish hand.

The outer curtain along the northeast flank (Fig. 185) stands 20–30 feet high along the top of the steep slope above the city. It is built of large blocks of uncut limestone, with an admixture of broken brick and poros, in parts thickly mortared. Certain sections are based for reinforcement on double stepped projections. Above runs a parapet of square merlons alternately pierced with steeply pitched, plastered musket holes, with a chemin de ronde little more than a foot wide. Toward the middle of the flank there is a round tower (Fig. 185) built partially solid so as to form, inside the enclosure, at ground level, an obtuse angle in the curtain wall, containing three case-mates: one a shallow, recessed arch, which turns into a concave, plastered niche, another a square recess, with a small hole in the outer wall, and another of more conventional shape, arched on the inside in alternating poros

Fig. 185. Mistra, the Castle: Northeast Flank of Outer Enclosure.

wedges and brick, and tapering to a smaller opening on the outside. This arrangement for artillery places the tower within the Turkish period. Its lower half on the outside is strengthened by an extra sheathing of masonry added later. Near the south end of the circuit is another reinforcement of the wall, in the form of a three-sided buttress built out on a small cliff, which has since sprung apart from the wall, but was originally intended to mask a cistern built within the curtain wall against it.

The outer enclosure ends, at the south, in a rectangular platform measuring 35 by 15 feet, built above a vaulted cistern, and a round bastion on a southward-pointing spur of cliff. This is strengthened also by a later, thickly plastered buttress. On top is a semicircular platform, raised 12 feet above the interior ground level, reached by a flight of steps carried on a quarter arch, a common feature among the Byzantine buildings of the town.[32] At the bottom of the semicircular parapet round the tower platform is one small steeply pitched gun embrasure pointing down the cliffs at a 60 degree angle toward the torrent 400 feet below. The curtain makes several turns westward from the round bastion for a space of 30 feet and then ends abruptly over the rocks, along whose line on the southwest no other defense is necessary. Toward the mid-point of this flank of the fortress, the wall reappears in a few small sections, sealing off fissures in the cliff.

The inner redout on the topmost crest of the hill is approached by a ramp (Fig. 186) and entered, near its southeast end, through a deep, depressed arch, vaulted in well cut voussoirs, with side walls of large, squared blocks. This door closely resembles those in the XIII century Villehardouin fortress of Chlemoutsi. To the southeast of the entrance, the enclosure is terminated by a large, rectangular donjon (Fig. 186), 30 by 40 feet wide, built over a semi-subterranean, vaulted cistern, 20 feet deep and as many square, to which a small passage in the upper part of its northwest wall gives access. It is covered with a depressed vault, and partly walled in brick. Round the top of the donjon's northeast and southeast walls, dominating the outer enclosure, runs a chemin de ronde surrounded by a parapet, in a form similar to that used over the hexagonal keep at Chlemoutsi. By these indications the donjon belongs to the original castle of 1249,

[32] A. K. Orlandos, "Τὰ Παλάτια καὶ τὰ Σπίτια τοῦ Μυστρᾶ," Ἀρχ. Βυζ. Μνη., III, 1937, January–June, p. 60.

though certain sections of it date to later periods. Its western corner is built of squared blocks, 2 feet long, the largest in all the castle walls, with cloisonné brickwork around them, suggesting a late Byzantine repair. The donjon's south corner is flanked by a narrow, hollow, assymetrically round tower (Fig. 187), made of small limestone rubble with broken tile in abundance, largely overlaid with plaster, in contrast to the more regular masonry of the donjon itself, with which it does not bond. The tower is riddled with scaffold holes, and bears traces of a domed turret in its upper portion.

The southwest curtain of the upper enceinte (left of Fig. 187) stands 10–30 feet high on the outside, supporting a 3-foot wide chemin de ronde and a much dilapidated parapet. Next to the donjon at the southeast end the chemin de ronde runs over the top of four blind arches

vaulted in wedge-shaped poros blocks. At the castle's northwest tip the curtain forms a round bastion, which hangs like the prow of a ship high in the air over the saddle of Dhiaselo (Fig. 188, right). This narrow, curved extrem-

FIG. 187. MISTRA, THE CASTLE: WEST CURTAIN AND SOUTH ANGLE OF DONJON.

ity is terraced on the inside into a platform 30 feet long and 5 feet above the interior ground level. At the tip end are remains of an artillery parapet containing wide, shallow embrasures pitched so as to allow fire down into the saddle below and on to the opposite hillside.

Both enclosures of the fortress are filled with ruins of houses dating from the Turkish period.[33] In the upper redout there are two small chapels, placed adjacently with a single dividing wall, set against the southwestern curtain, built with big blocks in the angles, which may be identified with the mosque "once a Christian church," mentioned by Coronelli. Interesting traces remain also of more recent habitation. The two openings of the outer gate shut off with newly raised walls, the embrasures along the ramparts which open on to the plain blocked against the fire of longer-range weapons than those of the Middle Ages, and the rude hutments of boards and tar-paper built up against the older walls all tell of a recurrent pattern of warfare, in which

FIG. 186. MISTRA, THE CASTLE: DONJON AND RAMP TO INNER ENCEINTE.

[33] A. Struck, *Mistra, eine mittelalterliche Ruinenstadt* (Vienna and Leipzig, 1910), p. 140.

the fortress was put to its old use again in the present day. At various periods during the civil war of 1943–1949 William Villehardouin's castle served as refuge for the families of Dhiaselo, Kato Khora, and the modern village of Mistra. In November, 1944, after Sparta fell to

ment to cover the perilous defiles of Taygetos, into which the Andartes had withdrawn, like the Slavic tribes in the Middle Ages. The peculiar geographical formation of Greece is the determining factor in a history rigid in its repetitions.

FIG. 188. MISTRA, THE CASTLE AND THE NORTHWEST WALLS OF THE UPPER TOWN.

the forces of ELAS, several hundred of the Security Battalions, formed under the German aegis, retired to Mistra, and among the ruins of the ancient city and its castle received the attack which was to prelude the December Revolution in Athens. For three days several thousand ELAS troops assaulted the mountain from their positions in the plain, and captured the citadel. The landing of British forces in Greece a week later ultimately restored Mistra to the hands of the Nationalists. These kept a garrison in the castle until 1949, using it as an observation post and machine gun emplace-

Exact chronological inferences about the fortress are hard to draw from its present state. Two centuries of Byzantine and three and a half of Turkish occupation have to a certain extent overlaid the brief fifteen years of Frankish possession. But the plan has remained fundamentally the same as when Villehardouin first laid it out. The scheme of a rock fortress with outer court, inner redout, and keep belongs to the XIII century. The rounded ends of the inner and the outer enceintes, the donjon, and the inner gate are Frankish elements placed at such points as to imply that the

Greeks and Turks did nothing more than rebuild or repair along the existing lines. During the Byzantine period (1262–1460) rings of fortifications were built to enclose the various levels of the hill, as the higher and lower towns grew up, while the castle itself became more testify to its revived importance during the late XV, XVI, and XVII centuries. While Mistra was attacked only once during Byzantine times, it received four attacks after 1460. For the Turks' position as foreign occupiers grew precarious as western expansion threat-

FIG. 189. MISTRA, THE NORTHWEST WALLS: REDAN AND UPPER GATE ABOVE DHIASELO.

and more a position of last resort. It is reasonable to suppose that little was done to improve or renovate it, while new defenses were being extended round the palaces and monasteries below. Probably for this reason we find little in the castle that can definitely be assigned to the centuries of the Despotate. By Turkish times the castle must have fallen into disrepair. The Turks restored the donjon, added a round tower and buttresses along the northeast flank of the outer curtain, and built new parapets with musket holes and artillery embrasures throughout the castle. These improvements

ened the Ottoman dominions. Stronger defenses were needed and so it is natural to find the Turks refortifying Mistra, and concentrating on the castle as its most defensible point.

From the summit of the fortress at the northwest end, 1865 feet above sea level, a thin, fragmentary line of curtain drops down the steep ledges; turns gradually north, and expands into a stout, tower-flanked wall descending all the way to the bottom of the hill (Fig. 188), and branching off at two points in parallel lines to enclose the town's upper and lower levels (Fig. 180).

Directly beneath the castle's northwest end, the wall forms a straight stretch 120 feet long, 30–40 feet high, through which, at its mid-point, a door leads out to the saddle of Dhia-selo (Fig. 189). This is covered by a triangular redan with slightly curving walls, whose angle, half way up, is recessed and flattened in the same way as in the redans of the Byzantine walls of Salonica. The foundations of the angle are of great, uncut limestone boulders. The door is covered with a depressed arch, masking a higher round arch within. The two walls of the redan are extended within the curtain to form a square tower (Fig. 190). The interior of this structure is topped with a barrel vault, which diminishes toward the redan's outer point. The inner face contains a second gate; a low, depressed archway set within a high, round, recessed arch. In the wall space formed

between the two was a window whose sill rested on the top of the lower arch. The collapse of the keystone involved also the fall of the window sill, so that now a vertical opening pierces the wall from the upper arch to the lower. Both of these are made of wedge-shaped blocks, alternating with double bricks. The tower platform bears traces of a crenellated parapet, probably Turkish, with double loop-holes placed low and plastered inside, with a slope to allow for downward fire.

To the north of the upper gate a thin, low curtain follows down the sloping cliff top to a line of flanking towers dominating the ruins of the Jewish suburb. The first of these is a hollow, square tower 50 feet high, covered with a compressed barrel vault. Its front is set on a triple stepped base 20 feet wide, and is marked with several single and double string courses of

FIG. 190. MISTRA, THE NORTHWEST WALLS: THE UPPER GATE, INTERIOR.

FIG. 191. MISTRA, THE NORTHWEST WALLS: SQUARE FLANK-ING TOWER.

brick (Fig. 191). Slightly over half way up the face is a broad course of dark red limestone. Above this is a blind recess, arched in alternating wedge and brick construction. The north flank contains an entrance arched in poros, masking a higher archway in the interior section of the wall behind it. The inner and outer sections of this flank do not bond together. A fissure in the masonry can be seen between the two arches of the door, extending up to the platform above. On the inside of the tower face can be seen a loophole, which the masonry of the recessed arch masks on the exterior. These features show the structure to be in reality two towers, the early one high and narrow, with a loophole in its face and an archway in its flank, around which was built, for added thickness, the present tower to encase it.

Fig. 192. Mistra, the Northwest Walls: Round Flanking Tower.

Further on is a round tower (Fig. 192) standing 40 feet high, streaked with single and double brick courses. Beneath the platform is a small vaulted chamber. The masonry is the same as in the outer shell of the square tower above it. If this is not an addition of the Turkish period, but antedates the year 1460, it must be one of the rare instances of a Byzantine tower being built round.

Twenty feet of curtain, uniformly plastered, with a low, crenellated parapet pierced with loopholes set low underneath the merlons, leads to a third tower, rectangular, standing 40 feet high and projecting 12 feet from the curtain. It is built of big limestone blocks, rough in outline but flat in surface, with courses of brick running between them. In the face, 25 feet wide, are two tall, deep, recessed arches built in the same way as those in the

flanking tower by the castle gate. The upper section of the tower contains two small vaulted chambers.

Beyond, the curtain projects out over a spur of rock to form a tower of roughly square shape, and then continues for 60 feet with a crenellated parapet and chemin de ronde, 7 feet wide, descending to a narrow, irregularly shaped tower (Fig. 193, right) built out on a cliff, containing two miniature chambers, one above the other, with loopholes in each level. An unusual feature, at the bottom of the tower face, is a form of relieving arch spanning a steeply pitched facet of the rock foundations. The arch is made of flat stones built out over each other and topped with a flat piece of slate. Inside, over the sloping rock, it is rudely curved and thickly plastered, with a square vent, now blocked, issuing from the interior of the tower. The whole structure has the eccentric, piecemeal quality of Turkish building.

At this point the line of fortification divides. Next to the tower the curtain turns a right angle eastward and curves round to the great northwest gate of the upper town, through

Fig. 193. Mistra, the Northwest Walls: Flanking Towers above the Nauplia Gate.

which the high-road to Nauplia once passed. Immediately below the corner thus formed, the cliff drops 20 feet. At the foot of the rock, another wall continues the northward line of the previous stretch above it (Fig. 193, left),

and then curves round, with pronounced indentations, to meet the curtain proper on a
lower level. Between these two walls a court
is formed outside the main town gate. The
outer wall carries a crenellated parapet and a
narrow chemin de ronde, strengthened inside
by three plain buttresses. Three square towers
flank it on the north side. The first, containing
like many of the other towers along the wall a

This wall serves as a screen for the large bay,
studded with towers round and square, which
contains the Nauplia Gate: a sector built of
rough but flat-faced stone, with an abundance
of terra cotta, set in a strong, gray mortar.
The towers are marked with single and double
courses of brick at intervals of 3–5 feet. Vertical bricks are used in such profusion as to
give the effect of cloisonné masonry. The

FIG. 194. MISTRA, THE NORTHWEST WALLS: THE NAUPLIA GATE.

vaulted chamber in its upper section, is reinforced by two buttresses, 10 feet thick, placed
against its front. Above and below it, on the
outside, the ground is terraced and covered
with the ruins of the Jewish quarter. Two
other towers are built out on projections of
the cliff. The third has the form of parapet
characteristic of all the walls of Mistra, and
belongs to the period of Turkish refortification,
with loopholes thickly plastered inside, some
facing two ways, placed low at platform level.

12

tower angles are built with short lines of flat
brick at 6-inch intervals. The southwest side
of the bay is flanked by a round tower built
entirely of cloisonné masonry (right of Fig.
194). A house was built against it on the inside,
so that the chemin de ronde became the level
of the upper storey. Instead of a parapet, the
tower supports the high, plastered walls of an
upper chamber lighted by large windows of
XVIII century dimensions. In the south corner of the bay, remnants of the original

crenellated parapet are preserved in a piece of walling built on top of it. The gate itself consists of an archway flanked on either side by towers (Fig. 194). These measure 20 feet square, with walls 6 feet thick. Each tower is set on a triple stepped base extending round the face and both flanks. The plan of the lower storey is identical in both towers. They consist of two high, narrow barrel vaults, separated by a transverse arch, the southeast side of which is carried on a stout pilaster. The opposite side of the chamber, or interior of the tower face, is thicker than the other sides, obviating the need for such a support. The chamber of the southwest tower has a door in the flank of the entrance passage. The chamber in the northeast tower lacks an entrance in any corresponding position, but has a small arched opening high up in its rear wall, similar to that in the large cistern of the inner castle redout. A hole in the roof testifies that this vaulted chamber also was used as a cistern. The upper storey, standing only in the southwest tower, consists of a chamber with vaulted niches and windows in the front and rear walls and in the side wall of the passage. Fragmentary walls with wide window-sills also remain of a house of the Turkish period built on the platform above. The gate between the towers is made of successive arches one behind the other. The outermost of these, 12 feet high, is made of alternate wedge-shaped poros blocks and double bricks. There is a gap for portcullis, and another arch slightly higher and wider than the first, behind that a flat beam, and then a third arch, depressed but taller than the others. Above the gate, the two inner flanks of the towers show the springing of a corbel support (Fig. 194) for a timber bridge between the two upper chambers.

The curtain curves out, serving as back wall for several houses and vaulted chambers, as far as a round tower at the north salient angle of the bay. This is built in the prevailing Byzantine manner, with single and double brick string courses. Here, as in the other round tower on the bay's opposite side, a later house has been built up against its interior. The outer curtain or screen wall in front of the Nauplia Gate, follows past it along the top of steep rocks, and continues on round the Despots' Palace.

The upper section of the town is bordered by a curtain wall (Fig. 197) which follows, with some lapses, along its whole eastern flank as far as the cliff over the Pandeleimona Gorge on the south side of the hill. It is mainly a simple retaining wall, which winds back and forth in wide-angled, broken arcs around the projections and indentations of the terrain. Standing 6–20 feet high on the outside, it spans the rocks and open fissures by means of a variety of relieving arches of wedge and brick construction, round-topped, depressed, and pointed. Several of the wall's obtuse corners are

FIG. 195. MISTRA, THE MONEMVASIA GATE.

built with projecting bases for reinforcement. Above runs a crenellated parapet 5 to 6 feet high, with square merlons 3 feet wide. Opposite the Despots' Palace it rises above the terrace which it forms, and the chemin de ronde detaches itself from the interior ground level. Southward from the Palace the wall disappears amid the general ruin, but further

Here the detached chemin de ronde is carried on three relieving arches, depressed and round, and leads up to the top of the tower. This contains two gates: the inner double, depressed on the outside and round within; the outer round (Fig. 195), and divided by a gap for portcullis. Small casemates in the outer flank cover the lower sections of the town and

Fig. 196. Mistra, North Sector of the Lower Town Walls: Aphendiko Monastery.

on re-emerges as a retaining wall for a cobbled way, leading down to the eastern entrance to the upper city.

The Monemvasia Gate is not drawn on the Grimani plan, which shows in this sector only an area of "houses some destroyed, some standing." It is a rectangular tower, 17 by 24 feet, abutting on the natural rock along its southwest side. The curtain joins it by changing from a retaining to a free-standing wall which rises, like a ramp, inversely as the cobbled way descends.

the cobbled way, which curves round below the tower and follows back underneath the upper wall.

Beyond the Monemvasia Gate the wall is obliterated in the debris of fallen houses, and begins again at the upper south corner of the Pandanassa convent. From here it stands upwards of 20 feet high; its top, in almost total absence of a parapet, is flush with the ground it serves to retain. Three hundred feet from the Pandanassa it projects forward and forms a redan pierced by a round archway, 10 feet

12*

high, with a short, depressed, vaulted passage behind it. Above the Perivleptos Monastery at the lowest south corner of the ruined city, the wall of the upper town contains, as the Grimani drawing shows, a small quadrangular gate, 12 by 15 feet, built against the rock on one side, with wedge and brick arched openings in the other three. Inside, it is vaulted. Above the front door at platform level, are two brackets,

a drop of 80 feet (Fig. 197). A thin wall, made with grey mortar at the bottom and white along the upper sections, follows down the incline to the enclosure of the Aphendiko Monastery (Fig. 196). Here the chemin de ronde is carried on arcades, a construction which the Turks used in their curtains of New Navarino, but which the Byzantines had used before them. The parapet runs with a straight top, without

Fig. 197. Mistra, the Castle, Despots' Palace, Curtain of Lower Town, and Aphendiko Monastery, from the North.

serving once as supports for the balcony of an upper storey. Beyond, the tiny wall winds its way to the edge of the Pandeleimona cliffs. Near the end is still another small gate, which once offered communication between the outer sections of the upper and lower town, and now stands deserted on the wasted slope of the hill.

The circuit wall of the lower town begins, as Plate XXXIV shows, under the north angle of the Despots' Palace, where the cliff makes

loopholes or crenellations. This appears to be a Turkish parapet on top of a Byzantine wall. Opposite the front of the Aphendiko Church, the wall rises to a height of 40 feet. Near the bottom are two small, brick-arched openings for a house built against it on the inside. Outside are the remains of a large, rectangular tower, whose lower flank is based on both a stepped projection and a talus, and whose face contains traces of the same form of tall, recessed arch as is seen in the flanking towers at the castle gate and in the upper town circuit. The flanks do not bond with the curtain, and this arch and talus are non-Byzantine features, so that the tower is probably a later Turkish addition.

Opposite the north corner of the Aphendiko is a confusion of ruined fortifications piled one on top of the other. The northernmost extremity of the circuit is marked by a tower (Figs. 196, 197, 198), shown on the Grimani plan as a small square in the wall. This contains five storeys and rises 80 feet high, a dimension that assigns it rather to the Turks than to the Byzantines. The face, which is all that remains intact, contains deep, tapering lancet windows. The north corner is underpinned with a curving talus of big blocks of stone.

For the space of 120 feet, the path which leads up from the communal fountain in the gulley, past the ruined tower, to the houses of Kato Khora marks the line of the circuit wall. Southeastward from the tower, opposite the church of Sts. Theodore (Fig. 196, right), it reappears and continues along the backs of low, clustered houses and small terraces of cultivated land, showing here a chemin de ronde, there a flanking tower, or a gate with cloisonné arch.

The enclosure of the Metropolis presents a front integral with the circuit wall of the lower town (Fig. 178, left). Just to the south is a large tower, 15 by 20 feet, shorn of its upper chamber but still showing the sills of lancet windows in its truncated face. Beyond this, the circuit can be traced down to a fortified house, which brings the wall forward over the olive groves of the Lacedaemonian plain. At the settlement of houses called Marmara, there is a 50-foot high tower with a fountain built into its flank. Its face is heavily decorated with brickwork. Near the top are eight stone brackets, which once supported a balcony. The windows are mere loopholes; the walls between

them are strengthened with tall interior buttresses. The curtain continues south from Marmara without chemin de ronde, flanked by two small towers, as far as the Perivleptos

FIG. 198. MISTRA, TOWER IN NORTH CORNER OF LOWER TOWN CIRCUIT.

Monastery, where it vanishes at last before the cliffs begin their precipitous ascent back to the fortress on the summit.

This elaborate system of town walls belongs to the centuries when Mistra was the capital of the Byzantine Morea. The earliest section is that which encloses the upper town, descending from Dhiaselo to the Nauplia and Monemvasia Gates. Except for certain Turkish additions, it dates for the most part to the first years of the Despotate, or the end of the XIII century. Later, when the capital was expanding and the Aphendiko, Sts. Theodore, the Metropolis, and the Perivleptos were built on a lower level of the hill, a new wall was extended to link up their enclosures. Discounting again the Turkish constructions round the Aphendiko, the circuit of the lower town may be assigned to the early XIV century. The Turks added a number of towers along the northwest flank of the city, and rebuilt all its parapets. Except for a depressed arch in a wall near the Perivleptos, supported on spirally carved pilasters, and bearing an inscription with the date 1714, the Venetian occupation of Mistra seems to have left no trace. Though the place served as a center of local administration, it is unlikely that the Venetians, interested chiefly in the artillery defenses of harbor towns, would have spent much effort on repairing a fortress already four and a half centuries old, originally built for the subjugation of local tribes in the depth of the country far from the sea.

CHAPTER XVI

CHALKIS

(Plate XXXV)

An attack on Euboea was first considered by the Venetians in August, 1687, before the fall of Mistra. During September and October, with the Peloponnese secured for all but Monemvasia, the war council continued debating the possibility. To capture the city of Negroponte would drive the Turks out of their strongest position in northern Greece, and give the Venetians a new bulwark for the Morea.[1] The scheme was postponed, however, and the Venetians invaded Attica instead. During the winter of 1687–8 they occupied Athens, and then after six months abandoned it as strategically useless, leaving the ruins of the Parthenon as a memorial of their barren victory.

Morosini, after his election as Doge, was anxious to bring off a victory at Negroponte and reconquer the island for Venice. Königsmark opposed this plan, claiming that Negroponte would be a useless possession, since the Turks would still hold the mainland, and the Venetians lacked troops to drive them off. Moreover the Turks had been preparing for a Venetian offensive since 1686, increasing the garrison of Negroponte and enlarging its defenses. Outside the walls of the town all the trees had been cut

down to form an open plain without cover. Trenches had been dug all round the city, protected by palisades, and four batteries of guns set up on near-by hills, so that 400 paces from the walls a strong line of outer defenses stretched from sea to sea. On the mainland immediately opposite the city a fort had been built on the hill called Karababa, dominating the bridge across the Euripos and connecting with it by a rock-cut way 300 paces long. It was considered an awkward work, but was well garrisoned and stocked with some 40 pieces of cannon. The operations had been carried out under the direction of an Italian renegade, a certain Girolamo Galoppo of Guastalla near Mantua, a dragoon in the regiment of the Marquis de Corbon, who because of losses at the gaming table and a quarrel with Daniele Dolfin, had gone over to the Turks at the time of the Venetian siege of Nauplia.[2]

In spite of Königsmark's objections, the armada set sail and on July 13, 1688, disembarked at Negroponte. The allied army numbered 15,000 against 6,000 of the Turks. Immediately a divergence arose between the leaders, whether or not to attack the new fort on Karababa. Against the better judgment of Königsmark, who wanted first to drive the

---

[1] Locatelli, I, p. 345; Laborde, *Documents inédits ou peu connus sur l'histoire et les antiquités d'Athènes* (Paris, 1854), pp. 160, 162, 165 f.

[2] Locatelli, I, p. 280; II, p. 95; Garzoni, I, pp. 268 f.; Foscarini, pp. 290 f.; Laborde, *Documents inédits*, p. 160.

Turks out of that vital position, the Venetians decided, on hearing it had no water supply, to pass it by and concentrate their forces instead against the city on the island.[3] So the fleet was sent, under the command of Lorenzo Venier, to occupy the bay north of the Euripos, while four galleys held the mouth of the southern channel. The troops set up their positions on the north shore to the west of the city (see line E, E on Plate XXXV).

The Venetians had reckoned without the natural conditions of the region. Encamped in the swampy lowlands of Chalkis 4,000 of the troops succumbed in a few days to the malaria which cost the lives of Daniele Dolfin and of Königsmark himself. The command of the army passed to a Frenchman, Charles Félice de Gallean, Duc de Guadagne, a veteran of Turenne's wars.[4]

The Venetians made little headway, their numbers halved by fever within a month of their landing, and their plans frustrated by quarrels among the military factions of different nationalities. They set up five batteries to the south and west of the city (Plate XXXV, A, D.), but were continually harassed by enemy sorties, while reinforcements from the Seraskier at Thebes made their way uninterrupted across the bridge into the city. Finally, however, the arrival of 4,000 auxiliaries from Venice inspired the allied forces to assault the Turkish palisades in the plain (Plate XXXV, I, I). After three attacks the Turks were driven from their outer line of defenses, leaving behind them, it was claimed, 1,500 dead and 39 pieces of cannon on the earthworks. This drew the circumvallation tighter round the city (line F, F), while new batteries were set up, one on the small island in the southern bay (point B), one on the small point of land north of the town against Karababa (K), and two against the town's land front (G and L). Now they concentrated their fire on the Turkish strongpoint, the sea bastion at the north extremity of the town circuit, where a breach was finally opened. On September 8 a band of 50 men assaulted it, planted the banner of St. Mark upon its walls, and then, for lack of support, were driven back.[5]

The allied army was reduced at this point to a dangerously low number, first by the effects of the fever and next by the departure of the Florentine and Maltese contingents. Those actively fighting amounted now to only 6,000, whereas the garrison of the city was being strengthened all the time from the mainland guarded by Karababa. Finally the Venetians pushed their trenches up to the edge of the counterscarp at the south end, where they set up a battery of eight guns (H) to open a breach in the opposite wall. After two months the casualties had reached such proportions that Morosini now decided to stake everything on a final assault. The breach was brought down to what was considered a scalable height, and the counterscarp was exploded in order to provide a crossing over the ditch. The chief attack was to be launched against the breach, while, to divert the enemy, a secondary attack was prepared against the north sea bastion already once taken. A feint was to be made by ships and troops sent against Karababa to prevent the Turks on the mainland coming to the relief of the city. On October 12 the signal was given. The Venetians captured the sea bastion on the north side with heavy losses, and once again, lacking support, were driven off. The main breach in the moment of assault was discovered to be still too high. A band of Albanians and Dalmatians nevertheless took one tower, but this was too high to afford descent into the city enclosure, and too narrow to be held. They abandoned it of their own accord, and the Turks drove back a Venetian force which came to attack it a second time. In the space of an hour and a half over 1,000

[3] Journal of Anna Ackerhjelm, in Laborde, Documents inédits, p. 245; Locatelli, II, p. 92; Garzoni, I, p. 289; Cappelletti, XI, p. 65.
[4] Garzoni, I, p. 271; Cappelletti, XI, p. 66.

[5] Garzoni, I, pp. 279 f.; Foscarini, pp. 293 ff.

of the Venetian army died at the breach. The assault was at last abandoned. Morosini at the final moment proposed to redeem the disastrous failure of his undertaking by setting up winter quarters and tightening the siege. But the German auxiliaries refused to stay, and so what was left of the allied army was embarked. Five thousand of the Greeks of Euboea, fearful of Turkish vengeance, crowded also on board the Venetian vessels, bound for the safer Peloponnesian shore.[6]

*　　*　　*

Negroponte in the XII century was noted by Benjamin of Tudela[7] as "a large city . . . where merchants come from every quarter," with a Jewish community of 200 souls, the second largest in Greece. The island itself was rich enough in 1170 to provide six galleys for the fleets of Byzantium, and Chalkis' fortifications resisted a Venetian raiding party several years before the Fourth Crusade.[8] The first formal claim which the Venetians established to the island was made in the Partition Treaty of 1204, by which they were to be assigned Oreos at the north and Karystos at the southern end.[9] However, in 1205 Euboea submitted not to the Venetians, but to Jacques d'Avesnes, who, descending through Greece in the wake of the conquering Frankish forces, stopped long enough at Chalkis to build a small fort in the middle of the Euripos channel.[10] Upon his death without heirs at the siege of Acrocorinth, Boniface of Montferrat, ignoring Venice's claim, divided Euboea among three Veronese nobles, who took the title of *terzieri* or triarchs, and swore allegiance to Guillaume de Champlitte.[11] The death of one and the departure of another left the third triarch, Ravano dalle Carceri, master of the

whole island. Venice exercised her usual cunning first by waiving her claim to Oreos and Karystos, which it would have required force to occupy, and then by lending Ravano naval aid in a rebellion of the Franks of northern Greece against the Latin emperor of Constantinople. In return for this favor she received the hommage of Ravano, the right of free trade and a church and warehouse in every town in Euboea.[12] A bailie was appointed from Venice to administer the Republic's affairs. Then, as usually happened in the places where Venice established a business interest, trading rights brought political power, which finally developed into control of the whole island. She began in 1216 on the death of Ravano by dividing Euboea among six claimants. Venetian weights and measures were introduced, and a church of St. Mark was founded in the city of Chalkis which, by a corruption of Euripos to Egripos, became known as Negroponte. Venetian officials arrived to take over the administration, and Lombard nobles, relatives of the original triarchs, to acquire lands, build castles, and live off the profits of Aegean piracy.[13]

Euboea was placed subject to the Principality of the Morea in 1236, when the emperor Baldwin II made Geoffroy II Villehardouin its suzerain,[14] and the triarchs swore to contribute eight knights or an armed galley to the Prince's forces.[15] These relations were further tightened when William Villehardouin took as his second wife Carintana dalle Carceri, baroness of the northern third of the island. When she died in 1255, he laid claim to her barony, but the other two triarchs and the minor Lombard nobles leagued together against him under the leadership of the Venetian bailie, putting up a candidate of their own to take over the northern estate. Villehardouin occu-

[6] Locatelli, II, pp. 139–143; Foscarini, pp. 297–301.

[7] *The Itinerary of Benjamin of Tudela*, p. 10.

[8] Miller, *Latins*, p. 22.

[9] Tafel und Thomas, *Urkunden*, I, p. 469.

[10] Niketas Choniates, ed. Bonn, p. 806.

[11] X. τ. M., lines 1550–1556; *C. di M.*, p. 424; *L. de C.*, § 221; *L. de F.*, § 102.

[12] Tafel und Thomas, *Urkunden*, II, pp. 89–96.

[13] J. B. Bury, "The Lombards and Venetians in Euboia," *J.H.S.*, VII, 1886, pp. 319f.; Miller, *Latins*, pp. 35, 45f., 73, 77ff.

[14] *L. de F.*, § 207; Hopf, *Geschichte Griechenlands*, I, p. 272.

[15] Sanudo, in Hopf, *Chroniques gréco-romanes*, pp. 99f.

pied Negroponte, which the Venetians re-captured after a thirteen months' siege. The barons of Achaea defeated the Venetians at Oreos, while Villehardouin harrassed the borders of their colony at Corone, and kept four galleys at Monemvasia, manned by Genoese, to prey on their shipping. Finally the bailie at Negroponte received instructions to come to terms, but by then Villehardouin had been defeated by the Greek emperor at Pelagonia and taken prisoner to Constantinople. Euboea at last had respite from war, and fell, as Sanudo says, "into a state so peaceful that the enemy of the human race would have had it in envy."[16]

The Lombard barons and the Venetian bailie soon had recourse, however, to a new defensive alliance, when a certain knight of Karystos named Licario, who had incurred the scorn of his high-born Italian compatriots by his marriage with the widow of one of the triarchs, sold his services to the emperor Michael VIII, and waged a guerrilla war against them in Euboea. With the capture of most of the castles he succeeded in establishing the Byzantine authority over a large part of the island. The city of Negroponte, fortified and defended by the Venetian bailie, held out against Licario, who ended as Grand Duke of the Byzantine navy, and kept Euboea, the neighboring islands, and the coasts of Attica in a state of upheaval for several years more.[17]

After 1261 when the Greek Empire was restored in Constantinople, Euboea took on new importance as an outpost of Latin rule in the Eastern Mediterranean. The Venetians doubled the salary of their bailie in Negroponte, and in 1304 forced the Jews to pay for the building of walls round the Venetian quarter of the town. Gradually they extended their sway over the whole of Euboea, buying up lands that fell vacant, assuming the admin-istration of the original baronies which descended to female heirs, and recapturing by the end of the XIII century all the castles which Licario had occupied.[18] Negroponte was developed into a naval station against attacks from the neighboring Catalans of Attica, whose alliance the Venetians nevertheless sought by a succession of treaties.[19] In 1317 the Catalan leader, Don Alfonso Fadrique, married the daughter of one of the triarchs, Boniface of Verona, who died shortly after, giving Fadrique the chance to invade Euboea and lay claim to his wife's inheritance. He occupied the castles of Karystos and Larmena and even captured Chalkis, until a Venetian fleet forced him to withdraw.[20] This disturbance, together with Turkish raids and a war with the Genoese, who fell on Negroponte and burned the suburbs, gave the Venetians the excuse to assume further jurisdiction over the island in the name of common defense. In 1365 they bought back from the Catalans Larmena and Karystos, and in 1388 the Senate ordered the heightening of the walls of Negroponte. The advance of the Turks across Macedonia into northern Greece in the early XV century made the Venetian's position increasingly dangerous in Euboea. In vain Manuel II sought their help for the defense of the Peloponnese: their attention was concentrated on their northern outpost. In preparation for the coming attack, they were busy, at the eleventh hour, lowering the taxes of their Greek subjects in an effort to win their co-operation, training the serfs in archery, and settling colonies of Albanians on the land. But the Turkish depredations continued and so disrupted the common life that the inhabitants begged Venice to make the island tributary to the Turks. Meanwhile Euboea grew poorer under the effects of plague and of

[16] *Ibid.*, pp. 103, 106, 119; Miller, *Latins*, pp. 102–108.

[17] Hopf, *Chroniques gréco-romanes*, pp. 119–131; Nikephoros Gregoras, ed. Bonn, I, pp. 95f.; Bury, *op. cit.*, pp. 325–340; Miller, *Latins*, pp. 136–141.

[18] *Ibid.*, pp. 78, 208 ff.

[19] Rubio i Lluch, *Diplomatari de l'Orient Catala* (Barcelona, 1947), pp. 132 ff., 141 ff., 196 ff.

[20] *Chronicle of Muntaner*, tr. Goodenough (London, 1921), chap. 243; K. M. Setton, *Catalan Domination of Athens*, (Medieval Academy of America, 1948), pp. 28–30.

raids from both Turks and Catalans. The fortifications of Negroponte declined, the harbors silted up, and the Albanian settlers grew restive before the danger.[21]

In 1458 Mohammed II stopped at Negroponte on his final campaign against the Morea, and carefully scanned the defenses of the city which he was to wrest from the Venetians twelve years later. The year 1463 marked the beginning of the long series of Turkish wars which were to cost Venice her empire. Argos was the first of her colonies in Greece to fall to the Turks, and on June 15, 1470, a Turkish fleet of 300 vessels appeared at Negroponte. Mohammed arrived from Thebes, set up his batteries on Karababa, and threw two pontoon bridges across the channel to the island where he dug his circumvallations. The population in the city numbered 2,500. Added to these were 700 fighting men from Crete and 500 Albanians. The number of the Turkish army was placed between 120,000 and 300,000. On June 25 Mohammed called on the city to surrender, on reasonable terms. The Venetian bailie, Paolo Erizzo, sent back a defiant rejection, and the defenders on the wall shouted abuse to the Turkish sultan. Mohammed launched three attacks against the town, but the arrival of a Venetian fleet of 71 vessels on July 11 seemed likely to bring deliverance. The ships could have charged the northern bridge of boats and shut Mohammed up in the little island fort, but the admiral, Canale, hesitated, and the tide turned in the Euripos. Mohammed sent out troops to line both Euboean and Boeotian shores against Canale's landing, and the next day attacked the city walls across a moat filled with corpses and debris. While the Turks fought their way street by street into the town, Canale's fleet still waited outside in the channel. The defenders at last surrendered, and the place was given over to a carnage in which the bailie and all the inhabitants over eight years old were killed.

With Negroponte, the whole of Euboea was lost to Venice.[22]

Travellers from Western Europe who visited Negroponte during the XVII, XVIII, and early XIX centuries testify to its continuing importance under Turkish domination. From their descriptions it is possible to gather some idea of the great citadel which modern town planners have taken such care to obliterate. George Wheler,[23] who saw the place twelve years before Morosini's abortive siege, wrote:

The city *Egripus* then is upon or hard by the place where *Chalcis* stood formerly; that is, on a *Peninsula* of the Island anciently called *Euboea*, and is there separated from *Boeotia* by a narrow streight: which is passed over first by a small Stone-Bridge of four or five Arches, to a little tower built by the *Venetians* in the middle of the Chanel; from whence to the Town is a Draw-Bridge, no larger than to let a Gally pass thorough. The Walls of the Town are not above two Miles about: but there are more Buildings and People in the Suburbs of the Christians beyond, than in the City, where only *Turks* and *Jews* inhabit. The Turks have two Mosques within, and two without; where the Christians have also their Churches. The City is separated from the Suburbs by a deep Ditch; and the Inhabitants of both may amount, probably, to fourteen or fifteen thousand people. There are six or seven Families of the *Francks* among them; and a seminary of *Jesuits*, who pretend to be there only to teach their Children; but withal, to do as much service to the *Romanists* as they can.

This is the chief residence of the Capitan *Basha*, or General of the *Turkish* fleet, who is Governor both of this City and Island, and the Adjacent parts of *Greece*; having a *Keiah*, or Deputy under him. A Fleet of Gallies still lie here, to be ready upon all occasions to go out against the Pyrates, and those of *Malta*. His Palace is without the Town, upon the Shore, North-East off the Bridge; Fortified only by the Gallies fastened to the Shore above it. His Brother *Achmet Basha* lives in the Town, at the Palace, which was the residence of the *Proveditore* of the *Venetians*, before this Island was taken from them, by *Mahomet* the Second. This is situate on the shore on the Eastern-side of the Bridge, and therein we were shewed some Vaults, with secret Passages to go out with Boats to the *Euripus*; where the *Proveditore* of that unhappy time of the Family *Erizzo* endeavoured to escape, but

---

[21] Miller, *Latins*, pp. 300 ff., 365 f., 376, 460.

[22] *Ibid.*, pp. 443, 471–476.
[23] *Op. cit.*, pp. 457 ff.

was discovered by Spies, taken, and most barbarously put to death by that Cruel Tyrant and Enemy to Christendom ...

On the Walls of this Palace we found an Inscription ...

ANNO AB INCARNATIONE DÑI NR̄I IH̄V XPI
MILLE CCLXXIII MĒS MAIO HOC OPVS FEC.
INCHOARI NOBIL. VIR DÑVS NICOLAVS
MILIANI BAIVL. NIGROPONTIS ET EIVS CONSI
LARII DÑI MĀHEL DE ANDRO ET PETRVS NAVAI
ARIO IN HONORĒ DEI ET BEATI MARCI
EVĀG.

By the Water on the same side of the City is an old Castle[24] where we were shewed among other great Guns several Mortar-pieces of such a prodigious Bore, as are capable to fling stones of two Foot and three Inches Diameter.

The observations of Wheler and Spon are echoed in the descriptions of Coronelli[25] and Garzoni,[26] who also gives the dimensions of the ditch as 20 feet deep and 100 wide, and in the accounts of the travellers Dapper[27] and Thompson[28] in the early XVIII century. Pouqueville[29] states that the sanjak of Negroponte comprised the whole of central Greece, with Chalkis the capital of an area including Euboea, Attica, Boeotia, Phokis, and Aetolia as far as the mouth of the Achelous river. In the time of Leake[30] the Turks and Jews were still the only inhabitants of the old walled city or Kastro. The Christians, who formed only a third of the population of the town, occupied the suburbs which were largely ruined and deserted. Speaking of the Kastro, Leake[31] writes:

This fortress is a construction of different ages; square towers erected before the invention of gunpowder are mixed with Venetian bastions of antique construction, or with Turkish white-washed walls and battlements. There is a dry ditch, intended to be

flooded at pleasure, but which is now filled with rubbish. The glacis of the Castle is occupied by the Turkish burying-ground, beyond which is the Christian town surrounded by walls, in a wretched state of dilapidation, encircling the promontory of the Kastro in a semilunar form from bay to bay; beyond these the Turks have lately thrown up a palisaded rampart of earth across the isthmus ...

The *Euripus*, which strictly speaking is no more than the narrowest part of the strait between Mount Karababá and the western walls of the kastro is divided as to its breadth into two unequal parts by a small square castle, founded on a rock, and having a solid round tower at the north-western angle. A stone bridge, 60 or 70 feet in length, connects the *Boeotian* shore with this castle, the entrance into which is by a drawbridge at the north-eastern angle. Another wooden bridge about 35 feet long, which may be raised at both ends for the purpose of admitting the passage of vessels, communicates from the small castle to the gate of the Kastro, which is in a tower projecting from the walls. The inner channel is said always to afford a depth of eight or nine feet: under the stone bridge the water is much more shallow.

Buchon[32] in 1841 noted the many carved lions, some of them re-used as building blocks placed upside down by the Turks, and the Venetian coats of arms still adorning the walls.[33] He failed to find the inscription noted by Wheler, though he saw another Latin inscription[34] in the church of Ayia Paraskevi, the early Christian basilica which the Franks converted into a Gothic cathedral.

* * *

To-day all that remains of Chalkis' defenses is the fort of Karababa on the mainland west of the city. Its plan is pear-shaped, extending

[24] Wheler probably refers to one of the bastions of the circuit wall.

[25] *An Historical and Geographical Account of the Morea, Negropont and Maritime Places*, pp. 206f.

[26] I, p. 268.

[27] *Description exacte des isles de l'Archipel* (Amsterdam, 1703), pp. 290f.

[28] *Travels* (Reading, 1752), I, pp. 423f.

[29] *Voyage*, III, pp. 316f.

[30] *Travels in Northern Greece* (London, 1835), III, pp. 254–257.

[31] *Op. cit.*, pp. 255–257.

[32] *Voyage dans l'Eubée, les Iles ioniennes et les Cyclades en 1841* (Paris, 1911), pp. 20–30.

[33] *Atlas des nouvelles recherches historiques sur la Principauté française de Morée* (Paris, 1845), plate XL, figs. 6, 9, 12, 13, 15, 19, 32.

[34] Buchon wrongly read its date as 1393. A correct transcription is

HIC IACET NOBILIS ET EGR
EGIVS VIR DOMINVS PETRVS
LIPPOMANO NEC NON HONORA
BILIS CONSILIARIVS NIGROPO
NTIS A VENETORVM DVCALI
DOMINIO CONSTITVTVS
QVI AB HOC SECVLO MIGRA
VIT DÑI SVB ANNI S·M·CCC·
LXXXXVIII DIE SEPTIMO
MENSIS SETEMBRIS· EX SVORVM
HEREDVM

some 500 feet long from east to west, defended by large bastions at both ends and two smaller terrepleined redouts in either flank. It is weak and poorly built, showing every sign of haste in construction, but is distinctive nevertheless as a complete, if slipshod, example of late artillery fortification. The masonry is homogeneous, consisting of small, well squared poros and more roughly cut limestone blocks, set in some approximation of coursing, with a quantity of broken tile in courses and ladders between the joints. The parapets are made of smaller rubble. Large, squared limestone and a few marble blocks are used in the angles of the bastions. Smaller, cut poros blocks form the angles of the embrasures. A thick coating of plaster still adheres in patches to the walls.

in the wall behind it, which leads into the fortress enclosure. To the right of the gate the wall curves round, bearing a ruined parapet of narrow, slot-like embrasures, to the large east bastion. This is the strongpoint of the fortress, and in fact its reason for being. Dominating the Euripos and the two bays of Ayios Minas and Bourkos to the north and south respectively, the bastion's guns were able to secure the bridge and the supply routes from the mainland, while at the same time warding off any ships that might try to approach the city. It is a polygonal bastion with five battering sides, terrepleined except on the south, which contains a long, vaulted chamber reached by a descent of steps. The parapet, which encloses a platform 75 feet across, is largely ruined. Measuring 6 feet thick, it contains seven embrasures, two of which are still occupied by old pieces of cannon.

FIG. 199. CHALKIS, NORTH CURTAIN AND FLANKING BASTION OF KARABABA. IN THE BACKGROUND, THE EURIPOS CHANNEL.

The entrance is in the southeast corner, a plain round arch made of two rows of poros voussoirs, masking the higher, vaulted passage

The curtains are low, standing to a height of not more than 20 feet, and only 5 feet thick. They support a 3-foot wide chemin de ronde and a parapet of peculiar scalloped outline (Fig. 199) whose undulating crest gives the impression of crenellation, without however providing the advantage of proper merlons. It is too high to allow for fire between the rounded tops, which nevertheless are pierced by a regular succession of tall, narrow loopholes with tapering sides made of big, cut poros blocks thickly plastered.

Two thirds of the way up the slope of the hilltop toward the western end of the enclosure, the north curtain is defended by a four-sided, terrepleined redout (Fig. 199), 60 feet across, reached by a ramp from the interior of the fortress. The face and flank of this bastion which cover the northern channel carry two embrasures five feet deep. The salient angle is flanked by two small embrasures raised 1½ feet above the platform level. The bastion's west face contains one embrasure, and the west flank, adjacent to the curtain, on the side least exposed to attack, supports only a thin parapet with musketry loopholes. The east flank contains a postern now blocked up.

The south curtain is almost entirely ruined or re-built. Toward the upper section of the fortress, where both curtains draw together, the scalloped parapet stands intact, with loopholes less frequent than on the north side, being set at intervals of three or four undulations of the parapet. A second terrepleined bastion, higher up the hill than the similar one in the opposite curtain, with one face and two flanks, projects also into the interior of the enceinte, forming an irregular pentagonal platform, reached here again by a ramp. Four embrasures in a half-demolished parapet cover the bay of Bourkos. A collapse of the masonry in both flanks of the bastion at the re-entrant angles, discloses an earlier construction which the walls of the present bastion serve to mask. The cavity in the eastern flank reveals a well

made casemate of cut poros blocks in the interior wall. This opening is blocked up on the inside. It may be presumed the original form of the redout was a simple, two-sided redan, hollow inside, with provision for guns at ground level. This was subsequently – probably soon after its building – encased and terrepleined by the bastion which stands to-day.

The west bastion at the highest point of the hill commanding the road from Thebes, is a hollow, slightly irregular heptagon 100 feet in diameter, with battering walls 20 to 30 feet high. It is built with some ingenuity, with a round archway of poros voussoirs on the east side within the circuit admitting to two concentric galleries built round a mass of masonry containing a cistern, which supports the gun platform above. A central hole and five channels in the outer rim of the platform conduct the rain-water into the cistern. The narrow inner gallery which encircles it is only 6 feet wide, separated from the outer by a heavy arcade 7 feet thick, carried on great piers of unequal size, measuring up to 15 feet long. The outer gallery is 10 feet wide, and opens on to a ring of vaulted casemates (Fig. 200), one

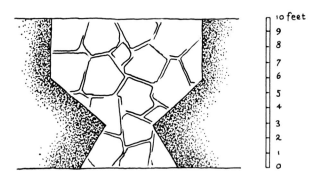

FIG. 200. CHALKIS, KARABABA: CASEMATE IN HEPTAGONAL BASTION, PLAN.

in each of the bastion's six flanks outside the fortress enclosure. Both galleries are covered with barrel vaults. In the outer the angles of the vault are spanned by ribs of cut poros blocks, springing from carved corbels (Fig. 201). Double rows of poros voussoirs are used in both the arcades and the embrasure arches.

A flight of steps to the left of the entrance leads up to the great gun platform above. This is enclosed by a parapet 2½ feet thick and 5 feet high, pierced by fourteen shallow embrasures, two to each side of the heptagon.

pond exactly with the batteries as drawn on Grimani's map of Negroponte. In the open country to the east of the city may be seen a section of the aqueduct marked in red on the plan. The conduit is carried on a line of fifteen

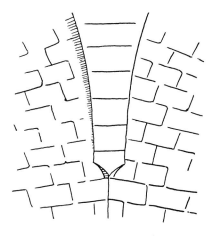 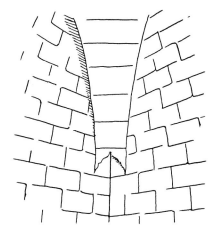

FIG. 201. CHALKIS, KARABABA: TRANSVERSE RELIEVING ARCH (INNER AND OUTER SECTION) AT ANGLE OF OUTER VAULTED GALLERY IN HEPTAGONAL BASTION.

Around the north and west sides the fortress is guarded by a raised earthwork or glacis extending from the east round to the west bastion, following the indentations and projections of the walls and bastions. The steepness of the slope along the south flank makes such a defense unnecessary. The rock-cut way mentioned by Garzoni[35] and Locatelli[36] may still be seen following in a straight line from the fortress gate down the hill toward the Euripos bridge.

Except for Karababa little remains to-day which can be identified with any of the works shown on Plate XXXV. Examination of the two hills on the peninsula south of the city (Plate XXXV, C, C) "fortified with batteries by the Turks," reveals traces of trenches and ruined habitation, though nothing to corres-

tall, pointed arches made of alternating wedge-shaped blocks and brick, of characteristic Turkish pattern. The wells which can still be seen in some of the houses of the old town, notably in one opposite the church of Ayia Paraskevi, must have been considered insufficient for the city's needs after 1470, when this aqueduct would have been built. Of the town walls, one isolated fragment of the east curtain still stands within the army compound. Except for this, all the sea and land walls have gone, the moat, the bridge, and the Euripos fort. These works, magnificent and irreplaceable, have been systematically demolished in order to give way to the tasteless uniformity of provincial boulevards. The city of Chalkis has spread out over the plain where the Turks once built their palisades and the Venetians dug their trenches; and the place where the armies met is a wide and dusty suburb.

[35] I, p. 269.
[36] II, p. 95.

CHAPTER XVII

MONEMAVSIA

(Plates XXXVI, XXXVII A, B)

By the late summer of 1687 all of the territorial Peloponnese was in Venetian hands. Mistra had fallen, and with it the interior highlands of the country. One place only remained to the Turks, the island rock of Monemvasia, a stone's throw from land off the southeastern extremity of Lakonia. At the beginning of September the Venetian fleet made its appearance there, in the hope that the long series of Venetian victories and a show of force would bring the place to terms. The first summons to surrender was rejected, and the second called forth a volley of musket fire. So Morosini ordered twelve of his largest ships to discharge a full salvo against the town. The Turkish guns answered by sinking one of the Venetian galleys. More ships were sent in to continue the bombardment, but after a few days Morosini decided time was being wasted to no effect, and the armada sailed on to Corinth. There the council decided to carry the war north of the Isthmus.[1]

Two years later, in the summer of 1689, after both Athens and Negroponte had been abandoned, the Venetians returned to consolidate their gains in the Morea. The forces of the Holy League, reduced by the departure of the Hanoverian, Florentine, and Maltese contingents, consisted now of only 11,000 men.

The council deliberated the possibility of attacks on Canea in Crete, Salonica, or the Dalmatian cities of Valona and Dulcigno. But the opinion of Morosini, as general and doge, prevailed in favor of a blockade of Monemvasia which, in Turkish hands, remained a thorn in the side of the Venetian Morea.

The contemporary Foscarini[2] describes how the fortress[3] is situated on a precipitous mountain set off by itself, from which one crosses to land by means of a stone bridge of twenty-three arches. At the bottom stands the lower town, facing south, bathed by the sea. On the other side toward the north are unscalable cliffs. Nature has made it impregnable to any force of arms, because to advance to attack the lower town, there is a narrow way without terrain for cover, open to the fire of the enemy who, besides musket and cannon, inflict grave damage from above with rocks. It was decided therefore to starve it out by siege.

In May, 1689, the first troops were disembarked on the Lakonian coast. Two forts were built, one on the mainland south of the rock, in view of the lower town, and another at the head of the bridge which joined the rock to land, to prevent the Turks escaping. From here the Venetian artillery was trained on to the Turkish positions on the cliff top and on to a certain "bonnet on a high position beyond the bridge," traces of which can still be seen

---

[1] Locatelli, I, pp. 352–357; Garzoni, I, pp. 214f.

[2] *Op. cit.*, pp. 327f.

[3] Traquair gives the dimensions of the rock as one mile long, 600 feet high; the cliffs are nowhere lower than 250 feet. *B.S.A.*, XII, 1905–1906, pp. 259 ff.

on a lower spur of cliff, accessible by sloping ledges on the north side. Another battery of mortars was set up near the bridge to fire on the town. The bombardment began on July 12, enabling the Venetians to capture the bonnet and advance their trenches beneath the south

Morosini himself was on the point of leaving the siege to go off in pursuit of the Turkish fleet in the Aegean, when he was taken with fever, and on September 13 set sail for Venice, leaving his command to Girolamo Corner.[4]

The siege continued,[5] while the war was pro-

FIG. 202. MONEMVASIA, FROM THE WEST.

flank of the cliff. On the night of August 11 a squadron of fire ships was sent in against the sea walls, while the infantry massed at the head of the bridge in readiness for an attack. But a northwest wind frustrated the action, and the Turks fired down from the cliff on to the heads of the troops. On this occasion Francesco Grimani was wounded by a rock hurled from above, and the commander of the fleet, Lorenzo Venier, was shot by a Venetian renegade.

The Duc de Guadagne pressed for an attack on the lower town, but Morosini overruled him, preferring to starve the place out gradually by siege rather than risk excessive loss of life.

secuted without great success in Dalmatia, until summer of the following year. New vigor was instilled into the Holy League by Pope Alexander VIII, himself a Venetian, who sent out galleys and reinforcements to press the siege of Monemvasia. The Duc de Guadagne now began to carry out his scheme of attacking the lower town. Detachments made their way out along the south side of the island with materials for mining the walls, but were checked by a sortie and caught between fire from the town and volleys of rocks from the

[4] Locatelli, II, pp. 205–247; Garzoni, I, pp. 326–332; Cappelletti, XI, pp. 71 f., 75.
[5] The Proveditor Antonio Molin claims to have commanded the siege for eighteen months, Δελτίον, V, p. 432.

13

cliffs above. However, they held their ground and succeeded in digging themselves in. Guadagne, meanwhile, set up positions on the rocky eastern end of the island, in an attempt to enclose the town in a pincers movement.

coste dela senextre on the right side of the drawing) and concentrating on the line of attack west of the town (*le coste dextre*, drawn on the left side). The eastern positions, he claimed, were mutually indefensible, and open to at-

Fig. 203. Monemvasia, the Lower Town, looking Southwest.

A month after they had entrenched themselves in this order, still without success, Guadagne sent one of his engineers, a Frenchman named Erault Desparées, to report on the state and efficacy of the positions in both sectors. Plate XXXVII B shows a section of the rock of Monemvasia, in a quaint combination of plan and elevation, with the Venetian emplacements on either side of the town. On the reverse side of the drawing Erault Desparées wrote out his elaborate report and the proposals which were to form the basis for the final attack. He recommended abandoning the positions at the eastern tip of the island (*le*

tack from three sides: sorties could be made either through the town's east wall, from above, down the easternmost cliffs, or by way of the steep slope, sealed off by a wall, marked *Mura Rossa* on Plate XXXVI, to intercept the Venetian supply route along the base of the cliffs on the north side. This could be cut off by two simple trenches, which would isolate the eastern positions and force them to rely solely on support from the sea. He proposed, instead, doubling the manpower of the western positions. Although the cliff top gave an almost aerial view of the Venetian trenches on this side, they were laid out with greater skill than the positions on the other. Covered ways had been built with fascines, allowing for intercommunication even by daylight between the different posts, which received protection from certain rocky outcroppings on the slope below would still be impossible to storm the upper fortress. They proposed instead to abandon the attack on the lower town, withdraw to the two original forts, and wait for the garrison's gradual starvation. Reports were leaking out

FIG. 204. MONEMVASIA, WEST CURTAIN AND GATES OF LOWER TOWN, FROM THE UPPER FORTRESS.

the cliffs and at the sea's edge. Desparées himself had reconnoitered beyond the advance position marked B on Plate XXXVII A, and found the terrain there more suitable for trenches, covered by a line of rocks, to which he suggested making the next advance.

The arrival of the fifteen Papal, Genoese, and Maltese galleys sent at the instigation of Pope Alexander VIII required first a council of war, in which Guadagne had to confront the opposition of the other commanders. These denounced his mode of attack as exposed and uncertain, objecting that if the Venetians were successful in capturing the lower town, it

from the fortress that the defenders were growing mutinous through hunger. The Venetians began moving back to the mainland, but the artillery commander, Mutoni di San Felice, claimed that since the Turkish guns were weak and their powder short, it would be possible to advance a double trench protected by sandbags to within 30 geometric paces of the town's west wall. The scheme was adopted, and within eight days three batteries were set up to destroy the enemy's defenses, cover the approach of the trenches, and, with the help of the bomb ketches out at sea, open a breach in the large sea tower at the lower west corner of the walls.

13*

The Turks, frightened at the progress of these operations, and not trusting the strength of the town walls, finally asked for a parley. On August 12, 1690, they surrendered, after fourteen months of siege. Twelve hundred Turks came out of Monemvasia, 300 of them soldiers, and handed over to the Venetians their store of

wars and foreign invasions like a sea-mark in a tide pulling now East, now West, always the last corner of Greece to succumb to its successive conquerors. Its beginnings are hidden in the general obscurity of the early medieval period. At some time during the centuries when Greece was turning into a wilderness,

FIG. 205. MONEMVASIA, SQUARE BASTION BELOW CLIFFS AT HEAD OF WEST TOWN WALL.

78 cannon and other munitions, and all the Christian slaves and renegades. While a Te Deum was celebrated by the conquerors, the Venetian, who twelve months before had shot Lorenzo Venier from the height of the fortress, was attached by his extremities to four galleys rowing in opposite directions and quartered alive. The Venetian conquest of the Morea was now complete.[6]

*   *   *

A geological eruption of rock destined Monemvasia to play, many times over, one unique role in the annals of medieval Greece. Its history is repetitious to the point of constancy, standing out among the long fluctuations of

the place must have drawn its first settlers, like a magnet in the dark, to live in the shadow of its impregnable isolation. A late medieval source[7] states that refugees from the invading Avars, in the VI century, found "a place on the coast, strong and inaccessible, where they settled with their own bishop, and which they named Monemvasia because of its single entrance" (διὰ τὸ μίαν ἔχειν τῶν ἐν αὐτῷ εἰσπορευομένων τὴν εἴσοδον, or μόνη ἔμβασις). Phrantzes,[8] writing in the XV century, makes the mistaken assertion about his birthplace that in the reign of the Emperor Maurice (582–602) Monemvasia became an independent metropolis. Neither of these sources are authen-

[6] Garzoni, I, pp. 362 ff.; Foscarini, pp. 342 f.; Daru, V, p. 156; Romanin, VII, p. 503.

[7] N. Bees, Τὸ "Περὶ τῆς Κτίσεως τῆς Μονεμβασίας" Χρονικόν, Βυζαντίς, I, 1909, p. 64.

[8] *Annales*, ed. Bonn, p. 398.

ticated, but by the XI century at least Monemvasia had advanced to the foreground of Greek history. As the Crusaders from Europe began their gradual infiltration into the Byzantine Empire, the Comnenos Emperors came to recognize the advantage of Monemvasia's position as an outpost against the West. A large measure of self-government was granted to the place, which together with its enormous natural strength developed in the inhabitants a spirit of resistance and political responsibility rare in the Greece of the Middle Ages.

In 1147 Monemvasia repulsed its first attack, from the Normans of Sicily.[9] In 1249, nearly half a century after the rest of the Morea had fallen to the Franks, Monemvasia capitulated, at the end of a three years' siege, to the combined Frankish and Venetian force of William Villehardouin. Its inhabitants retained, however, exemption from all feudal services except those on the sea.[10]

But Villehardouin kept his prize for only thirteen years. In 1262 it formed part of his ransom, claimed by Michael VIII together with Maina and Mistra. With these three places, as Phrantzes wrote,[11] the Greeks gained the foothold from which they were to recover the whole Peloponnese. Monemvasia became the landing place for Imperial troops coming in to strengthen the new Greek Despotate of Mistra, the headquarters for attacks on the Frankish Principality, and the center of a flourishing piracy that grew rich on the trade routes of the Venetians. The Imperial governor of Monemvasia also exercised authority over the Catalans in Attica, who in the pay of the Byzantine Emperor had dealt the death blow to the Frankish Duchy of Athens. In the early XIV century Monemvasiote corsairs captured Salamis from the Catalans and forced it for a time to pay tribute.[12]

The natural advantages of Monemvasia were increased by ecclesiastical and financial benefits, which purposed to make it the chief city in the Empire west of Constantinople. In 1293 Andronikos II issued a golden bull, which elevated its bishopric to the rank of metropolis, with jurisdiction over all the Peloponnese. Next, it was raised to the tenth see in the Empire, and given rights to ordain bishops at Methone, Corone, and Androussa, establishing an ecclesiastical hegemony which it kept until the XVII century.[13] These favors were a pious accompaniment to the more practical economic measures which enabled Monemvasia, as commercial capital of the Byzantine Morea, to compete with Venice's two stations in Messenia. Under Andronikos III further bulls were issued, exempting the Monemvasiotes from taxes and forced labor, and giving them the rights of free trade throughout the greater part of the Empire.[14] The place's prosperity was increased by the export of Malvasie or Malmsey wine, which was shipped to all parts of Europe.

The chief benefit which Monemvasia enjoyed was to develop its own rule and institutions in almost complete independence of the centralized and bureaucratic authority of Byzantium. But this freedom proved in the end a curse. The hereditary archons of Monemvasia were among the chief agents of disorder in the Despotate of Mistra at the time when that state was most in need of unity. One of these, Paul Mamonas, tried to make his city autonomous. When the Despot Theodore I expelled him from Monemvasia, he took refuge with the Turkish Sultan, who ordered his reinstatement. This was the time when Greeks were ceasing to decide the issue of their own affairs. Losing their Empire, with the conqueror already at hand, they were entering the long, progressive phase of divided national aims and dependence

[9] Niketas Choniates, ed. Bonn, p. 97.

[10] X. τ. M., lines 2905–2984; *C. di M.*, p. 437; Miller, *Essays*, p. 233.

[11] *Annales*, ed. Bonn, p. 17.

[12] Miller, *Essays*, p. 236; Zakythinos, *Despotat*, I, pp. 41, 43.

[13] Phrantzes, ed. Bonn, p. 399; K. N. Papamichalopoulos, Πολιορκία καὶ Ἅλωσις τῆς Μονεμβασίας ὑπὸ τῶν Ἑλλήνων τῷ 1821 (Athens, 1874), pp. 11 f.; "Ἡ Μητρόπολις Μονεμβασίας," Θεολογία, VIII, 1930, p. 230.

[14] Phrantzes, ed. Bonn, pp. 399 ff.

on foreign powers, which was to reach its worst aggravation in the XX century.

On the eve of the Turkish conquest, in 1442, Theodore II of Mistra ratified Monemvasia's ancient privileges, and renewed the system of death duties, called τὸ ἀβιωτίκιον, by which

Fig. 206. Monemvasia, West Curtain and Angle Bastion of Lower Town.

the property of those who died without heirs should go to the repair and refortification of the castle.[15] In 1458 and again in 1460 it daunted the energy of Mohammed II, after Mistra had fallen and all the Morea was overrun. Only Monemvasia remained out of what had been the Byzantine Empire. There the wife and daughter of Demetrios Palaiologos took refuge, while the beaten Despot attached himself to Mohammed's retinue and offered up his daughter to the Sultan's harem. An emir

was sent to Monemvasia to demand the place's submission. The women were handed over, but the Monemvasiotes under the command of Manuel Palaiologos sent back the reply: "Nature has bestowed its gifts upon this place. From God and its desert situation it owns its strength and surety. When the desire and plan are of the Lord above, His will is done and we can not withstand. To whom He wills He gives. We have no power to give away what He has built."[16] The Turks withdrew without attacking.

The Monemvasiotes then transferred their allegiance to the other Despot, Thomas. After a brief occupation by a passing Catalan pirate, they placed their citadel, with Thomas' consent, in the hands of Pope Pius II. In 1463 or 1464, with the outbreak of the Turco-Venetian war, Monemvasia came into the possession of Venice,[17] as Phrantzes writes, "not so much by the free desire of its (Papal) commander, as by the necessity of his helplessness."[18] This first Venetian occupation, lasting 77 years, was prosperous at the outset, but a second war with the Turks lost Monemvasia her dependent castles of Rampano and Vatika and all her lands outside the rock itself. The loss of trade routes and the expansion of Ottoman power marked the beginning of the disintegration of the Venetian empire in the Levant, while the decline of Venetian commerce gradually reduced Monemvasia to obscurity. A third Turkish war cost Venice her islands of Aegina, Mykonos, and the Sporades, and her last two possessions on the mainland of Greece, Nauplia and Monemvasia.[19]

The Turks held the great rock against attempts to win it back, first by the Knights of Malta in 1564,[20] and then by the Venetians in 1653 under a certain Foscolo, who succeeded

[15] Miller, *Essays*, p. 238; Zakythinos, *Despotat*, I, p. 215.

[16] Phrantzes, ed. Bonn, pp. 396f.
[17] *Estratti degli Annali Veneti di Stefano Magno*, in Hopf, *Chroniques gréco-romanes*, pp. 203f.
[18] Phrantzes, ed. Bonn, p. 415.
[19] Paruta, pp. 412, 451ff.; Miller, *Latins*, p. 509.
[20] Wace and Hasluck, "Laconia, Topography," *B.S.A.*, XIV, 1907–8, pp. 168–182.

only in capturing two Turkish forts "outside the town" and carrying off the cannon that covered the harbor.[21] The Venetians of the early XVIII century were less successful in keeping the περιώνυμον καὶ ὑπερνεφελὲς φρούριον which they won so laboriously in 1690. Twenty-five years later, after the rest of the Morea was lost, the Venetian governor of Monemvasia, Federigo Badoer, surrendered this last fortress without a struggle.[22] In 1821, however, when the Greeks began their War of Independence, the fortress which their ancestors had given up last was the first which they recaptured. Monemvasia capitulated from hunger, after a four months' blockade. The leading Greeks in the place, who had known the secret of the approaching Revolution, previously persuaded the Turks to empty the granaries and make a general distribution to the inhabitants roundabout.[23] And so, the last time it was to figure in history, Monemvasia fulfilled the pattern which Coronelli[24] described: "If in the passage of years it was subjected to many changes of rule, it was by the will of destiny and not by force of arms."

*   *   *

Plate XXXVI of Monemvasia, drawn by Levasseur, shows the few simple elements of the fortifications. On the mainland is the "port for small boats," guarded by a curving mole, which the Venetians built during the siege of 1690.[25] Around this harbor the new village has grown up, while life and activity are fast receding from the old walled town on the island. The plan shows the bridge of 14 arches built during the first Venetian occupation, which in 1889 was replaced by one of iron, with the watch-

tower at its head, flanked by a parapet on either side. The *Città Bassa* and *Recinto Superiore* are shown full of houses, with the "covered way and gate communicating with the upper enclosure." The southeastern sector of the cliff top is shown girt with a wall, which extends to a gun position on the seaward-pointing tip of the rock. At this point on the drawing is written in pencil, almost illegible, the word *Torioni*. Two buildings in the eastern part of the upper fortress are also marked in pencil *Cisterna* and *Magazin*. At the western end of the rock is a second gun position described in the legend as *Battaria che domina il Ponte*. On the highest point of the rock is the rectangular castle (Fig. 202) with three square corner towers and another round tower near by, joined to it by a wall. Near the latter is written in pencil *moulin*. Below it on the north side is a stretch of wall marked *Mura Rossa*.

At the bottom of the cliff a steep talus slopes down to the sea round the whole island. On the southern side, near the east end, the lower town occupies a well defined portion of this sloping belt, with the cliff for a back wall (Fig. 203), neatly enclosed by two ramparts which descend to the water and a long sea wall parallel to the rocks above it. This is the most completely fortified section of Monemvasia.

A road from the bridge, following the line of the Venetian trenches of 1690, leads along the island's south flank to the west curtain of the town. This begins immediately below the cliff, in the form of a rectangular bastion (Figs. 204, 205, 206), in whose west face an arched opening leads into a large, vaulted passage giving access to the town's upper quarter. This vault carries a 20-foot square, paved platform, reached by a ramp from below and enclosed on the two outer faces by a 4-foot parapet pierced with a gun embrasure in either side. In the northwest corner a flight of narrow stairs leads up to a small terrace built into a cranny of the cliff. This is masked by a thin parapet, and projects out beyond the building's west face to

[21] Coronelli's *Morea, Negroponte, & Adiacenze* (Venice, ca. 1708) contains a map of Monemvasia, wrongly labelled *Napoli di Romania*, numbered 65, which shows on the mainland two tenaille forts, no trace of which remains now, but which were probably those captured by Foscolo.

[22] Daru, V, p. 192; Romanin, VIII, p. 45.

[23] Finlay, *History of the Greek Revolution*, I, pp. 260f.; Papamichalopoulos, *op. cit.*, pp. 65–90.

[24] *Memorie*, p. 98.

[25] Δελτίον, V, p. 491.

cover its entrance. The bastion's salient angle, the corners and walls of the embrasures, and the arch of the doorway are all made of carefully squared poros blocks. The masonry of the wall faces is less regular, a combination of rectangular poros blocks and roughly squared

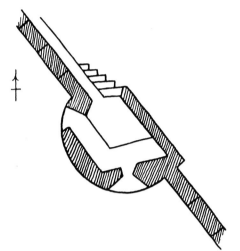

FIG. 207. MONEMVASIA, WEST WALL OF LOWER TOWN: ROUND FLANKING TOWER.

limestone. At the point where the curtain wall begins its descent from the redan's southeast corner is a tiny platform in the shape of a quarter circle (Fig. 205), raised several feet above that of the redan itself, supported on a circular squinch construction of cut blocks.

From here the west curtain of the town descends in an almost straight line to the sea. It is built with a slight talus on to a projecting base

FIG. 208. MONEMVASIA, WEST WALL OF LOWER TOWN. CURTAIN OF UPPER CITADEL ON TOP OF CLIFFS.

and carries, above a torus molding, a stepped parapet (Fig. 204) whose corners and sloping crests are made of cut poros. Nearly half way down the curtain is a large platform, extending 55 feet within the city enclosure, terraced by a battering retaining wall of poros ashlar. This is topped with a parapet pierced by one embrasure 12 feet wide at its narrowest point. A chemin de ronde, measuring only $1\frac{1}{2}$ feet in thickness, travels down from the platform to a small, round tower (Fig. 207) built on a piece of living rock, projecting through the talus of the wall. It carries a parapet of irregular width (Fig. 208) pierced by two gun embrasures set one lower than the other to follow the slope of the terrain beneath.

The main gate of the town is placed near the sea, a plain archway set in a square of poros ashlar bordered by a rolled molding. Above the right hand corner of this is an inverted cone of ashlar masonry which once carried a turret. Within the gate (Fig. 209) is a long

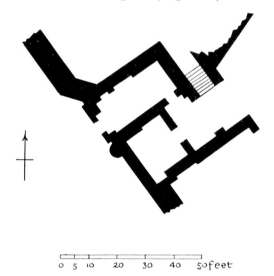

0 5 10   20   30   40   50feet

FIG. 209. MONEMVASIA, WEST GATE OF LOWER TOWN, PLAN.

passage, vaulted in clean poros ashlar, whose north wall contains two recessed arches. Next to it on the south side is another vaulted passage, partly walled off at a later period, into which one passes to emerge into the city enclosure. Immediately to the left of the inner opening, stairs lead to the platform above the vaults. Below the gate the curtain descends, with a tall, straight-topped, loopholed parapet, to a small platform furnished with a domed turret and a gun embrasure in the two outer corners, with a flight of steps in the inner leading down to the platform of the large sea bastion marking the town's southwest corner. This is the tower whose angle is reported by Garzoni[26] to have been destroyed by the Venetian bomb ketches in 1690 (Plate XXXVII B, *G. Brechia principiata dalle palandre*). Its battering walls are built almost entirely of poros ashlar, with a rounded salient angle. It must have been at least repaired, if not entirely rebuilt by the Venetians around the turn of the XVIII century. The parapet is 4 feet thick, with three embrasures facing over the sea and the roadway, which were put to the use of pillboxes by means of steel girders and cement by the Germans of 1943, in preparation for an Allied attack on the Balkans.

In the platform's southeast corner, steps lead under a low poros arch to the chemin de ronde of the sea wall. This stands 20–30 feet high over the rocks at the water's edge, which add themselves some 10 or 20 feet to its height. It is built of rough limestone and squared blocks of poros and sandstone, with variously vertical and battering faces. Large, squared poros blocks are also used in the angles of the numerous jogs along the wall. At the mid-point of the curtain is the sea gate, a small, plain arch of poros blocks, set deep into the talus of the wall, backed by two other wider arches behind it. The chemin de ronde, measuring 6 feet wide, is at some points level with the terraced ground within the circuit, at others rises from 6 to 10 feet above it. The parapet, 5–6 feet high, is as narrow as in the rest of the town circuit, measuring only 1½ feet wide, built with merlons of varying breadth, with pointed copes. For one stretch the parapet runs straight without crenellations.

The southeast corner of the town circuit is

26 I, p. 364.

formed by the east curtain rising up the cliff at right angles to the sea wall (Fig. 210). Here the parapet is built into a small, square, domed pavilion which straddles the chemin de ronde at the point of juncture of the two walls. The salient angle is built with a slight curve, which

FIG. 210. MONEMVASIA, EAST CURTAIN OF LOWER TOWN AT SOUTHEAST ANGLE.

follows up to the top of the pavilion. The inner corner is built concave. Each of the two outer sides contains a window, opening on to the sea and the rocky shore, while the inner sides are built with depressed arches affording passage for the chemin de ronde. The arches, the dome, and the wall faces are made of cut poros blocks. Poros ashlar is also used in the two sides of the salient angle, contrasting with the rougher masonry of the adjacent curtain. At ground level, on either side of the corner, are two large casemates vaulted in poros, with double arches of wedge-shaped poros blocks showing on the interior face of the wall, a form of construction used also in the Turkish fortifications at Patras and New Navarino.

The curtain climbs up in a straight line from here to the base of the cliffs (Fig. 211). A third of the way up the slope is a door, a small, depressed archway set in a square of masonry. The chemin de ronde of the curtain ascends by long, sloping steps, carefully built with a cobbled paving of limestone and squared poros blocks along the edge, reminiscent of the ramp

FIG. 211. MONEMVASIA, INTERIOR OF EAST TOWN WALL,
LOOKING UP TO CLIFFS AND UPPER FORTRESS CIRCUIT.

in the sea bastion of New Navarino. The parapet is irregular in outline and measures 1½ feet wide, at times reaching the disproportionate and ineffectual height of 12 feet. In the lower third of the wall the merlons are wide and covered with pointed copes, sloping parallel with the hillside, and containing each a small, square musket hole. The upper parapet is stepped as is that of the west curtain.

The wall leads up to a small, high, two-storeyed building at the top of the slope, covered with a depressed barrel vault of Turkish form, with windows and a door framed in cut poros blocks (Fig. 212). A ramp leads round it to a long terrace built up against the cliff base, with a string course round the retaining wall and a parapet pierced with two embrasures, covering the slope and the eastern sea approaches.

This circuit of town walls, with scarped face, torus molding, and careful angle construction, gives an impression of Venetian building, without however showing its real substance. No trace remains of any Frankish or Byzantine enclosure, though we know that a lower town

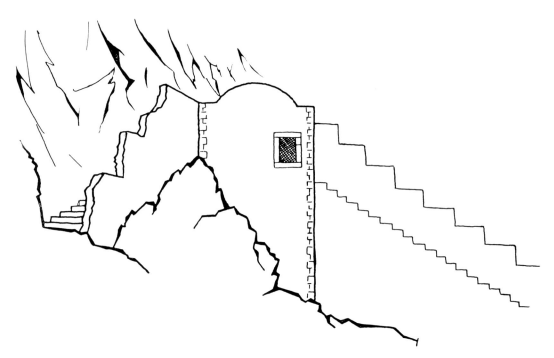

FIG. 212. MONEMVASIA, CONSTRUCTIONS AT HEAD OF EAST TOWN WALL, BELOW THE CLIFFS.

already existed in Byzantine times and that it was burned by Roger de Lluria in 1292.[27] The circuit that stands to-day does not antedate the year 1463. But during the occupation of 1463–1540 the Venetian *podestà* had his residence in the castle.[28] Does this mean that the lower town was not sufficiently defended, or that the Venetians had done nothing to fortify it? One is struck at any rate by the absence of the Lion of St. Mark, imprinted so abundantly in all other Venetian citadels. Comparison with Nauplia, Methone, Corone, and the Cretan fortresses, all built by the Venetians during the same period as their occupation of Monemvasia, reveals these walls as the work of another nation of builders: flimsy, awkward, and ill-suited to the uses of artillery. There are only sixteen gun embrasures in the entire circuit. Most of these are set in shallow parapets affording little protection. The walls themselves are thin, as the defenders of 1690 realized when the Venetian guns were drawn up close. The talus of the walls is slight, and the circuit abounds in those irregularities of construction absent from Venetian, and common in Turkish, architecture. A number of analogies with Turkish work in other fortresses leads to the conclusion that the town walls of Monemvasia were built, at least in large part, by the Turks during the XVI century. Had the Venetians enclosed the town with a wall, it would have been built to stand. The Turks must have destroyed whatever defense remained from Byzantine times in order to erect the present enclosure on its foundations.

The upper central section of the town reaches into a bay of the cliffs, up which leads a cobbled path, zigzagging in ten turns. It has a parapet on one side, of rubble masonry, with squared blocks at the corners, pierced by two round arches and by numerous loopholes framed in large, cut poros. At the height of the ascent is the fortress gate, a big, box-like structure in

[27] Miller, *Essays*, p. 235.
[28] *Ibid.*, p. 240.

the form of a redan in the wall running along the cliff top (Fig. 213). It stands 35 feet high and measures 33 by 27 feet wide. Its façade, facing southwest, batters in its upper half, and contains in the lower an archway set, like the two town gates, in a square of poros ashlar

FIG. 213. MONEMVASIA, GATE TO THE UPPER CITADEL.

framed in a bead molding. A square block is set into the wall above the arch, decorated with a cross and the ecclesiastical formula IC XC NI KA carved in the spaces quartered by its arms. Beneath the cross runs a row of smaller letters now obliterated. The salient angle of the redan is strengthened by a widely battering buttress which projects out on to a spur of cliff. Within the entrance is a long, vaulted passage, with a vaulted chamber alongside it on the south, three of whose walls are built with wide recessed arches, as in the passageway of the west town gate. Here also the vaults are of ashlar. In the vault of the side chamber, in one corner, may be seen embedded a block carved with a Venetian coat of arms. The upper storey has three vaulted chambers of different sizes, with windows arched and square on the southeast side of the redan. The platform above is enclosed by the remains of a parapet containing, on the same side, one small gun embrasure. The construction seems to be, by analogy with the lower gates, Turkish. The use of a Christian decorative fragment over the arch is not evidence to the contrary, when one recalls the winged lion re-set into the Turkish water gate at Methone. Venetians, on the other hand, would never have used in their vaults one of their own armorial bearings.

The curtain of the upper fortress is a thin wall which stands along the cliff top round the southeast sector over the town (Fig. 208). There are three gun positions at the east and west ends of the rock. One wall on the north side seals off a possible ascent. The cliff is un-assailable, and these bare defenses are enough, both for artillery against the mainland and the open sea, and for musket fire at closer range, in case of an attack on the lower town.

To the left of the upper gate, the curtain climbs for a short space to the height of the cliff, battering on to the rock, with a parapet of different masonry (Fig. 213), ascending in steps like those of the curtains below, containing three tall, poros-framed loopholes. Along the cliff top the wall stands 2–5 feet above the interior ground level, measuring 1½–2 feet in width, and pierced with loopholes at 4–foot intervals set at waist-level. On the outside it is upwards of 15 feet high around the bay in the cliff over the town. Further to the west, the exterior height rises to a maximum of 20 feet, the parapet grows lower, and the loopholes are set closer to the ground and spaced more widely. Both faces of the parapet and the interior of the loopholes are liberally coated in mortar. The wall is made of small limestone

and broken tiles held in a strong mortar, which still adheres in patches to the outer face. The parapet runs straight for all but a few stretches where it develops crenellations with merlons of curving outer slope.

The wall juts forward on a point of cliff over the western quarter of the lower town, forming a pronounced angle. The construction is un-usual, with both its faces battering and made of poros ashlar, topped with a sloping crest, level with the ground within, of long, squared blocks laid side by side. Two wide, shallow gun embrasures face out over the town. Directly above the line of the western town wall, there is a small guard chamber on top of the cliffs (Fig. 214), measuring 12 by 15 feet, and dating,

FIG. 214. MONEMVASIA, SOUTHWEST SECTOR OF UPPER CIRCUIT.

together with most of the upper parapets, from the Turkish period after 1540. It has a vault of cut poros blocks, covered by a gable roof made, like that of the building at the top of the east town wall, of tile chips and small limestone held in a thick plaster. This is a common form of surfacing in Turkish parapets. There is a small arched window, of a form both Turkish and Byzantine (Fig. 215, left) made with an arch filled toward the exterior with blocks of stone set one lower than the other. The door is made of two slanting poros blocks with joints bevelled to fit (Fig. 215, right).

Toward the western end of the rock, under

the summit of the hill, is an artillery parapet, 4 feet high on the inside, rounded at one end to form as it were a bastion (Fig. 216), and extending on the other in a long, broken line round the edge of the cliff. It is made of small limestone rubble, heavily plastered, and con-

Immediately beneath the second battery is a ledge extending out 40 feet over a lower spur of cliff, covered with a complex of walls, among which may be distinguished the traces of a small church, a tower, and two cisterns (Fig. 217). The apse of the church is built against

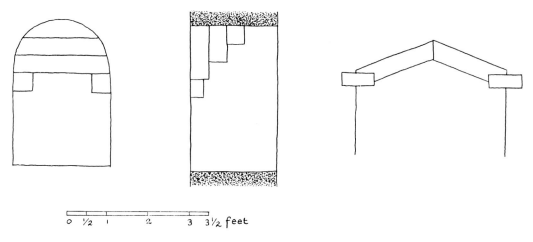

FIG. 215. MONEMVASIA, UPPER FORTRESS: WINDOWS IN GUARD HOUSE ABOVE SOUTH CLIFFS.

tains six embrasures $3\frac{1}{2}$ feet deep. At the westernmost extremity of the rock is the gun emplacement marked on Levasseur's plan, Plate XXXVI, *Battaria che domina il Ponte*. It is a parapet similar to the preceding, uniformly plastered, in two arms 50 and 70 feet long, built with a flat top and containing five embrasures measuring up to 12 feet wide. Both these positions are Turkish, from the materials used, the thick coating of mortar, and the width and shallowness of the embrasures.

the upper cliff. The rest of its walls show in lines of mortar still attaching to the rock foundations. Its south side contains a piece of ornamental brickwork in the masonry. Ad-

FIG. 216. MONEMVASIA, UPPER CIRCUIT: ARTILLERY BASTION IN SOUTHWEST SECTOR.

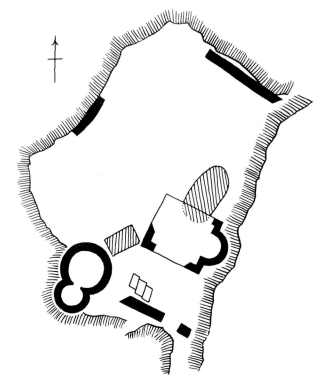

FIG. 217. MONEMVASIA, CONSTRUCTIONS ON LEDGE AT WEST END OF CLIFFS.

jacent to it, on opposite sides, are the two small cisterns lined in pink plaster, both originally vaulted. At the edge of the cliff, in the southwest corner, are the remains of a double round tower, with walls 12 feet high, which is probably the bonnet captured by the Venetians in 1689 as the first step in their advance against the town. Between this and the upper cliff three steps descend to a precipitous chimney in the rocks which could have afforded

FIG. 218. MONEMVASIA, FORT AT SUMMIT OF CITADEL, NORTHEAST VIEW.

an ascent from the south, now blocked by a wall. Other walls enclose the ledge on the more accessible north side.

At the top of the hill stands the ruin of a large fort (Fig. 218), dominating the long, undulating plateau above the cliffs. This consists of a slightly irregular quadrangle of walls (Fig. 219), roughly 100 feet square, defended by square towers at three of the corners. The walls are 5 feet thick and stand up to 20 feet high on the exterior face. The towers are hollow and measure 20–30 feet square. The masonry is of large, rough limestone blocks with an admixture of squared poros and broken brick. Cut poros blocks are used in all the angles of the corner towers and in the adjacent sections of walls. Brick is used both vertically and horizontally, approximating courses, and as decoration round a projecting Byzantine marble capital on the south side (Fig. 220). On the west side, facing the causeway and the mainland, is a tall, narrow door (Fig. 221), covered with a depressed vault of poros voussoirs. Just beneath the rocks of the

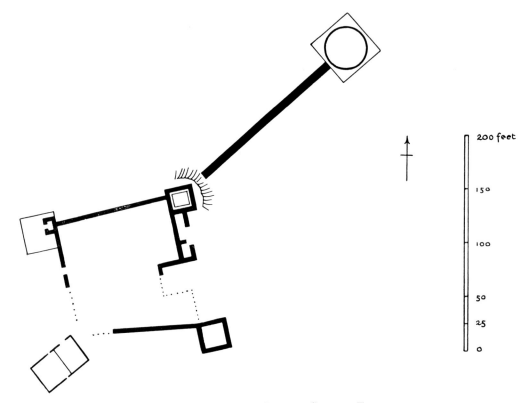

FIG. 219. MONEMVASIA, PLAN OF CITADEL FORT.

Fig. 224. Mon

4 feet high ab(
pierced with lo(
vals. The tip of
terrace, bounde
battering on to
holes set at grou
these two arms
guardhouse (Fi
ogram in plan,
roof with flatte
to the Turkish
a small turret i
ing, and anothe

14

northeast corner (Fig. 218) a wall, 8 feet wide, extends out along a rocky ridge for 250 feet northeastward, to another tower at the head of a great spur of the northern cliffs. This is set on a base measuring some 35 feet square with curved corners. Its north corner batters down 20 feet into a cleft between the rocks, and the east corner is made of both curved and rectilinear stepped projections. On top of this base stand the ruins of the tower itself. The fragments *in situ* and those lying about around the base show that it was round and hollow, and indicate a sudden destruction. Locatelli[29] mentions on July 24, 1689 the explosion of a powder store known as *molino da vento*, which in all probability coincides with this tower, indicated on Levasseur's plan as *moulin*. The plan and the masonry of the quadrangular fort appear to be Byzantine. The re-use of a carved marble capital in one of its walls might assign it to the period of the Slavic invasions, as in the case of Acrocorinth, where the re-use of Byzantine fragments indicates previous destruction. But Monemvasia remained consistently in Greek hands, and carved architectural members must have been frequent in any case. It is reasonable to suppose that the fort dates from the first Byzantine period, answering to Edrisi's description in the XII century of "Maliassa, defended by a very high castle above the sea, from which one may look across to Crete".[30]

Some fortification on the highest eminence of the rock must have existed among the defenses which withstood for three years the siege of 1246–1249. The construction is hardly Frankish, though again it is possible that it belongs in the second Byzantine period after 1262. The southeast corner of the quadrangle is completely demolished. In its place is a tall, rectangular building, measuring 30 by 45 feet, probably used as a barracks or storehouse. It is built with rubble walls and squared poros

29 II, p. 228.
30 *Géographie d'Edrisi*, p. 124.

angles, with a low door arched in two curved poros blocks and two small, poros-encased windows. It is covered with a vault and a curved roof with flattened sides, like the building at the top of the east town wall, which would assign it to the XVII or XVIII century.

Fig. 220. Monemvasia, Citadel Fort: Carved Bracket and Decorative Brickwork.

On the north side, below the fort, the ground falls between two headlands of cliff, forming a precipitous cavea. This is sealed off, halfway between the summit and the sea, by a wall (Fig. 222) 200 feet long and 60 feet high at its mid-point, which was built to prevent any ascent of the steep ledges reaching up to it from the water. The lower half of the wall is made of square blocks which show, in the characteristic Venetian honeycomb pattern, through the thick, red mortar of the joints. The color of this lower section justifies the

lower section of the *Mura Rossa* gives a strong impression of Venetian building, but the majority of the fortifications, almost the whole of the lower town circuit, all the parapets in the upper fortress, and the artillery emplacements at both ends, fall within the Turkish period. The Venetians of 1690–1715 made Monemvasia the capital of the Lakonian province, and developed the mainland harbor as an outlet for south Peloponnesian exports. But their only addition to the fortifications seems to have been repair-work on the large sea bastion in the lower southwest corner of the town walls, which their guns had bombarded during the siege.

FIG. 225. MONEMVASIA, NORTH SECTION OF ARTILLERY BASTION ABOVE EAST CLIFFS.

vasia in 1526 and 1538, the coat-of-arms and initials of Sebastiano Renier, *podestà* from 1510 to 1512, and the date MDXIV.[31] The

[31] Miller, *Essays*, p. 243; note in *J.H.S.*, XXVII, 1907, p. 300.

CHAPTER XVIII

CANEA

(Plate XXXVIII)

In the spring of 1692 the war between Venice and the Turks broke out once more. Full control of the Peloponnese had been secured two years before with the capture of Monemvasia, but the three fortresses which Venice had retained in western Crete since the War of Candia, earlier in the century, were now being menaced by a resumption of hostilities on the part of the Turks. The 1,200 deported from Monemvasia had formed themselves into marauding bands to oust the Venetians from their last possessions on the island, laying siege to Souda and Spinalonga, and capturing Grabousa with a bribe. At this time, however, Turkish reverses along other fronts of the War of the Holy League, particularly in Hungary, encouraged Venice to press a new offensive of her own. Negroponte was proposed for a second attack, but the recent fortification of the Isthmus of Corinth was considered enough to protect the Morea from the northern danger. The distant islands of Chios and Mytilene were also passed over in favor of Canea, where a successful attack, it was hoped, might not only raise the siege from the two Venetian outposts, but also lead eventually to the recapture of Crete itself.[1]

* * *

The city had already once owned a long Venetian occupation, dating from the year 1252, when the first colony was sent out from Venice, and gave to the town of Χανιά its Italian name, Canea. The settlers came with orders to rebuild the castle, which stood on the high rock over the port, and in the following century new town walls were raised around a wider area. These in time grew obsolete, and expenditures were made for refortification in 1475, and again in 1503. The spread of Turkish invasions drew ever closer to the shores of Crete, and finally in 1538 the Venetian Senate sent Michele Sanmicheli, the foremost military engineer in western Europe, to refortify the cities of Crete, including Candia, Rethymno, and Canea. Plate XXXVIII shows the town and harbor enclosed within a rough quadrangle of walls, with four large bastions at the corners. The years 1538–1540 saw the building of the San Salvatore bastion in the northwest corner; then the west curtain from 1540–1543; next the bastion in the opposite corner on the southeast, known as the Santa Lucia, from 1543–1546; the Schiavo, or San Dimitrio bastion in the southwest from 1546–1549; and finally in the northeast the bastion called Mocenigo, or Sabbionara. By *ca.* 1570, when Venice was losing Cyprus to the Turks, and enjoying their defeat at Lepanto, Canea's de-

[1] Garzoni, I, pp. 451–466; Cappelletti, XI, pp. 77–79; P. Kriares, Ἱστορία τῆς Κρήτης (Athens, 1931), pp. 81–83.

14*

fenses were brought to completion, and Crete began to wait for the Turkish attack.[2]

On June 11, 1645, a ship arrived in Canea with news that the Venetian bailie in Constantinople had been imprisoned, and that a fleet of 80 Turkish galleys and 440 smaller vessels were massing in the Bay of Navarino. This armada[3] put into the island of Kythera, announcing it was westward bound for Malta, but was sighted from Crete on June 13. The following day the Turks surrounded the island fort of St. Theodore, a few miles west of Canea, and took it by force after the Venetian commandant had exploded both himself and 600 of the attackers. In Canea the garrison and the inhabitants tried to add to the defenses of the walls, hastily building up a terreplein behind the Rethymno Gate[4] in the middle of the long south curtain, while others crowded on top of the ramparts, looking out to sea, believing every cloud on the horizon to be the sails of the Venetian fleet. An account of 1676[5] describes how

Canea was famed throughout the world as being in excellent state of defense, but in actual fact was not. It was an uneven work of fortification, with five imperfect bastions and four curtain walls of enormous length enclosing it on the landward sides. Toward the sea, it was bounded by an ill defended mole. Around the harbor mouth the parapets were lacking, which condition exposed it to any and all attack. The ditch, riddled with imperfections, was neither deep nor wide enough, lacked faussebraye and lower level, and had its counterscarp in ruins. There was no covered way, and the terrain of the surrounding country was dangerous to the fortress in many ways, with hills that overlooked the walls, and depressions by which an entire army could approach with adequate cover up to the ditch itself. Several years before, the place had been examined by other engineers, and pronounced indefensible not only in

face of a great army, but of a hundred picked troops, unless new exterior lines were built. In the alarm of the Turkish advance, the Proveditor Navagiero had not failed to make these defects known publicly, and to request the General's own supervision of the fortress. Yet all that was done was to send some new engineers to observe the situation. It was resolved to send out munitions and a sufficient garrison, but in the end the only action taken was the building of a small outer wall ("Muretto della Ronda") — a construction useless in time of siege, a ravelin equally inadequate, and the partial repair of the parapets. Even this was not brought to completion, because the General had ordered the Proveditor to keep the galley-slaves and forced laborers for fighting service only, where in fact they could be put to no constructive use. Moreover, the fortress suffered from a woeful dearth of gun carriages, the guns being in large part dismounted. In the hour of need this was Canea's greatest misfortune...

Perhaps more serious were the structural defects of a fortress already a century old. Another account, published a year after the siege, tells how, for all their thickness, the curtain walls were ill defended by the bastions, which were placed too far apart, and how the ravelin, newly built across the ditch from the Rethymno Gate, was set on ground too low to serve a useful purpose.[6]

The Turkish army of 40,000 spread out around the city, and set up their first battery of six cannon on a hill opposite the Rethymno Gate, which they bombarded, destroying its drawbridge. The Venetians in their turn set up a battery on the projecting platform, or small angle bastion above the gate (Fig. 228), which produced such a vigorous counter-barrage that an assault on the ravelin was averted, and the Turks, who had cut their oars into scaling ladders, were driven off, not daring for the time being to attack again. Their next efforts were launched against the Schiavo, or San Dimitrio bastion in the fortress' southwest corner, so that the Venetians were forced to abandon the ravelin and concentrate their resistance in this other quarter. More Turkish galleys were constantly arriving, which raised the spirits of the attackers, while rumors were

[2] G. Gerola, *Monumenti Veneti nell' Isola di Creta* (Venice, 1905), I, pp. 15, 223, 414, 418.

[3] Romanin, VII, p. 360, puts the number of the Turkish fleet at 78 galleys and 120 lesser ships.

[4] G. Brusoni, *Historia dell' Ultima Guerra tra Veneziani e Turchi, 1644–71* (Bologna, 1676), p. 24: "Terrapienate le porta di Sabbionara e Rettimiotta, il portello e il rivellino, e provedute di travi, e pietre le parti delle mura più esposte alla scalata..."

[5] *Ibid.*, p. 25.

[6] C. Cigala, *Successi della Canea* (Rome, 1646), p. 14.

rife within the city that the Venetian admiral at Souda, Marino Capello, feared to come to its aid, and that the Venetian ships, based only a few miles away, had sailed home. Meanwhile, the Turks were pressing forward mining operations beneath both faces of the San Dimitrio bastion. As soon as a breach had been opened, they attacked, but were driven back after a battle of three hours, in which all the citizens, including the women, took part. The Venetian general tried to recruit reinforcements in the country round about Canea, but found most of the local population had decamped into the hinterland of the Lefka Ori. A small force of 300 made its way into the city from the side of the eastern shore, insufficient, however, to replace the losses already sustained among a garrison which had numbered only 1,000 at the outset. The Turks tightened their grip at the San Dimitrio, building first a great mound on the counterscarp, with trenches behind it for their own protection, and then on July 22 descended into the ditch. The Venetian pieces, lacking their mounts and improvised into mortars, were of no avail against the mining, which now exploded the front and shoulder of the bastion. At the same time breaches were opened at the Sabbionara and Rethymno Gates, while the falling walls and terreplein of the San Dimitrio filled the ditch, and provided a crossing for the attackers. On July 30 the Turkish galleys bombarded the port, and then a general assault was launched by land and sea against all four breaches. The Turks were driven off at the two gates, and at one of the breaches in the San Dimitrio, but at the other they penetrated, aided by the traverse and the trenches behind them, on August 7, 1645. Yet even then they were repulsed after a furious resistance, lasting seven hours, on the part of the inhabitants and the garrison, a third of whose number perished. There followed a council of the Venetian captains, who, most of them bleeding from their wounds, voted the proposal to surrender, "this being not the first

time God had allowed the nobler cause to be vanquished by the greater power." On August 9 the garrison marched out with the honors of war, after a siege of fifty-five days, during which the Turks had lost 35,000 men. A force of 5,000 Turkish infantry and 500 horse entered Canea, and restored its defenses as a base of operations for the siege of Candia, which was begun later in the same year.[7]

* * *

Plate XXXVIII of Canea in the Grimani collection, drawn in 1692, shows a complete XVI century Italian fortress, untouched by the devastating effects of the modern Greek civic consciousness. To-day only a few bare fragments of architecture remain to tell us the shape of Sanmicheli's citadel. Almost nothing is left of the original Venetian fortifications on the summit of rock above the harbor, though below it on the west stand seven great, vaulted arsenals, part of a line of nineteen erected during the last quarter of the XVI century. At the eastern extremity of the harbor are two more of the same construction, with the façade standing of a third. The earliest plans of Canea, published in Gerola's study of the fortress, show that the port was open at this end, and only partially enclosed by a string of shoals and islets forming a lagoon. A plan of 1599, however, shows the channel filled in at the eastern end between the largest of the islands and the shore. Upon this extension of the mainland were built five parallel, vaulted structures, described on the plan as *Cinque corpi d'arsenale*.[8] From this northeasternmost angle of the quadrilateral fortifications the mole projects westward to the harbor mouth: a broad, paved wall defended on the outside by a parapet, which batters 15 feet high over

[7] Cigala, *op. cit.*, pp. 8–40; Brusoni, *op. cit.*, pp. 24–35; Nani, *op. cit.*, II, pp. 44–58; Cappelletti, X, p. 254; Romanin, VII, pp. 360–363; M. B. Sakellariou, Χειρόγραφος Ἔκθεσις περὶ τῆς πολιορκίας καὶ ἁλώσεως τῶν Χανίων ὑπὸ τῶν Τούρκων, *Byz.-Neu. Jahr.*, XV, 1938–1939, pp. 141–174.
[8] Gerola, *op. cit.*, I, p. 440, fig. 248.

the half-submerged rocks. Near the eastern shore a gap is bridged by an arch, whose outer section is strengthened, on each side, by a rough buttress, similar to those flanking the outer gate at Chlemoutsi. Near its midpoint the mole is guarded by a big, triangular cornices. A Turkish structure, resembling more a minaret than a beacon, it is set on a base in whose battering walls an empty niche would have once enclosed the seal of Venice, the winged lion of St. Mark.

Back at the northeast corner, the rear wall

Fig. 226. Canea, from the Air, looking West.

defense, built with battering walls of huge ashlar blocks in the lower courses, indicated on a plan of 1572 as *Rivellino di S. Nicolò*. Beyond it the parapet is built with a curved crest, and contains on its inner side a number of old cannon, embedded mouth downward in the masonry, which once served to carry the chains shutting off the harbor. At its entrance the mole terminates in a lighthouse (Fig. 227), decorated with crescent moons and acanthus leaves under its wide, molded, saucer-like of the five arsenals extends southward for 100 feet to connect with the large demibastion named Sabbionara, or Mocenigo, which projects from it at right angles. This angle was originally — before the drawing of the Grimani plan — the central re-entrant angle of a tenaille bastion (of which the existing structure is only a half), whose two outer faces were once intended to be brought out to meet in one salient angle. The plan, however, was not completed, but in 1591 an orillon was added to the south corner, converting that section into an independent bastion, while the north half remained in the form of a ravelin, of which the north wall disappeared in the subsequent building of the five arsenals.[9] The wall of the

FIG. 227. CANEA, THE TURKISH LIGHTHOUSE.

orillon contains a plaque of the lion of St. Mark, with four shields and an inscription bearing the date of building and the name of its builder, the Proveditor Giovanni Mocenigo. Plate XXXVIII shows a round cavalier with a vaulted entrance and seven embrasures in its parapet. To-day there is no trace of any such building, nor does it figure in any of the sources quoted or plans reproduced by Gerola.

The fortress' east curtain stands mostly intact from the Sabbionara to the Santa Lucia bastion. The great, terrepleined rampart, some 45 feet thick, has crumbled on its inner side, but the outer scarp is a masonry wall of monumental construction, with a talus of big, square blocks set in strong mortar. The Sabbionara Gate once pierced the curtain at a point near the bastion of the same name, where now a

150-foot stretch of wall has been demolished to make way for a modern road into the city. A plan by Coronelli, reproduced by Gerola,[10] makes up for its omission from the Grimani drawing. The gate itself, still standing in the early part of this century, was a small, arched opening, which had been blocked up since an uncertain date by the Turks.[11] A massive torus molding marks the level of the rampart platform, which supports the remnants of the parapet, a vertical, terrepleined defense, walled in ashlar masonry of blocks 1 foot square. The section of parapet immediately above the breach which marks the site of the gate belongs to the *Cavaliere della Sabbionara fatta dai Turchi, 1686*, indicated on the Coronelli plan.[12] At the mid-point of the curtain the parapet contains, above the torus, three empty shields, 5 feet high, flanked by two roughly stippled plaques on either side. It is at this point, where the line of shore (Plate XXXVIII, *Sabbione*) rounds out eastward into the bay, that the rising elevation of the land begins to form the counterscarp, now only a low slope of earth without masonry revetment.

The Santa Lucia bastion in the southeast corner of the citadel appears on Plate XXXVIII as a sharply pointed, spade-shaped structure, with an orillon covering its west flank. The work as it stands to-day exemplifies the process of dilapidation and encrustation by which monumental cities crumble. Its short north flank still stands, with the two gun embrasures shown on the plan of 1692, and a torus molding which stops 10 feet short of the bastion's northeast angle. This is built of great, squared, rusticated blocks. But the angle is truncated on its other side by the road from Khalepa, which crosses into the town from the side of the counterscarp over a broad dyke that closes the ditch. The bastion's eastern face, thus isolated, extends for 100 feet, diminished both

[9] *Ibid.,* I, p. 431, fig. 247; pp. 432, 438.

[10] *Ibid.,* I, p. 447, fig. 251.
[11] *Ibid.,* I, p. 453, fig. 256.
[12] *Ibid.,* I, p. 447, fig. 251.

by the filling in of the ditch and the complete levelling of the terrain on all sides, and by the ruin of the upper sections of the wall itself, which ends at ground level in two courses of curved stone, which is all that remains of the salient angle. The east face serves as back wall to the accumulation of sheds and shanties, which attach themselves around the base of older, stronger buildings like a growth of barnacles. Nothing is left of the bastion's south face, although its trace is evident in the line of shacks once built against it, still standing after the actual wall has disappeared.

Within the gorge of the bastion is a vast mound of earth, three quarters quarried away, even to the blocks of stone which once encased it, and the parapet whose six embrasures covered the southeast approaches to the town.

The whole eastern and central section of the fortress' long south curtain has gone, a barrier for the tide of modern building to slide over and obscure all traces. As the plan shows, this curtain was broken into halves by a widely obtuse angle at its mid-point. This was guarded by a small, slightly projecting bastion, flanked by two cavaliers on the rampart behind it (Fig. 228). A ramp communicated with the top of the eastern of these, while beneath that on

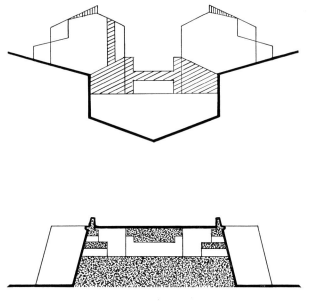

FIG. 228. CANEA, RECONSTRUCTION OF ANGLE BASTION AND CAVALIERS IN SOUTH CURTAIN.

the west a vaulted passage led to the lower platform, or *piazza bassa* of the bastion itself. Two such sunken levels in both of its flanks, communicating by a passage underneath the bastion's platform, provided for an upper and a lower gun emplacement to enfilade the ditch on east and west.[13] Immediately to the west of the bastion the Rethymno Gate, built in 1564, communicated by a drawbridge with the

FIG. 229. CANEA, THE SOUTHWEST BASTION, SALIENT ANGLE.

ravelin on the opposite side of the ditch. All this has vanished, but in the western sector a stretch of the original rampart and ditch still exist, half buried among the habitations of the city, and cut through by one of its streets.

The west flank of Canea's fortifications remains mostly intact. The San Dimitrio bastion is considerably preserved, despite its fatal position in the siege of 1645. The faces, flanks, and orillon are built in the prevailing masonry of square and rectangular oblong blocks of an average size of 1 by $1\frac{1}{2}$ feet. Other sections of the wall show the patchwork of repair. The salient angle is built pointed at the bottom, but toward the top rounds into a curve, crowned with a circular torus molding. The

13 *Ibid.*, pp. 456–460, figs. 260–264.

angle blocks are bigger than those in the wall faces, and their courses are alternately rough-dressed and smooth. A wall of small, square blocks, standing 5 feet high, extends along the bastion's south face and rounds the curve of the salient angle, supporting a minor torus molding of its own (Fig. 229). Above and around it is a cluster of small dwellings which fill the bastion's platform. Its north shoulder is now in complete ruin, together with the parapet of five embrasures indicated on Plate XXXVIII. The small lower platform, or *piazza bassa*, drawn at the re-entrant angle on the western side, has disappeared in the general collapse, while a similar piece of construction in the opposite corner, behind the orillon, has been filled in, and its lower level of casemates blocked. Behind the bastion rises the great earth hill which once served as cavalier. Traces of its facing wall may be seen, made of small stones covered in mortar, and a ramp curving round to the top, where the platform was once guarded with a battery of nine cannon.[14] The ditch which runs along the fortress' west curtain measures approximately 80 feet wide. Plate XXXVIII shows a thin line of green following down the middle of the moat from an aqueduct on the south to a point half way along the west side, described as *un po' di cunetta*. This is a water channel, used for the purpose of irrigating the market gardens to which the ditch is now given over. The moat is blocked, just north of the San Dimitrio bastion, by an earth dyke supporting the road which provides the western entrance to the city. The point where the road cuts through the rampart is marked on Coronelli's plan of 1689: *Luogo rotto colle mine da Turchi nel quale diedero la scalata*.[15] The counterscarp stands to a height of 20 feet, partially ruined opposite the San Dimitrio bastion (Plate XXXVIII, 5, 6), and lacking the ravelin opposite the mid-

point of the west curtain. The rampart in this section supports a big, square cavalier, embedded in shanties, whose walls stand 20 feet high above the level of its platform, a construction rebuilt by the Turks in 1647.[16] On either side, the top section of the curtain, cordon, and parapet have crumbled.

Near the north end of the curtain stands another mound of earth, which answers in shape if not in exact position to the oval cavalier indicated on Plate XXXVIII, though not on the other plans of the same period published by Gerola.[17] These agree in placing here a square cavalier, called Santa Caterina, which occupies the space between the ruined, terrepleined structure and the platform of the large northwest terminal defense known as the Gritti, or San Salvatore bastion, which was the earliest of the fortifications carried out after Sanmicheli had visited Canea. It is the lowest and smallest of the four main corner bastions. The salient angle is built in much the same fashion as that of the San Dimitrio, with big blocks pointed at the bottom and rounded at the top. Faces and flanks are built of smaller material than is to be found elsewhere in the circuit of the fortress. Within the re-entrant angle on the west side there is a sunken platform with curved walls, in whose masonry appears the trace of an early crenellated parapet. Plate XXXVIII shows a vaulted gate in the bastion's north face, but this now has disappeared, and there remains only the fragmentary shell of the small, round tower near the sea, which carries an interior chemin de ronde on machicoulis, and on its outer wall an inscription of 1477. It is incorporated into the large work which once guarded the entrance to the port, and is now the municipal prison.

* * *

[14] *Ibid.*, p. 463: the parapet with its nine embrasures was still standing *ca.* 1900. Plate XXXVIII, however, shows only six.

[15] *Ibid.*, p. 447, fig. 251.

[16] *Ibid.*, p. 464.

[17] *Ibid.*, p. 18, fig. 7; p. 156, fig. 75; p. 420, fig. 246; p. 431, fig. 247; p. 440, fig. 248; p. 446, fig. 250.

Plate XXXVIII represents the siege of 1692 in progress. Canea had been suggested to the Venetian war council as an objective by Domenico Mocenigo, a veteran of the War of Candia, who succeeded Francesco Morosini, now dead, and Girolamo Corner as *Capitan Generale*, or commander-in-chief. With 12,000 foot and 800 horse he landed at a place called Platania, three miles to the west of Canea (Plate XXXVIII, E). The local population, particularly that of the wild and untamed district of Sphakia, whose ancestors had once spent three and a half centuries rebelling against the Venetians, now rose to join their old against the new and worse oppressor. They besieged and captured the neighboring castle of Kissamo, while the Venetians moved in towards Canea, occupying the suburb outside the fortress walls (Plate XXXVIII, D). In all but its outcome, the siege followed the pattern of the Turkish assault 47 years before. Trenches were extended in arcs round the south and west of the city (I), while a line of small outworks, or bonnets at 100-yard intervals defended the Venetian rear. The cavalry and Cretan auxiliaries took up positions on the hills to the southeast (K), which commanded a general view over the town. The lines of trenches and batteries were tightened round the San Dimitrio bastion. The revenge failed, however, which Mocenigo hoped to stage upon the exact scene of the Turkish breach of 1645. The troops lagged in pushing the trenches forward, and large numbers fell ill under the sudden changes of the Cretan atmosphere from the heat of day to the damp of night. Though the population inside the fortress amounted to only 3,000, and the garrison 800, confidence was nevertheless gained from the slowness of the besieging operations, while a force of Turks from Candia under Kara Musa, another veteran of 1645, entered the city from the east by way of the Sabbionara Gate, covered by a sortie on the opposite side. The Venetians kept up a heavy bombardment from their batteries, but the infantry was not sent in to follow up with assaults. After a fortnight, a small Turkish ravelin (Plate XXXVIII, 2) opposite the San Dimitrio was taken with heavy losses on both sides. A new line and bonnet (3) were raised above the ditch in an effort to consolidate this gain, and a section of the bastion's west face and opposing counterscarp demolished (5, 6), beneath which the Venetians advanced their underground gallery. A large breach in the bastion's walls was opened by the mines, but at the moment when all was ready for the attack, Mocenigo halted the operations and ordered the siege to be raised. Rumors had reached the Venetian camp that in the Peloponnese Argos and Nauplia were threatened by a Turkish offensive, and that enemy troops were massing in the direction of Rethymno. The army had suffered great losses from sickness and desertion, and the Turks, if not strong within Canea, were certainly more than a match for the Venetians in the rest of the island. The reconquest of Crete was forgotten: Mocenigo was more concerned for the Morea. Behind his incapacity in pressing the siege lay the knowledge that Venice's need was first to guard her possessions nearer home. Over the objections of his lieutenants, and to the indignation of the soldiers, he transported his entire force to Nauplia, taking with him 2,000 of the Cretan rebels, leaving the population to suffer the reprisals of the Turks, and Crete to another two centuries of Turkish domination. This was Venice's last offensive in the Levant. She had entrusted its leadership to a figure typical of the Venetian decadence; a man who remembered the great resistance of Candia, urging first an expedition that recalled old glories, then failing for lack of energy to carry it through, but still clearsighted enough, like Venice's earlier, more successful sons, to realize the weakness of her old age, and the shrunken limits of her power.

CONCLUSION

The castles of medieval Greece show the evolution of military architecture through the upheavals of a thousand years and the building styles of a variety of nations. From the salient features of the Peloponnesian fortresses, separately described in the preceding chapters, we shall attempt to establish the relation of their masonry, plans, and defenses to one or the other of their builders, or to a date or a general period. Our conclusions are offered with caution and reservations. No chronology can be absolute in the face of the scarcity of historical reference, the lack of excavation on the sites, and the confusions existing in the architecture itself. Since fortification is the most functional of all forms of building, it is the geological formation and content of the land itself which influences most the character of the structures built to defend it. The same geology, likewise, tends repeatedly to reduce the masonry of the walls to a lowest common denominator of rubble or free-stone in which the secret of their authorship is lost. Numerous also are the cases of imitation, or the instances where certain methods of fortification transcend purely national styles, or where a particular form, grown obsolete in one place, lingers on in another. Nevertheless it is possible to proceed from limited certainty to wider conjecture. The art of fortification develops through the centuries according to a recognizable pattern, and certain distinct peculiarities of building exist in enough known cases to make us familiar with the general style of the different nations of builders.

For the purpose of archaeological chronology, the history of the medieval Peloponnese may be divided into the following main periods:

Early Byzantine (IV century A.D.–1204)
Frankish (1205–1430)
Late Byzantine (1262–1460)
Early Venetian (1206–1540)
Turkish (1460–1828)
Late Venetian (1685–1715)

I. EARLY BYZANTINE. Our point of departure is the IV century after Christ when, in the dusk of the Roman Empire, new walls were raised about the cities of Greece, whose defenses the Romans themselves had destroyed five hundred years before.[1] It is now a country menaced by invasions, insecure behind the boundaries of empire, lying outside the main routes of communication between the eastern and western Mediterranean, bypassed by the Via Egnatia linking Rome with Constantinople through Macedonia, and gradually abandoned to agriculture and economic self-suffiency.[2]

New fortresses arise where the *Pax Romana* once demanded desolation. Barbarian inroads make a frontier of every province and every fortified hill. To-day few traces remain from these defenses; little, indeed, to support the

---

[1] See *Corinth*, III, ii, pp. 127, 129 note 5.
[2] For a description of the Peloponnese at the end of the Roman Empire see Bon, *Le Péloponnèse byzantin*, pp. 1–25.

equally few historical indications of Prokopios: that the emperor Justinian "secured and rebuilt the walls of the cities of the whole of Greece within the defense-lines of Thermopylae," and on learning "that all the cities in the Peloponnese were without walls, fortified the Isthmus with a rampart defended by towers and bastions."[3] None of these works are definitely known to us. Whatever may have remained from this earliest post-classical period exists in fragments only, about which we can only offer the broadest generalizations.

Plans. Although the fortresses of classical Greece had lain in ruins since the Roman conquest, their socles of ashlar and polygonal masonry still remained in many places, showing the outline of curtain and square flanking towers, girdling an acropolis, such as at Pylos, Zarnata, Nauplia, and Corinth, and occasionally the plan of a concentric enclosure on a conical hilltop such as Argos. It is unlikely that Justinian's refortifications would have failed to utilize these massive foundations or departed from the plans already laid out, themselves lessons in the adaptation of hewn stone to living rock. For the Early Byzantine fortress plan we must look to those castles which resisted the Frankish conquest and so must antedate the year 1204: namely Corinth, Argos, Nauplia, Monemvasia, Kalamata, Corone, Methone, Arkadia, and Patras. All these places have been so overlaid with subsequent constructions that little is left that can be definitely assigned to this period. The first three, however, obviously follow the classical plan of plain circuit or concentric enclosure. At Monemvasia, crowning the summit of the rock, is a small, quadrangular fort, which may date from this period,

defended by large square towers at three corners (Figs. 218, 219, 220). The plan of donjon, inner redout, and outer court seems to be exemplified in the castles of Kalamata and Arkadia, where portions of all three elements appear in the fabric of the later Frankish rebuilding. The north flank and northeast corner of the castle of Patras indicate a similar pattern of redout and outer enclosure. Isolated stretches of curtain at Methone (the southeast half of the inner landward wall with the square flanking tower) and Corone (the west flank of the inner enclosure, and possibly the curtain immediately west of the main gate) are too few to afford an idea of their whole plan in Byzantine times. The Venetians of the XIII century established themselves too strongly in these two places to leave behind much trace of the fortifications which had surrendered so easily in 1205. It is notable that all nine fortresses mentioned are either on or near the sea: it was the cities on the coast which kept up contact with Byzantium and trade relations with the outside world, while the rest of the Peloponnese came under the sway of Gothic and Slavic invaders.

Materials. Where plans are insufficiently represented, there still stand a number of walls from which we may learn some of the characteristics of early Byzantine masonry and construction. It is natural to suppose that during the unquiet centuries of the early Christian era the first materials used would have been those lying ready to hand from the ancient Greek or Roman buildings ruined during the barbarian invasions. A glance at the walls of the medieval castles will indicate that these were plentiful at a time when they were quickly needed. Where this need was so great, it is most probable that, in the earliest period, the Byzantine Greeks made use of all such materials they could find. The Franks and Venetians, who came later, may have used them once again in their repairs and rebuildings. Generally, however, we may as-

---

[3] Prokopios, *De Aedificiis*, IV, 2, ed. Bonn, pp. 272 f.
Καὶ πόλεις δὲ τῆς Ἑλλάδος ἁπάσας, αἵπερ ἐντός εἰσι τῶν ἐν Θερμοπύλαις τειχῶν, ἐν τῷ βεβαίῳ κατεστήσατο εἶναι, τοὺς περιβόλους ἀνανεωσάμενος ἅπαντας . . . Ταῦτα δέ διαπεπραγμένος Ἰουστινιανὸς βασιλεύς, ἐπεὶ τὰς ἐν Πελοποννήσῳ πόλεις ἁπάσας ἀτειχίστους ἐμάνθανεν εἶναι . . . τὸν Ἰσθμὸν ὅλον ἐν τῷ ἀσφαλεῖ ἐτειχίσατο . . . φρούρια δὲ ταύτῃ ἐδείματο καὶ φυλακτήρια κατεστήσατο.

sume that the appearance of classical elements in medieval walls assigns them to the seven or eight hundred years preceding the Fourth Crusade.

A certain variety in their re-use reflects the changes which overcame Greece between the fall of West Rome and the high Middle Ages. Apparently the earliest form of post-classical wall construction is an ashlar masonry of large, rectangular blocks of stone, measuring approximately 4 feet in length, sometimes marked with the bevelled joints or clamp-holes of the classical buildings from which they were taken, laid, without mortar, in regular courses, with joints alternating at even intervals. Such a wall exists on Acrocorinth, in the lower western section of the poros screen sealing the north gulley (Fig. 151), which has been dated between the IV and VI centuries.[4] At Corone, the powerful north wall of coursed, rectangular blocks, measuring 2 feet high and upwards of 8 feet long, together with the adjacent west flank of the entrance pylon (Fig. 3, right), may date likewise to the period of Justinian or his predecessors. The monumental and meticulous style seems fitting to the first inheritors of the classical tradition of fortress architecture. Soon there comes a change. Large, cut blocks continue to be used, their cuttings and dowel-holes indicating still their classical provenance, but they are no longer fitted together in courses; instead they are set one upon the other without respect to levels. Small stones fill in the interstices between the larger blocks of disparate size. Pieces of thin tile begin to appear between the vertical joints. Examples of this form may be seen in the upper and eastern section of the north screen wall of Acrocorinth (Fig. 151), in the southeast inner rampart with the flanking tower at Methone (Fig. 66), the west corner tower of Arkadia (Fig. 93), and the donjon and southeastern inner curtain at Kalamata. All attempt

at regularity finally disappears among the walls thrown together with mortar out of blocks of stylobate, orthostate, and architrave, column drums, and carved marble fragments, such as we find in the north curtain of Patras castle (Fig. 144), the west curtain of the inner enclosure at Corone, the south tower at Arkadia (Fig. 91), the buried north angle of the outer curtain of Kalamata (see above p. 32), and the wall built around the shrunken village of medieval Sparta. These are the memorials of the Slavic invasions of the VI–IX centuries. A different form of masonry is distinguishable for the next four hundred years. The supply of building blocks has been mostly exhausted from the ancient structures now quarried to the point of total ruin. The materials of walls show a progressive decrease in size from the end of Antiquity. The constructions of the Imperial officials and the native landlords are made of smaller, flatter rectangular blocks of poros and limestone, measuring one foot or less, laid in regular courses with mortar and an increasing amount of broken terra cotta, and an occasional fragment, marble colonnette or window mullion that tells of the destruction of earlier Byzantine buildings. From these indications certain walls of Acrocorinth, Argos, Arkadia, and Kalamata appear to belong to the period following the Slavic invasions. At this time also we begin to find walls built of regular, squared, coursed blocks of moderate size (1–2 feet long), separated by thin brick or tile between the joints and courses in the cloisonné pattern most generally characteristic of Byzantine masonry.

Walls and parapets. The faces of the walls appear to be vertical, without talus, although stepped projections at the base may date as far back as the early Byzantine period. The chemin de ronde may be upwards of 8 feet broad, sometimes ascending by steps, protected by a crenellated parapet of evenly spaced merlons measuring 2½ feet in width, without archer-slots but sometimes, as in one case on

[4] See *Corinth*, III, ii, pp. 23–27, 210–215, figs. 18–20, 151–159.

Acrocorinth[5], pierced by small, square holes at the base. It is improbable, however, that many of these early parapets have survived the constant restorations so weak an element would constantly have needed.

Towers. Square flanking towers of varying sizes project boldly from the trace of the walls, but do not rise above them (Figs. 66, 138, 140, 153, 155). Some are hollow, containing single or parallel vaulted chambers in one or two storeys, supporting platforms above. The smaller towers are either hollow or terrepleined. Other variations, triangular or polygonal as at Argos (Fig. 123) may also belong to this period preceding the Fourth Crusade.

Openings. The gates may be either in the form of a two-storeyed tower or redan which projects the trace of the wall and provides a passageway parallel to it (Fig. 159), or else lead directly through it, with flanking towers on both sides (Fig. 160, upper left). The second and third gates of Acrocorinth show examples of each.[6] The doors, on the outer and sometimes the inner face, are simple rectangular openings. One case of a Byzantine postern shows battering jambs.[7] The lintel generally consists of a large, re-used classical block or, more often, one or two column shafts. Within these flat-topped entrances the passageway carries a barrel vault of well cut poros blocks laid in ashlar courses, sometimes strengthened with a reinforcing arch. In the north postern of Acrocorinth the vault carries through to the inner face, with a line of tile forming a decorative repeating arch over the exposed voussoirs. Windows are mostly small and rectangular, nearly square, with marble blocks or shafts of colonnettes for lintel. The square donjon at Arkadia (Fig. 96) and the north gate-tower in the third line at Acrocorinth contain tall, thin, splayed archer slots.[8]

II. FRANKISH. The span of the Frankish Principality of Achaea, from its foundation in 1205 to its obliteration from the map of Greece in 1430, falls into two unequal halves. The first is a period of early strength, complementing the unwarlike spirit of the inhabitants and the weakness of their resistance. It coincides with the establishment of princely and baronial families in the New France of the Morea, the practice of a rigorous feudal system, the building of castles for the subjugation of the inhabitants. For the first fifty years it is a period of military occupation. Racial exclusiveness perpetuates the rift between both races. The northerners' strength is gradually sapped in a country where a special and very different vitality is required for self-preservation. In 1259 the resurgence of the native power comes to a head with the capture of the Frankish Prince, and increases with the foundation of an expansionist Greek state in the southeastern Peloponnese. The foreigners now not only rule over the passive hostility of the population, but face an organized and actively hostile neighbor. From 1262 onwards the scheme of conflict changes from master against slave to masters against each other. The prevailing Greek pattern of civil strife reasserts itself, as the foreigners gradually vanish from the scene, losing their castles to their erstwhile subjects.

Plans. For an examination of the plan of Frankish fortifications in Greece, we must turn first to the fortresses which we definitely know to have been built by the members of those west European baronial families whose original purpose of crusading in the East was supplanted by a more permanent sojourn. The most important relic of this occupation is the castle of Chlemoutsi, built in 1220–1223 by Geoffroy de Villehardouin, in circumstances clearly told in the *Chronicle of the Morea*. The plan (Plate XXXIII), to which little change has been made, comprises a great, hexagonal keep enclosing an inner court on the summit of the hill, with an outer court extending

[5] *Ibid.*, fig. 113 (upper right) and plate VIII, no. 4.
[6] *Ibid.*, figs. 112–114, plates VI, VII.
[7] *Ibid.*, figs. 169, 170.
[8] *Ibid.*, fig. 132.

round the side of it most exposed to attack. The castles built by the Frankish barons of Achaea during the early XIII century, Karytaina, Passava, Kalavryta, and the castle on the lower peak of Acrocorinth, together with the little fort erected on Pendeskouphi during the Frankish siege of 1205–1210, are hilltop fortresses, consisting of a square donjon or keep set on the highest point of the rock or in a position to command the saddle between it and the neighboring altitudes, generally forming a part of the court that surrounds it. The castle built by William Villehardouin in 1249 on the summit of the precipitous hill of Mistra comprises a donjon and inner redout on the topmost ridge, with a lower court beneath it. Old Navarino, built around 1278 by Nicholas II de St. Omer, is a simple edifice of upper and lower enclosure which, because of its pre-eminent position, may not have needed as strong a donjon as the others.

Next, we are faced with the fortresses built by the Greeks before 1204, which the Franks took over after the conquest. At Kalamata, Arkadia, and Argos it is hard to tell whether they departed from the original Byzantine plan. At Acrocorinth they departed not at all, except to add outworks and a castle keep. Likewise at Patras the recurrence of early Byzantine walls throughout the circuit make it plain that Guillaume Aleman, who transformed the Latin archbishop's palace into a fortress, had in reality little to change from the existing quadrangular keep and outer court. Nauplia, according to the *Chronicle*, was at the time of its capture in 1210 a "castle in two enclosures," one of which was weaker than the other. Nauplia was a subsidiary appendage of the Burgundian Dukes of Athens, from whom it passed, after the Battle of the Kephissos, into the hands of bailies; the Venetians who bought the place in 1388 refortified it so thoroughly as to leave little trace of Frankish possession. Finally, at Monemvasia planning was unnecessary. On the whole, nature in Greece

made plans a simple matter. A vertiginous cliff could dispense with the need of more than a thin parapet wall along at least one flank of Acrocorinth, Nauplia, Monemvasia, Kalamata, Arkadia, and Old Navarino. The keep and one or two enclosures disposed themselves with ease about the summit and more accessible slopes.

Masonry. During the 225 years of Frankish rule we find a variety of building styles, of which some are inherited from Byzantine predecessors, others transmitted to succeeding Greeks, Turks, and Venetians. It is hard to tell what is exclusively Frankish, since there is little that is not borrowed or left to later builders. The materials used are the prevailing poros and limestone; where careful cutting is required, as in angles and openings, the softer poros appears more often. The way in which these are put together is the result of local conditions. There are few distinct differences of schools or periods to clarify the task of chronology. On one hand are the walls of small, trimmed limestone blocks in the earliest Frankish constructions, Pendeskouphi and the castle keep on Acrocorinth (Fig. 156). At Chlemoutsi, built soon after, we find large, carefully cut poros in the gates, angles, pilasters, windows, and ashlar vaults (Figs. 173–177). At Kalamata the donjon and south flank of the inner enclosure were rebuilt by the Franks out of materials[9] from the neglected Byzantine fortress (Figs. 32, 33). In the originally Byzantine castles at Patras, Arkadia, Kalamata, and Nauplia there are walls of small, oblong field stones set in courses, lacking in any distinctive feature, which probably belong to the Frankish period. At Argos there are two forms of masonry which may date to either the Frankish or Byzantine: one (Fig. 122) of roughly rectangular limestone laid in an approximation of coursing, with small chips of tile embedded in the mortar between the joints; the other

[9] The Frankish castle of Salona also contains a number of classical blocks re-used. See Bon, "Forteresses médiévales de la Grèce centrale," *B.C.H.*, LXI, 1937, p. 180, fig. 29.

(Figs. 125, 126) of limestone blocks of uniform size, carefully coursed with the aid of flat pieces of tile laid in long strips between them. It may be repeated that variations of rubble are to be found throughout the castles of Greece, whatever the condition, history, or domination of the time.

Walls and parapets. During the XIII century Frankish walls continue vertical, with occasional use of stepped projections at the base.[10] Battering walls come into use late in the XIV century, when the rapprochement between Greek Despots and Florentine Dukes presumably reflects itself in portions of the Acrocorinthian circuit wall, in a quasi-Byzantine masonry of roughly rectangular blocks and large, flat tile.[11] The walls are 4–5 feet thick. Parapets of the XIII century have only remained at Chlemoutsi, where the crenellations of the keep were preserved by the heightening of the wall crown. Here the merlons are square, without loopholes, and separated by crenels of equal width. Machicoulis is used only at Karytaina.

Towers. The Franks continued the Byzantine system of tall, square, flanking towers, projecting forward, but generally not higher than the level of the walls, open at the gorge or containing a vaulted chamber in the upper story. Such may be seen in the south flank of the keep at Patras (Fig. 147) and the curtain of Acrocorinth over the north cliffs. From the beginning of the XIII century round towers make their appearance in the fortresses of Greece for the first time since Antiquity. The tall, circular, vertical towers at Argos (Figs. 117, 118, 120), Chlemoutsi (Fig. 172), and the Castel de Franchi at Nauplia (Fig. 99) contrast strongly with the general aspect of squareness in Byzantine fortifications, which always retained some of the rigidity estab-

lished by Justinian and canonized by his biographer, Prokopios. A round tower on a battering base at Arkadia (Fig. 95) likewise belongs to the period of medieval warfare, despite the later gun embrasures built on top of it. These flanking towers belong to the XIII century, or more particularly to the time of Frankish ascendance. The same period may be given for the square castle keeps: on Acrocorinth the donjon on its characteristically Frankish pyramidal base, at Pendeskouphi, at Mistra, and at Kalamata (Figs. 32, 156, 186). At Mistra and Chlemoutsi a chemin de ronde and parapet ran round the top of the keep. The northeast curtain of Acrocorinth contains solid towers and bastions with carefully built corners, which appear to belong to the second half of the Latin domination of the Peloponnese.

Openings. Entrances were secured, simply, by wooden doors closed with beams. An important exception is the outer gate at Chlemoutsi, which was originally a rectangular pylon with portcullis set into a recess of the main curtain wall. The early Frankish gate is a plain passage covered with a depressed vault of cut poros voussoirs (Fig. 164). This is also the basic form of smaller doorways in the other Frankish castles of XIII century Greece, examples of which may be found in the east curtain of Chlemoutsi, the keep on Acrocorinth, and the inner redout of the Villehardouin castle at Mistra, as well as in the east flank of the summit fort at Monemvasia (Fig. 221). Still smaller doorways may be round or flat-topped. A more elaborate gate is the entrance to the hexagonal keep at Chlemoutsi, where wide, depressed archways in either face of a great avantcorps mask a high, round-vaulted inner passage. The huge, ovoid vaults of this keep (Figs. 173–175) are a local variation on the round or pointed vaults in use at the time in western Europe.

Again Chlemoutsi, as the purest example of French architecture in Greece, offers the

---

[10] For an analysis of French military architecture in the Peloponnese see A. Bon, *La Morée franque*, chapter "Architecture civile et militaire."

[11] For possible constructions of Niccolò or Nerio Acciajuoli see *Corinth*, III, ii, p. 277.

greatest variety of windows employed during the early XIII century. Some are tall and narrow, topped with flat lintel-blocks. Others are smaller and square, encased in limestone jambs, sill, and lintel on the outer wall face, fitted together with bevelled or drafted edges (Figs. 168, 169) built with flaring sides and sloping interior sill. The most notable form of window is a tall, wide, opening in the shape of a passage through the wall, with a depressed vault of poros voussoirs, into which is fitted, on the wall's outer face, a screen of poros pierced by twin lancets (Figs. 176, 177). Relics of the same type of window exist in Hugues de Bruyères' fortress at Karytaina. The outer curtain of Chlemoutsi is pierced by several splayed and vaulted round-topped lancet windows (Fig. 167). Four windows giving on to the hexagonal courtyard are of the prevailing pattern of double arches, covered, however, not under the depressed-vaulted passageway, but under a three-quarter pointed arch.

These castles belong to the century of the great Gothic cathedrals of western Europe. Yet in all the Frankish Morea the pointed arch only appears in these four windows of Chlemoutsi, in the vaults of the rude Latin church at Andravida, and the two monasteries of Isova and Vlakhernai in Elis. Decorative features of the Western or Gothic schools are almost totally absent. For decoration there are only the chamfered edges of impost-blocks and reinforcing arches, and the alternating play of tile and stone in the faces of walls, the latter of Byzantine origin. Here we realize how the Franks in Greece were unable to build exclusively according to the traditions of their own race and place. Chlemoutsi and Andravida show the conquerors cut off from their own land, building in a semi-Romanesque style which in France already belonged to the preceding century, and which local materials and native artisans could only, as if in adumbration of future events, mold to the rooted and living traditions of their subjected country.

15

III. Late Byzantine. In the year 1262 the Lakonian province of the Peloponnese returned into the Byzantine orbit, and recovered its relation to the Empire of the East. The Frankish domination of this region had only lasted fifty-seven years. It had left its mark, on the opposing mountain-slopes of Parnon and Taygetos, in the two castles of Geraki and Mistra, which the returning Greeks immediately made their headquarters. In each place we see to-day a Frankish castle of the XIII century isolated on a hilltop, with the ruins of an extensive Byzantine city of the late XIII, XIV, and early XV centuries displayed over the lower slopes. During these two last centuries of the Empire, the focus of its power receded from its Anatolian limits, shifted back toward Constantinople, then gradually westward over Macedonia, Epiros, and the Peloponnese to encircle the Aegean once more. As in a figure of multiple scales, the power of Byzantium diminished in the East, while further west it grew, and Frankish fortunes sank in their turn with a minor rise and fall among themselves.

The territories recovered from Greece expanded under the impetus of a vigorous and centralized administration, an artistic and intellectual renascence, and the vacuum caused in the Frankish principality itself by the centrifugal chaos of obsolescent feudalism. We have seen how the early XIII century was a period of foreign military occupation dedicated, against odds, to subjugating and rooting itself into a country materially and spiritually hostile. In contrast, the quality of later Byzantine rule in the Morea was systematically aggressive. The Despots of Mistra stimulated steady tension along the borders of the Venetian colonies in Messenia and Argolis, occupied one by one the citadels which the Franks could no longer hold, and carefully avoided outbreaks that might set them back on the defensive. Safe behind a policy of aggression, it was unnecessary to do more than embellish and fortify their new administrative centers. In 1262 the Greeks returned to a region already well stocked with fortresses, while their expansion was staked out by the successive capture of castles, built either by their ancestors or their opponents, which guarded the strategic points of the country. And so it is that we find no important new castles dating from the hundred and ninety-eight years of the Byzantine Despotate, other than a few rock forts in the hinterland such as Ano Sokha, Molaoi, Vatika, and Zaraphona, which are all later than the XIII century. Each follows the basic fortress plan of tower, or strongpoint, with subsidiary enclosure.

Plans. The one complete work of Late Byzantine fortification is the circuit wall round the city of Mistra (Fig. 180). The defenses are planned to take every advantage of a unique terrain. The face of the hill is triangular: at its apex sits the castle of William Villehardouin; the entire south side drops in a cliff over a plunging gorge which forms its own wall; on the north, the wall descends from the opposite end of the castle to the saddle below the castle rock, and follows down the steep edge of a gulley, which serves as an enormous natural moat, to a point some hundred feet above the Lacedaemonian plain, where it turns southward along the base to meet the bottom of the cliff on the other side. Half way up the hill another parallel wall turns southward from the north gulley along the top of a line of rock, dividing the city into an upper and a lower level.

It is not always easy to tell the precise date of these three sections of wall, which belong mostly to the later XIII and early XIV centuries. There are certain additions and repairs of the Turkish period after 1460, but the destruction of the entire town in 1770 has allowed a medieval wall to remain standing, where so many other walled cities of Greece have had to wait until the present century for their destruction to be decreed by municipal law.

Walls and materials. The masonry is of three different kinds: the usual rubble of poros, limestone, and broken tile; cloisonné; and a careful fitting of flat-surfaced poros and limestone blocks, separated by single, double, or occasionally triple courses of large, flat brick or tile at regular intervals. Larger blocks and tile more carefully set are used in the construction of corners. Walls are almost all vertical, from 7–10 feet thick, often pitted with scaffold holes in a more or less uniform pattern, strengthened with one, two, or three stepped projections at the base, especially in the angles. The chemin de ronde may be carried on a recessed arcade.

Towers. The trace of the Byzantine wall system of Mistra resembles an outline of crenellations, so numerous are the flanking towers. As at Salonica and Constantinople, they project both out and above the curtain, two or three storeys high. The bottom courses are built to protrude in two or three steps. They are all hollow, and contain either high, vaulted passageways for gates or vaulted chambers within. The smaller towers, which measure 8–10 feet across, generally contain a vaulted room in the upper storey. The larger ones, with a width of 20–30 feet, and upwards of 50 feet high, may contain a habitable chamber in the upper storey and a cistern in the lower, covered with two parallel vaults separated by a transverse arch. Of the fifteen towers that flank the north city wall of Mistra, three are round. Two of these are Turkish. The other (Figs. 188, 192), a short distance above the Nauplia Gate, is an exception to the normal tradition of square Byzantine towers. Nowhere in the Morea does a polygonal tower appear dating from this second Byzantine period. The face of the towers show a variety of structural and decorative features. The parallel lines of brick (Figs. 191, 194) or occasional string course in different stone are a modest reflection of the massive striations of the wall faces of Byzantium. Some are ornamented with elaborate tile-work, blind arches (Fig. 191) or rows of brackets for huchettes or the balconies of upper rooms. A more imposing feature is the deeply recessed arch, one or two to each face, which may be seen in the same north city wall, and on the top of the hill flanking the outer gate of the Villehardouin fortress. This latter is solid, and built with slightly battering sides (Figs. 183, 184), a departure which may also indicate Turkish authorship. Where the upper rooms are not vaulted in stone, they are supported on wooden floors on beams or on a balcony formed by a slight reduction in thickness of the tower wall inside, a construction used to this day in the fortified houses of the Mani.

Openings. The later Byzantine entrances either penetrate the main wall at right angles, or pass parallel with it through the flank of a redan which projects the wall-trace forward (Mistra, castle), or else, in the line of a Z, through a flanking tower, parallel first to the outside, then to the inside of the curtain (Kalamata, second gate, Fig. 30). The first kind of entrance consists of a plain doorway through a wall, often with arches of different size built one behind the other, as in the Nauplia Gate at Mistra, whose opening is constructed in four successive sections. Gates are flanked by one or two towers, or else actually placed inside a tower, in which case archways in both the inner and outer faces serve to screen the higher vaulted passageway within. The Monemvasia Gate (Fig. 195) and the outer castle gate of Mistra are examples of the latter form. A rare kind of gate appears at the top of the northwest town wall (Figs. 189, 190): a small door in one flank of a tringular redan backed by a square tower on the inside, with a second door in the interior face. The barrel vault of the tower keys into the tapering vault of the redan. The arch of gates may be divided by a gap for portcullis. In gates, doors, recessed arcades, and windows, the arch is often made of alternating wedge-shaped poros voussoirs and single or double bricks (Figs. 184, 195). The vaults are of

15*

small ashlar blocks, rubble, or rough, flat fieldstones, marked with the regularly spaced lines of tile string courses. Reinforcing arches are used where the vault is specially wide. Windows are round-topped, or else masked on the outside by a lower depressed arch. Loopholes are placed in small embrasures with flaring sides and slanting vaults or roofs made of a succession of lintels set one below the other.

Many of these characteristics of late Byzantine building are not confined to the period before 1460, but continue in use, without major change, during the domination of the Turks, who learned their architecture from the Greeks.

IV. EARLY VENETIAN. Venice began her history as a foster-offspring of Byzantium: tied to the Eastern capital first politically as a Roman outpost, in the land where Rome itself had fallen; then, as the independent Republic, drawn eastward by the irresistible tide of commerce down the Adriatic. After the collapse of the Western Empire, it was only Venice, in a Europe submerged in tribal barbarism, that kept touch with the distant East, where Antiquity had fused into the civilization of Constantinople. The city floating in the sea had its existence in the hulls of ships during centuries when the rest of Europe was landbound. Her galleys, plying back and forth through the Adriatic and Aegean Seas, brought to Europe its only material knowledge of an Empire, still existing, which had long since vanished from the West; brought to Venice a substantial part of its splendor, and to the territories of Byzantium a legion of merchants and pilgrims.

This watery dominion gravitated to the harbors which lay between Venice and the Hellespont. In every place Venetian traders installed themselves to draw out a stream of produce to be marketed by Venice to an unproductive continent. In each place they kept close watch on the balance or unbalance of power along the Dalmatian, Greek, and Asiatic coasts, that Venice might know when to proffer, when to remove her aid. With her unique commercial and naval might, Venice grew both indispensable to the individual Emperors and inimical to the actual fabric of the Empire. At a critical moment, when the Normans had seized the last Byzantine possessions in Southern Italy, and carried their attack to Monemvasia, Corinth, and Constantinople itself, Venice lent the Emperor her warships in exchange for free trading rights in the Imperial lands. This entrenchment in the centers of eastern Mediterranean commerce enabled Venice finally to carve up the Byzantine Empire, leaving to her allies the task of conquering and governing its separate regions, while she laid claim to the only thing she needed, harbors. The Partition Treaty of 1204 allotted her originally whole coastal territories, which she soon after relinquished in favor of certain isolated posts, easily taken, easily held, that secured her the mastery of the sea. The Islands were bestowed on Venetian families. A Venetian bailie was installed in Euboea, and a Venetian naval force possessed itself of the two chief ports of Messenia. Venice's single concern was for her monopoly of the trade routes, to which the fortified harbors of Greece to-day bear witness. In 1214 the purchase of the whole island of Crete marked a new development in the history of her Levantine rule. With the gradual spread of control over the island of Euboea, the direct acquisition of Argos and Nauplia in 1388, of Patras, Naupaktos, and Navarino in the early years of the XV century, territorial increase led to political responsibilty, and finally to the military leadership which made Venice the last Christian power to withstand the Turks in Greece.

Plans. Venetian fortresses are a departure from the mountain castles of the Franks and the Byzantines. Those guarded the land, these the sea. With their back, as it were, to the land, they must nevertheless be so strong that no land force could take them. Where a bay took a deep enough bite out of the coastline,

the Venetians encircled it whole, extending the opposite lines of shore by mole or embankments to draw the fortifications tight round the harbor mouth. Such are the defenses of Candia, Canea (Plate XXXVIII), and Kyrenia, which present a wall against the sea and heavy ramparts against the land. Naupaktos is unique in utilizing a great, steep hill, cliff-edged in the rear, from whose summit two ramparts descend straight to the shore and out like curving arms into the water, to embrace a tiny harbor. Like the rings of a tiara, crenellated walls cross the hill-slope horizontally, forming three levels of enclosures. Where, on the other hand, a port was only formed by a long, narrow, straight peninsula projecting from the shore of some much larger bay (Fig. 61), the Venetians occupied the peninsula, with whatever existed on it of previous Byzantine fortifications; walled it about from end to end; built moles, with here or there the use of rock shoals or islets, to create a smaller, safer shelter in the heart of the wider refuge of the coastline; and finally cut the peninsula off at the neck with a moat from sea to sea, protected by massive defenses against the hostile tides of the Byzantine, then Turkish mainland (Plates I, II, XIV, XVI, XVII, XIX–XXIII).

Early constructions. Examples of the latter type of site are Methone, Corone, and Nauplia which, occupied by the Venetians from the XIII to the XVI century, show better than any other fortresses in Greece the transition from medieval to artillery fortification. The latter style has overlaid the former at the most strategic positions. Yet we have from the XIII and XIV centuries, at both Methone and Corone, the entrance gates with pointed arches (Figs. 6, 68), the simple medieval curtain and crenellated parapet along sections of the outer enclosures which the Venetians were still trying to make over for artillery in 1700 (Plate XVI, B, D, E, I, and N), and the tall, narrow, rectangular and vertical, or chamfered, round, and battering flanking towers (Figs. 83, 84, 85), built of rubble or ashlar, with big, squared blocks set always in the angles. We learn little of early Venetian building from either Argos, which retained its Byzantine and Frankish character until the Turks took it, or from Negroponte, whose Venetian fortresses have disappeared.

Nor was it till after these two places were lost in the first Turkish war that Venice, once protected by the discord of her neighbors but now face to face with a single enemy, at last transformed her remaining citadels to the uses of modern warfare. The present Venetian fortifications in Greece date almost entirely to the two periods 1470–1540 and 1685–1715.

Artillery defenses. In medieval fortification the prime factor was always height. Previous to the XV century castles are either placed on top of a hill, or built to simulate one, enabling the defenders to pour a rain of arrows or vertical missiles upon an attacker struggling upwards; and to escape scaling ladders and grappling towers effective against walls in the lowland. With the introduction of artillery the basic conception of fortification changes. Eminence becomes a target for destruction by fire-impelled projectiles. Stone walls with chemin de ronde and simple parapets for archery give way to thick, low, earth-filled, terrepleined ramparts faced with a battering masonry scarp generally of ashlar, set low into the ground, their defensible height still preserved by the sinking of a ditch below it, with a stone-faced, battering counterscarp on the other side (Fig. 63). The earth from the ditch is thrown up on the counterscarp to form an embankment, or glacis, screening the scarp itself; grazing fire from the ramparts sweeps its long, gradual slope over the outer country. The gun emplacements on the walls are defended by thick parapets of stone and earth, with deep, flaring embrasures, originally vaulted (Fig. 107, left), but in the later period left open to the sky. Instead of simple walls defending the curtain by sealing off accessible

slopes, as at Acrocorinth, the artillery curtain is protected, in the ditch, by a long parallel embankment, or faussebraye, and by traverses, caponiers, and ravelins, or demi-lunes, beyond it. Flanking towers gradually give place to massive bastions, at first terrepleined, then hollow in order to provide two levels of cannon emplacements, set at the strategic corners, to enfilade the ditch. In the XVI century with the innovations of Sanmicheli, the long, straight, bare curtains are broken up into angles, with added bastions to cover the lines of approach (Fig. 228). The chief purpose of defense was to prevent the enemy arriving at the counterscarp, from which he could build up the glacis into a parapet for himself, begin operations in the ditch, and dig the tunnels or galleries beneath it to the point under the curtain or the bastion itself where the powder barrels could be detonated.

The earliest dated Venetian artillery constructions are those of Vettore Pasqualigo at Nauplia. The island fort in the Bay, built in 1471, consists of an octagonal tower with battering walls and a gun platform, with two lower emplacements on either side. A string course molding encircles the platforms at the level of the embrasures. At the same period also the Venetians strengthened the north and east flanks of the Castel de Franchi with a talus and squat flanking bastions, round and angular (Figs. 99, 103). They extended the fortress eastward by the addition of a third enclosure with a gate and round flanking bastion on a battering base (Fig. 104). So far the parapets in these constructions, as well as in the contemporary curtain of Old Navarino, are crenellated in a characteristic Italian style of notched, or swallow-tail, merlons, alternately pierced with loopholes (Figs. 45, 105). The apex of the third enclosure of Acronauplia is occupied by an immense, round double bastion built with widely battering ashlar walls, which dates to the late XV or early XVI century (Fig. 106, 107). Its double gun platform is surrounded with a heavy cordon, or torus molding, the most characteristic, though not an exclusive, element of Venetian military architecture. The early artillery parapet is narrow and irregular in outline, with shallow embrasures, vaulted and tapering to a small hole on the outside.

To the last quarter of the XV century may be assigned the colossal talus walls of Corone (Figs. 7, 16, 20) and the larger part of the land defenses of Methone (Figs. 63–65, 74). An inscription of *ca.* 1480 in one of its bastions and an account of 1494 describing the works in progress tell the story of the Venetians' increasing political instability and architectural prowess on the eve of the second Turkish war. We see them at Methone masters of artillery fortification, employing a complete system of a rampart in two levels, bastions, ditch, faussebraye, counterscarp, covered way, and glacis. But by the time these works were completed, the earlier artillery defenses at Nauplia were already outdated: their parapets too shallow for guns of ever larger caliber, and the Bourtzi tower too prominent for safety. After 1500 the Venetians built a lower city at Nauplia on what had previously been water and marsh, and fortified it with a sea wall and heavy ramparts, ditch and outworks on the east side facing the land. What remains of the wall is flanked with circular bastions, all built with a slight talus of both rubble and ashlar masonry.

Openings. The openings reflect the changed emphasis in construction. There are no windows. Ramparts are only pierced by vaulted casemates. Land gates are monumental structures placed at the head of a drawbridge over the moat. Sea gates and smaller doors are plain round archways, made of a few big, curved, wedge-shaped blocks of limestone (Figs. 101, 102). The doors and talus faces generally bear sculptured plaques of the lion of St. Mark, the seal which Venice set upon so many harbors of the Eastern Mediterranean.

V. TURKISH. The Peloponnese was ruled by foreigners from 1205 to 1828, with a partial interlude of two centuries under the Byzantine Despotate. The Turkish conquest of 1460 initiated a period of military occupation which first expanded, with the expulsion of the Venetians from Greece and the sweep of Turkish arms westward into the Mediterranean and Europe, then gradually retreated to a defensive position in the XVII century. The architectural activity of the Turks belongs almost entirely to the first period.

The prototypes of this architecture are the XV century Turkish fortifications at Constantinople and the Bosporos. The high, vertical walls are built of rectangular blocks measuring $1\frac{1}{2}$–2 feet long, laid with mortar in courses of varying width, here or there striated with double or multiple courses of brick in the traditional Byzantine manner. The parapets are crenellated, with outline parallel to the slope of the chemin de ronde. The merlons are tall and narrow, with pointed copes made of two sets of flat stones tilted against eachother. The walls are flanked with round, square, triangular, and polygonal towers, which project above and sometimes inside, as well as outside, the curtain. Large round or octagonal towers defend the angles, built often in two levels, the inner and the outer both crowned with a ring of crenellations. The big corner towers are hollow, with stairways spiralling up to their first level through the immense thickness of the outer walls. These are pierced with deep, tunnel-shaped loopholes. The vaults and arches of doors, windows, and passageways are built of great fans of long, flat brick. Arches are round, depressed, and pointed, sometimes springing from molded corbels.

Features such as these appear among the military constructions of the next four hundred years in Greece, sometimes helping to identify the Turkish hand. More often, identification is confused by the variety of Turkish imitations both of medieval and artillery,

Greek and Venetian forms, as well as by the restricted activity of the Turks themselves among the many fortresses throughout the country, which needed only occasional repairs and renovations.

Plans. To their fortress plans the Turks seemed to have devoted either too little or too much attention. The caprice of a Mohammed II, who built Rumeli Hissar on the plan of his own Arabic initial, is matched by the rigid symmetry of the star-shaped defenses of Yedi Kule at Constantinople, the three-tiered octagonal fort at Methone (Fig. 82), the octagonal towers at Corone and the Castle of Morea (Plates I, XXX), and the toy-like, hexagonal fort at New Navarino, shaped like a snow-flake with its six projecting bastions pointing at every corner (Plates XI, XII). The studied regularity of the Castles of Morea and Roumeli, New Navarino and Zarnata, and the tidy rectangles of Kelepha and the lower town at Monemvasia contrast with the expedient and skillfull irregularity of the fortresses of the Greeks, Franks, and Venetians, who knew better how to fit their walls to the terrain.

Materials. Turkish masonry reflects the evolution of four centuries of architecture. The styles are many. The most characteristic is a masonry of rubble and broken tile, generally mortared, sometimes pocked with scaffold-holes, which varies in appearance according to locality and period. With a model at Mistra of late Byzantine provincial architecture, the Turks continued the use of rubble wall faces, decorated with string courses of flat brick or broken tile. At Patras the Turkish works can be recognized by heavily mortared rubble, heterogeneously compounded of limestone, poros, and brick. Zarnata is built of small, rough stone, with an abundance of broken tile set horizontally, approximating courses (Fig. 22). The ramparts of Kelepha are made of rough blocks of limestone, fitted together tightly without filling of tile or mortar, presenting a uniform wall surface of flat-faced stone (Fig. 36). These two XVII century castles seem not, as frontier-posts in Mani, to have merited the particular skill or care devoted to more important fortresses. The XVI century Turkish constructions at Methone, New Navarino, and the lower town of Monemvasia are distinguished by masonry of roughly squared, oblong blocks in courses, with large, carefully squared blocks in the angles and quoins of the arches, vaults, and casemates (Figs. 50, left; 53, 55, 56, 78).

In other places the Turkish builders copy the more refined techniques of Byzantine cloisonné and Venetian ashlar. Examples of the former are the polygonal southeast corner bastion at Patras (Fig. 136), and the gates of the inner enclosure and Bourtzi at Methone (Fig. 82); of the latter, the scarped faces of the Castle of Roumeli, the chamfered interior bastion of Patras, and Methone's southern sea gate (Figs. 80, 146, 149). At Corone the great Turkish artillery defenses on the eastern side, built after 1500, follow the Venetian model with walls of squared blocks of different height and width, fitted carefully together in a strong, white mortar visible at all the joints (Figs. 10, 11). Terra cotta is extensively used in Turkish fortification, whether in the form of chips of broken tile reinforcing the mortar, string courses streaking the wall face, or the long, flat brick in the arches, the vaults of casemates and passageways, and the great, hollow domes of the artillery bastions.

Walls and parapets. The Turkish fortifications of the XV, XVI, and XVII centuries in Greece attest the long, fumbling effort of the Turks to learn the principles of artillery warfare. Their misunderstanding of its needs and purposes is revealed in the innocent rigidity of their plans, the clumsy disposition of their bastions, too close together or too far apart, and the defenseless construction of their walls. Even in their artillery fortresses the curtains follow the obsolete Byzantine or medieval form: at New Navarino, Mistra, and Monem-

vasia tall, narrow masonry walls, not even
solid to the full width of the chemin de ronde,
but diminished by arcades of recessed arches
on the inner side (Fig. 51). A coating of plaster
over the wall faces, liberally applied with the
trowel, is a characteristic of the XVII and
XVIII centuries. Rarely do we see the full,
terrepleined ramparts such as the Venetians
were building during the same period. The
legends on the Grimani plans bear eloquent
witness to this defect with the urgent insist-
ence, *La Mura ha bisogno del suo terrapieno.*

Parapets continued for centuries after the
Turkish conquest to provide a defense only
for archery and small arms. Most of the parapets in the Greek fortresses to-day, both simple
crenellations and artillery bulwarks, belong to
the Turkish period, as the element always first
destroyed and first to be rebuilt. As at Constantinople and the Bosporos, we find at
Monemvasia, New Navarino, and Argos tall,
narrow merlons with pointed copes, following
the slant of the terrain (Figs. 51, 124, 129). In
the XVII century parapets tend to lose their
crenellations and become simply thin, straight-
topped walls pierced by single or double loopholes. The artillery parapets vary in thickness
from $2\frac{1}{2}$ to 15 feet, pierced with flaring embrasures and often long, square or vaulted holes
for musketry aligned to cover the vulnerable
base of adjacent walls. In outline the parapets
are either curved or angular, with a sloping
top (Figs. 10, 59). At Methone and Corone
(Fig. 10), flat, square tiles form a covering
over the top, embedded in the mortar. The
two great bastions at Patras and a tower in
the outermost line at Acrocorinth support a
peculiar form of parapet in two levels, the
lower containing deep, vaulted, tapering casemates, which support a chemin de ronde and
a thinner parapet of elaborately notched and
slotted crenellations (Fig. 136). The fort of
Karababa at Chalkis, built by the Turks in
1686 under the direction of a Venetian renegade,
has musketry parapets of scalloped outline,

whose undulations serve no more purpose than
a straight-topped wall (Fig. 199). At Nauplia
in the XVIII century, after driving the Venetians out, the Turks added on to the Bourtzi
and the east postern gate of the Palamedi
artillery parapets walled in the regular cloisonné masonry which they had begun to
imitate from the Byzantines three hundred
years before.

Towers and bastions. The Turks perpetuated
the use of flanking towers: at Mistra (Figs.
185, 187, 193, 194, right) and Methone, in the
dividing wall between the two enclosures,
quadrangular, round, and hollow in the upper
storey; at Zarnata (Fig. 23) and Kelepha
straight, round, and hollow, containing cisterns. It is characteristic of Turkish ineptitude,
both here and elsewhere, that the vital necessity of resistance, water, should be stored
in this most crucial element of defense, and
chief target of the attacker. At Old and New
Navarino, Patras, and Chlemoutsi the medieval
form gives way to round towers with gun
platforms and embrasured parapets, occasionally hollow for a lower level of casemates,
sometimes built with string course and talus
base, reflecting the advance of artillery fortification.

Detached, individual towers are also a
Turkish feature, of which the outstanding
example is the island fort at Methone (Fig.
82). This belongs probably to the XV century,
with its high lantern form in two levels each
ringed about with crenellations, and stairway
winding up through the thickness of its outer
wall. Separate, polygonal towers also exist at
Corone and the Castle of Morea. A later kind
is the high, square πῦργος in several storeys,
with turrets supported on corbels at the four
corners, characteristic of the fortified houses
of the Mani (Fig. 24).

With greater attention paid to artillery defense in the larger fortresses, flanking towers
give way to elaborate, massive bastions. At
the Castle of Morea, at Corone on the eastern

ments, as is the ca
projected for the
(Plate XXV). W
development of fo
medieval, and ea
point and curtai
combination or
forts. New Navar
transition betwee
set at the crucia
hexagonal enclosu
lery ramparts; th
by a tower-flanke
independent basti
points along the
standing example
medi citadel of 17

Materials. The
walls is of three
rough stones fitte
mortar covering
used in the first
Kalamata (Figs.
the Palamedi fort
and caponier at
A masonry of rou
in regular course
Drepanon (Fig. 2
piazza bassa, ou
north defenses at
87). In all these
ment stands out
masonry: the con
The outer gate of
rectangular bloc
Methone the late
on foundations
mental ashlar blo
salient angles. At
pears in the uppe
angles of the Gr
lower section is k
rusticated ashlar
the corner (Figs.
used in the angle

flank, at New Navarino, and Kelepha these project boldly from the angles or the curtain, chiefly round and low, measuring between 25 and 90 feet in diameter, built hollow with huge, ovoid tholoi, domed in brick, containing cisterns or lower levels of gun emplacements pointing through deep casemates in the walls (Figs. 8–12, 50, 52, 56, 150). New Navarino and the Castle of Roumeli guard their respective channels with bastions so complex as to be almost separate forts, with great gun platforms carried on deep, vaulted arcades, presenting formidable fronts of double levels of guns along the water's edge (Figs. 53, 54). Other emplacements are terrepleined, such as the big, round bastion at Argos (Fig. 124), the XVII century constructions at the eastern and western ends of the cliff-top of Monemvasia, and along both flanks of Karababa (Figs. 199, 216, 225). The great polygonal bastion at Karababa, with its concentric, vaulted galleries, central cistern, line of lower vaulted casemates, and ring of embrasures in its upper parapet, is a sophisticated, if constricted, example of late XVII century artillery fortification. At Methone may be seen three cavaliers, two on the east ramparts of the inner enclosure (Fig. 86), and one at the southeast corner of the outer curtain (Fig. 78). The latter is a lofty, rectangular tower consisting of two wide, open arches, built with considerable care with molded cornices and quoins of cut voussoirs, and serving almost no other purpose than a precarious watch-post. The two on the inner ramparts are semicircular structures, with outer stairs leading to ill guarded gun platforms on top. Inside they are divided into two chambers by a wall down the middle, covered with lopsided, curving, diminishing vaults, a construction visible also in a hollow, semicircular bastion at Kelepha. Some of the later Turkish defenses carry turrets and guard houses. The turrets may be, as at Patras, wide, hexagonal, and domed, or plain sentry-boxes lined and domed in thick plaster, as at Monem-

vasia. The guard houses are small, rectangular buildings, generally set on top of the bastions, covered with a depressed vaulted roof (Figs. 212, 225), and pierced with numerous loopholes.

Openings. A typical form of Turkish gate marks the east curtain of Patras castle (Figs. 134, 135). A small, depressed arch of poros blocks is set under a ponderous, brick-arched huchette in the side of a great, square flanking tower, through which one turns at right angles into a wide, high chamber covered with a barrel vault of brick, and passes into the outer enclosure through a pointed arch occupying the line of the curtain wall. This form of zigzag entrance may be seen also in the gate to the upper enceinte of Kalamata (Fig. 30). Gateways are also built in the form of straight, depressed vaulted passages, as in the southern water gate at Methone: an elaborate, rectangular building flanked with towers on the outer face (Figs. 80, 81). The construction of a recessed pointed arch enclosing a round or depressed arch seems to be, at Methone, both a Venetian and a Turkish feature (Figs. 68, 76, 81). The pointed arch is an originally eastern form, which the Turks used extensively. At Methone also, the gates of the inner dividing curtain and the island fort are distinctly Turkish, with their pointed arches of brick in multiple layers and surrounding wall faces of cloisonné masonry.

The gateways of the XVI century are a Turkish interpretation of artillery models. At Monemvasia the entrances to the lower town and the upper citadel are each contained in a square bastion through which a round arch, framed in a square of poros ashlar, gives access to a long, ashlar vaulted passageway occupying one half of the bastion's area. Next to it, in each, is a twin vaulted chamber (Figs. 209, 213). A similar construction of a square section of poros ashlar, framed by a rolled molding and pierced by a door, appears also in the eastern side of the town wall. The lower western gate

con
for
ma
by
wh
red
tin
tio
sec
sha
arc
of t
ern
cer
iall
poi
ses
Ge
bri
wh
the
wir
per
wh
lint
pla
tio
hol
cas

tio
yea
por
Eu
Ea

Pel
wa
tha
citi
the
une
nes
ter

contribution to the art of fortification, the Palamedi. Its five separate castles, built as Sagredo wrote, "di grossezza estraordinaria e della più massima struttura,"[14] are each of different size and plan according to position and terrain, but all of one construction. Each encloses a court in one, two, three, four, or five sections. The ramparts around them are either plain masonry walls or colossal structures containing series of high, narrow, parallel vaulted chambers, the line of whose sides and vaults carries through to the inner faces of the courtyard walls; in each chamber are a door and oval window, with a circular window beneath the arch. Upon these vaults is carried the gun platform, 30–40 feet wide, surrounded by the double parapet for large pieces of artillery and musket fire (Fig. 115). The parapets are all of brick, containing flaring, vaulted embrasures on the lower level, above which runs a broad chemin de ronde, defended by a straight-topped, uncrenellated parapet with many loopholes pointing in two, three, and four directions, and communicating with the lower platform by means of a series of separate stairways carried on barrel vaults, 5 feet high and 8 long, in the manner of certain Byzantine stairways at Mistra. The gun platforms themselves are reached by long stairs and ramps from the courtyards below, and beneath the courtyards are long, vaulted cisterns. At the

[14] Gerola, *Napoli di Romania*, p. 396.

southern end of the citadel is a fort stretched out in successive sections, containing the old state prison, now ruined, defended by a moat drilled in the rock; beyond this a long bonnet de prêtre, or three-cornered outwork, extends to the edge of the mountain's accessible slope.

Openings. The Venetians, who demolished the castle of Kalamata in 1685, soon after repaired the damage and added a new gate to the outer enceinte (Fig. 26). This is a simple structure consisting of a square tower set in a redan, with a vaulted chamber and two plain, round, poros-arched doorways in the inner and outer flanks. The platform above the tower is guarded by a thin parapet without provision for artillery. The construction shows no great advance over the gateways of the medieval or Turkish period. Equally simple are most of the doors and windows of the later Venetians: unadorned openings, with flat lintels or round or depressed arches, generally framed in cut blocks of stone. The gate to the Palamedi is as plain as this, though flanked by battering buttresses with massive, rusticated angles, and topped with an inscription and the winged lion of St. Mark. Only in the walls of the lower fortress of Acronauplia does the Sagredo Gate of 1713 (Fig. 112), with its pyramidal pillars and Palladian architrave, give any hint that these fortifications, otherwise as functional and bare as in the early days of Byzantium, belong now to the world of the Renaissance.

APPENDIX A

THE ARGOLID PORTS

(PLATES XIX, XX, XXIV–XXVII)

The Peloponnese is represented in thirty-seven out of the forty-one Grimani plans, of which nine cover the south shore of the Argolid peninsula. A quarter of the collection devoted to this twentieth part of the Peloponnesian coastline emphasizes the strategic importance, for the Venetians, of its peculiar geography.

The capital of the Morea at the head of the Argolid Gulf, full in face of the Arkadian mountains, was of all the maritime cities in the Peloponnese closest to the heart of the country. Apex of the historic Argos-Corinth triangle, Nauplia commanded quick reach of Monemvasia across the Gulf, while the sea provided the shorter route of winds and currents round to Mani and Messenia on the far side of the interior highlands. The Argolid coast southeast of Nauplia, with its string of landlocked harbors concealed along the recesses of the Gulf, provided the havens for the Venetian fleet, upon whose decks conquest and rule depended. Here, as in all her history, Venice obeyed the sea which she commanded, and centered her new dominion around a water-girt citadel and the succession of ports which formed its lines of defense.

In addition to three elaborate plans of the fortress of Nauplia, the collection includes two maps of Nauplia Bay (Plates XIX, XX) and three simple charts of the Argolid shore showing the ports of Karathona and Tolos (Plate XXIV) near Nauplia, the mouth of the bay of Drepanon (Plate XXV), the harbor of Porto Kheli, or Porto Bisato (Plate XXVI) opposite the island of Spetsai, and the heavily indented line of coast opposite the islands of Dhokos and Hydra, forming the bays of Koverta and Hermione, or Kastri (Plate XXVII).

Reports of the Venetian governors attest the importance of these places. Writing in 1692, Tadio Gradenigo[1] mentions the six harbors of the Morea: Navarino, Poro, Bisato, Trapano, Tolon, and Napoli di Romania; the last five, all in the Argolid, are the only ports in the eastern Peloponnese. In 1701 Francesco Grimani writes:[2]

The necessity of ports to shelter the fleet deserves Your Excellencies' most serious consideration. The harbor of Nauplia, if it is not dredged, is lost. In several despatches I have indicated this need, and have sent also a drawing showing its depth, the condition of the sea floor, and the opinions of the experts.

He also recommends works to secure the harbors of Poros and Drepanon. Karathona is mentioned in a contemporary Venetian publication as sizable enough for the light ships of

[1] Δελτίον, II, pp. 231 f.
[2] *Ibid.*, V, pp. 491–3. See Plate XX.

the navy ("Porto Caretan ... capace per l'armata sottile").[3]

In the early XIX century the French traveller, Pouqueville,[4] wrote the following description of the south and east sections of the Argolid:

La distance de Damalas à Castri, qui est l'ancienne Hermione, est de quatre heures trente minutes de marche. Cette ville était ruinée du temps de Pausanias... Son port... vaste baie, divisée en plusieurs mouillages, est comme le canal d'Hydra, un abri commode aux vaisseaux, qui peuvent laisser tomber l'ancre partout...

A une heure trente minutes de Castri par terre, et à une lieue par mer, on arrive d'un côté à Cranidi, et de l'autre à Bizati, qui est son port. Cette place, habitée par six cents familles chrétiennes, ne repose sur le terrain d'aucune ville ancienne, quoique Halice et Philanorium aient existé aux environs. Quelque personnes croient que Masès, ville citée par Homère, exista vers le port dont un des côtés est formé par le promontoire Struthuntium... Pour ce qui concerne Bizati, nous dirons que c'est le plus grand port du golfe d'Argos. M. de Champmartin, commandant la frégate du roi la Flore, qui y était de relâche au mois d'Avril 1776, est le premier qui en ait levé un plan

digne de figurer dans un portulan. Il peut contenir la flotte la plus nombreuse, qui y serait à l'abri de tous les vents. On y trouve à y faire du bois, et c'est ordinairement l'endroit où les Hydriotes en prennent les provisions nécessaires à leur navigation.

En descendant vers Nauplie, on trouve, à six milles audessous de Bizati, Drapano, port où cinquante bâtiments de guerre seraient à leur aise. On y entre par un goulet large de soixante-deux brasses, après avoir contourné une pointe sur laquelle les Vénitiens avaient bâti un fort qui est démoli. On peut ammarer à terre sans courir aucun danger, il y a partout dix-huit et vingt brasses, fond de coquillages. Nous avons fait connaitre les ports Tolon ou Avlon et Caratone, qui sont les derniers qu'on trouve sur cette côte avant d'arriver à Nauplie. Ces stations intérieures étaient essentielles à indiquer aux navigateurs à cause des obstacles qu'ils rencontrent de la part des vents de N.E. et de N.N.E. qui défendent l'entrée du golfe d'Argos où ils sont presque réguliers, surtout en hiver; temps où leur impétuosité rend son accès difficile.

L'importance de la partie orientale de l'Argolide que nous venons de décrire, sera facilement appréciée comme point de défense de la Moree, si on fait attention aux forteresses dont elle fut autrefois hérissée, et aux ports ouverts sur ces côtes. Elle avait été sentie en 1693 par François Morosini, doge et commandant de la flotte vénitienne, lorsqu'il conseilla de fortifier Salamine, Egine, Hydra, Spezzia, qui auraient avec Corinthe formé une ligne de défense presque insurmontable...

---

[3] P. Pacifico, *Breve Descrizione corografica del Peloponneso ò Morea* (Venice, 1704), p. 39.

[4] *Voyage*, V, pp. 260 ff.

APPENDIX B

DREPANON

(PLATE XXV)

In 1701 Francesco Grimani reported to the Venetian Senate on the condition of the Argolid ports and the unique position of Drepanon bay, in process of being improved for the work of dry-dock repairs, urging the need to secure the harbors of Drepanon and Poros by "two forts at the entrance of each, or at least heavy, well stocked towers."[1] An account of 1704 again mentions Drepanon "where the fleet undergoes repairs."[2]

Poros is not included in the Grimani collection, which contains no drawing either of its bay or Bourtzi, but Plate XXV of this series shows a plan for the fortification of Drepanon which, though not marked with Grimani's crest, may well have been executed at his command; in 1701 he was already speaking of improvements in progress.

Drepanon is a sickle-shaped inlet stretching $1\frac{1}{2}$ miles parallel with the sea behind a long arm of land, entered by a narrow mouth at the eastern end. A low-lying, waterless island called Plateia faces this mouth accross a mile of water.

One of the panels of Plate XXV shows a plan for improvement in the bay's innermost section, where "the repair work on the hulls *(concia)* could be made safer and easier by dredging and driving in palisades." The shallowest part of the bay could thus have been closed off by a kind of dyke, through whose entrance ships could come into dry-dock. There is no indication to-day that this was ever accomplished. The other panels of Plate XXV show a three-point system of fortification based on either side of the bay's mouth and on the island of Plateia opposite. The forts proposed for the island and the eastern point of the harbor entrance were never built. In 1714, however, the governor, Agostino Sagredo, mentions in his report the building of a fort big enough for twenty-eight pieces of artillery to protect ships undergoing dry-dock repairs.[3]

On the western point stands a small, irregular fort with six gun embrasures facing east across the bay's mouth (Fig. 230) and four on the side of the open sea. Of presumably the

---

[1] Δελτίον, V, p. 491: "Trapano merita una singolarissima stima, perchè unico alle tante utile concie di tutta l'Armata, ma chiama riparo all' imbonimento che vi si va facendo, anzi aperto e senza alcuna difesa lascia libera l'adito all' insidie e alle rimarcabili conseguenze, che ho più volte considerate. I porti di Trapano e Poro chiedono d'esser assicurati, o con due Forti, in ognuno all' ingresso, o almeno con grosse Torri ben munite."

[2] Pacifico, *Breve Descrizione*, p. 39: "Porto Trapano vi siegne assai comodo, dove si da la concia all' armata."

[3] Δελτίον, V, p. 377: "A sicurezza dell' Armata, quando l'attrova, sotto la concia a Trappano, stabilij un Forte capace di vintiotto pezzi d'Artiglieria, che serve a tutelarla, stando, per l'effetto della concia medesima in quel Porto, ma non ad impedire quando non s'attrovasse in vigore di sortire al cimento, che il Nemico non possa tenirla rinchiusa, ed in tal modo togliere le sue assistenze alla difesa de Stati, che fossero assaliti."

FIG. 230. DREPANON, FROM THE EAST.

FIG. 231. DREPANON, EAST BATTERY, LOOKING SOUTH.

same size as that proposed in the upper left corner of the Grimani drawing, this fort is built according to slightly different plan, though with certain features in common. It is built on a slope of rock directly over the water. On the east and south are the two embrasured flanks, built with battering walls (Fig. 231). A cistern is built against the wall on the east, providing a gun platform reached by steps from a lower level behind it. The salient southeast section contains the ten gun embrasures. The upper section of the fort is a platform built on the higher level of rock, held in by a battering retaining wall. At the top is a small, square, pyramidal-roofed chamber. The upper apex of the fort is occupied by a small, irregular platform from which descends a wall, battering both inside and out, with parapet and chemin de ronde, in the line of a Z to another round platform on the water, facing the interior of the bay. The masonry is uniform: uncut blocks of limestone, with broken tile. This is the work noted in Sagredo's report, written one year before the Turks returned into the Peloponnese, and described by Pouqueville a century later to guard that bay where "fifty warships could anchor at ease."[4]

[4] *Voyage*, V, p. 262.

APPENDIX C

CATALOGUE OF PLATES

RACOLTA DELLI DESEGNI DELLA
PIANTA DI TUTTE LE PIAZZE
DEL REGNO DI MOREA E PARTE
DELLI PORTI DELLO STESSO

I. CORONE: PIANTA DELLA FORTEZZA DI CORON.

A. Porta Principale, B. Torrion detto Castel di Mar, C. Porta della Lenguetta, D. Falsa Braga e Torrioni della linguetta, E. Brechia picola detta Maltese, F. Batteria della Brechia Grande, G. Piazza bassa della detta Batteria, H. Torre Ridotta in Kaualiero, I. Muraglia del Recinto antico, K. Chiesa della Madona delle Gratie, L. Opra principiata p serar la gran Brechia della qualle parte è fatto come deue stare e parte Serata di Muro Secho e parte fatto Solo il Bassamento.
Scalla di Passi Veneti nọ. 100

59×42.5 cm. Francesco Grimani's crest and coronet drawn surrounded by elaborate scroll-work in lower left. Signed: A. D.

The drawing of the fortress is meticulous and accurate. Various features of the environs are marked on the plan itself: south shore, Sabionera; tongue of land east of the fortress, Penisola con diuersi Pozzi, e conserue senz' Aqua; aqueduct west of citadel, Condoto della Fontana; the peninsula ridge, Sito Eminente alto dal pian del Mare piedi Veneti nọ. 146, bounded on its north side by Baricatura dalla parte alta; the site of the present town, Sito doue ui e piantato il Borgo, bounded on the west by Baricatura alla fronte del borgo.

II. CORONE: PIANTA DI CORON RELEUATA SOTO IL COMANDO DEL ILL^mo· ECC^mo SIG^ro FRANCESCO GRIMANI PRO^ro GENERALI · IN · MOREA ·

A. Forteza, B. Castelo, C. Bastion Nouo, D. Piaza Bassa, E. Lingueta, F. Porta di forteza, G. Fontana, H. Burgo, I. Mollo, K. Sito di bataria, L. Moschea, M. Strada di modon, N. Torrion di marina, O. Recinto del Castelo, P. Bastion nouo, Q. Mezeluna.
Scala (1–100)

51.5×37 cm. Grimani shield and a monogram held as pendents in either hand of a winged victory. Signed: Beler–F.

Above the legend in lower left is a small, low panel, showing a section of the fortress (Profil) with the items N, O, P, and Q. On the plan in lower right is written: Fontana. The details are careful, but the plan of the fortress is out of proportion. The drawing is floridly decorated.

III. ZARNATA: PIANTA· DE· ZARNATA· RELE-VATA· SOTO· IL· COMANDO· DEL· IL^mo ET· ECC^mo SIG^ro FRANCESCO· GRIMANI· PRO^ra GENERALI· IN· MOREA.

A. Forteza, B. Batterie, C. Porta, D. Aqua, E. Uila Campa, F. Uila Albe, G. Maltis, H. Uile uaruchi, I. Calliue, K. Uaruchi piculi, L. Mulin da uento, M. Strada di calamata, N. Madona, O. Batteria, P. Porta di forteza, Q. Strata di forteza.
Scala di Pasi Geometrici (1–100)

36.5×51.5 cm. Grimani shield, capped with a coronet held up by a winged cherub over the legend in the lower right corner. Signed: Beler F.

A small-scale plan showing the fortress lying amid hills, villages, wheatfields and olive yards. A narrow panel at the top of the plan shows a view of the fortress from the south: Prespetive de Zarnata.

IV. ZARNATA: PIANTA D' ZARNATA

A. Fortesa, B. Batteria, C. Porta, D. Cisterna, E. Villa Campa, F. Villa Albi, G. Maltis, H. Villa uaruchi, I. Calliue, K. Varuchi Piculi, L. Molino da uento, M. Strata d' Calamata, N. Madona, O. Bateria, P. Porta d' fortesza, Q. Strata di forteza.

Scala di Passi Geometrici N° 100:

43 × 63.5 cm. Grimani shield on lower edge of plan, next to legend. Signed in longhand: Beler.

Similar in scale and dimensions to Plan III. Lists same features in legend, with slightly different wording. A narrow panel along the top contains a view of Zarnata from the south.

V. KALAMATA: No title or legend.

73 × 49 cm. Grimani crest in lower left corner. No signature.

The castle is only two inches square, accurately drawn, on this map of the Kalamata region, where the Venetians won their third victory in the Peloponnese, September 1685. The map shows the alignment of the Turkish and Venetian forces. Items indicated *in situ* are: Mare, Campagna, Bosco, Colline, Monti Altissimi, Torrente che discende da Monti, Accampamento, Battaria, Prima Battaglia Pñtata a Turchi, Battaglia e Rotta datta a Turchi, Fortezza di Calamata, Primo Recinto, Porta, Monte che Domina la Fortezza.

VI. KELEPHA: PIANTA D'CHELAFA

A. Fortesza, B. Chieza, C. Corpo di guardia, D. Cisterna, E. Magasin delle arma, F. Magasin d fromento, G. Porta Stupa, H. Porta di S marco, I. Borgo d chelafa, K. Falche braga proposta, L. Borgo d Vitulo, M. Caualliri, N. Magazin d Pulure.

Scala d' Passi Veneti N° 100.

47 × 70.5 cm. Grimani crest in central panel. Signed: Vasieur·F.

This plan is divided into three panels. The large central panel contains the plan of the fortress, with the Grimani arms in the lower left corner. The upper section contains the title and legend, the lower a careful elevation, which reverses the positions as shown in the actual plan from east to west, drawn to show a cross-section from within the fortress enclosure. This shows, on the east, the low, uncrenellated, slotted parapet of the proposed faussebraye (K in the legend); the round, hollow bastion in the S. E. corner; the long flank of the guardhouse (C); the south curtain with its ascent of steps and crenellated parapet; the raised crenellations of the

16*

semicircular bastion, the short gable-end of the storehouse (F); the S.W. corner bastion, and finally the short wall, pierced with six loopholes and an opening, sealing off the area between the postern gate and the steep drop of the Milolangadho ravine at the extreme right. This elevation is marked Profilo, beneath which is written: Scala del Profilo Passi Veneti N° 30.

VII. NAVARINO BAY: DISEGNO DEL PORTO DI NAUARINO

A. Bocca del porto, B. Scoglietto alla bocca, C. Scoglio Grande, D. Falsa bocca, E. Nauarin Vechio, F. Peschiera, G. Bocca della Peschiera, H. Argine serve p Strada, I. Scoglietto nel porto d° dei Sorzi, L. Fortezza di Nauarin nouo, M. Villa corbei, N. Porto.

Scalla de Passa Geom.^ci N° 1000.

56.5 × 42 cm. Grimani crest in lower left corner. No visible signature, but beneath the legend is written is written in a cursive hand: ... dal originalle del qualle fu copiato... (next word scratched out).

VIII. NAVARINO BAY. No title or legend.

Features of Navarino region written on the plan: Mare, Granda Isola, Granda Bocca, Bocca Falsa, Bocca falsa con poca Aqua, Porto dy Nauarin, Isola, Pesquiere, Nauarin Vechio, Mandrachio, Nauarin Novo, Condotta d' Aqua, Petitte Pianure, Villa.

Scala.

110.5 × 40.5 cm. No Grimani arms. Signed: Levasseur Ing fecit.

The map is inaccurate, the Bay, Sphakteria, and the Osmanaga Lagoon clumsily elongated, and the compass directions some 30 degrees off.

IX. OLD NAVARINO: PIANTA DE NAVARINO VECHI RELEVATA SOTO IL COMMAND' DEL ILL^mo ET ECC^mo SIG° FRAN^co GRIMANI PRO^ra GENE' IN MOREA

Discrition. A. Fortesa, B. Castel, C. Porta dela Fortesa, D. Porta del Castel, E. Batteria, F. Peschira, G. Bocha falshi.

(No scale)

59.5 × 45 cm. Grimani arms and coronet above the legend, filling the lower right corner of the plan, held in one hand by a dragon-fly-winged, woman-breasted satyr, who holds in the other a brace of thunderbolts, amid a cluster of cannonballs, drums, and flagpoles. Signed in longhand: beller F and Beiler.

The drawing of the fortress, occupying only a few square inches of the map, shows its basic elements, though the two enclosures are compressed together. A long, low panel along the bottom of the plan gives a view of the castle from the east. A scroll floats in the air above it, marked with the words: Propetive di Nauarino Vechi.

X. OLD NAVARINO : ADI 30 SETTENBRE 1706. S. N. PIANTA DI NAVARIN VECHIO CON LI NOMI DELLI POSTI ET L'ARTEGLIARIA CHE, ESSISTENTE LE MVRE IN DIFESA DELLA MEDEMA COME DAL ALFABETO SARA DICHIARATO GENERE PER GENERE ET LI POSTI BISOGNIOSI CHE RICERH' ARTEGLIARIA LI NVMERI DEST: INQE-RANO LE CASE, E LE DISTANZE DELLE COLINE PIV CIRCONVICINE ALLA FORTEZA.

A. Prima Porta Magior, B. Seconda Porta, C. Tore sopra la Porta, D. D. Posto S.ª Barbara, E. Cannon Di Bronzo Da 60 Segado, F. Cannon Di Bronzo Da 40 Segado, G. Passavola.º Di Bronzo Da 9, H. Bataria Moresina, I. Cañon Di Bronzo Da 60, K. Cañon Di Bronzo Da 40, L. Falconeto Di Bronzo Da 3, M. Posto Precipicio, N. Canon Di Bronzo Da 40 Segado, O. Falcon Di Bronzo Da 6, P. P. Trauersa, Q. Porta Del Castello, R. Posto Bel Veder, S. Falcon Di Bronzo Da 6, T. Posto Alla Lupa, V. Cañon Di Bronzo Da 14, X. Periera Di Bronzo Da 12, Y. Periera Di Ferro Da 14, Z. Turion S. Marco uole un Cañon da 12, &. Posto uole due Colunbrine da 20.

1. Turion S. Gaetano uel una periera da 12, 2. Turion Del Sendardo, 3. Turion Serue per pregion, 4. Tore Antiche, 5. Porta Stopa, 6. Casa Del Proueditor, 7. Caualaria, 8. Quartier de Soldati, 9. Forno Del Proueditor, 10. Stalla Del Proueditor, 11. Cisterna Granda, 12. Deposito Di poluere, 13. Chiesia Grecha la Madona, 14. Ci-sterna, 15. Casa del Ajutante, 16. Casa del Capo Pric̃ipal, 17. Chesia Latina Spirito Santo, 18. Casa Del Guuernator, 19. Cisterna, 20. Monecion, 21. Ceruicho, 22. Couento Del Frate, 23. Casa Del Magior, 24. Forno Publicho, 25. Qartir de Cap . . ., 26. Stala scopert . . ., 27. Tezon p Apresta (mento) da Artegliaria, 28. Casin del Oficiale de Guardia, 29. Quartier de Soldati, 30. Sepoltura de Tur(chi), 31. Mura Anticha, 32. Strada Della Fo(rtez)za, 33. Pozo con Aqua, 34. Grota.

At the end of this legend is written: La linea rossa . . . ara Le Coline; La Scala se. . . . . . Passa 100 p Mesurar Fora del Recinto . . . Forteza. Scala di piedi — 100 p la Pianta

81×55.5 cm. No Grimani coat of arms. Unsigned.

The plan is accurate in all respects, drawn to show the fortress in a complete state of defence, with its gun-positions and other points still lacking artillery. On the plan are written Scoglio Gioncho (Sphakteria), Peschiera (Lagoon of Osmanaga), and Sa(bbionar)a, or the beach of Voidhokilia.

XI. NEW NAVARINO : PIANTA · DI · NAVARI-NO · NOVO · RELEVATA · SOTO · IL · COMA-DO · DEL · ILL.ᵐᵒ ET · ECC.ᵐᵒ SIG.ʳ FRA.ᶜᵒ GRI.ⁿⁱ PRO.ʳ GENERALI · IN · MOREA.

Discrisione: A. Forteza, B. Castel, C. Burgo, D. Bateri a marini, E. Porta di forteza, F. Lazareta, G. Fontana del Basa, H. Tiza greca, I. Condutta daqua, K. Strata di mudon, L. Strata di nauarini uechi, M. Arsenal del Castel. Scala (upper left corner).

59.5×45 cm. Grimani arms held in one hand by a reclining Victory, who holds in the other an olive branch, surrounded by the paraphernalia of war, above the legend in the lower left corner. Signed twice: BELER F and Beler in lower right corner.

This is a companion piece to Plan IX, drawn by the same hand, to approximately the same scale, and with balancing decorative elements. At the bottom of the plan is a long, low panel containing a simple elevation, Profilo di Navarino Novo.

XII. NEW NAVARINO . No legend as such.

Marked on the plan are the features of the southern end of Navarino Bay: Isola (Sphakteria), Torre projettato, Cisterna (on the small rock island in the mouth of the Bay now marked by the monument to the French Philhellenes killed in the Battle of Navarino, 20 October, 1827), Mare, Porto d' Nauarin, Bocca del porto 700 a 800 passy, Pianta di Nauarin Nuoua con y projetty marcatto jn jallo, Castel (the hexagonal fort), Opera a Corno projettatto, forte S Barba, S Marco (the two sea bastions), Bourg. Scalla di passy G. 100

41×55 cm. No Grimani arms. No signature appears on the plan itself, but on the reverse side is written, in longhand: Vassor.

XIII. OLD and NEW NAVARINO. No title or legend. Two views in ink wash.

40.5×49 cm. No Grimani arms. No signature.

Drawing of New Navarino shows south end of Sphakteria; mouth of the Bay; N. E. sea bastion; east curtain with entrance and flanking towers; hexagonal fort with parapets, turrets, and chief gate; within the enclosure mosque, houses, and gardens; to the south the suburb and the arches of the aqueduct at the extreme left. In the foreground is a small harbor where two houses occupy the site of the present town of Pylos, or Neokastro.

Old Navarino appears in a rude sketch, divided into two panels showing the fortress from the east and south. The former is drawn from the sandbar dividing the Osmanaga Lagoon from Navarino Bay, indicating the steep cliff on the

XXII. NAUPLI
FRONTE DI
POLI DI R(
PROPRIO SI
A. Porta d
qualle si far
per coprirsi,
D. Pezzo sta
che arriva si
qual riusira
Strada cope
con Fossa b
sada, I. Scal
lamida, K. I
per impedir
L. Cima più
dello stesso
cauare prof
naui, N. Fo
far piazza p
Scala di Pas
103×53 c
Written i
Castel da I
Mollo fatto
Strada che
Palamedi),
Strada (twi
This plan
XXI in th
during the
plia. On pa
across the p
approach fr
proach from
tween the I
with three
palisade (H
suggested in
L), with a fli
ing is reco
passage und
None, howe
by the Ven
Dolfin Bast
east city w:
Despite the
plan belong
bably to th
veditore Gen

XXIII. NAUPI
FORTEZZA
COLLE NU(
IORI FATTI
MEDEMO.
A. Piazz
Ant°, C. Cl

castle's east flank and the gap in the curtain above it, together with one corner of the Lagoon and the bay of Voidhokilia beyond it. At the top of the picture floats a scroll inscribed: Veue du Vieux Navarin. The right-hand drawing shows the path climbing the incline from a small, barely distinguishable complex of buildings at the bottom (on Plan X marked 31. Mura Anticha) to the first gate in the outer curtain. Above this appear the flanking towers of the inner redout.

XIV. BAY OF METHONE : PORTO DI MODON
Dichiaratione: A. Città di Modone, B. Castel da Mare, C. Mandrachio, D. Ponte che passa il Fiume, E. Spiaggia, F. Principio delle Colline in Terra Ferma, G. Scoglietto, H. Promontorio delle Sapienze, I. Loco dove aggredono le Galere ma non possono metter scalla jn terra p mancanza di fondo, K. Punta, L. Collina, M. Monte più alta della sud^{tta} Collina, N. Monte alto sopra il sudetto, O. Canal delle Sapienze.
Scala di Passi n°. 100
54×38.5 cm. Grimani arms in lower left corner. Unsigned.

XV. PORTO LONGO : PORTO LONGO NELLE SAPIENZE.
Dichiaratione: A. Bocca grande del Porto, B. Sitto dove due Galere possono Sicura far Scalla in ...., C. Grotta con abbondanza d' acqua, D. Altra Grotta con acqua in minor quantità, E. Sitto p ogni sorte di gran Bastimenti, F. Grebani che dal mare si van alzando verso li Monte, G. Grotta con abbondanza d' acqua, H. Scoglieto, I. Loco p il qualle può passar in ...... piccole Bastimenti, K. Altro Luoco p .... con Magg^r fondo, L. Scoglio Grande, M. Altra bocca p picoli Bastime^{ti}.
Scala di Passi n°. 500
54×41 cm. Grimani arms in lower right corner. No signature.
Fontana is written twice *in situ* on the map, in lower left and upper center. The harbor itself is filled with soundings. Plans XIV and XV appear to be done by the same hand, both of them naval charts, and each with the legend written in the same faded script.

XVI. METHONE : PIANTA DELLA CITTÀ DI MODONE CON LA DISTINTIONE DELLE STRADE ET ISOLE DE FONDI E CASE E SITTUATIONE DELLE FABRICHI PUB^{ci} FATTE PRINCIPIATE E DA FARSI IN DETTA CITTÀ ORDINATE DALL ILL^{mo} ET ECC^{mo} SIG^r FRANCESCO GRIMANI PROVED^r GEN^{le} DELL ARMI IN REGNO DI MOREA.
A. Porta di terra Ferma, B. Terrapieno da Farsi alla cortina della stessa Porta, C. Posto alla Porta Stoppa, D. Terrapieno da farsa alla Cor-

tina dello stesso, E. Terrapieno da farsi al posto d°. la Piazzeta, F. Porta del Mandrachio, G. Corpo di guardia da Farsi alla stessa Porta, H. Magazini che si fara da nuovo, I. Terrapieno da farsi al posto S. Filipo, K. Ospitale da farsi, L. Forni pub^{ci} da farsi, M. Porta di S Marco, N. Terrapieno da Farsi alla stesa porta, O. Quartiere che si fabrica su la piazza della sud^a Porta per una Compagnia, P. Quartiere nouo gia fatto, Q. Quartiere che si Fabrica su la piazza grande d' Armi, R. Altro Quartiere simile capace di due Compagnie, S. Casa seruira per il Sarg^{te} Magior della Piazza, T. Deposito per poluere, V. Fabrica per il Consiglio della Comunità, X. Chiesa Grecha, Y. Chiesa Latina de Frati, Z. Chiesa noua p conuente de F. F. Minori os ... anti, &. Sitto del Palazzo Gouernalitio, 1. Porta de Castel da Terra, 2. Quartiere da farsi in d°. Castello per una Compagnia, 3. Casa del N. H. Proueditore, 4. Fabri antichi rouinati, 5. Casa abita il Capo Principale, 6. Fabriche rouinate.
No scale of measurements or compass directions.
91.5×37 cm. Grimani crest. No signature.

With detail and accuracy Plan XVI shows the alignment of the streets in the medieval fortress town. With the collapse of the buildings these have all disappeared, though an air view picks them out clearly (see Fig. 61). This plan also shows the fortress as it stood before the Venetians added important works to the fortifications of the landward side shortly before 1714.

XVII. METHONE: LA CITTÀ DI MODON
No legend. Scale (100 passi) written on plan. 26×18 cm. No Grimani arms. Unsigned.
On the drawing are marked *in situ*: La Città di Modon, Porto piccolo, Il Porto grande, Li Borghi, and Mare Mediterraneo. A lower panel contains a view of Methone from the S.W. In the foreground of this is written: Mare Mediterraneo, di Morea. Above the drawing of the fortress is a scroll inscribed: Prosp: di Modon, per mare 1731.
The plan postdates the expulsion of the Venetians from the Peloponnese, and therefore would not belong to the original Grimani collection. Probably a later insertion, this small but detailed plan shows some of the late Venetian additions to the defenses of the landward front made shortly before 1715, and after the drawing of Plan XVI where they do not appear. A scheme of dotted lines shows the proposal for hornwork and bonnet de prêtre off the N.W. end of the counterscarp. The upper left corner of the plan indicates the river that runs below the modern village with its two bridges and the hexagonal Venetian well-head on the farther side.

to be seen at Nauplia. It is notable chiefly for the extent of its proposed fortifications, which represent an advance over those of Plans XXI and XXII. Most of these proposals remained on paper. The presence of Grimani's crest and the absence of any of the works actually built during the period of Daniele Dolfin (1701–1704) and later, combine to assign this plan to the years 1699–1701, when Grimani held his first official post in the Peloponnese.

XXIV. KARATHONA and TOLOS: DISEGNO DELLI PORTI CARATONA E TOLLONE.

A. Porto Carretona, B. Scogieto, C. Chiesa e Monastero, D. Punta Carretona, E. Porto Tollone, F. Scoglio, G. Chiesa e Monast.^{io} sun il Scoglio grande, H. Scogieto, I. Fontana, K. Altro Scogieto, L. Città Anticha, M. Strada. Scalla de Passi Geom.^{ci} N.° 1000.

57 × 41.5 cm. Grimani arms and coronet with flagpoles in upper center. Signed: Nicolo Franco.

An accurate topographical map of the point of land eight miles S.E. of Nauplia, with its two fine bays used by the Venetians. In the right half of the map appears a plan of the Homeric Asine, marked *in situ* L. Paleocastro.

XXV. DREPANON. No single title or separate legend. Divided into four panels, a plan for the fortification of the bay of Drepanon and the nearby island of Plateia.

70 × 47 cm. No Grimani arms. No signature. On the reverse side is written: N.° 5 Chiam.^a nella lessn. del n.° 66

1) Upper left panel: FORTE PER LA PUNTA DI PONENTE DEL PORTO TRAPANO. The interior of the bay is distinguished from the channel between Plateia and the mainland by: Parte interiore del Porto Trapano, Parte esterna del Porto. Two lightly drawn lines indicate the distances between this and the fort on the other side of the bay's mouth, and the fort on the island opposite: Distanza dal Forte opposto Passi 305, Distanza dal Forte di Platià Passi 1610.

This western fort is in the shape of a rough triangle, with sides broken to fit the geography. Its N.W. apex is built up into a platform on which sits a small, square tower (Torre), reached by a flight of steps. Beneath this is a battery of four guns covering the interior of the bay. From this side, steps lead up from the water to a gate in the re-entrant angle of the N.E. flank. The eastern corner contains a platform for three pieces of artillery, also reached by steps, providing cross-fire over the mouth of the bay. The long south flank contains five gun positions covering the channel between the mainland and Plateia.

The Venetians built a fort in this position, of slightly different plan, on the eve of the Turkish reconquest (see Appendix B, Figs. 230, 231).

2) Upper right panel: FORTE PER LA PUNTA DI LEVANTE DEL PORTO TRAPANO. Bay and sea are again distinguished as: Parte interiore del Porto, Parte esterna del Porto. The distances from the other two works are again marked on dotted lines: Distanza dal Forte opposto Passi 305, Distanza dal Forte di Platià 1510.

The eastern fort is a small, irregular work, with two bastions on the landward side, protected by a ditch, across which a bridge leads to the entrance in the east flank. On the seaward side, facing west, is a quadrangular platform for four guns, reached by steps in its south corner.

3) Lower left panel: FORTE PER LO SCOGLIO SOPRA LA RIVA VERSO GRECO NELLA META IN C.^a DELLA SUA LUNGHEZZA, PER DOMINARE LO SPATIO DI BUON TENIDORE E COPERTO, TRÀ ESSO SCOGLIO, E LA BOCCA DEL PORTO. Behind the work is written: Parte dello Scoglio de Sorzi nominato da Greci Platià. Two diverging lines from its center are marked: Passi 1510 dal Forte di Levante, Passi 1610 dal Forte di Ponente.

This island fort is a modified form of bonnet de prêtre, built on the advantage of a projecting shore, with three guns in each of the equal wings (these closed by a simple tenaille) and five guns in the curved central section. Its rear is protected by a bastion surmounted with slotted parapets and a tower.

Neither of these last two forts was ever built.

4) Lower right panel: PARTE DELLA LAGUNA DEL PORTO TRAPANO, CHE PUÒ RENDERE MAGGIOR COMODO, E SICUREZZA ALLA CONCIA DELL' ARMATA, ESCAVANDO IL BISCOGNO, E FACENDOVI LE PALEFICATE SEGNATE DI GIALLO. A scheme for dredging and shutting off the inmost section of Drepanon Bay. The section enclosed is filled with soundings, and marked: Tutto il fondo è fango tenero, & al Boccaso giarina. Li Numeri denotano le Profondità in P.^{di} Veneti. On the upper shore a church is drawn: Chiesa Latina fabricata nel 1696. A separate scale is given for this section: Scala de Passi Veneti per questa sola Pianta.

There is no sign to-day of either the dredging, the shutting-off by piles, or the Latin church.

XXVI. PORTO KHELI: DISEGNO DI PORTO BISATO.

A. Porto Bisato, B. Canale, C. Scoglio Gligniza. (These three items are also written *in situ*).

Scalla di Passi Geo: n.º 1000

58.5×42.5 cm. Grimani shield, left. No signature.

A simple chart of the land-locked harbor of Porto Kheli S.E. of Nauplia. The Grimani arms, the north arrow, and the contour markings resemble those of Plans XIV and XV, also plain topographical charts. The printed handwriting is also not dissimilar.

XXVII. KOVERTA and KASTRI (Hermione): DISEGNO DELLI PORTI COUERTA E CASTRÌ.

A. Porto Couerta, B. Spiaggia, C. Porto Castrì, D. Villa Castrì, E. Ruine di Fabrica antica, F. Spiaggia, G. Punta di Termisi, H. Scoglio Docho, K. Scoglio Jdra.

Scalla de Passi Geom.ci N.º 500.

59×43 cm. Grimani arms in lower left. Signed: Nicolò Franco.

An accurate topographical chart of the indented Argolid coastline, east of the Kranidhi peninsula. Ruins of the Classical Hermione (E).

XXVIII. ARGOS[1]: PIANTA DEL CASTEL D' ARGOS

Discripsio: A. Porta Principali Primo Recinto, B. Porta del Recinto Superiure, C. Porta del Recinto inferiore, D. Chieza Latin', E. Casa del Gouernator, F. Moschea.

Scala di Piedi N° 100.

63×42.5 cm. Grimani arms. Signed: Vandeyk.

Two cisterns are indicated *in situ*, marked Cisterna, each with three drainage holes, one within the inner redout, one in the flank of the outer west curtain. Within flank of inner redout a small building marked Cuartiiri. A large-scale plan, simple and clear as to detail, but wrong in proportion and orientation.

XXIX. PATRAS: TOPOGRAPHIA DELLA FORTEZZA E BORGO DI PATRASSO.

Scalla di Passi Geo.me N.º 100.

40.5×61 cm. Grimani arms. Signed in upper right corner: Vandeyk.

A general map of Patras and environs, accurately drawn in small scale. The city occupies only the high land west and south of the castle. It is surrounded by: Pianura Tutta Coltiuata. The site of the modern city is occupied by fields (Pianura), a church (S. Andrea), and a hospital (Lazareta) near the shore. Sixteen churches are indicated in and around the town, each identified by name. The fortress, clearly drawn, is surrounded almost entirely by a ditch (Fossa) and faussebraye (Falsa bruo). The lines of coast,

streams, streets, houses, and castle are impressed with a stylus, an early method of reproduction.

XXX. CASTLE OF MOREA (RHION): PIANTA DEL CASTEL D'MOREA.

61×41 cm. Grimani crest in lower left corner. Two signatures: Vandeyk and Vaseur – F. in upper and lower right corners of the lower panel.

1) Upper panel: a plan of the fortress on its point of land isolated by the ditch running from sea to sea. At the extreme right is marked: Fontana. South curtain crossed by line A–B. Scala del Pianta Passi N.º – 50.

2) Lower panel: a carefully drawn elevation showing a section of the enclosure, the curtain and parapet, and the ditch, with scarp, movable bridge, and counterscarp. Scala del Profilo Passi N.º – 20: Della Ligne A–B.

XXXI. ACROCORINTH: PIANTA DELLA FORTEZZA DI CORINTO.

A. Porta del Primo Recinto, B. Porta del Secondo Recinto, C. Porta del Terzo Recinto, D. Posto del Proueditor, E. Bel Veder, F. Posto S. Michiel, G. Porta Auerta, H. Posto auanzato del Proueditor, I. Porta stopa, K. Posto auanzato della porta stopa, L. Porta del posto auanzato piccolo, M. Posto auanzato piccolo, N. Posto alla Cisterna di S. Paulo, O. Posto alle Grote, P. Castello in tre Recinti, Q. Posto auanzato sopra la porta del p.º e secondo Recinto, R. Sepolture de Turchi, S. Strade.

Scalla de Passi Geometrici n.º 100

56×41 cm. Grimani arms in lower right. Signed: A.D.[2]

An exact drawing of the fortress, flawless but for slight prominence in salient and re-entrant angles. Only in small details does it differ from the Swiss survey plan of 1931 in *Corinth*, III, ii. The moat outside the first gate is not shown, though shadings indicate a gulley in its place. North postern not shown. A number of buildings are drawn within the circuit, which have to-day disappeared.

XXXII. ACROCORINTH: PIANTA DELLA FORTEZZA DI CORINTO CON LI NOVI PROGETTI FORMATI DAL TEN.te COLONEL LA SALLA REGIMENTO BORGAN.[3]

A. Lengueta doue deue esser formata una Bateria di 4 pezzi di Canoni e due Mortari da Sassi, B. Trauersa con una Torre per Serrare il

---

[1] For an accurate, modern plan of Argos see Fig. 119.

[2] See Venetian Drawing reproduced in *Corinth*, III, ii, fig. 99, a view of Acrocorinth from the west, which bears the same signature, A.D., in cursive capitals.

[3] Francesco Grimani in his report of 1708 mentions a drawing of Corinth by La Salle; Δελτίον, V, p. 541.

sitto oue si puol sorprendere il posto deto la Lenguetta, C. La stessa Lenguetta, D. Sito oue il Grebano fa scalla per montare al posto auanzato un huomo alla volta, E. Posto auanzato, F. Da questo sitto sino al Castel uechio segnato B+ la mura ha bisogno d'esser ristoratta, G. Lo stesso bisogno ha la mura da questo segno sin in F et il sudeto G significa il posto distacato, H. Dal sudeto posto distacato G sino a questo segno H la mura ha lo stesso bisogno di ristauratione, I. Altro Posto distacato grande che ha bisogno d'eser in parte rifatto, L. Sitto doue si deue dirrupare per impedire la sorpresa del posto, M. Dal sudeto Posto sino a questo segno la mura pure deue eser ristaurata, N. Il simile alle mura sino a questo sitto, O. Da detto sitto N sino a questo O la mura s'atroua inaccessibile per eser fondata su diruppo di Grebano, P. Porta aperta sino al qual sitto da O la muraglia si troua d'assa buona quallita, Q. Redotto per coprir la sudeta Porta aperta, R. Sitto doue la mura principia nouamente ad' hauer bisogno di ristauratione, S. Sitto sin doue da R ha bisogno la mura d'eser ristaurata in molti luochi esteriormente, et al interno fato la Bancheta e parapeta, T. Posto Beluedere sin doue da S la muraglia ha in qualche parte bisogno del suo Parapeto, e Bancheta, U. Fianco sino al qualle da V la mura ha bisogno quasi che dello stesso, X. Trauersa per impedire che gli abitanti non uadino nel Fianco, Y. Casa delli Rapresentanti, Z. Trauersa per impedire che gli abitanti non uadino nel Fianco de la Lengueta, 1. Ospitalle, 2. Quartiere fatto da nouo, 3. Quartier da continuar a S.ᵗ Paolo, 4. Quartier da farsi nel Posto distaccato G, 5. Altro Quartier da farsi nel Posto distacato I, 6. Quartier da farsi alla Porta aperta, 7. Altro Quartier da farsi nel Posto auanzato E, 8. Quartier da farsi nel Castel Vechio, 9. Magazen da Michia, 10. Altro magazeno, 11. Deposito da Poluere, 12. Moschea Serue per Biscoto, 13. Ospitall uechio serue per Quartiere, 14. Vltimi recinti doue deue esere serato da una torre all' altra con muraglia, 15. Fossa proposta con suo parapetto, 16. Recinto de gli habitanti da douer distrugere, 17. Fianco progetato con le sue piazze basse e casemate, che deue seruire per fianchegiare quell' altro Fianco opposto della Lengueta, 18. Muraglia che deue esere alle proue di cannoni, e che uada ad' atacarsi sino al Grebano del Fianco, 19. Fianco proposto sopra sitto uantagioso che deue seruire di difesa a il suo oposto n.° 17 e deue andare con una facia ad' atacarsi al posto della Lengueta per riceuer dalla d: il suo socorso con una porta di communicatione, 20. Primo recinto e porta che deue eser spianata per ritrouarsi senza eser fianchegiata da parte alcuna della Piazza, 21. Ci-

mitero che si troua per la sua eminenza comandare il p.° recinto, 22. Linea del Profillo n.° 23, e 24. nel Fianco n.° 17, 25. Profillo del Fianco n.° 19, segnato con la sua linea 26, 27, 28. Porta da farsi da nouo, 29. Ponte leuador proposto, 30. Altra porta proposta sopra la Fossa tra un Fianco e l'altero, 31. Le due linee puntegiate segnate D'azuro fanno uedere il luogo doue la Fortezza puol esser sorpresa se non ui si rimedia, 32. Recinto da spianare, 33. Vena di Grabano che si deue spianare all' altezza di due huomini sino al Grabano della Lingueta, 34. Sitto doue gli abitanti abandonando il proprio posono edificar le loro case, 35. Sitto tra la grabina, e S.ⁿ Paolo doue si deue romper il Grabano essendo facile la salita.

Tuti li luoghi segnati di Gialo sono li proposti. Scala di pasi geometrici: 100.

66.5 × 45.5 cm. No Grimani coat of arms. The plan is not signed, unless we are to take for a signature the statement in the title that the proposed works are those of Lt. Col. la Salle, and the name written on the reverse side of the plan in longhand: La Sale.

Plan XXXII is divided into three bands, horizontally. The upper contains a panorama of Acrocorinth from the west, entitled: Ueduta della Fortezza di Corinto uerso Ponente. This shows the three lines of defense, the relieving arches under the ramps leading to the first and second gates, a building between the second and third, the village within the enclosure, the Frankish keep on the western summit (drawn higher), and the watchtower on the further peak to the east.

The lower band contains the title and legend.

The central band is divided into three sections. The left-hand panel shows a section of the cliff that falls from the high wall of the third line of defense (at the south end) down to the first line immediately beneath it. A dotted line extends from the upper to the lower wall, passing also through the ledge (sitto uantagioso) on which is proposed a new wall (Fianco) to connect with the upper eyrie, or Lengueta of item 19. The right-hand panel shows the section of cliff immediately beneath the N.W. corner of the third line of defense, marked Profil del Fianco signato N. 17., together with a proposed outwork to occupy the accessible ledge already sealed off once in Byzantine times (see *Corinth*, III, ii, pp. 180, 272; figs. 112, 116).

The central panel contains the plan of the fortress itself, a copy of Plan XXXI, though here the North arrow points downwards, and the drawing is covered with proposals for refortification, as follows:

First line of defense to be demolished.

Second gate to be rebuilt.

A movable bridge for the second gate.

A wall (Fianco) with gun positions down the rocks between the eyrie at the S.E. corner and the first and second lines directly below it.

An outwork (Fianco) to seal off the accessible ledge north of the second line.

Houses between the second and third lines to be demolished. A ditch to seal off the area between these two lines, providing a barrier for the third.

A new gate to give access across this ditch.

Third line of defense to be terrepleined, walling up spaces between flanking towers.

A new village for the inhabitants behind the third line. A wall (Trauersa) — properly a short northward extension of the third line — to shut off the small N.W. section.

Barracks at five points along the circuit: in the inner redout (Castel Vechio); at the S.E. outwork (Posto distacato G); in the east outwork (Posto distacato I); at the N. E. postern; and at a point marked E in the legend, not drawn on the plan.

The cliff to be blasted away at two points, to protect the east outwork (L), and at a section not shown on the plan (35 in the legend).

A work to protect the N.E. postern (Q in the legend but not indicated on the plan).

Restorations in the curtain wall throughout the circuit along the north, east, and south.

An outwork to defend the castle's S.W. corner.

The plan shows this to have been accessible by a path up the southern slope (one of the Strade marked on Plan XXXI). A six-piece battery extends the re-entrant wall of the eyrie (Lengueta) above the vertical western cliffs. A wall (Trauersa) and tower project from beneath the S.W. tip of the inner redout. These together form a pincers to seal off the approach up the slope.

Fourteen of the items in the legend are not drawn on the plan, though it is not hard to tell their position. They are A, C, E, P (the N.E. postern), Q (the redan protecting it), T (Posto Beluedere, the N.W. headland, which appears also on Plan XXXI as E. Bel Veder), U, Z, 7, 11, 12, 13, 31, and 33.

Three features marked in yellow on the plan but not noted in the legend are: a building in the N.E. outwork, a long building behind the curtain of the N.E. headland, and some constructions round the N.E. postern.

The highest peak of Acrocorinth is called by the Venetians San Michiel, while San Paolo is the name given to the reservoir of Upper Peirene.

XXXIII. CHLEMOUTSI[4]: PIANTA DELLA FORTEZZA DI CASTEL TORNESE.

A. Porta principal della Fortezza, B. Chiesa con Cisterna, C. Porta di sortida ò di Socorso, D. Porta del Castello, E. Corpo di Guardia, F. Loco qual era Chiesa Grecha qual serue p: Monitione sotto della qualle e deposito di Poluere, G. Cisterna Grande, H. Due Pozzi p: il qualle si estra de l'aqua di d.ª Cisterna, I. Scalla per la qualle s'ascende sopra li Voltoni di d.º Castello qualli coperti di copi con condoti portano l'aqua nella Cisterna Grande, K. Borgo. Scalla de Passi Veneti n.º 20.

58×42 cm. Grimani crest above legend in lower left. Signed twice: beneath the shield, the initials A.D.; in lower right corner, in longhand, Vandeyk.

No compass directions. Drawing of the fortress inaccurate and out of proportion, especially in western half. The round flanking tower drawn in the outer curtain immediately under the keep on the south side does not exist. The angle in the south curtain is wrongly drawn. The acute S.W. corner of the outer curtain is drawn obtuse. The whole orientation of this sector is incorrect. The suburb is drawn to the northeast. The present village of Kastro lies to the west. The entire town within the walls has disappeared to-day, but for a few walls and foundations.

XXXIV. MISTRA[5]: PIANTA· D'·LA·FORTEZA· E· BORGO· DI· MESTRA.

A. Castelo, B. Forteza (upper town), C. Bazara, D. Pallaza d'carlo magna (Despots' palace); E. Archiuescouo (Metropolis), F. Uescouata (Pandanassa Convent), G. Conuente d'callori (Aphendiko), H. Cassa Parta distruta et Parta in Piede (lower town), I. Borgo diascolo (hamlet of Dhiaselo), K. Borgo di ebraicha (Jewish quarter outside N.W. town walls), L. Aquaduta, M. Borgo da bassi (New Mistra, or Exokhori), N. Pallaza di Reprezantante, O. Cartieron per la Caualeri, P. Conuente di Socolante (at the present Marmara). Scala Di Passi Veneti N. 100.

46.5×70 cm. Grimani arms, with flagpoles, in upper panel. Signed: Vasieur F.

XXXV. CHALKIS: ANOTATI¹ DELLE COSE REMARCABILE DELLA PIANTA, ET ATTACO

---

[4] For a modern plan of Chlemoutsi see Fig. 170.
[5] A modern plan of Mistra is given in Fig. 180.

DI NEGRO PONTE ATTACATO DAL' ARMI VENETI L'ANNO 1688.

A. Collina oue si piantorno le prime batterie e si batteua la colina Fortificata d'Tur.ᶦ, B. Scoglietto oue si fesce una batteria d'4 pezzi d'Cañ: e 4 morteri che batteua la colina fortificata da Turchi, C. Colina fortificata da Tur.ᶦ con batterie, D. Batterie auanzate dai nostri p battere le palisate con batte d'mortari, E. Le linee segniate di uerde sono d'auanzamento auanti preso le Palisate, F. Le linee segniate di uerde drento le Palisate sono p lataco della Piazza, G. Batteria di 16 pezi di Cannoni che leuò le difese al Nemico, H. Batterie di 8 pezi di cannoni sopra la contra scarpa che fecie la brechia, I. Palificate fatte da Turchi con batt, K. Batt.ᵃ di 12 pezi, che Batteua carababa con due morteri, L. Batt.ᵃ di 8 pezzi che fecie la brechia, M. Trinciera infilata da 4 pezi nemichi, N. Il Borgo adornato de Palazi e gardini.
Scala de Passi Giometrici n.ᵒ 300.

66.5×45.5 cm. Grimani arms, with palm branches, above legend on left side. No signature.

A fine, clear map of Negroponte and environs, showing the promontory of Euboea and the point of the opposite mainland. This is a plan of a siege in progress, with the Turkish and Venetian positions at successive stages. The items drawn on the map itself combine to make it a clearer source than any contemporary account. On the mainland is written: Tera Ferma; Forte Carababa; Bateria di 4 Pezzi di cannon nemiche. The original walled town[6] is marked Citta, and its suburb Borgo. The S.E. and N.W. sections of the Bay of Euboea are marked respectively: Mare dalla parte del Capo Colona, Mare dalla parte del golfo del Uolo. The narrows between the mainland and the point of Negroponte to the south is marked: Luoco oue era le Galeaze di guardia. The bay in the Euboean coastline south of the city is marked: Luoco oue erano le Galere doppo preso le Palisate. Below this the swampy shore is indicated: Paludo. The city's water supply is written: Aquadoto. Further south are: Accampamento de fiorentini, and Fontana d'aqua dolce abondante. On the right side of the map, the northern bay is marked: Luoco oue erano le Naue del Ecc.ᵐᵒ Venier.

XXXVI. MONEMVASIA: PIANTA DI NAPOLI DI MALVASIA

Dichiaratione: A. Città Bassa, B. Recinto Superiore, C. Castello, D. Mura Rossa, E. Ponte che unisce il scoglio con la terra Ferma, F. Mandrachio p picole Barche, G. Terra Ferma, H.

Torre che guarda e diffende il Ponte, I. Porta della Città Bassa, K. Strada Coperta e porta di comunication con li Recinti Superiori, L. Battaria che domina il Ponte.
Scala di Passi Veneti – N.ᵒ – 200.

71×46.5 cm. Grimani crest, with palm branches, in top panel. Signed twice: Veseur (longhand, lower right corner of right-hand panel); Vasieur F. (printed, lower left of central panel).

An accurate and simple plan to show the few simple elements of the fortifications.

XXXVII(A). MONEMVASIA : PLAN DES TRANCHEES DE NAPLE DE MALVESIE. LE COSTE DEXTRE EST MARQUE DE JAUNE, ET LE COSTE SENEXTRE EST ROUGE. ON Y VOIT LE BOURG, ET LA VILLE AVEC TOUTS LES POSTES ADVENCEZ FAICT LE 3.ᵉ JUILLET 1690. ERAULT SIEUR DESPARÉES INGENIEUR DE LA SERENISSIME REPUBLIQUE DE VENIZE.

Le costre dextre par Erault: A le poste du Coronel, B le poste du Major, C le poste des grenadiers, D le poste des petits Mortiers a grenades, E le poste des Esclavons, F le poste des Bandis, G Machine pour porter le Canon au poste du Coronel et ensuite partout ou on voudra a couvert.

Le Coste dela Senextre par Bernard: H le poste du Coronel, I le poste du Major ou fusilliers, K le poste des grenadiers, L le poste dela Marine, M le poste des Esclavons, N le vivandier, O la fontaine, P la Ville haulte, Q le Bourg, R le poste nouveaux des Esclavons.

87.5×29.5 cm. No Grimani coat of arms. Signed: Erault Desparées Jngenieur dela Serenissime Republique de Venize fecit.

A panoramic sketch of the eastern section of Monemvasia, drawn for combat use. The meticulous but stilted drawing gives the effect of an air view. It shows the southern cliffs, with the parapet wall running along the top as far as the tower on the west and the gun platform at the eastern end; the quadrangular walled town between the cliffs and the sea; the ascent to the upper town, and the Venetian siege-positions on either side as of 3 July 1690. The table to these positions is given in the upper left corner, in which the west or landward side of the drawing is called Dextre, while the eastern sector is referred to as Senextre. The colonel's post (A) is shown under a big rock near the mid-point of the island, which offers shelter from the cliffs above. Near the left of the drawing is the steep talus where the vertical cliffs are lowest and an ascent is not impossible. The tip end of the island shows a spring of water at the point now occupied by the lighthouse.

---

[6] All the fortifications have disappeared. Only the name Kastro is left to indicate this quarter of the modern city.

The reverse side of the plan is covered with the report, in minute longhand, of the same French engineer, Erault Desparées, recommending to the general, the Duc de Guadagne, to abandon the eastern positions (Senestre) and concentrate the attack against the town's west wall (Dextre), as follows:

Monseigneur le Duc de Gadagne General de l'armée dela Serenissime Republique de Venize m'ayant ordonne d'aller sur le senestre pour visiter les postes et le Terrain qui se treuve sur les lieux pour luy faire un fidelle raport de la Difficulté ou Utilitté qu'on en peut tirer pour le profit dela Serenissime Republique afin de continuer ou abandonner les travaux

Postes de la Senestre

Ayant tout considere et veu les dittes Situations, Jay remarque que touts les postes dela Senestre sont situez d'une maniere quelles pechent contre le maxime des fortifications puis quelles ne se deffendent pas les unes les autres et quelles peuvent estre coupées par les Ennemis sans qu'un poste puisse estre deffendu d'un autre.

Que les ennemis peuvent attaquer les postes par trois endrois diferens avec de tres grands aventages se servant de leurs hauteurs peuvent attaquer sans estre veu, et couper tel poste quils voudront et s'en rendre Mestre facilement. Que les Crestiens ne peuvent deffendre un poste par un autre sans sortir de leur poste et se faire voir a descouvert aux Ennemis

Les Ennemis peuvent faire sortie par trois endrois diferens

1. Par la Muraille du Bourg et attaquer les postes dela Marine et celles des grenadiers

2. Par la Tour d'en hault se glisant sur les Rochers attaquer les Esclavons et le poste du Coronel

3. Par la Muraille Rouge pour empescher la Communication et le secours du pont

Se fortifier dans le Chemin en y faisant deux tranchées sous le feu de leur Mousquetrie qui les favorisant empeschera toute Communication et seront a couvert de toute Insulte, les troupes ne pourront plus estre relevee que par le Marine.

Les raisons cy dessus avec celles de ne pouvoir relever les gardes que la nuict et de continuelles pertes m'obligent de conclure qu'il seroit plus apropos d'abandonner la Senestre et lever la garde pour doubler les gardes dela droite quoy que le lieu soit beaucoup plus veu estant en les formes ne fera pas la resistance sy aventageuse puis que les postes dela droite se deffendent comme on fera voir cy apres

Postes dela Dextre ou Tranchees

Raisons pour faire voir que le bourg de Malvesie ne doit estre attaquer que par le Coste d Extre

L'on est oblige de donner un Esclercicement dela forme du Terrain pour faire voir la force des Tranchees qui sont soustenues les unes les autres en toutes les regles — autant qu'on a peu suivre le terrain dans les Rochers Vifs

Depuis le pont jusques au poste du Coronel qui est le corps de reserve il y a une Blinde de facines sur chandeliers qui est paralele au coste du Rocher d'enhault qui a 455 pas geometrique de longeur qui met a couvert les gens qui montent et dessendent les gardes et par lequel chemin on peut donner secours en plain jour

Le Poste du Coronel est couvert d'un rocher et d'une muraille alaquelle il y a une banquette qui a plus de 20 murtriere qui flanquent le Rocher opose

Le dit poste n'est point veu du bourg a cause que le terrain est plus bas que le bourg et qu'il y a un glacis qui va toutjours se levant jusques au poste des grenadiers

Audevant dudit poste il y a quatre murtriere qui battent sur un grand chemin qui conduist ala porte du bourg et un peu plus avant, il y a un corps de garde d'un sergent avec 10 soldats qui gardent cette advenue lesquels sont entierement couvert du feu d'enhault

A Coste de ce grand Chemin cy dessus est la tranchee paralele au chemin d'enhault qui conduist au poste des petits Mortiers a grenades, grenadiers et du Major la ditte tranchee n'est point veue du bourg ni enfille d'aucun endroit

Le poste des petits Mortiers est soustenu et veu du poste du Coronel n'en estant qu'a 30 pas, les deux postes se soustiennent l'un l'autre, et le dit poste voit tout le Terrain d'en bas et la Muraille du bourg et deffent le poste du Major, et le poste du Major flanquent le dit postes des petits Mortiers

Le poste des fusilliers qui est entre le poste du Coronel et des grenadiers est soustenu par une Muraille qui est paralele au Rocher d'enhault sur laquelle est une banquette avec 20 murtriere qui flanquent le chemin voisin et qui bat en front le Tourillon d'enhault lequel poste soustient les grenadiers

Le poste des grenadiers est a 57 pas geometrique du poste de reserve et dont la tranchee qui s'y va rendre est paralele au Rocher d'enhault et va toutjours seslevant en dos d'ane sur toute la hauteur il y a une platte forme qui faict une gallerie couverte alaquelle il y a 9 murtriere qui flanquent et voit en front le bourg et deffent le poste superieur du Major

Le poste du Major a communication avec le poste du Coronel par la tranchée du poste des fusilliers et par consequent est deffendu et secouru des deux postes

Ce poste du Major dessend le long dun Rocher qui le met a couvert du Roc d'enhault et est advence de 20 pas plus que celuy des grenadiers du coste de la Marine, et a 20 pieds au dessus du dit poste il y a un corps de garde sur une gallerie couverte qui a 8 murtriere qui deffend le poste des grenadiers dont 3 murtriere deffendent le front dela Muraille du bourg et voit jusques a la Muraille du dit bourg

Par en bas au front du poste du Major il y a un gros parapet a l'Espreuve du Canon sur lequel il y a quatre Murtriere qui battent en front dela Muraille du bourg et qui est a couvert dela grande hauteur du Rocher d'enhault il sert de parapet a deux petits Mortiers de Bombes de Cent. Dans ce poste du Major l'on y peut mettre une double Batrie de Canon pour battre la Muraille du bourg — comme on peut voir par le plan

Je suis obligé Monseigneur de vous dire que jay este recognoitre a 60 pas plus avant que le poste du major, j'en ay remarqué le terrain qui se trouve favorable n'estant que du Sablon mesle de pierre dans lequel on peut s' enfoncer et couvrir en terre lespace de 20 pas de longuer apres quoy l'on trouve une Chesne de Rochers qui vous couvrent en partie de la grande hauteur du Rocher d'enhault et de l'angle rentrant qui y forme deux flancs, Il est veu du bourg et du Tourillon dela mer, le dit Rocher a 60 pas de longeur et conduist a 20 pas dela Muraille presques toutjours a couvert d'enhault

Au Millieu de ce Rocher il y a un renfoncement que forme la ravine qui vient d'enhault auquel lieu on y peut prendre un bon poste qui sera a couvert de l'angle rentrant d' enhault et soustenu par les bandis et Esclavons en leur faisant quelques feridor ala Coste et quelques petits couvertures de sart a terre.

Du poste du Coronel l'on dessend pour aller a couvert au poste des Esclavons le long des Rochers dela Marine et ensuite au poste des Bandis, comme ces postes sont enfillés du Tourillon dela Mer et battus de 3 pieces de Canons et qui n'ont point de communication avec les postes ny du Major ny des grenadiers je les tiens de peu de service et de dificile garde pour ne rien entreprendre de ce coste la, Mais peuvent bien servir pour les postes dittes cy dessus en cas qu'on Veuille avencer les travaux se sont les sentimens que j'avois mis sur le papier pour donner ala consulte generale quon me demande mon advis comme Ingenieur dela Seren. Republique.

XXXVII (B). MONEMVASIA : NAPOLI DI MALVASIA NEL MODO CHE SI RITROAUA QUANDO ERA ASSEDIATA.

A. Le Blinde o'uero Trinciere, B. Il posto del Collonelo, C. Il posto del Maggior, D. Il posto di Granatieri, E. Il posto di Schiauoni, F. La Batt^{ia} Suposta, G. Brechia principiata dalle Palandre.

55×23 cm. No Grimani arms. No scale of measurement. Unsigned.

A meticulous and accurate ink drawing showing a view of Monemvasia from the south, with the Venetian siege-positions (here on the west side only), the lower walled town with its flanking towers, the zig-zag path up the cliff, the gun positions at either end, the tower on the summit, and the extensive town in the upper citadel, whose ruins only are left to-day. The retrospective wording of the title, and the east end of the island drawn bare of siege-positions indicate that this drawing postdates Plan XXXVII(A), and that Erault Desparées' advice was taken.

XXXVIII. CANEA : PIANTA DELLA FORTEZZA DI CANEA ATTACCATTA DALL' ARMI DELLA SER^{ma} REP^{ca} DI VEN^{ia} L'ANNO 1692.

Dichiaratione delle cose più nottabili che si contengino nel presente Dissegno. A. Fortezza di Canea, B. Fossa assiuta con un pò di cunetta doue si uede il collor Turchino, C. Contrascarpa doue si uedono le operationi Ester^{ri} segn^{ti} con il Giall^o, D. Borgo di detta Fortezza, E. Parte doue tre miglia lontano è il Porto di S^o Todoro oue habbiamo sbarchata, F. Parte doue la seconda notte si siamo tratenutti con l'esercito, G. Torrente d'acqua, ouero Fiumara, H. Sitto che haño ocupato le Militie subito preso il Borgo, I. Linea di Contrauallatione e Bonetti diuersi dietro a Regi^{ti}, K. Sitto doue era la più parte della Caualleria, e Greci che scavano collà alla vista del Campo Inemico, L. Casa oue piantasimo 4: Morteri da 500, M. Sitto doue era Acampato il Sr Gñal delle Armi, e Sarg^{te} G. C. Mutie, N. Sitto doue era Acampato il Sig^r Prou^r del Campo, O. Sitto che era il Sr Sarg^{te} G. C. Repetta, e Sarg^{te} Magg^r di Batt^a, P. Primi posti fatti fuori del Borgo, Q. Battaria di 7: Mortari da 500, R. Battaria di 11. Pezzi di Cannoni da 50, S. Batteria de 4: Cannoni 2 da 50 e 2 da 30, T. Linee prolungate con un bonetto in ogni estremita, V. Mortaro da 1000 che si getaua Sassi, X. Opereta fatta p impedire al Inimico l' andata uerso quelle parti, Y. Batt^{ia} di 8: Cannoni p lauer li fianchi de Balloardi, Z. Batt^{ia} de 7: Cañoni 4 da 20 e 3 da 30 detta de (Maltesi?), &. Linea d'Approcchi, n°. 2. Mezzaluna del Inimico presa da nostri p Assalto, n°. 3. Linea fatta dopo presa la Mezzaluna con un bonetto nell' estremita, n°. 4. Locco doue l'Inimico fece uolare un forneleto, n°. 5. Terreno della Contrascacarpa riuersciato con mina da Nostri nella fossa con l' auanzam^{to} della galleria in detta fossa – – (last four words illegible), n°. 6. Spallamento fatto dalle Batta^ia^ R. et S. p hauer altro terreno nella Fossa, n°. 7. Trauerse che l'Inimico fece nella Fossa.

Scala de Passi Geometrici 200 (lower right corner).

67.5×47 cm. No Grimani arms. No signature. The wording of the title, the peculiarities of spelling and script in the legend, and the general draughtsmanship of the map bear a close resemblance to the signed drawing of Valona, Plan XXXIX. Canea also may reasonably be assigned to the hand of Bortolo Carmoy.

The plan shows the city of Canea, with its XVI century fortifications built during the previous Venetian occupation (1214–1645). The environs, suburb, and coastline are also shown. Over the surrounding countryside the abortive Venetian siege of 1692 is shown is progress, with all the items noted in the legend and indicated *in situ* on the map. The latter are: Sabbione, to east and west of the fortress; two hills to the west marked: Collina di Grebano coperta di Sabbione, Collina di Sabbione; in the suburb two buildings marked: Corpo di Caualleria, Due Reg^ti^ d'Infanteria aloggiati in questo sito. Southwest of the city are: Reg^ti^ Ausil^ti^, and on the beach to the east, or left-hand edge of the drawing: Parte doue passo il socorso.

XXXIX. VALONA (Vlore, or Avlona, Southern Albania) : PIANTA DELLE FORTEZZE DI VALLONA, E CANINA

Sbarco delle Gallere Galliazze e Galliote; Marchia de Christiani, e fuga de Turchi; Presa delle med^e^ Fortezze li. 17; e 18. Sett^re^ 1690. dall' Armi della Ser^ma^ Republ^ca^ di Venetia. Sotto il Glorioso comando e Valore dell' Illmo et Ecc^mo^ Sig^r^ Girolamo Corner K^r^ Pr Cap^n^ Ger̃al.

Dichiaratione delle cose più nottabili che ui sono nel presente Dissegno: A. Fortezza di Vallona, B. Fortezza di Canina, C. Castello di detta Fortezza, D. Gallere, Galliazze, e Galliote in Ordine di Battaglia, che cannonauano li Turchi quando uenero d'impedire il Sbarco, E. Luocco doue li Cimarioti comparsero, F. Acqua freda doue seguì il sbarco alla uista di detti Cimarioti, G. Marchia de Christiani doue nel medisimo luocco si trouauano li Turchi, e Scaricandole adosso li Christiani una salua di moschetate cessero il locco, H. Marchia dell' Ecc^mo^ Sarg^te^ Gr̃al Spar con li Schiauoni doue Scharamuzando con li Turchi Guadagno le Coline, e Montagne che detti Turchi haueuano ocupate, I. L'Ecc^mo^ Sarg^te^ Gr̃al Spar inssieme con l'Ecc^mo^ Sig^r^ Francesco Grimani Tenente Gen̄l che marchiauano con la Brigata, K. L'Ecc^mo^ Sig^r^ Ducca di

Guadagno con l'Ecc^mo^ Sarg^te^ Gr̃al Marchese del Boro, e l'Ecc^mo^ Ten^te^ Gr̃al Grimani e l'Ecc^mo^ Sig^r^ Bortolo Erizzo assieme con due Sarg^ti^ Mag^ri^ di Battaglia Co^te^ Pompei, e Lanoi con la loro Brigata, L. L'Ecc^mo^ Sig^r^ Gr̃al de Malta con sue Trupe, e Papalini, M. L'Ecc^mo^ Sig^r^ Sarg^te^ Gr̃al Co^te^ Rapeta col Sarg^te^ Mag^r^ di Battaglia Cte Montanari con la loro Brigata alla Coda, N. Turchi li quali uedendo li Monti ocupati da Christiani fecero una scarica de lor Schiopi, e poi si missero alla fuga, O. Marchia che fecero le due Brigate la matina seguente l'una sopra li Monti, et l'altra p la Strada doue à due hore di giorno si trouorono alla uista della Fortezza di Cannina, P. Turchi che vienssero attaccar li Christiani d^ta^ matina doue facendoli una scarica di Moschetatte si diedero alla fuga, & li Christiani occuporono poi il primo Borgo doue è d^ta^ lettera P, Q. L'Ecc^mo^ Sig^r^ Cap^n^ Gr̃al il qual andaua a caualo tutto'l giorno uedendo li posti, R. Li Sig^ri^ Maltesi, e Papalini collà Scquadronati, S. Il Sig^r^ Sarg^te^ Gr̃al Spar in un vallon con sua Brigata, T. L'Ecc^mo^ Sig^r^ Zuane Loridan Pro^r^ di Cauailli con la Caualaria dentro il Sud^to^ Vallone, V. Battarie di Otto Pezzi di Cannone fatta in una notte con l'assistenza dell' Ecc^mo^ Cap^n^ Gr̃al Tenente Ger̃al e Bortolo Erizzo Pro^r^ dell' Artigliaria, X. Il Borgo sotto le Mura della Fortezza doue fù ocupato il giorno dell' Assalto dalli Sig^ri^ Maltesi e Papalini, Y. La Dritta del Borgo che fù ocupato dal Sig^r^ Sarg^te^ Gr̃al Spar con sua Brigata, Z. La Sinistra del Borgo che fù ocupato il giorno dell' Assalto dal Sig^r^ Sarg^te^ Gr̃al Marchese del Boro e Ten^te^ Gr̃al Grimani con Sarg^ti^ Magg^ri^ di Battaglia Cte Pompei, e Lanoi con loro Brigata, &. Luoco oue s'attacco il Minatore, N°. 2. Acampamento de Turchi dietro la Fortezza di Canina, N°. 3. Fuga de Turchi, N°. 4. Altro Acampamento de Turchi apresso la Fortezza di Vallona.

62×44 cm. No Grimani crest. Signed: Bortolo Carmoy.

This is a combination of plan and panoramic drawing. It shows in progress the attack on Valona and Canina near the coast of Southern Albania, September 17 and 18, 1690, under the leadership of Girolamo Corner. This officer had succeeded Francesco Morosini as supreme commander (Capitan Generale) of the armies of the Holy League a year before at the siege of Monemvasia.[7] The description of the attack, given in the twenty-seven items of the table, mentions the Duc de Guadagne (K), who had succeeded Königsmark as general after the latter's death at Negroponte in 1688. Francesco Grimani

_____

[7] See Foscarini, p. 343.

figures actively in the engagement (I, K, Z) with the rank of Lieutenant General (Ten$^{te}_{.}$ G$\tilde{r}$al). The occupation of Valona for a few months during the winter of 1690–1691 was one of Venice's diversionary operations along the Adriatic.

XL. DULCIGNO (Ulcinj, coast of Montenegro) : PLAN, UND PROSPECTIVE VON DOLCIGNE, SO VON DENEN VENEZIANERN BELAGERT WORDEN AO: 1718.

A. Die Stad, B. Das Schlos alles auf felsen, C. Das Thor, e. Die Standarte, F. die gemahte Brechia, von einer neben ligenden Insel.

26 × 18 cm. No Grimani coat of arms. Signed : forte perti Fecit 1751.

The plan is divided into three panels. In the upper left corner the citadel is shown from the south. The lower left panel contains the plan, and the right-hand an elevation of the city as seen from the north. Over this a scroll is inscribed Prosp^a di Dolcigna da Tramtana forte perti Fecit 1751. This plan seems to have no place in the original *Racolta* of Grimani's engineers. It serves, however, as a footnote to the last of the Turco-Venetian Wars, the attempt of an exhausted Venice to avenge her loss of the Kingdom of the Morea.

APPENDIX D

CHRONOLOGY OF THE MOREA AND RELATED EVENTS IN THE LEVANT

146 B.C.–A.D. 1827

146 B.C.   Capture of Corinth by Mummius. Roman subjugation of Greece. Classical Greek fortresses dismantled. Local fortification forbidden within Roman Empire.

III–IX centuries A.D.   Period of greatest obscurity.

IV century   Late Roman refortification of cities within Empire. Vizigothic invasions of Greece.

527–565   Justinian, Emperor. Local refortification within Byzantine Empire. In Greece, two lines of defense, set at Thermopylae and Isthmus of Corinth. Fortified wall built across Isthmus.

583–586   First Slavic invasion of Peloponnese.

746   Greece ravaged by plague.

VIII century   Second wave of Slavic invasions.

805   Saracens and Bulgars attack Empire from both sides. Slavs of Peloponnese besiege Patras. Decisively defeated by Greeks. Slavic invasions halted.

X century   Byzantine authority reintroduced into Peloponnese. Country divided between Byzantine officials and hereditary local lords, or archons. Political chaos over period of two centuries. Coasts ravaged by pirates.

981, 995   Bulgarian invasions.

1082   Commercial treaty between Venice and Byzantium. Venetian merchants allowed rights of free trade in Imperial cities.

1099   First Crusade. Byzantine territories overrun by Crusaders from western Europe. Jerusalem captured. Latin Kingdom of Jerusalem founded in Arab-held Syria.

XII Century   Commercial prosperity in several coastal towns of Peloponnese. Piracy against European shipping encouraged by Emperor John II Comnenos to offset western power in Eastern Mediterranean.

1125   Methone raided, in reprisal, and destroyed by Venetians.

1147   Peloponnese raided by Normans of Sicily under Roger II. Venice lends naval assistance to Emperor Manuel I.

1180   Theodore Sgouros, archon of Nauplia, given Imperial fleet to clear Peloponnesian coast of foreign piracy.

1182   Massacre of Latins in Constantinople under Emperor Andronikos I. (Latin population estimated at 60,000).

1199   Second commercial treaty between Venice and Byzantium. Alexios III gives Venice special trading rights in Patras, Methone, Nauplia, Argos, and Corinth.

1203   Leon Sgouros, archon of Nauplia, makes himself master of citadels of Argos and Corinth.

1204   Fourth Crusade. Preached by Pope Innocent III to rescue Frankish principalities in Syria. Venice diverts Crusade to Constantinople. Byzantine Empire partitioned, by previous treaty, among Venetians and Crusaders, who set up feudal Latin Empire of Romania in its place, including the Kingdom of Salonica, Kingdom of Crete, Duchy of Naxos, Duchy of Athens, and lesser Counties and Marquisates in mainland Greece.

1204–1205   Frankish conquest of Greece. Boniface of Montferrat, King of Salonica, occupies Northern Greece, descends through Vale of Tempe, Larissa, Pharsala, Domoko, Lamia. Leon Sgouros plans resistance at Thermopylae, flees back to Peloponnese. Siege of Acrocorinth, Nauplia, and Argos begun. Geoffroy de Ville-

17

hardouin, crusader, blown by storm into Methone, invited by local Greek landlord to subdue rival archon. Then crosses Peloponnese, arrives at Nauplia, meets friend, Guillaume de Champlitte. Together Villehardouin and Champlitte conquer Peloponnese. 500–700 rout army of 4,000–6,000 Greeks at Battle of Koundoura. Villehardouin and Champlitte lead 100 knights into Messenia, capture Methone, Corone, Arkadia (Kyparissia) and Kalamata. Peloponnese becomes French Principality of Achaea. Champlitte first Prince, succeeded by Geoffroy I Villehardouin.

1206 Venetian fleet seizes Methone and Corone.

1209 Treaty between Venice and Principality of Achaea. Geoffroy I Villehardouin confirms Venice in her possession of Methone and Corone.

1210 Capitulation of Argos and Acrocorinth, after 5-year resistance. Suicide of Leon Sgouros.

1212 Nauplia falls to Franks.

1214 Venice buys Crete from Latin Emperor of Constantinople. (Venetian occupation of Crete 1214–1669).

1216 Venice begins to extend sway over Euboea, vassal state of Frankish Morea.

1220–1223 Chlemoutsi, fortress, built out of funds confiscated from Latin clergy of Morea by Geoffroy I de Villehardouin.

1249 Monemvasia falls to Prince William Villehardouin, who builds castle at Mistra to subdue Slavic tribes of Taygetos. Climax of Frankish rule in Peloponnese.

1259 Battle of Pelagonia. William Villehardouin, with most of the French barons of Peloponnese, defeated and taken captive by Greek Emperor of Nicaea, Michael VIII Palaiologos.

1261 Constantinople recaptured by Greeks under Michael VIII. Byzantine Empire re-established.

1262 William Villehardouin set free by Michael VIII in exchange for three castles of Monemvasia, Mistra, and Old Maina. New Byzantine province set up in S. E. corner of Peloponnese, governed by general, appointed annually, with seat at Mistra.

1265 Venice makes treaty with Byzantium, to insure safety of Methone and Corone.

ca.1278 Old Navarino, fortress, built by Nicholas II de St. Omer, Marshal of Achaea and husband of William Villehardouin's widow.

1293 Kalamata occupied by Slavs of Taygetos during reign of Florent of Hainault.
Golden Bull of Andronikos II elevates Monemvasia to ecclesiastical capital of Byzantine Morea.

1308 Byzantine military governor of Mistra appointed with life tenure.

1311 Battle of Kephissos. Frankish barons of Greece defeated by Catalan Grand Company, mercenary army of King James II of Aragon. Catalans take over French Duchy of Athens and Neopatras. (Catalan Athens, 1311–1385). Acrocorinth becomes frontier against hostile state north of Isthmus, retains this strategic position 1311–1458.

XIV century Morea divided among expanding Greek Despotate of Mistra, Navarrese Grand Company, Knights of Rhodes, Florentine merchant family of Acciajuoli, Venetian coastal colonies, and dwindling Frankish Principality.

1313–1316 Civil war in Frankish Principality between Burgundian and Catalan partisans: war of succession between grandson-in-law of William Villehardouin, Louis of Burgundy, and Villehardouin's younger daughter, married to Ferdinand of Majorca, leader of Catalan Grand Company. Louis, supported by Frankish barons of Achaea, defeats and slays Ferdinand at Battle of Manolada (1316), and succeeds to Principality.

1318 Greeks of Mistra seize three castles in province of Arkadia.

1326 Separatist tendencies, within Frankish Principality, of Catholic Archbishop of Patras.

1348 Mistra becomes appanage of Imperial family. John VI Cantacuzene appoints younger son, Manuel, as Despot of Byzantine Morea. Piracy and civil strife suppressed.

Mid-XIV century Niccolò Acciajuoli, Florentine banker, buys up lands and castles in Peloponnese, including Acrocorinth (1358) and Kalamata.

1381 Navarrese Grand Company enters Peloponnese, bases itself at Old Navarino.

1385 Nerio Acciajuoli becomes Duke of Athens, ousts Catalans.

1385, 7, 8 Turks raid Peloponnese.

1388 Venice buys Nauplia and Argos from last of Frankish line.

1388–1394 Offensive alliance between Nerio Acciajuoli and Theodore I Palaiologos, Despot of Mistra. Beginning of active hostilities between Greek Despotate and Venetian colonies in Peloponnese. Theodore seizes Nauplia and Argos. Venetians recapture Nauplia (1389) and Argos (1394).

1394 Acrocorinth returns into Greek hands after 184 years. Theodore takes possession of fortress on marrying Nerio's daughter.

1395 Turks under Sultan Bayezid I invade Northern Greece, raid Peloponnese. Theodore builds Hexamilion, wall across Isthmus of Corinth, on site of Justinian's defense line.

1397 Turkish army captures and abandons Argos.

1400–1404 Theodore leases Acrocorinth to Knights of St. John of Rhodes for maintenance of strategic fortress.

1404–1430 Centurione Zaccaria, last Prince of Frankish Achaea, now diminished to N. W. corner of Peloponnese.

1407 Theodore II Palaiologos, son of Emperor Manuel II, made Despot of Mistra. Venice buys Naupaktos (Lepanto), on north shore of Corinthian Gulf.

1408 Venice rents Patras from Latin Archbishop.

1415 Emperor Manuel II rebuilds Hexamilion. Venetians withhold assistance, concentrate on defense of Euboea. Desultory warfare between Greeks and Venetians on borders of Messenian colonies.

Turkish army under Turakhan scales and destroys Hexamilion, invades Greece.

Despot Theodore II makes war on Antonio Acciajuoli, Duke of Athens, and captures Centurione, Prince of Achaea.

Old Navarino fortress bought by Venetians, to keep Genoese away from Messenia.

1425–1448 Reign of John VIII, Emperor. Five sons of Manuel II: John VIII, Constantine XI, Theodore, Thomas, and Demetrios, last family of reigning Emperors at Constantinople and Despots of Mistra.

1427–1430 End of Frankish Principality. Constantine Palaiologos captures Chlemoutsi and Patras. Peloponnese unified under Greek rule (except for Venetian colonies at Methone, Corone, Argos, and Nauplia). Thomas marries daughter of deposed Centurione Zaccaria, fixes seat at castle of Arkadia (Kyparissia).

1443 Constantine, Despot of Mistra, rebuilds Hexamilion, takes offensive against Florentine Athens, captures Salona and attacks as far as Boeotia and Epiros.

1446 Sultan Murad II invades Greece, defeats Constantine and Thomas at Hexamilion, raids Peloponnese.

1449 Constantine XI, last Emperor of Constantinople. Leaves Despotate of Morea divided between his two brothers. Thomas, with capital at Patras, seeks help from Italy and the West. Demetrios, ruling at Mistra, seeks Turkish protection, and places Morea under tribute to the Sultan. Civil war between the two brothers.

1453 Fall of Constantinople, May 29. Constantine XI killed. Sultan Mohammed II places capital of Ottoman Empire in Constantinople.

Albanians in Morea revolt under high taxes. Demetrios calls in Turakhan to quell uprising. Archons of Morea withdraw allegiance from both Despots.

1458–1461 Turkish conquest of Peloponnese. Morea delays payment of tribute. Mohammed invades, and captures Acrocorinth, Patras, Kalavryta, and Vostitza. Thomas and Demetrios renew civil war. Mohammed returns (1460), Thomas flees to Italy, and Demetrios submits at Mistra. Venice makes treaty with Sultan to keep Methone, Corone, Nauplia, Argos, and Euboea.

1456–1487 Turks capture Belgrade, and subjugate Serbia, Bosnia, Herzegovina, and Albania.

1463–1479 First Turco-Venetian War. Monemvasia, last remnant of Byzantine Greece, places itself first under Papal, then under Venetian rule (1463–1540). Argos and Kalamata occupied by Venetians under Bertoldo d'Este (1463). Mistra attacked by Sigismondo Malatesta (1464). Mohammed II takes Euboea (1470). Venice, defeated, gives up Euboea and Argos.

1498 Vasco da Gama discovers sea route to Indies, commercial leadership passes from Mediterranean to Atlantic powers. Turks conquer Egypt, old Venetian trade routes cut off. Venice enters decline.

1499–1500 Second Turco-Venetian War. Sultan Bayezid II builds Castle of Morea and Castle of Roumeli, to guard Corinthian Gulf (1499). Methone, Corone, and Old Navarino captured by Turks (1500).

1531 Methone raided unsuccessfully by Knights of Rhodes.

1532 Corone occupied for a year by Andrea Doria, admiral of Holy Roman Emperor Charles V.

1537–1540 Third Turco-Venetian war. Venice loses last possessions in Peloponnese, Monemvasia and Nauplia.

1538 In Crete Venetians fortify Canea and other citadels under direction of engineer Sanmicheli.

1566 Turks capture Chios.

1571 Venetians lose Cyprus.

Battle of Lepanto (Naupaktos).

Turkish fleet defeated in Corinthian Gulf by combined Hapsburg and Venetian navies under Don John of Austria.

Don John raids Methone and Old Navarino.

1573 New Navarino, artillery fortress, built by Turks.

1645–1669 War of Candia. Turkish campagn against Venetians in Crete.

Turks capture Canea (1645) and begin siege of Candia (Heraklion). Venetians make diversionary attacks against Patras (1645) and Kalamata (1659). Candia surrendered (1669) by Francesco Morosini after 24-year siege. Venice loses Crete after 355-year occupation.

Retains three forts in Western Crete: Souda, Spinalonga, and Grabousa.

ca. 1670 Zarnata and Kelepha, castles, built by Achmet Kiuprili to contain inhabitants of Mani (Maina) Peninsula.

1683 Second Turkish Siege of Vienna.

1684 Holy League formed between Austria, Poland, Venice, Papacy, and Knights of Malta. King John Sobieski extends Poland eastward. Austria occupies Hungary, Slavonia, Transylvania, and Croatia. Venice leads attack on Turkish Morea, with allied army under command of Francesco Morosini. Armada of Holy League captures islands off N.W. coast of Greece, Leukas, Baltos, and Xeromeros, cities of Missolonghi and Preveza. Treaties with Duke of Brunswick and people of Cheimarra (Epiros) and Mani (Peloponnese).

1685 Morosini besieges and captures Corone. Castles of Passava, Zarnata, and Kelepha surrender to Maniates. Turkish army defeated at Kalamata. Venetians demolish castles of Kalamata and Passava.

1686 Old and New Navarino captured by Königsmark, Swedish general commanding forces of Holy League. Methone and Arkadia, Nauplia and Argos captured by Venetians. Turks begin to fortify Negroponte (Chalkis). Venetian renegade builds fort of Karababa on mainland opposite Chalkis.

1687 Patras, Castle of Morea, Castle of Roumeli, Naupaktos, Acrocorinth, and Chlemoutsi captured by Venetians. Turkish army abandons Peloponnese. Mistra besieged and taken by Maniates. All Peloponnese, except for Monemvasia, in Venetian hands by August 1687. Athens besieged by Venetians, Parthenon destroyed and Acropolis taken. Venetians make winter quarters in Athens.

1688 Morosini elected Doge. Venetians abandon Athens. Armies of Holy League besiege Chalkis (July–October). Königsmark dies, succeeded by Duc de Guadagne as General. Venetians abandon siege, return to Peloponnese. Departure of German, Florentine, and Maltese allies.

1689–1690 Siege and capture of Monemvasia. Morosini returns ill to Venice.

1690–1691 Venetians occupy Valona and Canina on Albanian coast.

1692 Venetians under Domenico Mocenigo besiege, then abandon Canea (Crete).

1693 Morosini resumes command of army in Greece.

1694 Morosini dies at Nauplia. Venetians capture, then abandon Chios.

1699 Peace of Carlowitz. Austria gains Hungary, Transylvania, Slovenia, and Croatia. Poland consolidates eastern gains. Venice gains new Levantine dominion: seven Ionian Islands, Butrinto, Parga in Epiros, Souda and Spinalonga in Crete, islands of Tenos and Aegina, and the Kingdom of the Morea.

1711–1714 Palamedi at Nauplia fortified with seven citadels by Agostino Sagredo.

1715 Turks reconquer Morea in three months campaign with army of 100,000. Morea defended by only 8,000 Venetians concentrated at five points of resistance, Nauplia, Methone, Monemvasia, Castle of Morea, and Corinth.
Turks capture Tenos, Corinth, Aegina, and Nauplia. Methone, Castle of Morea, and Monemvasia surrender.

1718 Peace of Passarowitz allows Venice to keep Kythera (Cerigo), Antikythera (Cerigotto), Butrinto, Leukas, Preveza, Vonitza. Venice loses three Cretan Forts, Aegean islands, and the entire Peloponnese.

1770 Russo-Turkish War. Revolt of Greeks in Peloponnese stimulated by Empress Catherine II, lead by Gregory Orloff. Mistra and Kalamata captured from Turks, Methone and Corone besieged. Russians driven out by Turks and Albanians. Mistra burnt to the ground.

1821–1833 Greek War of Independence.

1825 Mistra burnt again by Ibrahim Pasha.

1827 Battle of Navarino. Combined English, French, and Russian fleets destroy Ottoman Naval power. French occupation of west Peloponnesian artillery fortresses (Methone, New Navarino, and Castle of Morea) under Marshal Maison, who clears them of habitation and rebuilds towns outside their walls.

With the formation of the independent Greek Kingdom in 1834, the castles of Byzantine, Frankish, Venetian, and Ottoman Greece cease to play a role in history, until, during the Second World War and after, a number of these fortresses return once more to the uses for which they were built.

BIBLIOGRAPHY

K. I. Amantos, Ἱστορία τοῦ Βυζαντινοῦ Κράτους (Athens, 1939–47)

Le saint voyage de Jherusalem du Seigneur d'Anglure, 1395, ed. Bonnardot and Longnon (Paris, 1878)

N. A. Bees (Βέης), Τὸ «Περὶ τῆς κτίσεως τῆς Μονεμβασίας» Χρονικόν, Βυζαντίς, I, 1909, pp. 57–105

The Itinerary of Benjamin of Tudela, ed. Adler (London, 1907)

A. Bon, "Eglises byzantines de Kalamata," *Actes du VIe Congrès international d'Etudes byzantines* (Paris, 1951), II, pp. 35–50

A. Bon, "Forteresses médiévales de la Grèce centrale," *Bulletin de Correspondance Hellénique*, LXI, 1937 pp. 136–208

"Note additionnelle sur les forteresses médiévales de la Grèce centrale," *B.C.H.*, LXII, 1938, pp. 441f.

A. Bon, "The Medieval Fortifications of Acrocorinth and Vicinity," *Corinth*, III, part ii (Cambridge, Mass., 1936)

A. Bon, *La Morée franque. Recherches historiques, topographiques, et archéologiques (1205–1430)* (In preparation).

A. Bon, *Le Péloponnèse byzantin jusqu'en 1204* (Paris, 1951)

A. Bon, "La Prise de Kalamata par les Francs en 1205," *Revue archéologique* XXIX–XXX, 1949, (*Mélanges Charles Picard*, I), pp. 98–104

J. B. G. M. Bory de Saint-Vincent, *Relation du voyage de la Commission scientifique de Morée* (Paris, 1836–38), 2 vols.

B. Brue, *Journal de la campagne que le Grand Vézir a faite en 1715 pour la conquête de la Morée* (Paris, 1870)

G. Brusoni, *Historia dell' ultima guerra tra Veneziani e Turchi, 1644–71* (Bologna, 1676)

J. A. Buchon, *Atlas des nouvelles recherches historiques sur la principauté française de Morée* (Paris, 1845)

J. A. Buchon, *La Grèce continentale et la Morée* (Paris, 1843)

J. A. Buchon, *Nouvelles recherches historiques sur la principauté française de Morée et ses hautes baronnies* (Paris, 1843), 2 vols.

J. A. Buchon, *Voyage dans l'Eubée, les îles ioniennes et les Cyclades en 1841* (Paris, 1911)

J. B. Bury, "The Lombards and Venetians in Euboia: 1205–1303; 1303–1340; 1340–1470," *Journal of Hellenic Studies*, VII, 1886, pp. 309–351; VIII, 1897, pp. 194–213; IX, 1898, pp. 91–117

Cambridge Medieval History (Cambridge, 1924–1943)

Cambridge Modern History (Cambridge, 1907–1932)

Canon Pietro Casola's Pilgrimage (1494) (Manchester, 1907)

Cantacuzenus, *Historiae, Corpus Scriptorum Historiae Byzantinae* (Bonn, 1828–1832)

G. Cappelletti, *Storia della Repubblica di Venezia* (Venice, 1850–5), 13 vols.

Carnarvon, Henry John George Herbert, 3rd Earl of, *Reminiscences of Athens and the Morea: Extracts from a Journal of Travels in Greece* (London, 1869)

A. Castellan, *Lettres sur la Morée et les îles de Cerigo, Hydra et Zante* (Paris, 1808), 2 vols.

Laonikos Chalkokondyles, *Corpus Scriptorum Historiae Byzantinae* (Bonn, 1843)

Τὸ Χρονικὸν τοῦ Μορέως (*The Chronicle of the Morea*) ed. J. Schmitt (London, 1904)

Τὸ Χρονικὸν τοῦ Μορέως, ed. Kalonaros (Athens, 1940)

Χρονικὸν Σύντομον, *Corpus Scriptorum Historiae Byzantinae* (Bonn, 1832)

C. Cigala, *Successi della Canea* (Rome, 1646)

Constantine Porphyrogenitus, *De Administrando Imperio, De Ceremoniis Aulae Byzantinae, De Thematibus, Corpus Scriptorum Historiae Byzantinae* (Bonn, 1829, 1840)

V. Coronelli, *Description géographique et historique de la Morée*, French translation (Paris, 1686)

V. Coronelli, *An Historical and Geographical Account of the Morea*, English translation (London, 1687)

V. Coronelli, *Memorie istoriografiche del regno di Morea* 2nd ed. (Venice, 1688)

V. Coronelli, *Morea, Negroponte & Adiacenze* (Venice, ca. 1708)

Cronaca di Morea (Italian version) in Hopf, *Chroniques gréco-romanes* (Berlin, 1873)

O. Dapper, *Description exacte des isles de l'Archipel* (Amsterdam, 1703)

P. Daru, *Histoire de la république de Venise* (Paris, 1821), 8 vols.

C. Diehl, *Une république patricienne, Venise* (Paris, 1918)

E. Dodwell, *A Classical and Topographical Tour through Greece* (London, 1819), 2 vols.

Dorotheos of Monemvasia, in Hopf, *Chroniques gréco-romanes* (Berlin, 1873)

D. Doukakis, Μεσσηνιακὰ καὶ ἰδίᾳ περὶ Φαρῶν καὶ Καλαμάτας ἀπὸ τῶν ἀρχαιοτάτων χρονῶν μέχρι τοῦ Καποδιστρίου (Athens, 1905–1908)

Doukas, *Corpus Scriptorum Historiae Byzantinae*, (Bonn, 1834)

A. Duheaume, *Souvenirs de la Morée* (Paris, 1833)

Edrisi, *Géographie d'Edrisi, traduit de l'arabe en français ... par P. A. Jaubert, Receuil de voyages et de mémoires*, vol. VI (Paris, 1840)

C. Enlart, *L'art gothique et la renaissance en Chypre* (Paris, 1899)

C. Enlart, *Manuel d'archéologie française depuis les temps mérovingiens jusqu'à la renaissance*: vol. II, *Architecture civile et militaire* (Paris, 1904)

C. Enlart, *Les monuments des croisées dans le royaume de Jérusalem; architecture religieuse et civile* (Paris, 1925–8), 2 vols.

Expédition scientifique de Morée, ordonnée par le gouvernement français. Architecture, vol. I. (Paris, 1831)

G. Finlay, *The History of Greece under Othoman and Venetian Domination*; 1453–1821 (London, 1856)

G. Finlay, *History of the Greek Revolution*, Part I, A. D. 1821–7; Part II, *Establishment of the Greek Kingdom* (Edinburgh, 1861), 2 vols.

M. Foscarini, *Historia della Republica Veneta* (Venice, 1722)

J. Frazer, *Pausanias' Description of Greece*, translated with a commentary (London, 1898), 6 vols.

P. Garzoni, *Istoria della Repubblica di Venezia in Tempo della Sacra Lega* (Venice, 1705), 2 vols.

G. Gerola, *Monumenti Veneti nell' Isola di Creta* (Venice, 1905), 4 vols.

G. Gerola, "Le Fortificazioni di Napoli di Romania," *Annuario della Regia Scuola Archeologica di Atene*, XIII–XIV, 1930–1, pp. 347–410

D. Gritti, report of Venetian census-taker, Greek translation by P. Chiotes, Φιλίστωρ, II, 1861, pp. 218–230

Guillet de la Guilletière, *Lacédémone ancienne et nouvelle* (Paris, 1676)

M. Hadzidakis, Μυστρᾶς (Athens, 1948)

J. von Hammer-Purgstall, *Histoire de l'empire ottoman*, tr. J. J. Hellert (Paris, 1835–1843), 18 vols.

The History of the Venetian Conquests (London, 1689)

K. Hopf, *Chroniques gréco-romanes inédites ou peu connues* (Berlin, 1873)

K. Hopf, *Geschichte Griechenlands vom Beginn des Mittelalters bis auf unsere Zeit*, in Ersch und Gruber, *Allgemeine Enzyklopädie der Wissenschaften und Künste*, (Leipzig, 1867–1868) vol. LXXXV, pp. 67–465, vol. LXXXVI, pp. 1–190

A Journal of the Venetian Campaigne (London, 1688)

P. Kalonaros, "Khlémoutzi," *L'Hellénisme contemporain*, II, 1936, pp. 174–180

Kedrenos, *Corpus Scriptorum Historiae Byzantinae* (Bonn, 1838–1839)

P. M. Kondoyannis, Οἱ Ἕλληνες κατὰ τὸν πρῶτον ἐπὶ Αἰκατερίνης Β′ Ρωσσοτουρκικὸν πόλεμον (Athens, 1903)

P. Kriares, Ἱστορία τῆς Κρήτης (Athens, 1931)

L. E. S. J. de Laborde, *Documents inédits ou peu connus sur l'histoire et les antiquités d'Athènes* (Paris, 1854)

Sp. P. Lampros, Ἱστορικὰ Μελετήματα (Athens, 1884).

M. G. Lamprynides, Ἡ Ναυπλία (Athens, 1950)

T. E. Lawrence, *Crusader Castles* (Golden Cockerel Press, 1936), 2 vols.

W. Leake, *Travels in the Morea* (London, 1830), 3 vols.

W. Leake, *Travels in Northern Greece* (London, 1835), 4 vols.

W. Leake, *Peloponnesiaca* (London, 1846)

Libro de los Fechos et Conquistas del Principado de la Morea (Société de l'Orient Latin) ed. A. Morel-Fatio (Geneva, 1885)

Livre de la conqueste de la princée de l'Amorée. Chronique de Morée (1204–1305), ed. Longnon (Paris, 1911)

A. Locatelli, *Racconto historico della Veneta Guerra in Levante* (Cologne, 1691), 2 vols.

J. Longnon, *L'empire latin de Constantinople et la principauté de Morée* (Paris, 1949)

J. Longnon, "Problèmes de l'histoire de la principauté de Morée" (second part), *Journal des Savants*, July–December 1946, pp. 157–159

S. Luce, "Modon — a Venetian Station in Medieval Greece," *Studies in Honor of Edward Kennard Rand* (New York, 1938)

Stephano Magno: *Estratto degli Annali Veneti di Stefano Magno*, in Hopf, *Chroniques gréco-romanes* (Berlin, 1873)

J. Mangeart, *Souvenirs de la Morée* (Paris, 1830)

Μεγάλη Ἑλληνικὴ Ἐγκυκλοπαιδεῖα (Athens, 1926–34), 24 vols.

F. Miklosich and J. Müller, *Acta et Diplomata Medii Aevi Sacra et Profana* (Vienna, 1860–1890), 7 vols.

W. Miller, *Essays on the Latin Orient* (Cambridge, 1921)

W. Miller, *The Latins in the Levant, A History of Frankish Greece, 1204–1566* (London, 1908)

W. Miller, "Monemvasia," *Journal of Hellenic Studies*, XXVII, 1907, pp. 228–240

A. Mompherratos, Μεθώνη καὶ Κορώνη ἐπὶ Ἑνετοκρατίας (Athens, 1914)

A. G. Mompherratos, Σιγισμοῦνδος Πανδόλφος Μαλατέστας (Athens, 1914)

La Morea combattuta dall' armi Venete. Con li Successi in Levante, aggiuntivi il Diario di tutta la Campagna MDCLXXXVI ... del D.P.B.F. (Bologna, 1686)

La Morea combattuta dall' armi Venete (Venice, 1686)

Muntaner, Ramòn: *The Chronicle of Muntaner*, tr. Goodenough (London, 1921)

B. Nani, *Historia della Republica Veneta* (Venice, 1662), 2 vols.

Nikephoros Gregoras, *Corpus Scriptorum Historiae Byzantinae* (Bonn, 1829–1830, 1855)

Niketas Choniates, *Corpus Scriptorum Historiae Byzantinae* (Bonn, 1835).

A. Noiret, *Documents inédits pour servir à l'histoire de la domination vénitienne en Crète de 1380 à 1485* (Paris, 1892)

A. K. Orlandos, "Τὰ παλάτια καὶ τὰ σπίτια τοῦ Μυστρᾶ," Ἀρχεῖον τῶν Βυζαντινῶν Μνημείων τῆς Ἑλλάδος, III. January–June, 1937, pp. 3–114

P. Pacifico, *Breve Descrizione corografico del Peloponneso ò Morea* (Venice, 1704)

K. N. Papamichalopoulos, Πολιορκία καὶ Ἄλωσις τῆς Μονεμβασίας ὑπὸ τῶν Ἑλλήνων τῷ 1821 (Athens, 1874)

P. Paruta, *Historia Vinetiana* (Venice, 1703), 2 parts

J. M. Paton, *The Venetians in Athens, 1687–1688*, Gennadeion Monographs I, (Cambridge, Mass., 1940)

Pauly-Wissowa-Kroll, *Real-Encyclopädie der Klassischen Altertumswissenschaft*, 2nd ed. (Stuttgart, 1894 et sqq.)

Pausanias, *Description of Greece*, ed. Loeb (London and Cambridge, Mass., 1918–1935)

Phrantzes, *Annales, Corpus Scriptorum Historiae Byzantinae* (Bonn, 1838)

F. Pouqueville, *Voyage de la Grèce* (Paris, 1826), 6 vols.

Prodocimo, *Successi dell'Armi della Serenissima Republica di Venetia nella campagna di 1687. La Morea Combattuta e Vinta, e con l'acquisto della famosissima Piazza d'Atene* (Venice, 1687)

Prokopios, *De Aedificiis, Corpus Scriptorum Historiae Byzantinae* (Bonn, 1838)

Prokopios, *History of the Wars*, ed. Loeb (London and Cambridge, Mass., 1914–1928)

Prokopios, *Secret History*, ed. Loeb (London and Cambridge, Mass., 1935)

Provveditori Generali, Reports of Venetian Governors and officials in the Peloponnese, 1690–1716, published by Sp. Lampros, Δελτίον τῆς Ἱστορικῆς καὶ Ἐθνολογικῆς Ἑταιρείας τῆς Ἑλλάδος, vol. II (1885–89) reports of:

    1) Giacomo Corner (Provveditore Generale, April 1688–Dec. 1690) pp. 282–317;

    2) Tadio Gradenigo (Prov. Estraordinario di Morea, Provvr. Estraordinario in Morea, 16 April, 1692) pp. 228–251, 425–428;

    3) Antonio Molin (Proveditor Estraordinaro in Morea, Provvr. Genl del Regno di Morea, 30 May, 1693) pp. 429–447;

Vol. V (1886–1900):

    4) Francesco Grimani (Provveditor General dell' Armi in Morea, 8 Oct. 1701) pp. 448–532; Francesco Grimani, report to Provveditor Generale dell' Armi in Morea, da Mosto, "colla cessione della carica," 19 Jan. 1708, pp. 533–561;

    5) Giacomo da Mosto, report without heading or date, pp. 561–567;

    6) Daniele Dolfin (Provveditor Estraordinario d'Armata, Provveditor Generale delle 4 Isole, Proveditor Generale da Mar, Proveditor General in Terra Ferma) pp. 605–644;

    7) Angelo Emo (Provvr. Genl, 18 January, 1708) pp. 644–706;

    8) Marco Loredan (Provvedr. Genãl. dell'Armi in Morea, 11 Dec. 1711) pp. 707–714; Marco Loredan, report to Antonio Loredan (Provveditor General dell' armi in Regno, 20 Sept. 1711) pp. 715–735;

9) Agostino Sagredo (Provr. General da Mar, 20 Nov. 1714) pp. 736–765;

10) Daniel Dolfin (Capitan General, 14 April 1716; Provr. Capn General, 26 March 1716) pp. 765–810;

11) Anzelo Moresini, Giacomo Minio, Vicenzo Grimani, Marin Marini, census-takers, reports of (dated 25 June 1704, 4 August 1704) pp. 810–823

B. Randolph, *The Present State of the Morea* (Oxford, 1686)

L. von Ranke, *Die Venezianer in Morea*, Greek translation, Ἐρανιστής, τόμος Α' τοῦ Β' ἔτους (1842) σελ. 36-47, 96–111, 280–289; τόμος Β' τοῦ Β' ἔτους (1843) σελ. 829–869

Il Regno della Morea sotto i Veneti descritto da D.G.P.B. (Venice, 1688)

Relation de la Prise de Coron (Amsterdam, 1686)

G. Rey, *Étude sur les monuments de l'architecture militaire des croiseés en Syrie et dans l'Ile de Chyprel* (Paris, 1871)

S. Romanin, *Storia documentata di Venezia* (Venice, 1853–1861), 10 vols.

Rossi, *Successi dell'Armi Venete in Levante nella Campagna 1685. Descritto da N.N.* (Venice, 1686)

A. Rubio i Lluch, *Diplomatari de l'Orient Catala* (Barcelona, 1947)

A. Rubio i Lluch, Περὶ τῶν Καταλανίκων Φρουρίων τῆς Ἠπειρωτικῆς Ἑλλάδος, translated by G. N. Mavrakis (Athens, 1912)

M. B. Sakellariou, Χειρόγραφος Ἔκθεσις περὶ τῆς πολιορκίας καὶ ἁλώσεως τῶν Χανίων ὑπὸ τῶν Τούρκων, *Byzantinisch-Neugriechische Jahrbücher*, XV, 1938, 1939, pp. 141–174

Marino Sanudo, *Istoria del Regno di Romania*, in Hopf, *Chroniques gréco-romanes* (Berlin, 1873)

K. N. Sathas, *Documents inédits relatifs à l'histoire de la Grèce au Moyen Age* (Paris, 1880–1890), 9 vols.

K. N. Sathas, Τουρκοκρατουμένη Ἑλλάς (Athens, 1869)

F. Scalletari, *Condotta Navale ... del Viaggio da Carlistot a Malta del ... Gioanni Gioseppe d' Herberstein* (Graz, 1688)

G. Schlumberger, *Numismatique de l'Orient latin* (Paris, 1878)

R. L. Scranton, *Greek Walls* (Cambridge, Mass., 1934)

K. M. Setton, *Catalan Domination of Athens* (Medieval Academy of America, 1948)

G. Sotiriou, "Le château-fort de Chloumoutzi et son atelier monétaire de tournois de Clarentia," *Journal international d'archéologie numismatique*, XIX, 1918–1919, pp. 273–279

J. Spon, *Voyage d'Italie, de Dalmatie, de Grèce, et du Levant*, 1st ed. (Lyon, 1678), 3 vols.

Strabo, *Geography*, ed. Loeb (London and Cambridge, Mass., 1917–1932)

A. Struck, *Mistra, eine mittelalterliche Ruinenstadt* (Vienna und Leipzig, 1910)

G. Tafel und G. Thomas, *Urkunden zur älteren Handels- und Staatsgeschichte der Republik Venedig mit besonderer Beziehung auf Byzanz in die Levante*, in *Fontes Rerum Austriacarum, II. Diplomataria et Acta*, vols. XII–XIV (Vienna, 1856–7)

O. Tafrali, *Topographie de Thessalonique* (Paris, 1913)

P. Tafur, *Travels and Adventures, 1435–1439*, ed. Letts (New York, Harpers, 1926)

Theophanes, *Corpus Scriptorum Historiae Byzantinae* (Bonn, 1839–1841)

G. M. Thomas and R. Predelli, *Diplomatarium Veneto-Levantinum* (Venice, 1880–1889), 2 vols.

S. M. Thomopoulos, Χριστιανικαὶ ἐν Πάτραις Ἐπιγραφαί, Δελτίον τῆς Ἱστορικῆς καὶ Ἐθνολογικῆς Ἑταιρείας τῆς Ἑλλάδος, I, 1884, pp. 523–526

C. Thompson, *Travels* (Reading, 1752), 3 vols.

P. Topping, *Feudal Institutions as revealed in the Assizes of Romania* (University of Pennsylvania, 1949)

R. Traquair, "Laconia, the Fortresses," *Annual of the British School of Archaeology*, XII, 1905–6, pp. 259–276

R. Traquair, "Mediaeval Fortresses of the North-Western Peloponnesus," *Annual of the British School of Archaeology*, XIII, 1906–1907, pp. 268–281

A. A. Vasiliev, *Histoire de l'empire byzantin*, trans. Brodin and Bourgovina (Paris, 1932), 2 vols.

G. de Villehardouin, *La Conquête de Constantinople*, ed. Faral (Paris, 1939), 2 vols.

A. B. Wace and F. Hasluck, "Laconia, Topography," *Annual of the British School of Archaeology*, XIV, 1907–1908, pp. 168–182

G. Wheler, *Journey into Greece*, 1st ed. (London, 1682)

T. Wyse, *An Excursion into the Peloponnesus* (London, 1865)

D. Zakythinos, *Le Despotat grec de Morée*, vol. I (Paris, 1932)

P. Zerlendis, Τάξις Ἱεραρχικὴ τῶν ἐν Πελοποννήσῳ Ἁγίων τοῦ Θεοῦ Ἐκκλησιῶν (Hermoupolis, 1922)

Theodore Zygomalas, in Hopf, *Chroniques gréco-romanes* (Berlin, 1873)

INDEX

PLATES

PLATE I

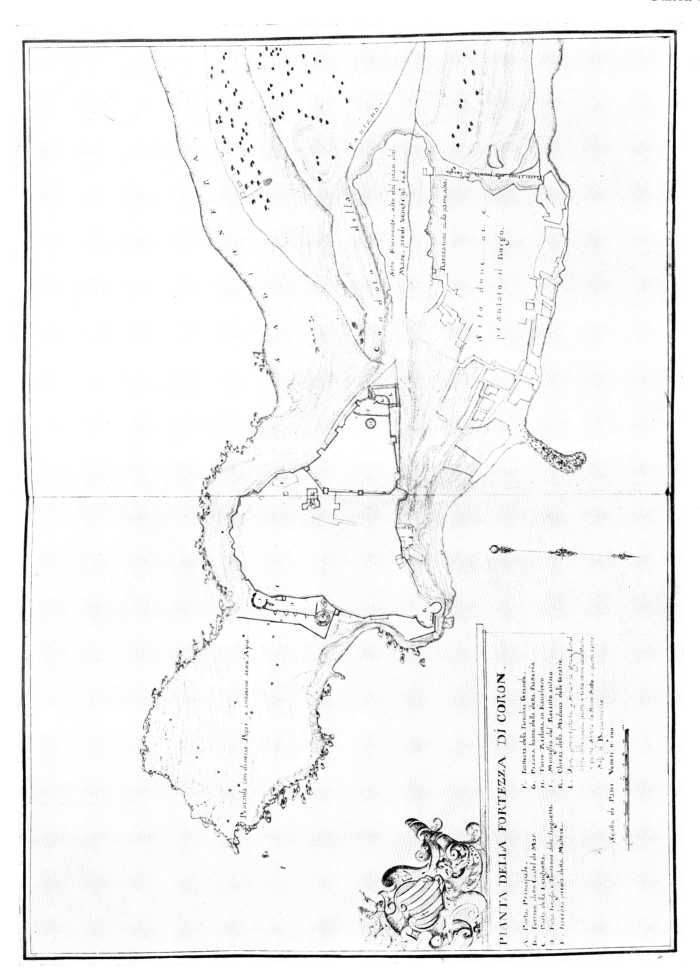

PIANTA DELLA FORTEZZA DI CORON.

A. Porta Principale.
B. Torrion detto Castel di Mar.
C. Porta delli Langnetta.
D. Sito luogo à Torrioni della Inguetta.
E. Iiuetta, ditta della Maltesa.

F. Batteria della Turchia Grande.
G. Piazza bassa della detta Batteria.
H. Torre Pardana, in Kanaltero.
I. Muraglia del Recinto antico.
K. Chiesa della Madona delle Gratie.
L. Por. principale.

Scala di Passi Veneti n. 100

CORONE

PLATE II

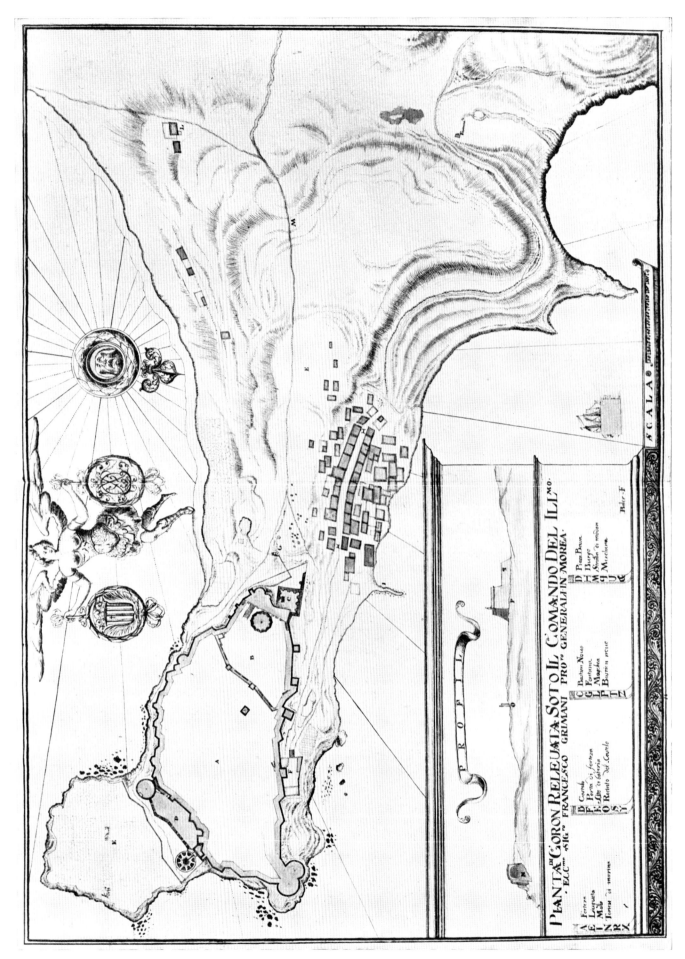

CORONE

PLATE III

PRESPETIVE · DE · ZARNATA

PIANTA·DE·ZARNATA·RELEVATA·SOTO·
IL·COMANDO·DEL·IL^{mo}·ET·EC^{mo}·SIG^{re}·FRANCESCO·
GRIMANI·PRO^{re}·GENERALI·IN·MOREA·Dele·F·

A Fortesa	B Batteria	C Porta	D Aqua
E Ubi Campo	F Ubi Alte	G Malto	H Ubi maruchi
I Caltre	K Ubi archipeschi	L Monicamento	M Strada veniente
N Macona	O Batteria	P Veria i fortesa	Q Sniui i fortesa
R X	S Y	T Z	V U

SCALA·DI·PASI·GEOMETRICI·

ZARNATA

PLATE IV

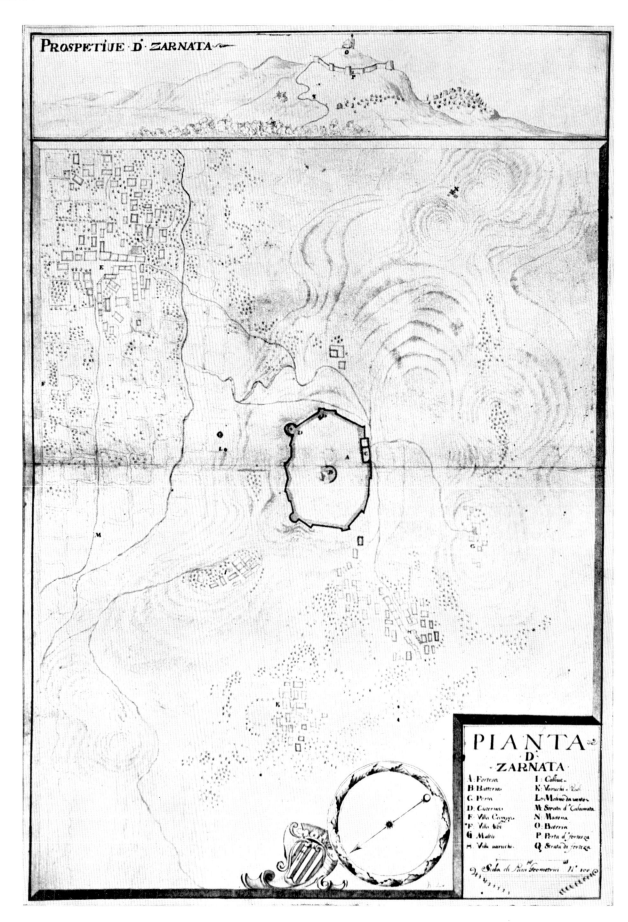

Zarnata

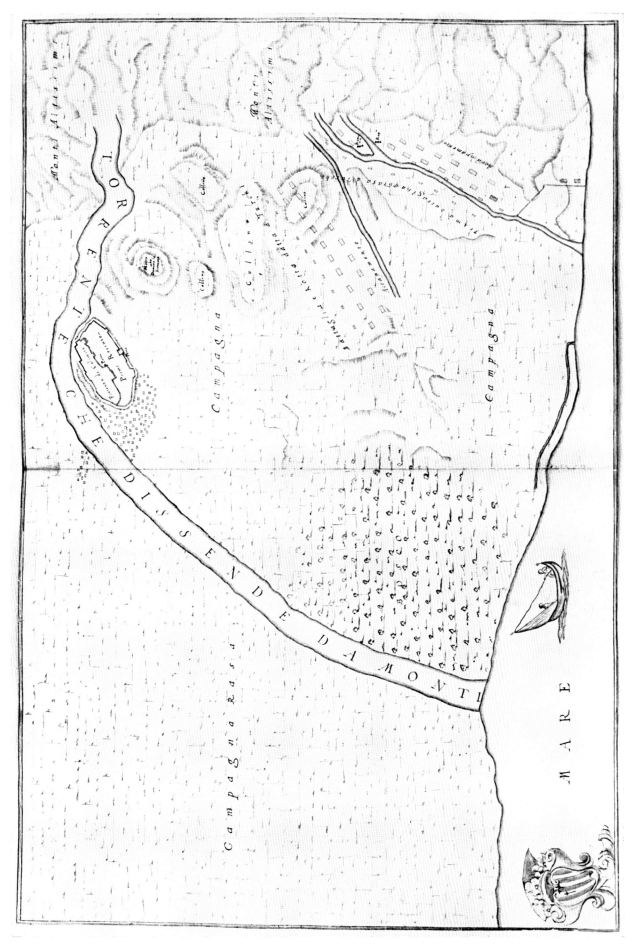

PLATE V

KALAMATA

PLATE VI

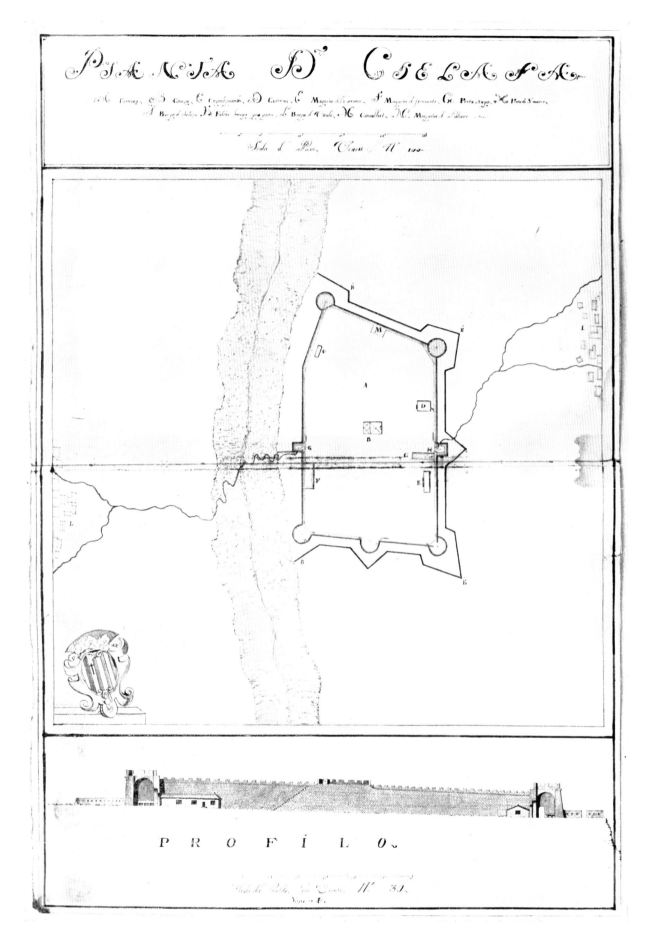

KELEPHA

PLATE VII

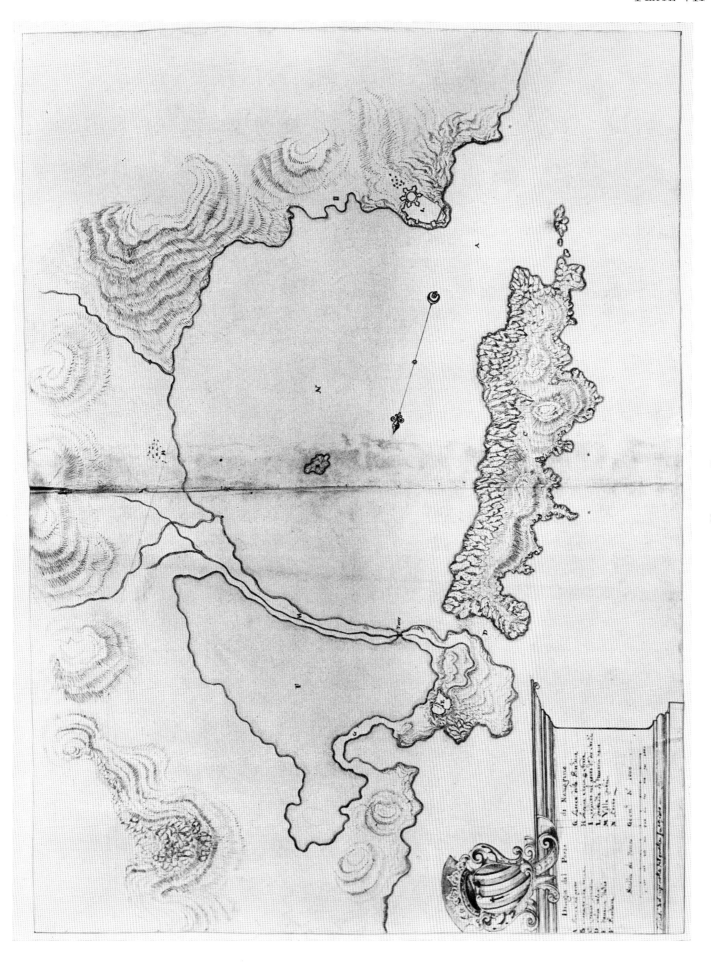

PLATE VIII

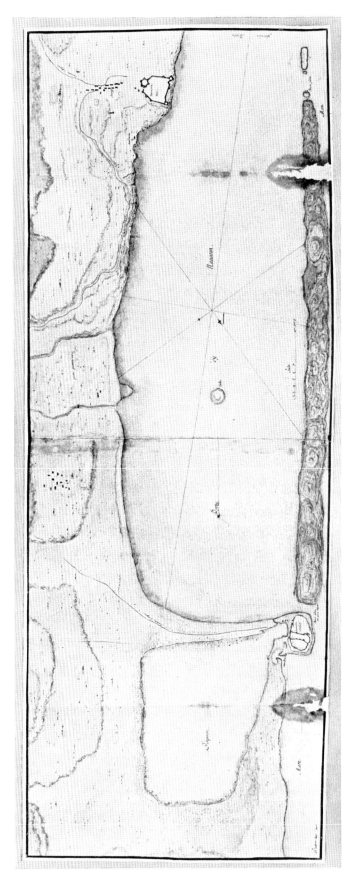

NAVARINO BAY

PLATE IX

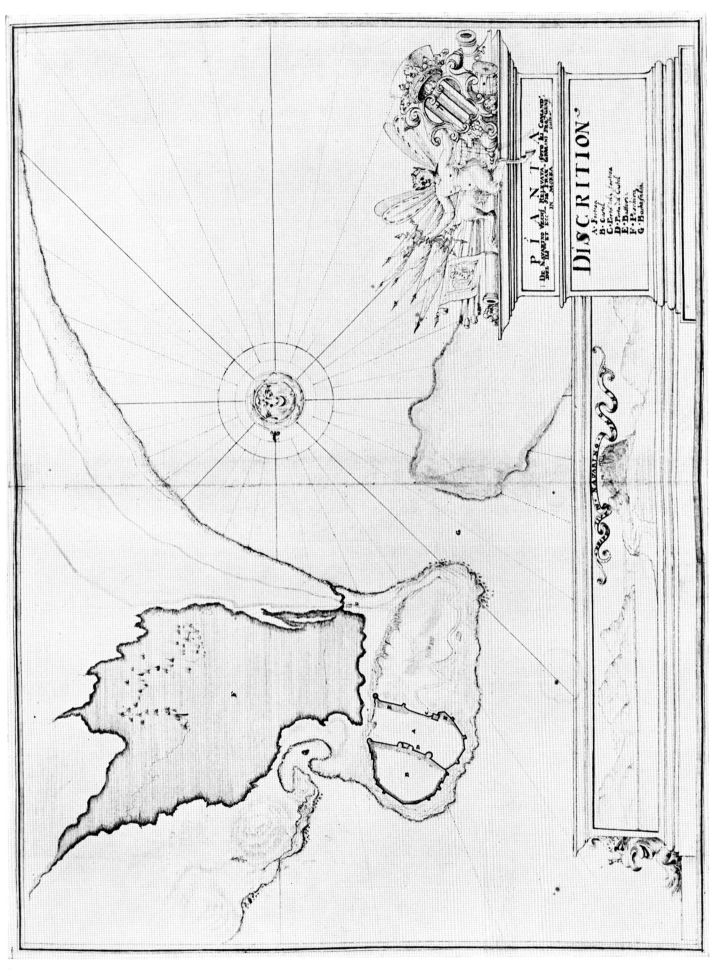

PIANTA
De Navarin Vechi, Ricavata sotto il Comando
del Illmo et Ecc.mo Sigr Fran.co Gibriani Prov.Genl
in Morea

DISCRITION.

A. Forteza
B. Castel
C. Terra della Barbaria
D. Porto del Castel
E. Batteri
F. P. Picciolo
G. Bocca Zan....

OLD NAVARINO

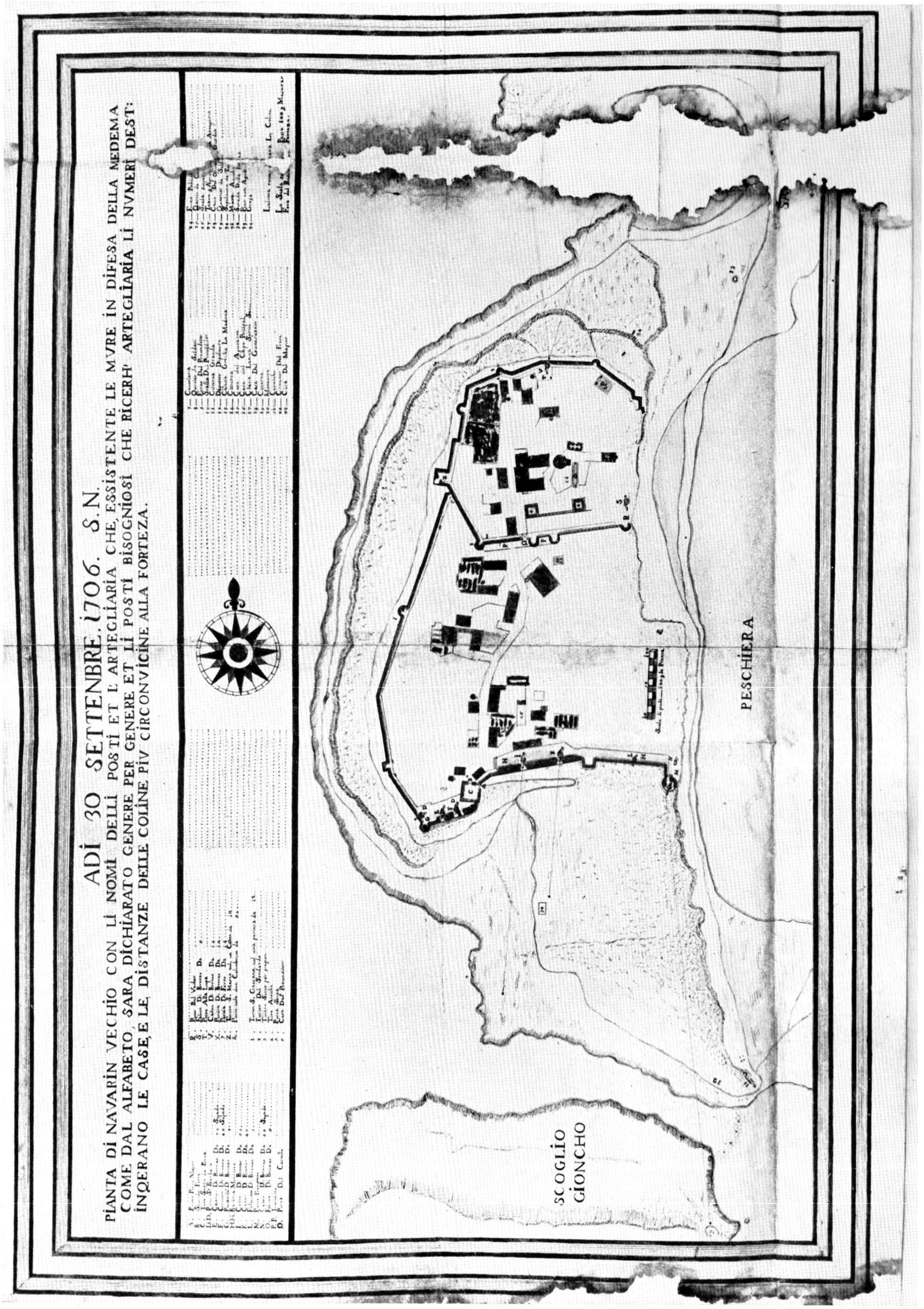

PLATE X

ADì 30 SETTENBRE. 1706. S.N.

PIANTA DI NAVARIN VECHIO CON LI NOMI DELLI POSTI ET L ARTEGLIARIA CHE, ESSISTENTE LE MVRE IN DIFESA DELLA MEDEMA
COME DAL ALFABETO, SARA DICHIARATO GENERE PER GENERE ET LI POSTI BISOGNIOSI CHE RICERH ARTEGLIARIA LI NVMERI DEST:
INQERANO LE CASE, E LE DISTANZE DELLE COLINE PIV CIRCONVICINE ALLA FORTEZA.

SCOGLIO GIONCHO

PESCHIERA

OLD NAVARINO

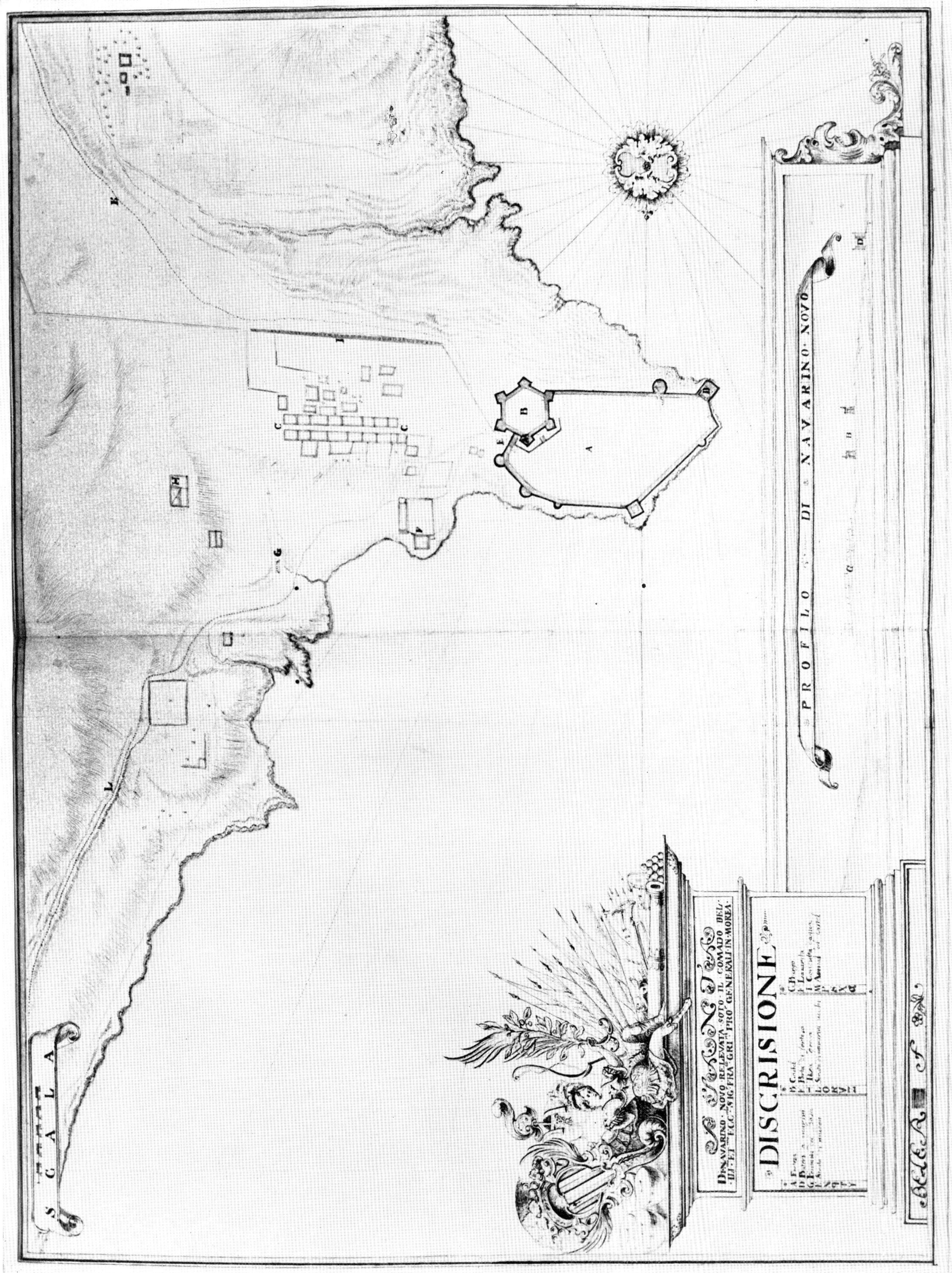

PLATE XI

SCALA

PROFILO DI NAVARINO NOVO

DISCRISIONE

Di Navarino Novo relevata soto il Comado del
Ill.mo Ecc.mo Sig.r Fra Gri Pro Generali in Morea

New Navarino

PLATE XII

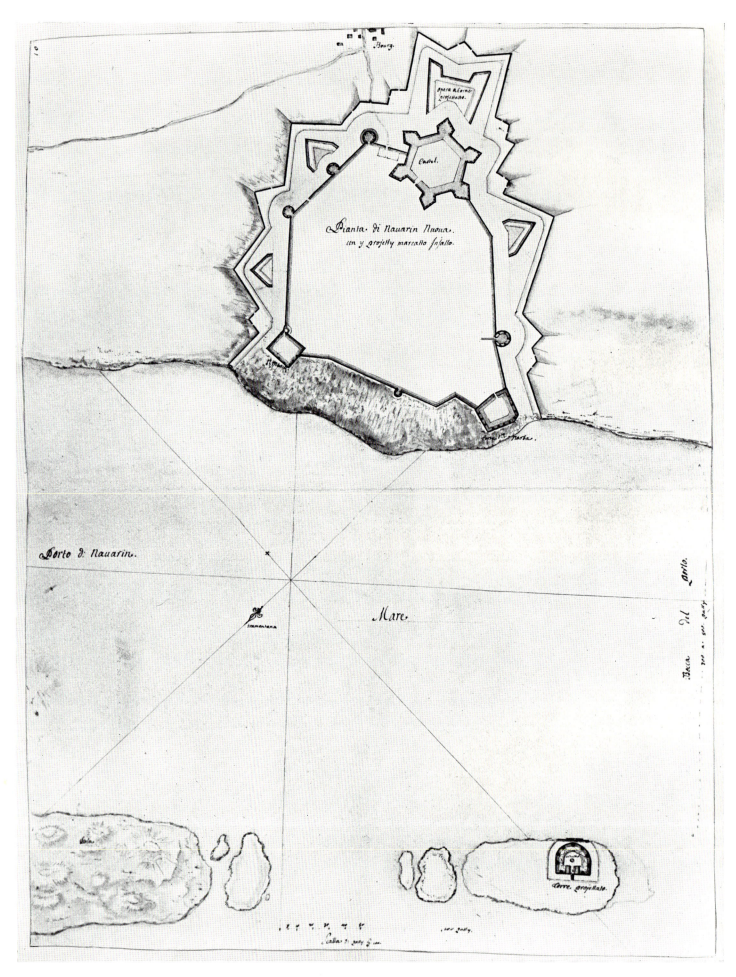

NEW NAVARINO

Plate XIII

Navarino, views of Old and New Fortresses

PLATE XIV

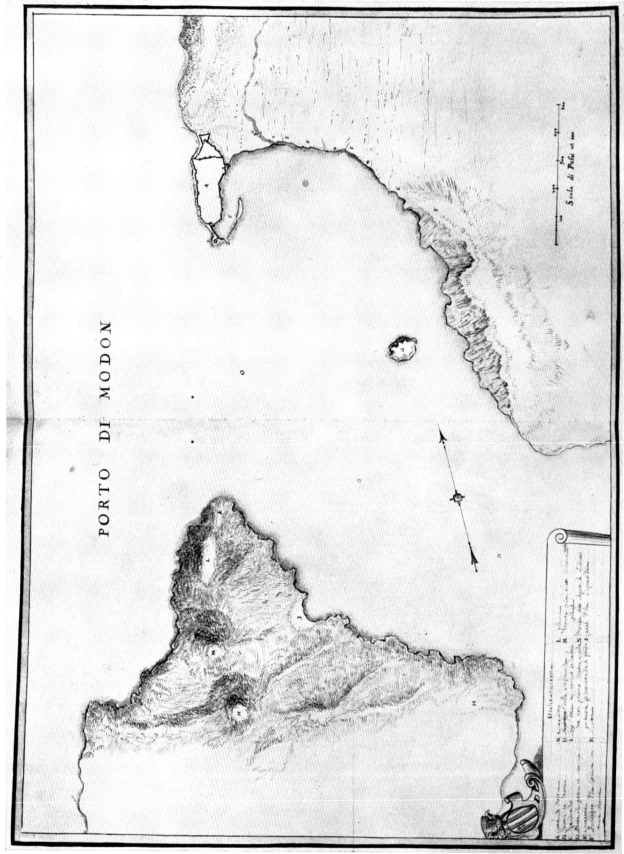

PORTO DI MODON

METHONE BAY

PLATE XV

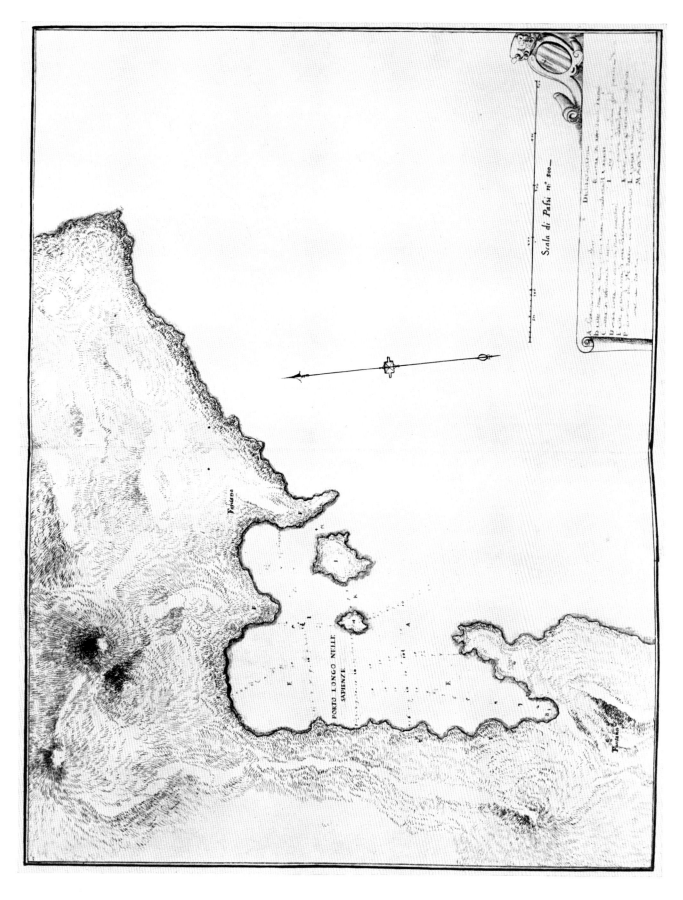

Scala di Paßi nᵢ 500

PORTO LONGO NELLE
SAPIENZE

Fontana

Fontana

Fontana

PORTO LONGO, SAPIENZA

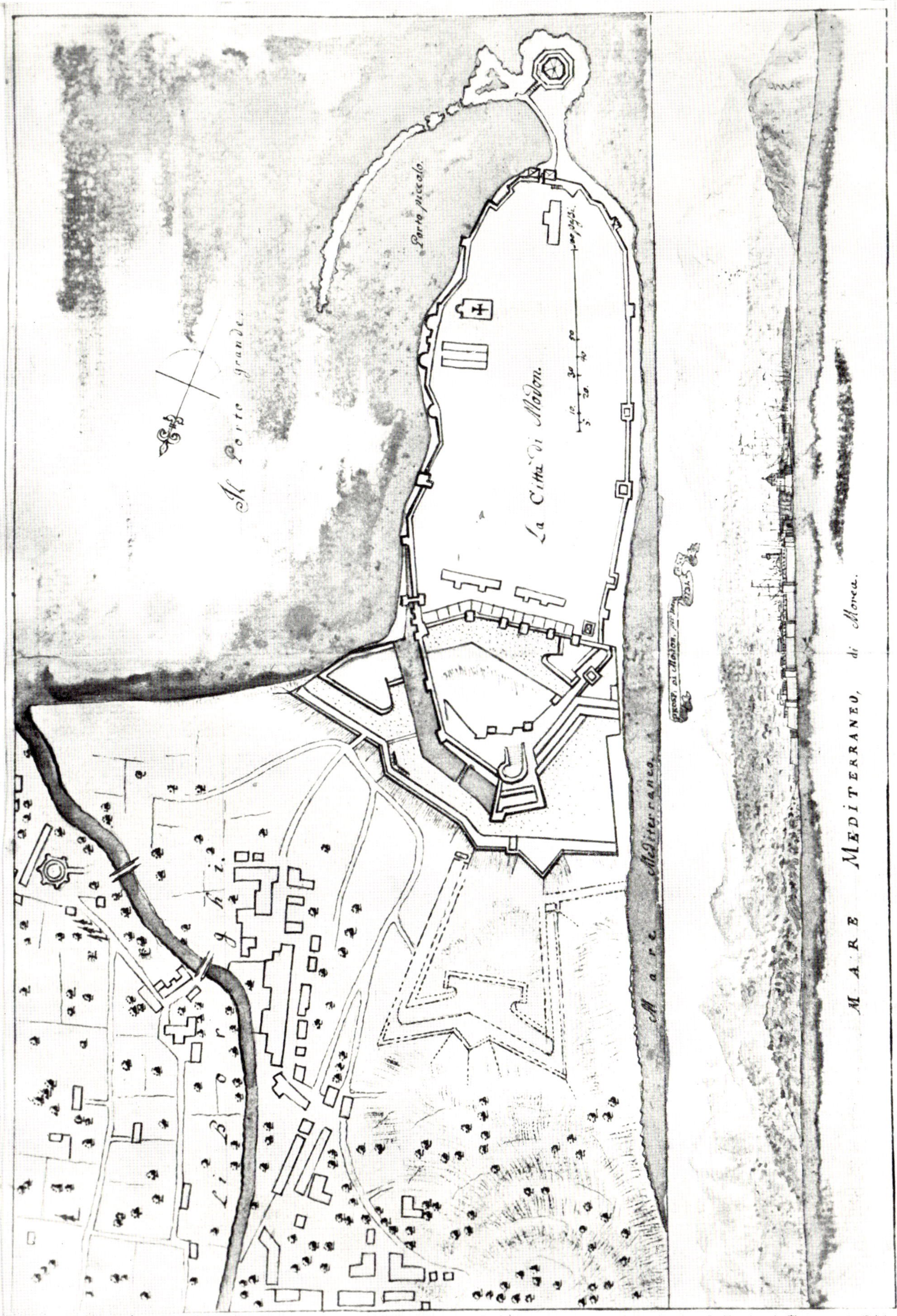

PLATE XVII

La Città di Moion.

Porto piccolo.

Il Porto grande.

MARE MEDITERRANEO, di Morea.

METHONE

PLATE XVIII

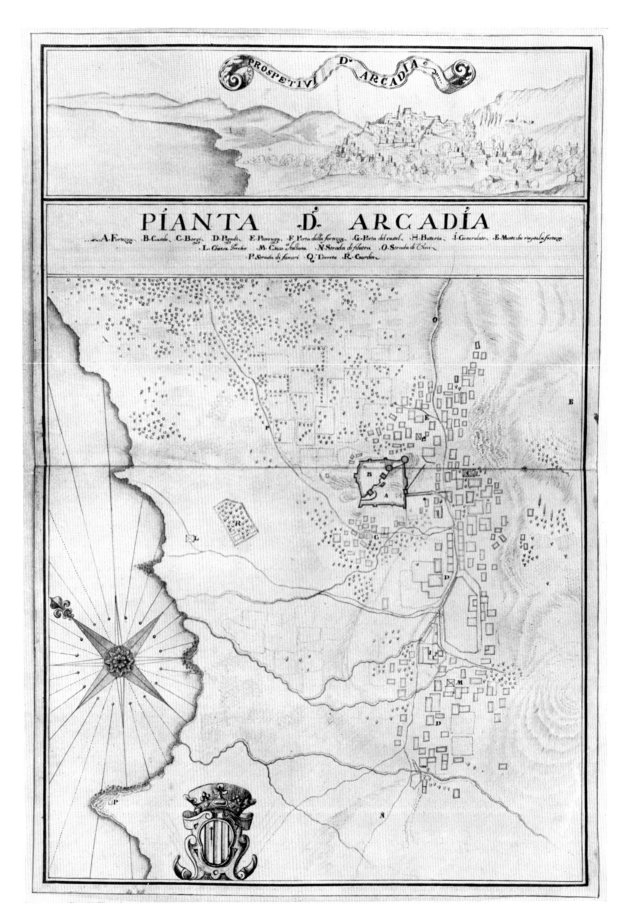

ARKADIA (KYPARISSIA)

PLATE XIX

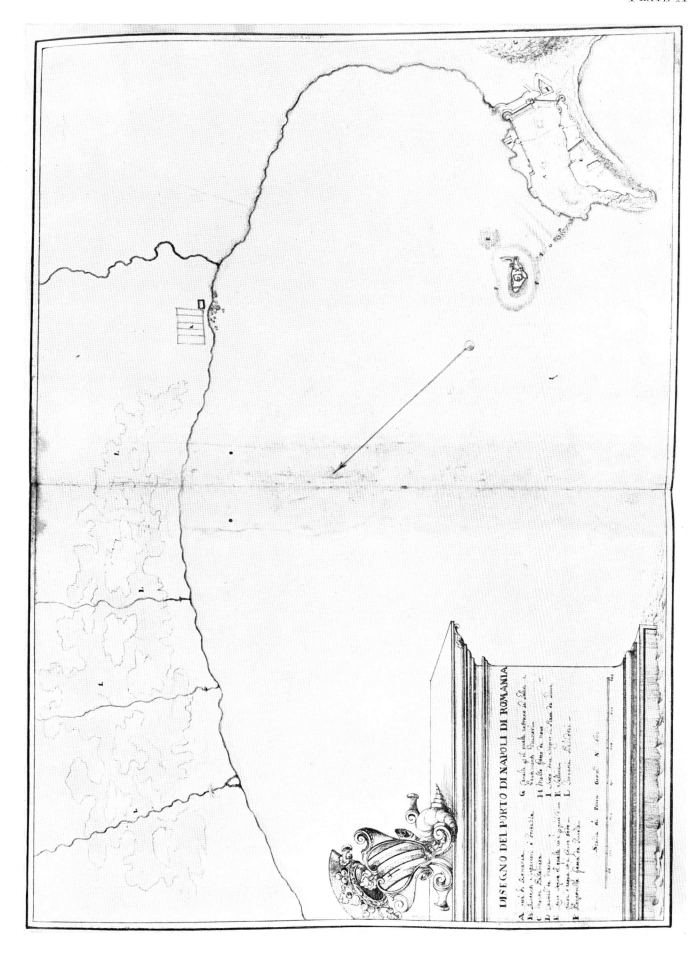

DISEGNO DEL PORTO DI NAPOLI DI ROMANIA

NAUPLIA BAY

Plate XX

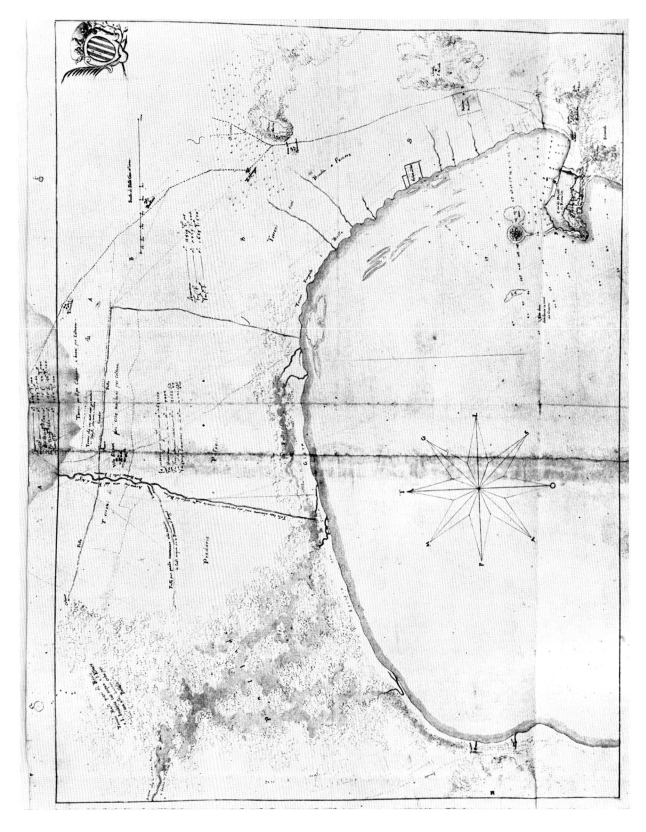

Nauplia Bay

PLATE XXI

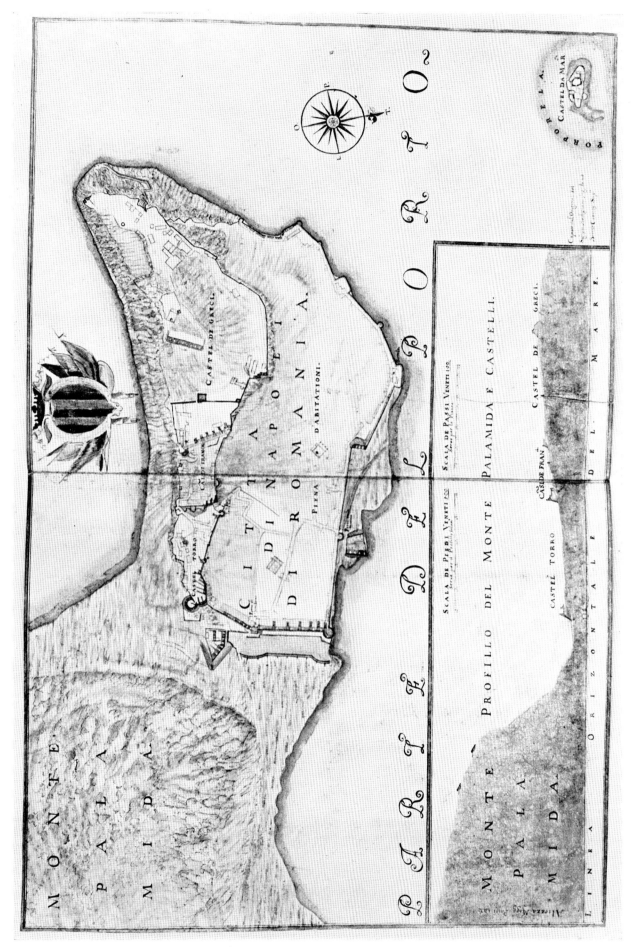

NAUPLIA (NAPOLI DI ROMANIA)

PLATE XXII

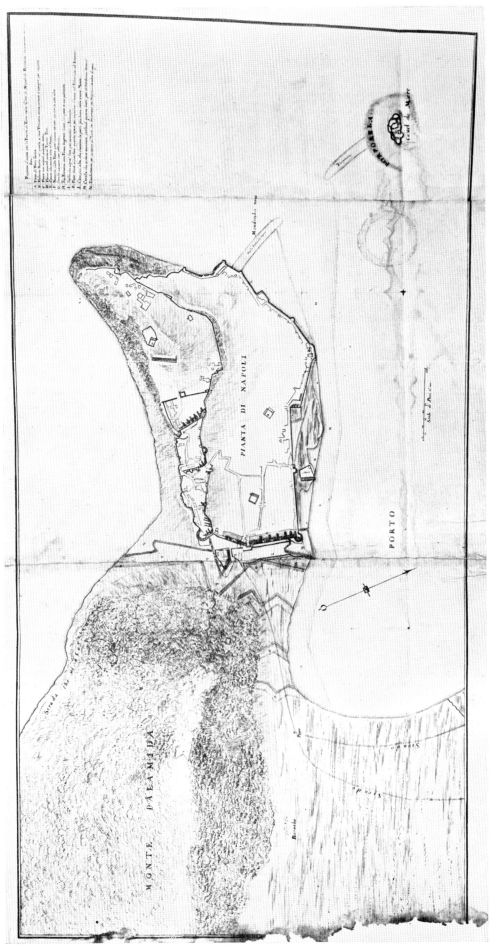

NAUPLIA

PLATE XXIII

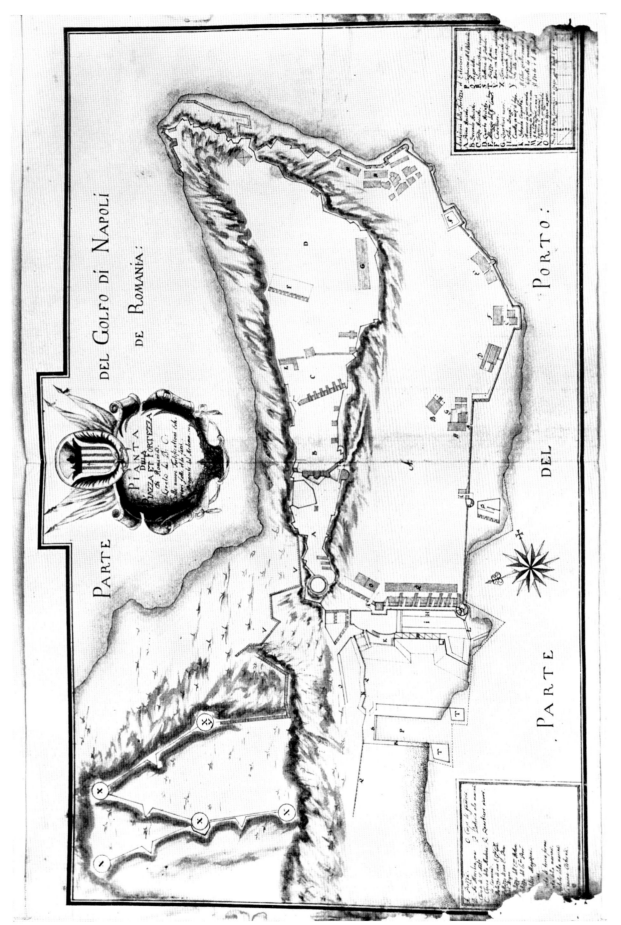

PLATE XXIV

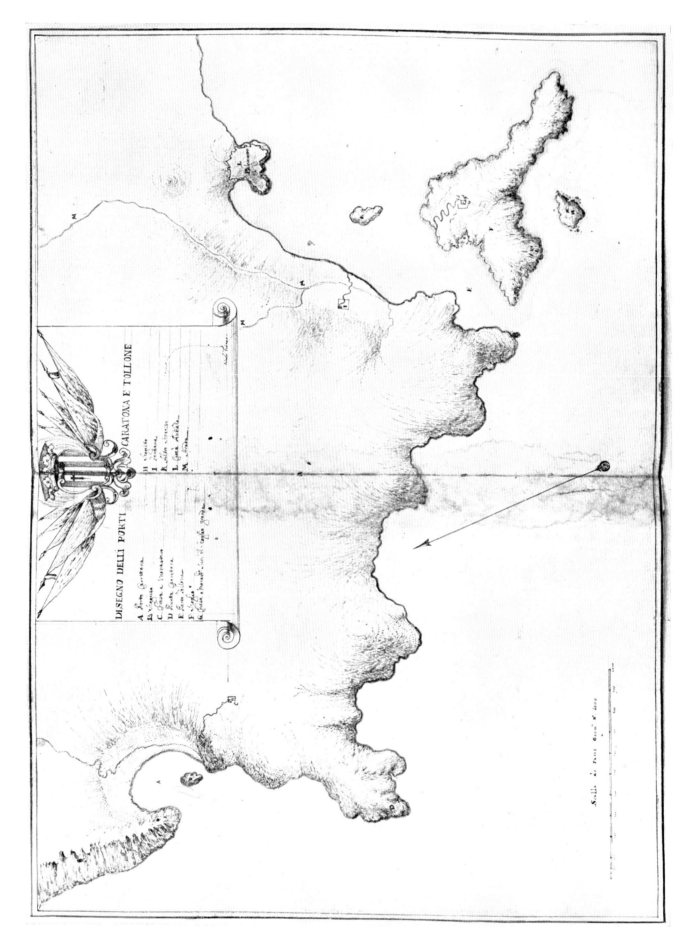

DISEGNO DELLI PORTI CARATONA E TOLLONE

A Porto Caratona
B Vergniere
C Fossa e Peniniera
D Punta Garidena
E Scro Salivan
F Vaglio
G Gotta Parada in il capta grande

H Cepida
I Anttana
K Aton Anicin
L Gota Anicle
M Croca

Plate XXV

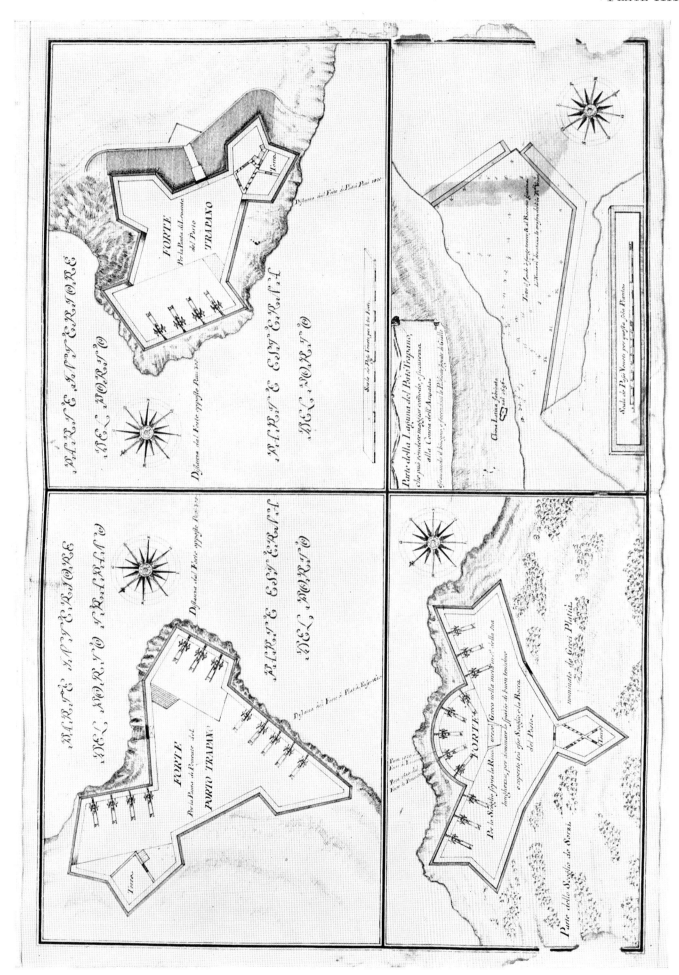

DREPANON

Plate XXVI

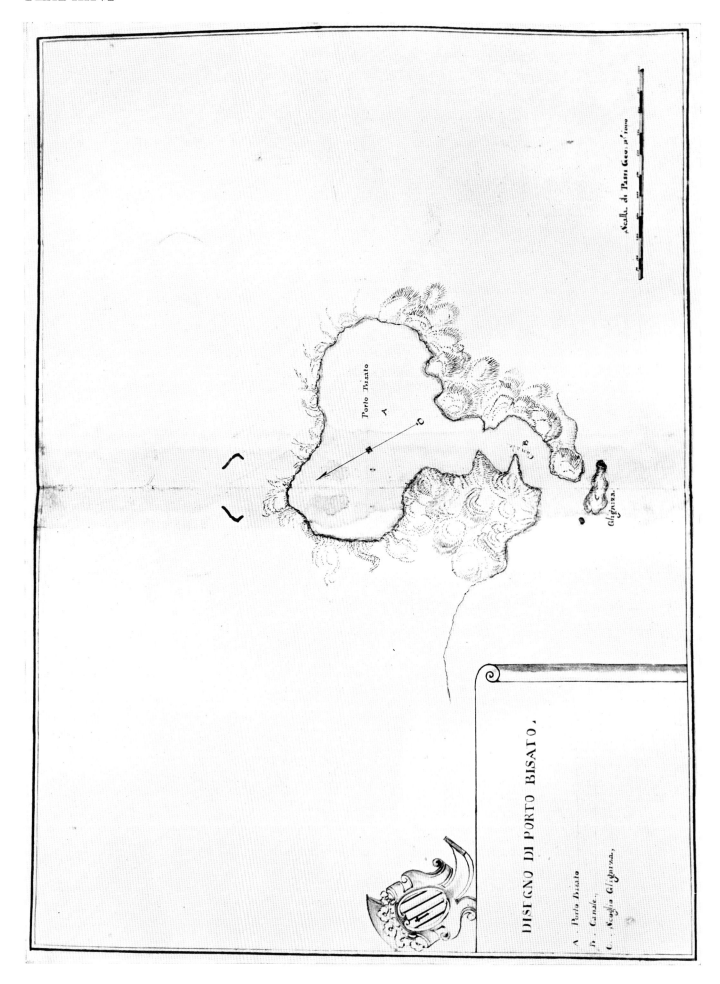

Porto Bisato

Gligniza.

DISEGNO DI PORTO BISATO.

A . Porto Bisato
B . Canale.
C . Scoglio Gligniza.

Scale di Passi Geo. p'oco

Plate XXVII

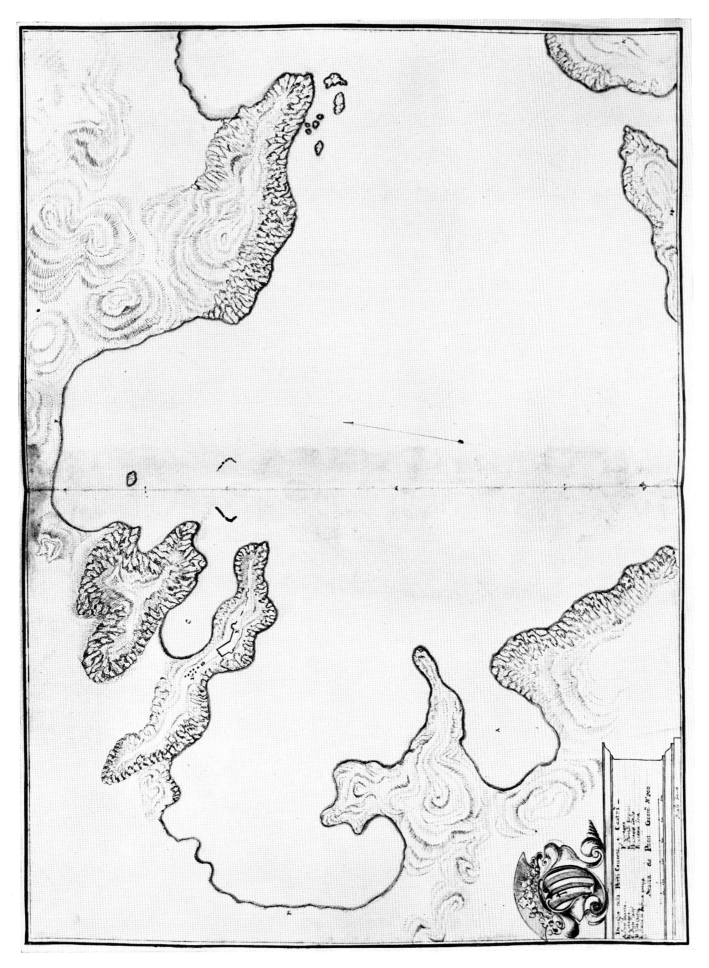

Hermione (Kastri) and Koverta Bays

PLATE XXVIII

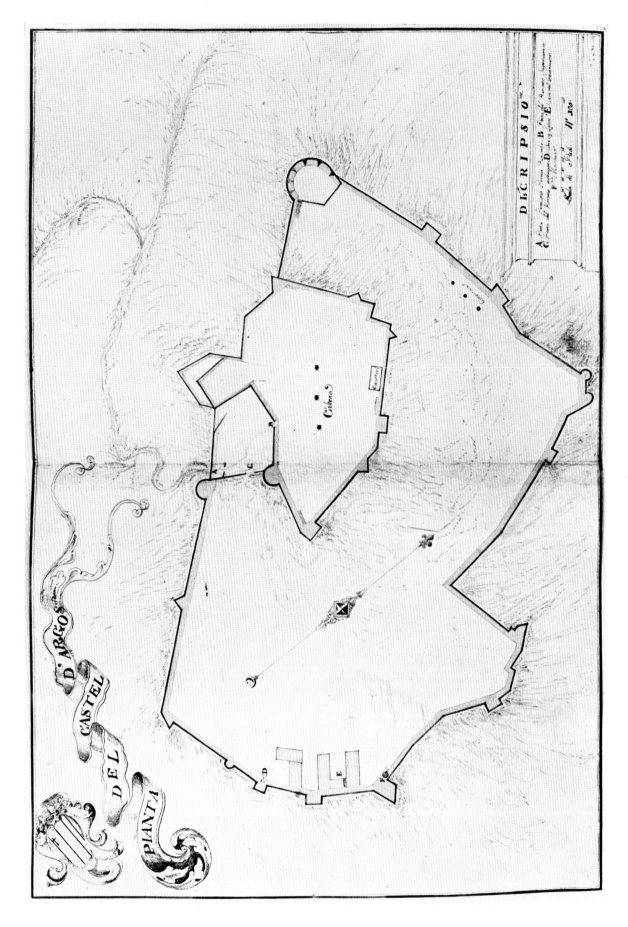

ARGOS

PLATE XXIX

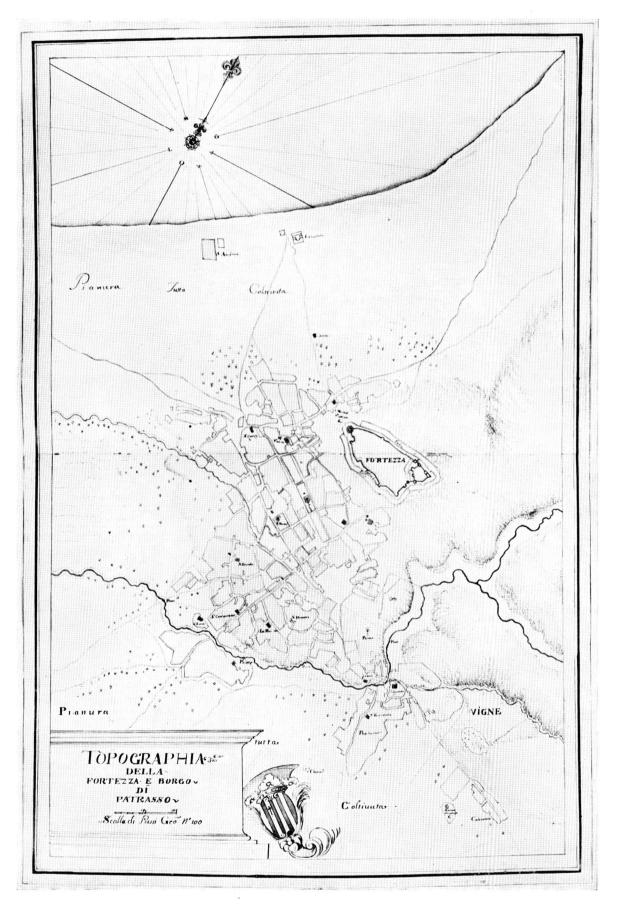

Patras

PLATE XXX

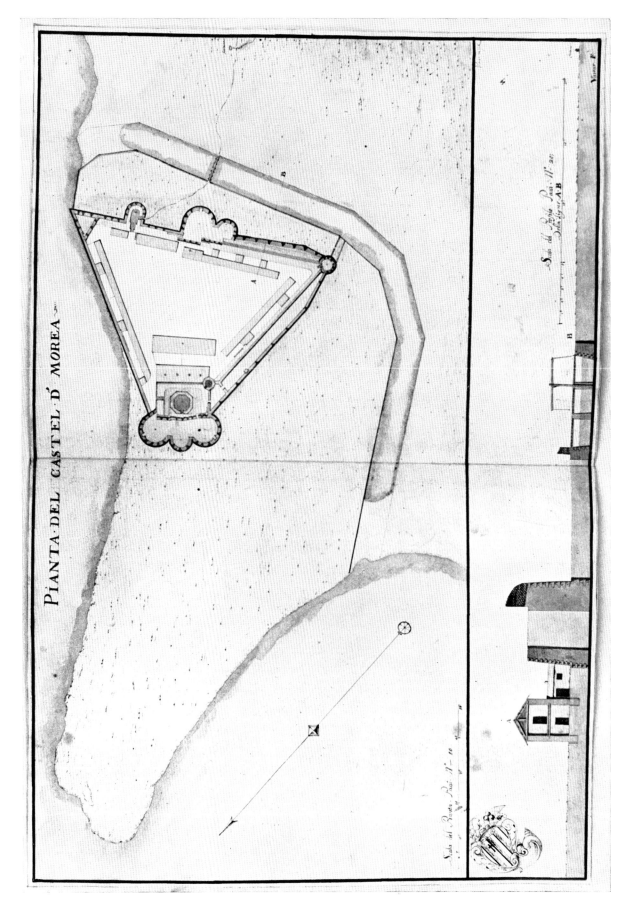

PIANTA·DEL·CASTEL·D'·MOREA

CASTLE OF MOREA (RHION)

PLATE XXXI

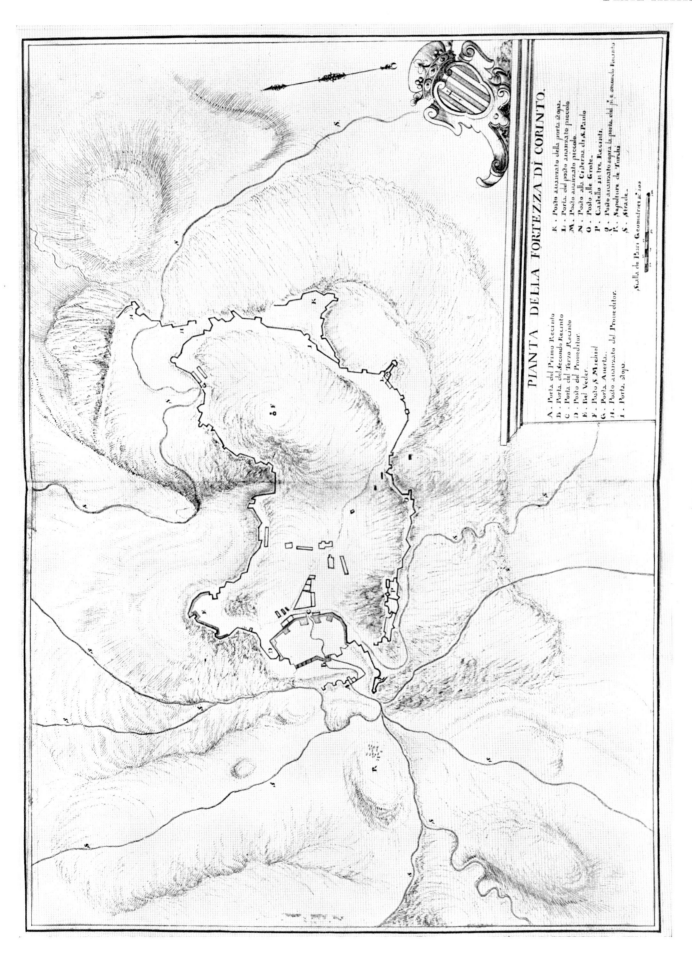

PIANTA DELLA FORTEZZA DI CORINTO.

A . Porta del Primo Recinto
B . Porta del Secondo Recinto
C . Porta del Terzo Recinto
D . Posto del Proueditor
E . Bel Veder
F . Posto S. Michiel
G . Porta Auerla
H . Posto auanzato del Proueditor.
I . Porta Sopa

K . Posto auanzato della porta sopa
L . Porta del posto auanzato piccolo
M . Posto auanzato piccolo
N . Posto alla Cisterna di S. Paulo
O . Posto alle Grote
P . Castello in tre Recinti
Q . Posto auanzato sopra la porta del pri e secondo Recinto
R . Sepolture di Turchi
S . Strade

Scalla de Passi Geometrici di 100

ACROCORINTH

PLATE XXXII

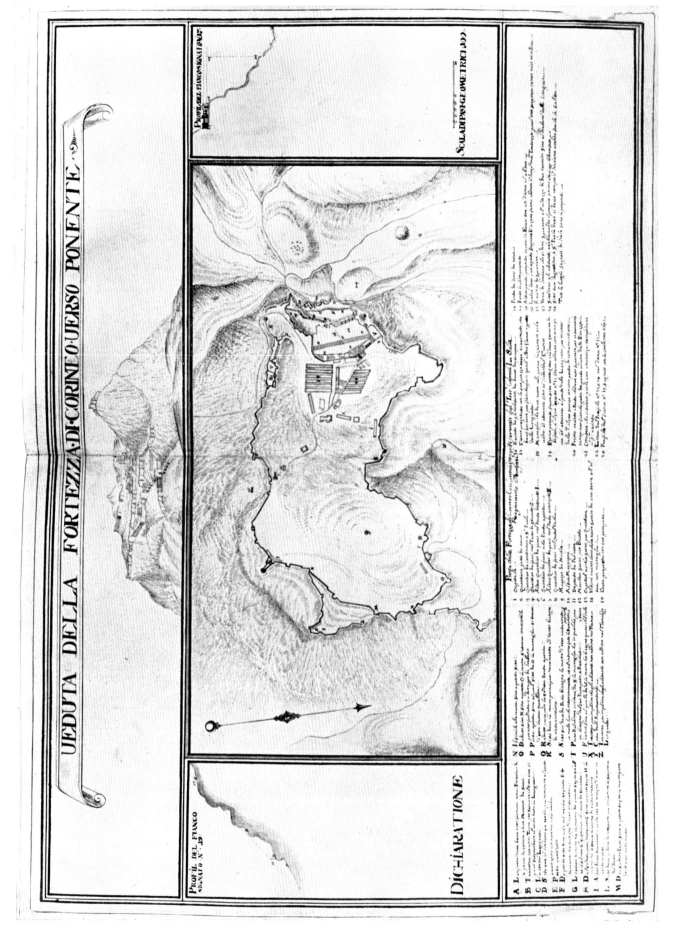

PLATE XXXIII

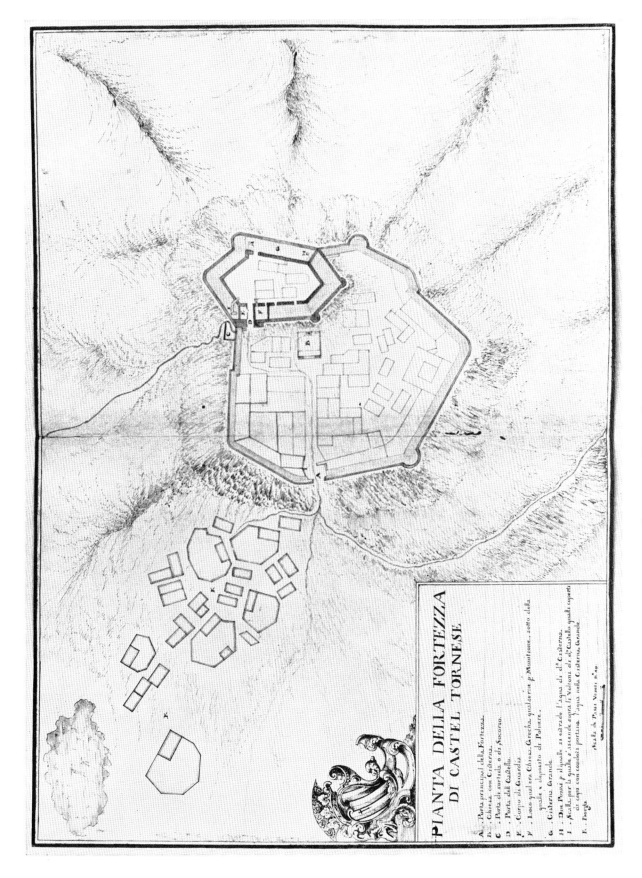

CHLEMOUTSI (CASTEL TORNESE)

PIANTA DELLA FORTEZZA
DI CASTEL TORNESE.

A . Porta principal della Fortezza.
B . Chiesa con Cisterna.
C . Porta di sortida o di Ancora.
D . Porta del Castello.
E . Corpo di Guardia.
F . Loco qual era Chiesa Greca, qualserue p. Munitione, sotto della
    quale e dicontro di Palmre.
G . Cisterna Grande.
H . Due Pozzi p liquali si entrade l'aqua di d.ª Cisterna.
I . Scalla per li quale è ascende sopra li Voltoni di d.º Castello quali coparti
    di copi con condoti portina l'aqua nella Cisterna Grande.
K . Torglo.

Scalla di Passi Venit. n.º 40.

Plate XXXIV

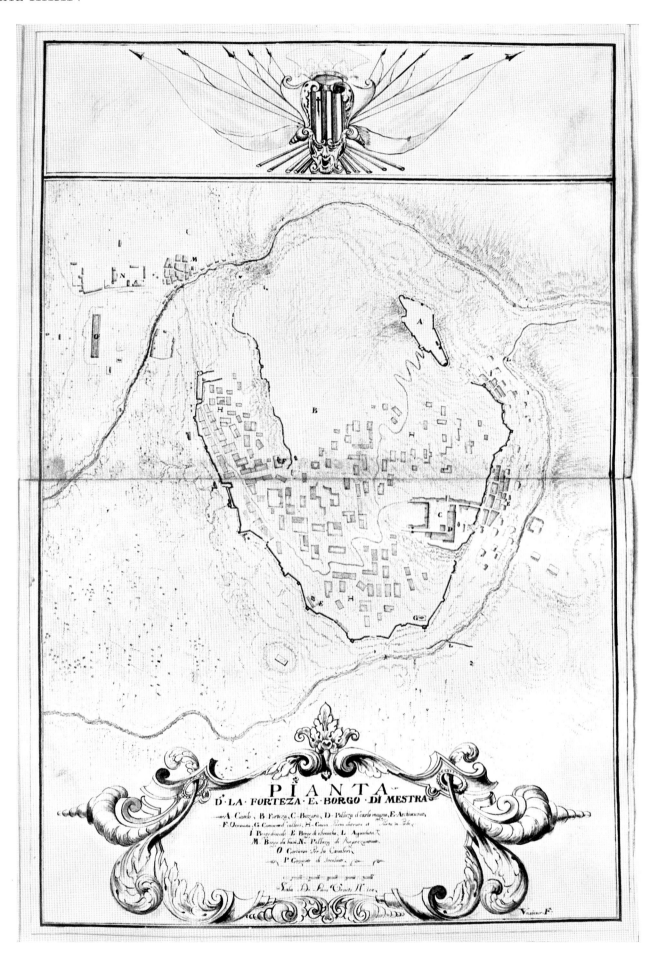

PIANTA
D' LA FORTEZA E BORGO DI MESTRA

MISTRA

PLATE XXXV

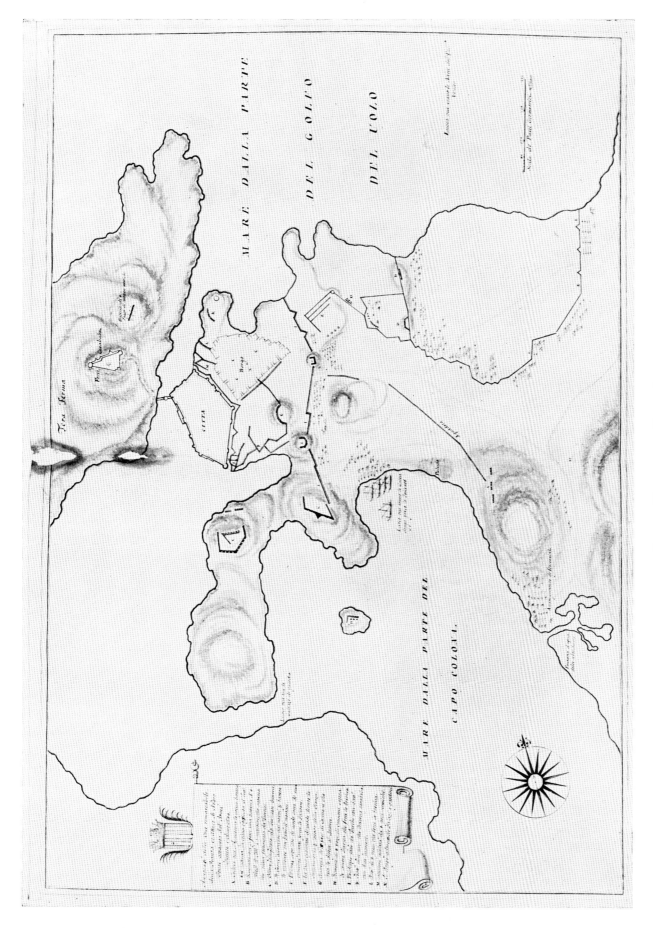

CHALKIS (NEGROPONTE, EUBOEA)

PLATE XXXVI

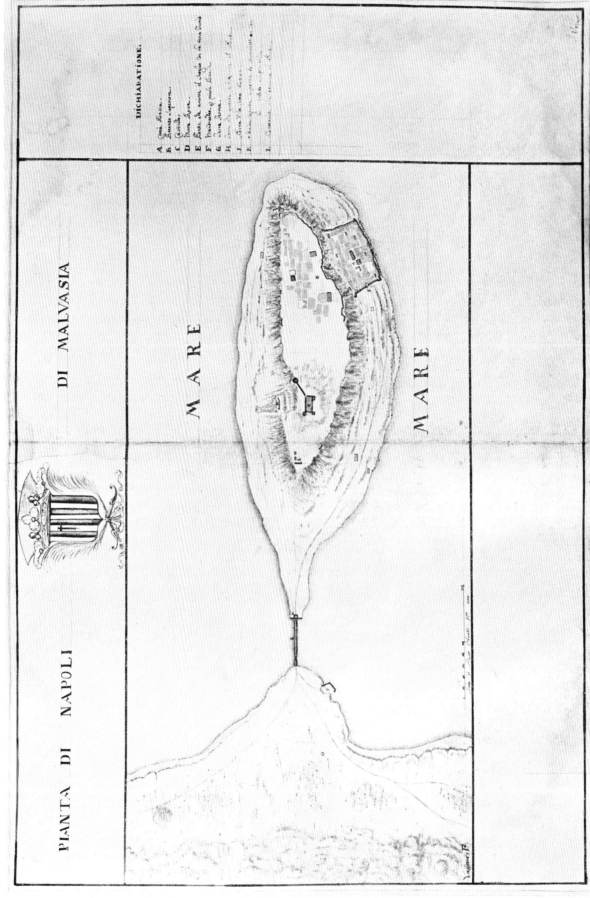

PIANTA DI NAPOLI DI MALVASIA

MARE

MARE

DICHIARATIONE.

A Cité Alta.
B Ponte e speroni.
C Castello.
D Porta bassa.
E Porta de acqua di legno in di Terra ferma.
F Fontana di quest' Isola.
G Città ferma.
H ...
I Strade di terra ferma.
K ...
L Cisterna...

MONEMVASIA (NAPOLI DI MALVASIA)

PLATE XXXVII

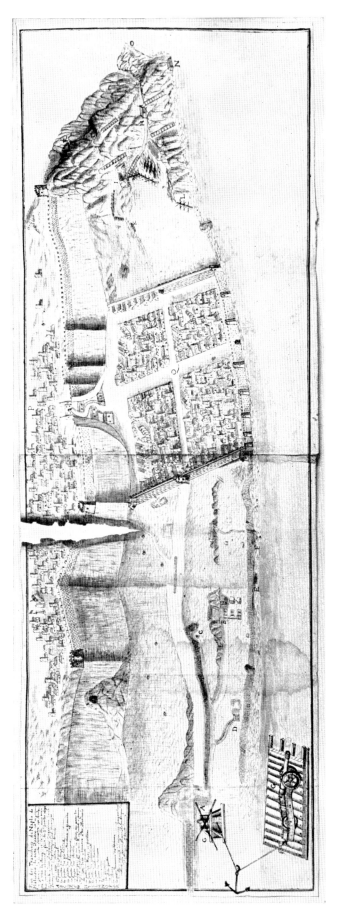

A. MONEMVASIA

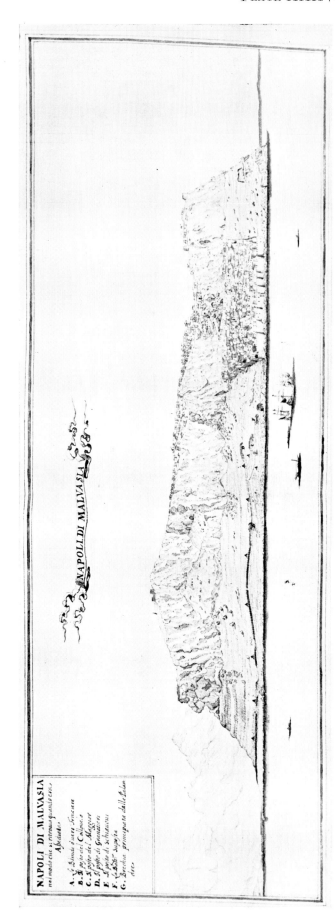

B. MONEMVASIA

NAPOLI DI MALVASIA
nel modo che si ritrova quando cine Abitata

A. Armata d'acqua Veneta
B. Piccoli Caiques
C. Posto del Maggior
D. Posto di Granatieri
E. Posto di Schiavoni
F. Falla Supria
G. Breccia principale dalla Lata etc.

PLATE XXXVIII

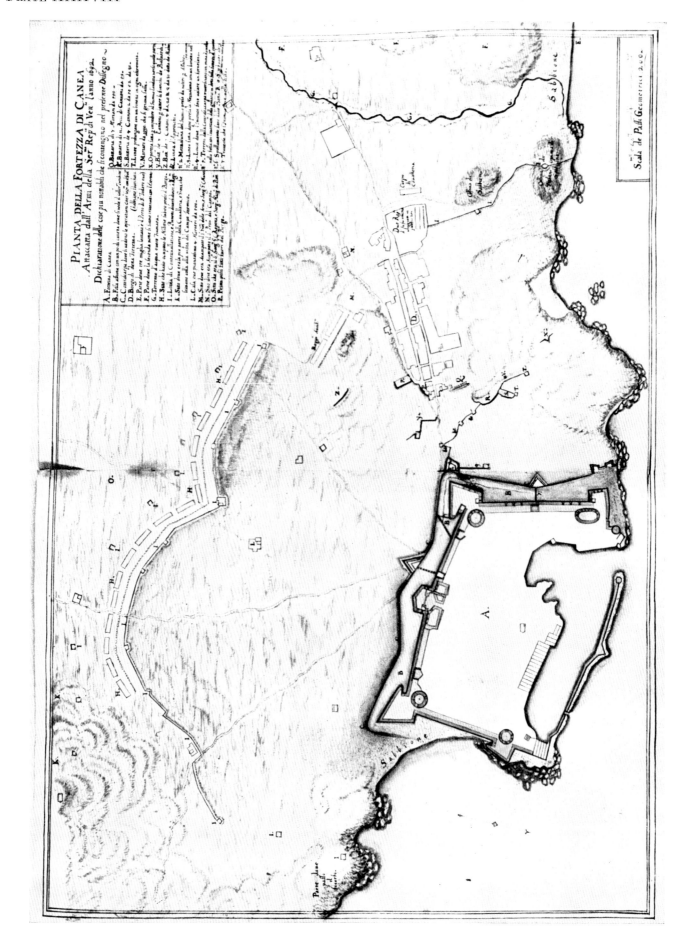

CANEA (CRETE)

PLATE XXXIX

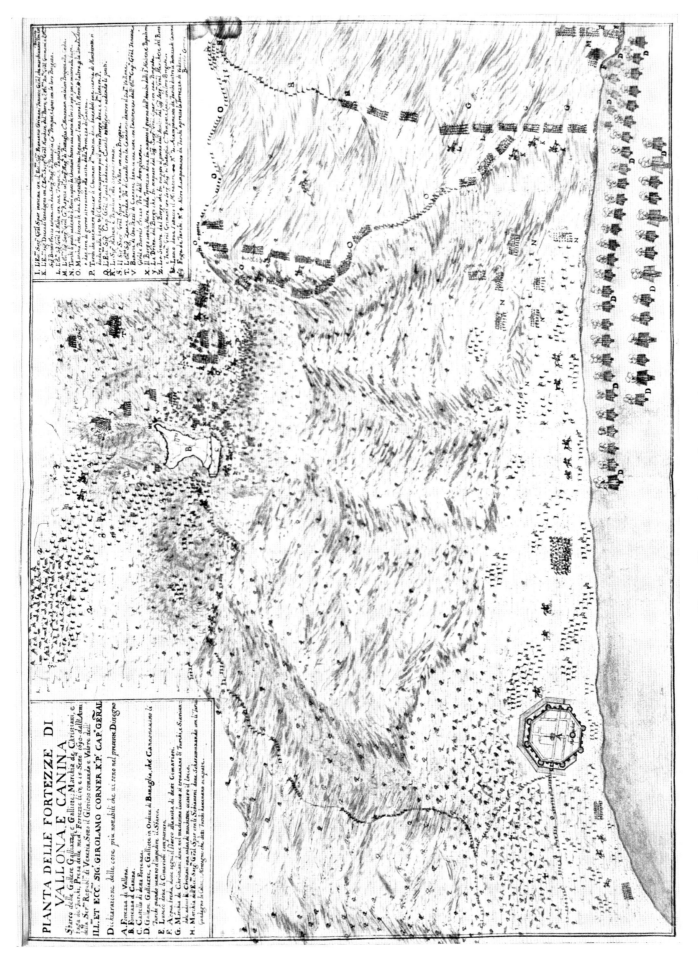

VALONA (VLORE, OR AVLONA, SOUTHERN ALBANIA)

PLATE XXXX

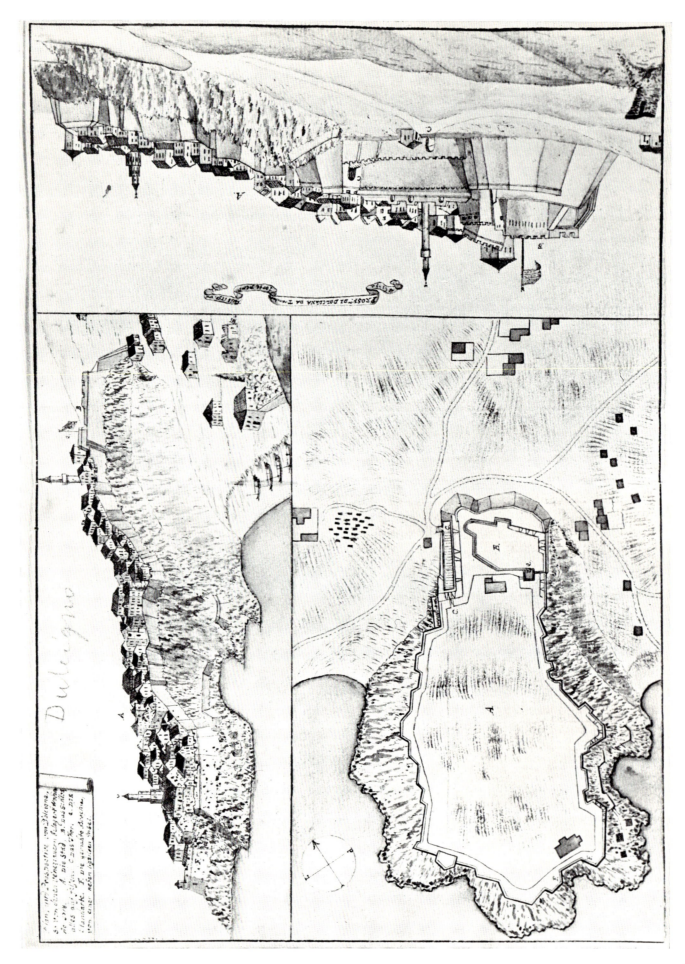

DULCIGNO (ULCINJ, MONTENEGRO)